The publisher gratefully acknowledges the generous
contribution to this book provided by the Jewish
Studies Endowment Fund of the University of
California Press Foundation, which is supported
by a major gift from the S. Mark Taper Foundation.

# Jewish Identities

CALIFORNIA STUDIES IN 20TH-CENTURY MUSIC

Richard Taruskin, General Editor

# Jewish Identities

*Nationalism, Racism, and Utopianism in Twentieth-Century Music*

Klára Móricz

UNIVERSITY OF CALIFORNIA PRESS

*Berkeley    Los Angeles    London*

University of California Press, one of the most distinguished
university presses in the United States, enriches lives around the
world by advancing scholarship in the humanities, social sciences,
and natural sciences. Its activities are supported by the UC Press
Foundation and by philanthropic contributions from individuals
and institutions. For more information, visit www.ucpress.edu.

University of California Press
Berkeley and Los Angeles, California

University of California Press, Ltd.
London, England

Library of Congress Cataloging-in-Publication Data

Móricz, Klára, 1962–.
    Jewish identities : nationalism, racism, and utopianism in
twentieth-century music / Klára Móricz.
        p.   cm. — (California studies in 20th-century music ; 8)
(Mark Taper Foundation Jewish studies imprint)
    Includes bibliographical references (p.   ) and index.
    ISBN 978-0-520-25088-8 (cloth : alk. paper)
    1. Jews—Music—History and criticism.   2. Music—20th
century—History and criticism.   3. Nationalism in music.
    4. Bloch, Ernest—Criticism and interpretation.   5. Schoenberg,
Arnold—Criticism and interpretation.   I. Title.   II. Series.
ML3776.M67   2008
780.89'924—dc22                                    2007002243

Manufactured in the United States of America

16   15   14   13   12   11   10   09   08
10   9   8   7   6   5   4   3   2   1

This book is printed on Natures Book, which contains 50%
post-consumer waste and meets the minimum requirements
of ANSI/NISO z39.48-1992 (R 1997) (*Permanence of Paper*).

*To the memory of my father*

# CONTENTS

# ILLUSTRATIONS

# ACKNOWLEDGMENTS

My interest in the topic of identities, their musical expression, their social basis and implications originates in my experience in Hungary, where in the years after the fall of socialism in 1988 newly discovered political, religious, and ethnic identities divided a population that had previously lived in the illusionary unity of the politically repressed. In the abrupt fracturing of society it was easy to recognize that human diversity can be eliminated only temporarily in favor of group identities, which can ultimately be maintained only at the price of trimming individual opinions and inclinations. Arriving in the United States in 1994, I was emboldened to tackle this subject by the critical approach and anti-essentialist intellectual atmosphere I encountered at the University of California at Berkeley.

I have many individuals and institutions to thank for their help with this project. For assistance with my archival work I owe thanks to UC Berkeley's excellent music librarians, John Roberts and Judy Tsou (now at the University of Washington), for their support during the semester I spent looking over the boxes of the library's Ernest Bloch Collection. Thanks are also due to the staff of the Arnold Schoenberg Institute, then still at the University of California, Los Angeles, especially to Wayne Shoaff, who shared valuable knowledge about the collection, provided me with photocopies, and offered much advice during my two trips to the Institute. From the Schoenberg Institute of Vienna I owe thanks to Eike Fess for prompt responses to my inquiries. It is hard to find the appropriate words to thank the staff at the Library of Congress. Lloyd A. Pinchback spent hours copying the entire sketch material of Ernest Bloch's opera *Jézabel*, a generous act without which I would not have been able to complete my research during my short stay in Washington. Elisabeth H. Aumann obtained permission from Suzanne Bloch to copy the draft of *Jézabel* by arranging to visit the composer's daughter in New York solely for my sake. Suzanne Bloch not only gave me permission to copy *Jézabel,* but also spent a delightful afternoon with me reminiscing about her father. Chana Mlotek provided me with invaluable guidance at the YIVO Institute for Jewish Research, as did Tova Gazete at the Judah Magnes Museum, Berkeley. Stanley Rabinowitz allowed me access to materials at the Amherst College Russian Culture Center and gave generous permission to reproduce the cover page of Alexander Krein's song "Natof natfah hadim'ah." He also helped me to organize a conference on Russian Jewish music at Amherst College in October 2004, which enabled me to discuss the topic of my first two chapters with experts in the field. I am thankful to Lawrence Schoenberg, the composer's son, for granting me permission to publish many unpublished documents, drafts, and sketches by his father.

I gratefully acknowledge the financial support I received during my research from the Mabelle McLeod Lewis Memorial Fund in 1998–99, and from the American Council of Learned Societies (Andrew W. Mellon Fellowship for Junior Faculty) in 2003, when I wrote the bulk of the book. A generous subvention from Amherst College has enabled me to set music examples for the book.

I thank Mary Francis of UC Press for her sober guidance and support in the publishing process, Kalicia Pivirotto for responding to millions of questions related to the preparation of the manuscript for submission, Rose Vekony, Dore Brown, David Anderson, and Sharron Wood for excellent editorial work, and Don Giller for his expert preparation of music examples.

It gives me the greatest pleasure to recognize and thank the individuals who helped the scholarly development of my work at various stages. My musicological colleagues and friends have done their share beyond the call of duty: Beth Levy and Alyson Ahern, members of the editorial board of *repercussions,* in which an early version of my argument about Bloch appeared, helped me not only with that article, but also read and commented on several chapters of the book. Danielle Fosler-Lussier spent many hours checking my German translations and giving me editorial comments about the text. James Loeffler and Paula Eisenstein Baker were always ready to answer any questions related to my first two chapters. Both were eager to share ideas, drafts, and sources. Eliyahu Schleifer and Mark Kligman helped me identify the source of the theme in Krein's Sonata. Robert A. Rothstein checked some Russian and Yiddish translations and Yiddish transliterations. He also generously lent me his copy of Kiselgof's *Zamelbukh,* which was an invaluable source for my first chapter. While visiting Berkeley in March 1998 Izaly Zemtsovsky listened to my ideas and called my attention to the volume of Yoel Engel's writings. David Biale read an early version of what became my chapters on Bloch and made me aware of the writings of Simon Dubnov. Tom Gray submitted my work on *Jézabel* to the scrupulous editorial process of *JAMS.* Chapter 4 profited greatly from his editorial expertise. Julie Brown edited and critiqued my ideas about Bloch as editor of a forthcoming volume, *Western Music and Race*. László Vikárius also did editorial work on what became part of chapter 8, which was published in *Essays in Honor of László Somfai on His 70th Birthday*. Dana Gooley made one of the first critiques of my argument in chapter 8. Joseph Auner and Eric Sawyer read all my chapters on Schoenberg and gave me valuable critical feedback. Alexander Knapp allowed me to cite one of his music examples. I benefited from the comments I received from my two anonymous readers and the reader of the press's Editorial Committee. Greg Hayes prepared reduced scores for my book, consulting with me about every example. My dearest friend Noemi Schwarz helped me with Hebrew and Yiddish texts and volunteered to be the first audience for my papers. Most of all she lent me the kind of support that only real friends can.

I am profoundly grateful to Richard Taruskin, whose seminars started me on the subject of Jewish nationalism. He has followed and encouraged my work from my early seminar papers to its present form, spending countless hours critiquing my ideas and editing my prose. Taruskin's work has inspired me to extend a critical eye over the conventions of our own field. Composers, Taruskin cautioned, however much we respect them for their music, are human beings, as prone to misjudgment as any of us. The encouragement of my former Hungarian mentor, László Somfai, has been a constant source of inspiration, even as my work has taken an American bent. His insistence on remaining close to the music and to primary sources in musicological arguments helped me not to get tempted by intellectually attractive theories that had little to do with my protagonists and their music.

I received the greatest support from my family during my work. My father-in-law, Thomas Schneider, read several chapters, helped me decipher difficult German passages, and gave me valuable editorial suggestions. Although my own father could not provide me with practical help, I owe him the most for bequeathing me his never-ending quest for understanding, his dissatisfaction with ready-made answers, his belief in the individual value of human beings, and his resistance to assuming identities dictated by groups or institutions. I dedicate the book to his memory.

The list would not be complete without thanking my husband, David E. Schneider, whose emotional and professional support made my work possible. He patiently listened to my ideas and rigorously criticized, questioned, and corrected me, providing me with the constant intellectual control I needed for shaping my argument. He read all the chapters, in several versions, edited the text, encouraged me when needed, but most of all he always believed in my work, which gave me the impetus to go on even in emotionally trying times. I should not leave out my daughter, Emma, who provided me with delightful opportunities of diversion. When she is old enough to read my work, I hope she will acknowledge that, despite her present belief, I have some imagination after all.

# ABBREVIATIONS

| | |
|---|---|
| ASI | Arnold Schoenberg Institute, Vienna. |
| *EBS Bulletin* | *Ernest Bloch Society Bulletin.* |
| *JASI* | *Journal of the Arnold Schoenberg Institute.* |
| Lazar | Lazar, Moshe. "Arnold Schoenberg and His Doubles: A Psychodramatic Journey to His Roots." *Journal of the Arnold Schoenberg Institute* 17, nos. 1–2 (June and November 1994): 8–150. |
| LC Bloch Col. | Ernest Bloch Collection, Library of Congress, Washington, DC. |
| Lew. 1 | Lewinski, Joseph, and Emmanuelle Dijon. *Ernest Bloch (1880–1959): Sa vie et sa pensée.* Vol. 1, *Les années de galères (1880–1916).* Geneva: Editions Slatkine, 1998. |
| Lew. 2 | Lewinski, Joseph, and Emmanuelle Dijon. *Ernest Bloch (1880–1959): Sa vie et sa pensée.* Vol. 2, *La consécration américaine (1916–1930).* Geneva: Editions Slatkine, 2001. |
| Ringer | Ringer, Alexander. *Arnold Schoenberg: The Composer as Jew.* Oxford: Clarendon Press, 1990. |
| *S/Reader* | Auner, Joseph. *A Schoenberg Reader: Documents of a Life.* New Haven: Yale University Press, 2003. |
| Stein | Stein, Erwin, ed. *Arnold Schoenberg: Letters.* Translated by Eithne Wilkins and Ernst Kaiser. Berkeley: University of California Press, 1987. |
| *Style/Idea* | *Style and Idea: Selected Writings of Arnold Schoenberg.* Edited by Leonard Stein. Translated by Leo Black. Berkeley: University of California Press, 1975. |

*S. Werke* B/19    *Arnold Schönberg Sämtliche Werke: Kritischer Bericht.* Edited
by Joseph Rufer. Kritischer Bericht. Abtl. V: Chorwerke.
Reihe B, Band 19. Edited by Christian Martin Schmidt.
Mainz: B. Schott's Söhne; Vienna: Universal Edition,
1977.

UCB Bloch Col.    Ernest Bloch Collection, University of California,
Berkeley.

# NOTE ON TRANSLITERATION

The transliteration of Russian words follows the system established by Gerald Abraham for the *New Grove Dictionary of Music and Musicians* (1980), described in volume 1. Modifications are applied according to those used by Richard Taruskin in *Musorgsky: Eight Essays and an Epilogue* (1993). If reference is made to a source in translation, the notes and the bibliography cite the author's name as transliterated in the publication (Sabaneev and not Sabaneyev; Dubnow and not Dubnov). Russian Jewish names of German origin appear in the main text according to their Russian spelling, usually taken from *Yevreyskaya entsiklopediya* (1906–13) (e.g., Gintsburg instead of Günzburg). Whenever the original Yiddish title page of sheet music was available to the author, the transliteration of Yiddish titles follows the post–World War II YIVO system. Otherwise titles are given as quoted in other sources. (An exception is table 1, in which all terms, titles, and names are given according to Kiselgof's transliteration.) Hebrew words and names of well-known Jewish personalities are generally transliterated as in *The New Standard Jewish Encyclopedia* (1992). When titles or passages are quoted from Bloch's or Schoenberg's compositions with Hebrew text, the transliteration follows the printed score.

# Introduction

In "Jewish Music and a Jew's Music," the penultimate chapter of his path-breaking book *Arnold Schoenberg: The Composer as Jew,* Alexander Ringer campaigns for Jewish music that goes "beyond more or less obvious affinities with liturgical or folk-tunes, not to speak of mere textual reference or the parochial effusions of composing chauvinists." Where this "beyond" leads composers Ringer is all too ready to declare. In the spirit of his protagonist, Arnold Schoenberg, Ringer denies the significance of the "what" (material) and elevates the "how" (treatment) in the creation of a uniquely Jewish music. Following Russian music theorist Boris Asafiev (1884–1949), Ringer dubs this specific treatment "intonation," and defines it as a quality reflecting "not merely the individual psyche but the total historical experience of the community, physical and spiritual, to which the artist belongs, whether he identifies with it consciously or not."[1] There are several assumptions behind Ringer's definition, most of them common in discussions of national or ethnic music. The most important are a preference for the expression of a community over that of the individual, or, to approach it from a different angle, the belief that the individual psyche reflects the communal experience; the conviction that the experience of a nation or an ethnic group can be reduced to some essence that is present in every member of the group; and the idea that works of art inevitably carry this essence, betraying the artist's national or ethnic origin. This approach, based on what Jehoash Hirshberg calls the "genetic-psychological model," demolishes the comforting, practical boundaries of Curt Sachs's 1957 definition of Jewish music as "music made by Jews, for Jews, as Jews."[2]

The present book is a study of Jewish identities in professional ("art") music, with an emphasis on their complex, often conflicting nature, something much ignored in essentialist studies of identity. I am not the first to argue against essentialist assumptions of Jewish identity. Recent works, such as Matthew Baigell and Milly Heyd's collection of essays *Complex Identities,* effectively show the untenability of the "ever-elusive and really non-existent Jewish essentialism that would lump together artists from different historical periods and geographic locations, let alone different genders, cultures, and degrees of religious observance." Instead of an undefinable essence, Baigell and Heyd offer "Jewish experience" as a common basis for Jewish identities.[3]

David Biale, Michael Galchinsky, and Susan Heschel, the editors of another collection of essays, confront the problem on a more fundamental level by questioning not only the content but also the very nature of identities, which they perceive not as monolithic and static but as multiple and fluid. Especially in the case of Jewish identity, they argue, one has to acknowledge "the multifaceted nature of identity without abandoning the importance of identity altogether." For, they write, "in a variety of ways . . . to be a Jew, especially at this historical juncture, means to lack a single essence, to live with multiple identities."[4]

The protagonists of this book also had multiple identities. Their Jewish ethnicity was certainly an important component of their identity, but what being a Jew meant in Russia, Switzerland, France, Austria, Germany, or the United States for composers of completely different temperaments, and of different degrees of involvement both in international modernism and in Jewish culture, varied a great deal. Examining these composers in the contexts of emerging Jewish nationalism, quickly spreading racial theories, and utopian tendencies in modernist art and twentieth-century politics reveals a trajectory that leads from paradigmatic nationalist techniques (such as the reliance on traditional Jewish music) through assumptions about the unintended presence of racial essences, to an abstract notion of Judaism that ultimately leads to utopian visions of purity. Since the protagonists of this study are separated in the three parts of this book, this introduction will consider them together in the general context of Jewish nationalism and in the light of particular definitions of Jewish music.

## HAZARDOUS DEFINITIONS

Although one of the oldest European nationalisms, that of the seventeenth- and eighteenth-century English, was modeled on the example of Old Testament Hebrews,[5] Jewish nationalism, when it finally emerged at the end of the nineteenth century, followed contemporaneous European political models rather than the ancient biblical one. From the time of its conception, Zionism struggled to find a basis for the movement's secular nationalist claims. What might seem to be the most concrete basis for a Jewish community, the ancient, shared religion, could not be used as a focal point for political leaders in the first phase of the new Zionist movement because Orthodox rabbis opposed its secular political orientation.[6] In the absence of religion, the notion of community in Jewish nationalist ideology was based on a supposedly shared cultural tradition, its definition necessarily vague, its boundaries necessarily elastic. In a 1933 lecture on Jewish nationalism novelist Lion Feuchtwanger (1884–1958) compared the indefinable character of Judaism to Israel's abstract, nonrepresentable God. Although he admitted that "Judaism is not a common race, not a common territory, not a common way of life or a common language," Feuchtwanger succeeded in finding the commonality of world Jewry in "a common spirit, a common spiritual attitude."[7] This assertion echoed others, including Sigmund Freud's invocation of the Jews' "common mental construction."[8]

By the 1940s the early debates about what was genuinely or authentically Jewish in music were partially resolved by a similarly general, accommodatingly vague definition. In the preface to Gdal Saleski's 1949 *Famous Musicians of Jewish Origin* (in its original 1927 publication entitled *Famous Musicians of a Wandering Race*), the author "wishes to make clear . . . that the words 'Jew' and 'Jewish' are not used in their religious or national sense. The method of approach," Saleski assures the reader, "is purely an ethnic one." The word "ethnic" here was an up-to-date substitute for "racial," the word used in the first edition of Saleski's book but which had fallen out of favor after World War II. This change in vocabulary did not solve the basic problem. If after Saleski's introductory statement about "ethnic" rather than "national" or "racial" considerations the reader expected a rigorously scientific method, the next sentence dashed this hope. Saleski's stated reason for collecting these musicians in one volume merely rehashed the old legend of shared spirituality: in his view all of the almost four hundred composers and performers included in his book—from the creator of Jewish operetta, Abraham Goldfaden (1840–1908), to the originator of twelve-tone technique, Arnold Schoenberg (1874–1951), and to the mistakenly included Max Bruch, Maurice Ravel, and Camille Saint-Saëns—"have in their souls that fire to which the Jewish prophets gave utterance in the time of old Jerusalem's glory."[9]

Saleski's was only one of many definitions of Jewish music or musicians. Such definitions, some descriptive, others prescriptive, have varied from technical ones to evasive references to a preternatural Jewish spirit or specific Jewish voice that supposedly infiltrates the compositions of Jewish composers. Thus while Joseph Yasser (1893–1981) tried to determine "Jewishness" in music at least partially on the basis of thematic material and its technical treatment,[10] David Ewen (1907–85) proposed an amorphous definition of Jewish music. Hebrew music is easily recognizable, Ewen argued, for "it becomes apparent to all those who have heard Hebrew music that there is something here, a voice far different from that to be found in any other music." In contrast to Yasser, Ewen considered technical details such as scales or intervals to be "superficial, inaccurate and of little importance." Definitions can hardly get more cryptic or complacent than his: "Hebrew music is a spirit expressed in music. That perpetual sadness, nurtured during two thousand years of the diaspora; that idealism which has kept a race alive despite the weight of centuries; that pride in one's traditions—these things are found in Hebrew music. Hebrew music is the audible expression of something that is in the heart of every Jew—a something by which every Jew must recognize himself. Listen to some music that is authentically Jewish and something within you will tell you that it belongs to you."[11]

Ewen's approach was not unique. The authors of a handbook prepared by the National Jewish Music Council to foster the commissioning of Jewish musical works confirm that "the *verbatim* utilization of folk song or liturgical melodic quotations . . . is no longer considered an absolutely indispensable part of Jewish music."[12] In the same handbook Isadore Freed (1900–1960), clearly working against stereotypes of Jews as overemotional, superficial, and exaggerating, describes the Jewish composer in terms as evasive (and as self-congratulatory) as Ewen's: "The serious Jewish composer is concerned with . . . clarity of thought, which is a Jewish essential; with the emotional depth of the Jewish spirit; with abstinence from flowery overstatement; with the expression of that indomitable sense of faith and hope which has kept the Jewish people alive during many dark centuries; with the prophetic demands for Justice and Freedom."[13] These sweeping, ambiguous definitions emphasizing the "Jewish spirit" of the music and the Jewish "essence" emanating from the composer owe much to Freed's teacher Ernest Bloch (1880–1959), the most renowned Jewish composer of the first half of the twentieth century, whose statements strongly influenced contemporaneous conceptions of Jewish music.

Such elusive definitions could serve not only as means of inclusion but also of exclusion, as the persecution of Jews during the Nazi era dismally demonstrates. Biological definition of Jews was combined with mystical concepts of Jewishness, the latter modeled on Richard Wagner's infamous essay *Judaism in Music* (1850). Wagner based his poisonous anti-Semitic ideology on the Romantic notion that a work of art expresses not only its composer's individuality but also his national or ethnic inheritance—a tautology if it refers to the composer's cultural tradition as a defining factor in the formation of his style, and racism if it ignores the cultural milieu in favor of vague racial characteristics. Neither Wagner's ideas about the racial determinism of art nor his anti-Semitic agenda were new at the time he published his article. The combination of the two in a public essay on music, however, signaled the infiltration of aggressive, political anti-Semitism into the sphere of culture.

Wagner's essay was so influential that rehashing his ideas became an obligatory ritual in every discussion of Jewish music. Surprisingly, though, the invocation of Wagner did not serve as a shibboleth, for opinions about his ideas hardly differentiated anti-Semites and the proponents of Jewish music. Ignoring, or for the moment pushing aside, Wagner's anti-Semitic agenda, authors of all stripes have often readily endorsed his essentialist view of Jewish composers. Ringer, for instance, who otherwise passionately fought anti-Semitic tendencies in musical discourse, was willing to explain Wagner's rejection of Jewish composers as a consequence of his "artistic destiny." Since "Jewish musical temperament is essentially Mediterranean in nature and hence, if not necessarily vocal, primarily melodic-rhythmic in essence," he wrote, "then the man [Wagner] destined to carry Central European harmony to its highest potential could hardly be expected to favour those most likely to interfere with his artistic-national mission, a mission he conceived and executed in an unremitting spirit of historical inevitability and moral rectitude." Acknowledgment of Wagner's anti-Semitism did not lessen his approval, because, Ringer insisted, "from a purely musical point of view, he scored a point or two in his predictions."[14]

Ringer relied heavily on the ideas of literary historian Heinrich Berl, who, inspired by Nietzsche's passionate attack on Wagner, wrote an anti-Wagnerian *Das Judentum in der Musik* in 1926. Yet even Berl, who in the preface of the book described himself as a non-Jew with Zionist convictions, agreed with Wagner's assumption of Judaism as a foreign element in Western culture. For him the basic question was whether this foreign element exercises a positive or a negative influence on the cultural development of the West. While Wagner answered the question in the negative, Berl proposed a positive interpretation. Berl's thesis is based on two basic premises: that the music of the East opposes the music of the West, and that Jewish music belongs to the Orient. He believed that in the music of Jewish composers the combination of the East and the West results in a "pseudo-morphosis" (the incongruity between "Eastern" content and "Western" form), which, he suggested, had been the "essential cause of the Asian crisis in European music since the Romantic era."[15] Contrasting Eastern (Jewish) and Western (European) music, Berl revels in binary oppositions: "melody" versus "harmony," "visual" versus "spiritual," "extensive" versus "intensive," "time-oriented" versus "space-oriented," "culture" versus "civilization" (the former in Berl's philo-Semitic account applied to the Jews, the latter to the Germans). Ringer celebrates Berl's approach, for, as he writes, it shows a "rare understanding of the intrinsically musical roots of the controversies that surrounded first Mahler and then Schoenberg."[16] By ignoring the sinister overtones of a "crisis" caused by Jews, Ringer demonstrates how aesthetic convictions (in Ringer's case the unconditional admiration of Wagner and Schoenberg) can hamper political judgment.

While others were still waiting for the Messiah of Jewish music, Berl had already found his hero in Arnold Schoenberg. According to Ringer, Berl believed that "hidden behind the new sounds and technical innovations [of Schoenberg's music], there lay a specifically Jewish intonation."[17] Berl saw the Viennese composers Gustav Mahler, Max Brod's teacher Adolf Schreiber, and Arnold Schoenberg as the first whose music contained the "voice" representing a primarily Jewish principle, and whose careers epitomized the fate of the Jewish composer in Western society. While Berl considered Mahler to have wrestled unsuccessfully with a Western form alien to him, and saw Schreiber's suicide as a result of his racially determined incompatibility with the norms of a European music he tried to master, he hailed Schoenberg as the one who overcame the handicap of his race by conquering the alien Western forms and opening new horizons. Despite Schoenberg's paradigmatic status in his conception, for Berl the solution to the "Jewish problem" in music was a Zionist one. His conviction that the Zionist movement should help Jews transform their "mechanical, non-organic existence" in exile to "organic reality" suggests a separatist solution that would mean that the Jews, while encouraged to find their own voice, would ultimately be excluded from the culture of the Diaspora.[18] Thus although Wagner's and Berl's essays were written with opposite intentions, their basic principles and proposed solutions hardly differed.

Flagrant though they may now appear, such correspondences between the premises advocated by propagandists for Jewish music and those of their anti-Semitic counterparts have rarely been noticed. Even Max Brod (1884–1968), whose analysis of German ideology exhibits political sensitivity, ignored the danger of labeling when he described Mahler's music as essentially Jewish. "It may be," he wrote in 1916, "that Mahler's music, though apparently German, is instinctively recognized as being non-German—which is indeed the case." At the time of its publication, Brod's revelation provoked angry protests from assimilated German Jewish music critics. Paul Stefan accused Brod of being "completely imbued with Zionism."[19] Stefan's aversion, typical of assimilated Jewish intellectuals, nevertheless signaled the danger of Brod's achievement.

Brod's efforts to save Mahler by labeling the characteristics of his music that were criticized by his contemporaries as typically "Jewish" exemplify how negative criticism played into Brod's and many others' way of thinking. The process is a characteristic one, repeated often as minorities accept and identify with the stereotypes applied to them by a dominant group in an attempt to turn negative critique into celebratory affirmation. Brod's tour de force, however, raises even more paradoxes, demonstrated by the Nazis' almost grotesquely favorable treatment of his research in the infamous guide to verboten musical territory, the 1940 edition of *Lexikon der Juden in der Musik*. "Brod," the authors write, "unlike his comrades of the same race, tries to explain the compositions of Jewish composers on the basis of their Jewish mentality."[20] To prove the point, the *Lexikon* quotes two long paragraphs from

Brod's article on Mahler, the stereotypical Jewish composer, who, however hard he tried, could not rid himself of his racial characteristics.

Brod did not deny that Mahler and Mendelssohn had been "keenly anxious to forget" their origin. Yet despite their efforts, Brod argues, the "demon is nevertheless present [in their music] and makes itself felt—in spite of all the polish—in a rather unruly manner." The image speaks for itself. The "demon," or as Brod puts it in another sentence, the "Jewish essence," irrepressibly reveals itself, especially in the music of Mahler, who, as Brod noted, draws deeply on subconscious sources. Similarly, in Mendelssohn's Violin Concerto the "Jewish tone—albeit used unconsciously—can be heard clearly, pervading the essence of the work rather than its details"[21]—a statement that, like all essentialist arguments, cannot be refuted empirically. Even when Brod tried to be more specific by collecting "Jewish traits" in Mahler's music, he could not free himself of all-embracing generalities. March rhythms, melodic lines fluctuating between major and minor, and slow beginnings of melodies may indeed be characteristic of Hasidic folk music, but the same features appear in the music of composers who have neither racial nor cultural relations with Jewish tradition.

The notion that the music of Jewish composers unconsciously expresses a "Jewish essence" served as the perfect fishing net for Brod; it was so general that it could snare absolutely every composer of Jewish origin. In fact, it must have caught composers of all stripes, but gentiles were thrown back without a word. By emphasizing the unconscious, Brod created not only the perfect shelter for gathering composers of Jewish origin under one roof, but also the perfect prison from which there could be no escape. The label "Jewish composer," which meant to liberate, was also a trap.

### THE PROTAGONISTS

This book critically examines three related topics: the birth of the notion of Jewish art music in Russia; the shaping of the idea of a racially conscious but not necessarily nationalistic musical idiom in the works of Ernest Bloch; and Arnold Schoenberg's abstract, utopian vision of music and politics as documented in his unpublished papers and his works with Jewish subject matter. Choosing Bloch and Schoenberg as the main characters of this historical narrative was no random decision. Bloch, who became the standard-bearing Jewish composer of the twentieth century, confirmed every stereotype reflected in definitions of Jewish music. Schoenberg did not correspond to Blochian stereotypes, for neither his personality nor his music fit into the image that Bloch propagated as "Jewish." He was drawn into the narrative of Jewish music both because his stature in the history of twentieth-century music marked him for appropriation and because his prominent role in German musical life and his subsequent expulsion from Germany made him a symbol of persecution. As debates surrounding Jewish art music show, the notion of Jewish music, though it descended from nineteenth-century ideas of national music, was nevertheless tightly bound to modernist tendencies. Jewish art music needed the prestige that a "high priest" of modernism such as Schoenberg could lend it. Moreover, even while Schoenberg's music remained outside the discussion of Jewish musical idioms, his figure loomed large in arguments about Jewish identity.

In previous studies of the history of Jewish music the placement of any two of these three topics in a single narrative has presupposed a historical continuum stretching from the ancient religious music of the Hebrews to the art music of the twentieth century. No data support this imagined continuity. Nor should it be assumed that a significant link existed between Bloch, Schoenberg, and the Russian originators of Jewish art music. As chapter 5 demonstrates, attempts to locate the origin of Bloch's style in the musical idiom of the Russian Jewish group have failed. Similarly, although Schoenberg had contact with some former members of the Russian group, he never established professionally significant relationships with them. In discussing such dissimilar composers as Bloch and Schoenberg under one banner, critics have shown only the strength of their own belief in the existence of a Jewish spirit that unites the music of all Jewish composers, however dissimilar their styles and methods.

In studies of Jewish music some authors have given equal weight to Bloch and Schoenberg, some have favored the one or the other. Whether Schoenberg or Bloch receives more praise demonstrates the authors' position in the debate about what style best epitomized Jewishness in art music. Even for the propagators of the notion of an essentially common Jewish idiom it has been easier to cast a vote for or against Schoenberg or Bloch than it has been to find their musical common ground.[22] Peter Gradenwitz is one of the few scholars who attempted to do so. To create a potential basis for a connection, Gradenwitz first tried to relate Schoenberg's musical style to characteristics of "Oriental music": "When Schoenberg argued that a certain tone-row should serve a musical composition as a key, as well as basic thought or theme, he may not have been aware of the fact that he was actually reintroducing into Western music the principles of ancient, traditional and still reigning oriental technique, although based on different scales. Some Israeli composers have rightly found that Schoenberg's twelve-tone music has distinct possibilities for the East and West synthesis sought after in Israel, and theirs is certainly one of the interesting and promising ways."[23]

Unwilling to deny Bloch the designation "Jewish composer," Gradenwitz ventured to link Bloch's musical style to Schoenberg's. The strange result reflects the difficulty of constructing a coherent narrative about Jewish art music: "In his late-period compositions—particularly the second String Quartet—he [Bloch] comes very near to Schoenberg's expressive twelve-tone melodic invention, and the synthesis between Blochian exoticism and Schoenbergian twelve-tone influence produces a stimulating proof of the latent Oriental roots of the twelve-tone technique. Yet while Schoenberg can hardly have been conscious of the Oriental heritage of his theory at the time of its formulation, Bloch would possibly deny an inner contact between his Oriental emphasis and Schoenberg's music."[24] In one respect Gradenwitz is correct: neither Bloch nor Schoenberg would have accepted a connection with the other. Schoenberg barely acknowledged Bloch's existence[25] and surely would have dismissed Bloch's Orientalizing music the way he dismissed, while working on his *Kol nidre*, the "violoncello sentimentality" of Max Bruch's *Kol nidre*, the best known "Jewish" instrumental piece before Bloch's *Schelomo*.

There was no other composer Bloch resented more than Schoenberg. Schoenberg's twelve-tone compositional method was claimed to have radically changed attitudes toward composition and thus rendered Bloch a musical conservative. By the 1940s Bloch had become an outspoken opponent of Schoenberg's music, which he not only considered harmful to his own musical career, but literally a danger to humanity:

> The "12-tone row," for me, is an *imposture!* Like the last paintings of *Picasso,* or *Cocteau* (alas, alas, all Jews, who have used the degeneracy of our Time, to cultivate it for *their profit!* After poisoning Europe, they have now come here, to this country, and poison it! We owe this to Mr. Hitler! A fine heritage. This goes with all the rest, with Atom bombs, and the next coming War. Art does not lie. I foresaw it all, I warned them, vainly, in my Lectures in Geneva 1911–1914. I saw it all coming, through the *degeneracy,* the *dishonesty* of the *cubism* and other "isms." R. *Wagner* was right in his "Judenthum"—horribly sad—but *true. Those* who put me, and my "modern" music in the same category as these "imposteurs" have never understood a note of my music, or what I *mean.* I am not a reactionary, but I believe in *Life,* in Tradition *and* Evolution, in *organic* form, in *integrated* mind and not in farcical elucidations made on an arbitrary system, mere *sensations* of nerves, versus *intelligence).*[26]

Considering how rejected Bloch felt in the 1940s, this antimodernist outburst is not surprising. More striking is that his outmoded convictions were mixed with Wagnerian anti-Semitism and that Schoenberg came to symbolize for Bloch all the negative attributes he labeled "Jewish" (even, unaccountably, in Picasso and Cocteau).

In the present work, the stories of the Russian Jewish group and the various aspects of Bloch's and Schoenberg's Jewish identities are presented as case studies, expressly countering essentialist assumptions by locating the continuity between these stories not in a shared essence but in evolving social milieus. It was due to the similarity between Bloch and Schoenberg's social status as assimilated Jews in a suspicious or hostile environment that made their relationship to their Jewish background equally peculiar.

Bloch and Schoenberg both absorbed the anti-Semitic tendencies of their surrounding culture and made frequent anti-Semitic remarks, especially when confronted with real or imagined opponents of their music who happened to be Jewish. Although they were well aware of the dangers of ghetto-ization, both were willing to essentialize Jews as a group representing a single set of ideas and attitudes. It was, however, no accident that both Schoenberg and Bloch developed a fear of "Jewish criticism" of their work. In nationally minded Jewish circles their modernist aesthetics could easily mark them, in the words of Abraham Zvi Idelsohn (1882–1938), as "renegades and assimilants" who "detest all Jewish cultural values."[27] Being seen at once as too Jewish in the dominant culture, and too assimilated among the nationalist or observant Jews, they remained outsiders both in their ethnic and in their adopted cultures, especially since both cultures understood identities as exclusive, determined by national or racial essences.

By connecting the inherent contradictions of Jewish musical nationalism with the intrinsic ambivalence of Bloch's and Schoenberg's Jewish identity, the narrative of Jewish art music emerges as a complex, sometimes contradictory and often unsettling story. It was neither Bloch's or Schoenberg's racial heritage, nor their variously looser or stronger bonds to Jewish culture, that defined their artistic personalities, but a web of interrelated social, political, and personal components—of which their Jewishness was only one. By showing the ideological currents that have colored Jewish nationalism in the first half of the twentieth century, I hope to supply a historical perspective that has often been missing even from scholarly discussions. I wish to question essentializing conceptions of Jewish identity as well as attempts to define Jewish music and musicians collectively. Bloch and Schoenberg deserve our attention not as "Jewish" or "universal" composers but as artists with multiple identities whose compositions serve us less well as expressions of a Jewish essence than as focal points for critical readings of their composers' uneasy personal relationship to both their ethnic and adopted cultures, an unease that amply demonstrates the contradictions inherent in the concept of "Jewish music."

# PART I

# Jewish Nationalism à la Russe

## *The Society for Jewish Folk Music*

# Chapter 1

# "Trifles of Jewish Music"

*Is it not from "trifles" that emerge all the important collections of national objects?*
*One must begin by first loving that which is small and modest . . . that which does*
*not attract because of its majesty and colossal forms . . . but where are hidden the*
*characteristic traits of that nation, hidden by the futile modes of despotism, ignorance*
*and persecution.*
    VLADIMIR STASOV, "Art israélite à l'Exposition Universelle" (1878)

In a 1924 article Russian Soviet musicologist Leonid Sabaneyev (1881–1968) announced that through the work of a group of Jewish composers Jewish music was approaching the phase Sabaneyev called "its artistic expansion."[1] Sabaneyev's account of the birth of Jewish art music reflected art publicist Vladimir Stasov's version of the development of Russian musical nationalism. Lest there be any doubt about this connection, the prophecy with which Sabaneyev closed his article demonstrated the strong effect of Russian national music on Jewish aspirations. Stasov shaped and propagated most effectively the Russian national ideals as the ideological basis for the *moguchaya kuchka* (frequently translated as "the Mighty Band"), a group of nationally committed Russian composers around Miliy Balakirev (1837–1910).[2] The Jewish group of composers, Sabaneyev claimed, has "many external features in common with the Russian national school" and "has many chances of becoming the 'mighty band' of Jewry."

Heir to Herderian ideals of nationhood, Sabaneyev, like most of his contemporaries, saw no contradiction between a belief in the fundamentally diverse characteristics of nations, on the one hand, and the uniformity of their evolution toward the expression of their national genius, on the other. The genius of the Jewish race, like that of the Russian nation, was supposed to have been carried unconsciously for a long period by the "music associated with the life of the people," in other words, by folk music. In Sabaneyev's view the appearance of an intelligentsia with national allegiances signaled that this "unconscious, semi-psychological" phase of national music came to an end, for members of the new Jewish intelligentsia, after recognizing in their native music *"the style of the national soul,* the style of its sentiments, its emotions, its historical existence," acquire "the irresistible conviction that the real creative power of music is always and in every case national." Sabaneyev's is only one of many variations of the same basic tale of origin, newly applied to the birth of Jewish national music. It suggests a natural development in which a conscious expression of the national spirit replaces an unconscious one, and in which the sophisticated art music of the intelligentsia supersedes the folk music of the uneducated masses.

Sabaneyev, like other historians of Jewish music, identified the origin of Jewish art music with the foundation of the Society for Jewish Folk Music (Obshchestvo Yevreyskoy Narodnoy Muzïki, henceforth OYNM) in St. Petersburg in 1908. The OYNM was an association of professional musicians and music lovers who sought to purvey Jewish music, both secular and sacred, to audiences both Jewish and non-Jewish. The organization was inspired in part by two of Russia's most influential musical figures, Vladimir Stasov (1824–1906), who encouraged Jewish artists to create Jewish art, and composer Nikolay Rimsky-Korsakov (1844–1908), who prophesized to his Jewish students about the coming of a Jewish Glinka. Both were intimately associated with the Mighty Band. In most narratives of the OYNM's history these two men have been given so much credit that their contributions have been allowed to overshadow the cultural and political factors that paved the way for a Jewish musical renaissance in Russia. The overemphasis on Rimsky-Korsakov's and Stasov's roles has also served to shift attention from the collection and popularization of folk music, the focus of the OYNM at its inauguration, to the creation of Jewish art music. The Jewish political movements and the Russian model, however, played equally important parts in the development of the OYNM. As the history of the OYNM cannot be fully understood without the context of Jewish nationalism in Russia, so the music created by its composers cannot be accurately interpreted without comparison to Russian national music.

The political vagaries within the Jewish national movement strongly affected the emergence and development of Jewish cultural organizations. The desire to preserve and revive culture as a substitute for political activity and the bitter fights over the nature of the culture that would provide a common identity for all Jews left their mark also on the OYNM. Revisiting the political debates helps us understand how the fate of the OYNM was tied to that of the Jews in Russia, in other words, to a gruesome political situation, the memory of which should not be eradicated by nationalist nostalgia toward a pre-Holocaust, intact Jewish culture within Russia's Pale of Settlement. As the spiritual focus of some of the factions of Jewish nationalism in Russia contributed to the process of gradually losing touch with the political reality that gave impetus to the movement in the first place, so composers' preoccupation with the creation of Jewish art music obscured the original nationalist goals of the OYNM.

The Russian nationalist model was crucial in turning the OYNM from an organization for the preservation and popularization of Jewish musical culture into a funnel for the creation of a specifically Jewish art music. The progress from simple folk song arrangements through pieces of art music that exhibited their composers' professional training and, finally, through modernist compositions with a neonationalist agenda mirrored the progress of Russian national music, evolving from *kuchkist* principles exemplified by the Mighty Band, through a modernist, neonationalist combination of stylistic elements, appropriated from folk music and modernist techniques, which reached its peak in the works of Igor Stravinsky. While the neonationalist phase of Jewish national music is the topic of chapter 2, this chapter focuses on the first, *kuchkist* phase. Ironically, the music written by composers whose ambition was to become the Mighty Band of Jewish music emulated their Russian models not only in technical details, but also in their willing embrace of stereotypes Russian composers exploited to depict the Oriental others, among them Jews. Instead of a Jewish Glinka, then, the OYNM produced several Jewish Borodins, who, using the Oriental style initiated by Glinka in his *Ruslan and Ludmilla,* cast themselves in the exotic garb of the Polovtsians of Borodin's *Prince Igor.*

## POLITICAL BACKGROUND:
## THE EMERGENCE OF JEWISH NATIONALISM IN RUSSIA

Albert Weisser (1918–82), an insightful chronicler of the Russian Jewish national movement in music, points to two Jewish cultural-political factors that stimulated the new Russian Jewish intelligentsia to create Jewish art music around 1900: *haskalah* (the Jewish enlightenment) and Herzlian Zionism.[3] What produced the intensity of the Jewish cultural renaissance was not the simple fact of the appearance of these movements but their transformation in Russia, where they had to adapt to the specific political situation of Russian Jewry. Precisely because of the oppressive policies of the tsars, culture came to serve as a surrogate for political activity among Jews in Russia even more than in Central Europe. This emphasis on culture, coupled with the belief in the existence of an intact, authentic Judaism in Russia, gave a special sense of mission to Russian Jewry.

Initiated by the German Jewish philosopher Moses Mendelssohn (1729–86) in Berlin at the end of the eighteenth century, *haskalah* gained ground in nineteenth-century Russia against the opposition of the Orthodox Jewish establishment, which feared the movement's secularizing effects. In Russia as in Western Europe, *haskalah* mediated between assimilation and Orthodoxy, advocating both the study of Western culture and internal Jewish reforms. The most important organization of the Russian *haskalah* was the Society for the Spread of Enlightenment among the Jews of Russia (Obshchestvo Rasprostraneniya Prosveshcheniya Sredi Yevreyev Rossii, henceforth ORP), founded in 1863 in St. Petersburg under the patronage of the philanthropic Gintsburg family.[4] Especially after a series of pogroms in 1881 that dashed the hopes of many assimilationists, organizations like the ORP began to attract members of the assimilated Jewish intelligentsia.[5] This new group became the primary inculcator of secular nationalist ideals, which appeared in Russia even before Theodor Herzl's Zionist movement.

When it reached Russia, Herzl's brand of Zionism inspired Russian Jewish nationalists to define their national ideals in opposition to those propagated in the West. Resistance to Herzlian political Zionism in Russia displayed the familiar dichotomy between Jewish existence in the East and the West: a dichotomy between an almost intact community with living traditions and a Westernized, relatively emancipated Jewish culture that engaged in political action to substitute for its vanishing national identity. The Russian counterparts of Zionism were distinguished from the Herzlian movement by their focus on spiritual values instead of political programs and their awareness of an existing Jewish culture. The cultural organizations that sprang to life to preserve and develop these Jewish cultural traditions reflected the relationship of the competing factions of Jewish nationalists to the culture of the Diaspora.

The most influential of these Eastern Zionist movements was founded by Asher Gintsberg (1856–1927), more commonly known as Ahad Ha'am (Hebrew for "One of the People"). The Jewish secular nationalism advocated by Ahad Ha'am opposed Herzl's political program, accusing it of sacrificing a living Jewish tradition for a utopian political future. Ahad Ha'am did not dispute the legitimacy of Herzl's objective to create a Jewish state in Palestine, but he mistrusted the political methods advocated by Herzlian Zionists. The diplomatic solution for which they strove, he believed, was divorced from the political reality of the Russian Empire, home of 70 percent of Europe's Jewish population. The realization of Herzl's utopia, Ahad Ha'am feared, would break the continuity of Jewish tradition in the Pale of Settlement. He warned that spreading Herzlian Zionism was not only false but also dangerous for the Eastern European masses because, by exchanging material and political interest for spiritual, cultural integrity, it distracted the Jews from their "loyalty to spiritual greatness."[6]

Ahad Ha'am did not limit Judaism to religious practice. Instead of religious observance or potentially disruptive Herzlian politics, he offered culture as the means for preserving Judaism's spiritual continuity, which, he believed, was already threatened by the disintegration of isolated ghetto communities. What needed to be saved was not the Jews but Jewish ideals, the Jewish national spirit that Ahad Ha'am constructed from Jewish traditions. Ahad Ha'am envisioned a Jewish Palestine not as a politically independent state that would give home to Jewish refugees, but as a cultural center in which an intellectual elite would cultivate the true Jewish spirit and where an uncorrupted, genuine "Hebrew" character would be created.[7] This center was supposed to radiate the "right kind" of Judaism and thus help keep it alive in the Diaspora.

Ahad Ha'am's focus on abstract spiritual and cultural values and his contempt for political programs were not unique in Russia. Next to Ahad Ha'am the most influential advocate for the revival of Jewish culture was the historian Simon Dubnov (1860–1941). Initially Dubnov, like Ahad Ha'am, was an ardent opponent of political Zionism, which he thought would raise false hopes in a people who needed all their strength for survival.[8] Dubnov believed that other means besides politics existed for helping the Jews. As Ahad Ha'am transformed political Zionism into spiritual Zionism, Dubnov promoted cultural nationalism in opposition to the political nationalism of the Zionists. As the founder of the autonomist movement, Dubnov fought for cultural as well as limited political autonomy in the Diaspora.

Dubnov formulated his theory of Jewish nationalism in a series of articles entitled "Letters on Old and New Judaism," published between 1897 and 1906 in *Voskhod* (Sunrise), a St. Petersburg Russian Jewish periodical that served as the most important forum for the new Russian Jewish intelligentsia until 1906.[9] Strongly influenced by French historian Ernest Renan's definition of a nation as a "spiritual principle,"[10] Dubnov distinguished three phases in the historical development of a people's national existence: the tribal, the political-territorial, and the spiritual. Only in the second, territorial phase did nationalism appear as an aggressive and oppressive force, familiar to the Jews who suffered its consequences. Dubnov rejected this aggressive nationalism by calling it "national egotism" and advocated a spiritual, "national individualism" in its stead. National egotism, Dubnov stated, aimed to repress the culture of the minorities, while national individualism would give cultural and political autonomy to all peoples.[11]

Both Dubnov's spiritual nationalism and Ahad Ha'am's cultural Zionism were attempts to give culture a role that would have been played under other circumstances (or in other countries) by politics. Dubnov and Ahad Ha'am's major point of difference lay in their conceptions of the time and place of the Jewish spiritual rebirth. Ahad Ha'am placed his hopes in Palestine, whereas Dubnov insisted that the Diaspora could become an autonomous cultural entity without any particular spiritual lodestar. Dubnov, who held the existing culture of the Diaspora to be more eternal than Ahad Ha'am's dreams about the future, rightly sensed disdain for the Diaspora in Ahad Ha'am's utopian vision of a purified Jewish culture.

The debate between Dubnov and Ahad Ha'am about the Diaspora came to a head in 1909, at a time when controversies among Jewish nationalists about the kind of culture that should be fostered reached a new level of divisiveness.[12] By the 1910s Jewish secular national movements in Russia were divided according to their position regarding the interrelationship of politics and culture and their attitude toward the Diaspora. While the Herzlian

Zionists' political program ignored the existence of Diaspora culture and Ahad Ha'am's cultural Zionism dreamt of its purification in a Jewish Palestine, Dubnov's cultural nationalism saw the Diaspora as its basis.

Only the *Bund*,[13] which represented the socialist faction in Russian Jewish politics, rejected the utopian tendencies of the nationalist movements. Jewish socialists focused on practical solutions to political and social problems and fought for freedom equally for Jews and non-Jews. Although in 1903 even the *Bund* adopted national-cultural autonomy in its program, Jewish socialists disapproved of the narrow outlook of political and cultural nationalists alike. Representing the interests of the masses instead of an intellectual elite, Ber Borochov (1881–1917), founder of the socialist Poale Zion (Workers of Zion) party, lashed out at utopian Zionism in the revolutionary year 1905:

> I confess that my mind is not capable of grasping what benefit would redound to poor, hounded Yankel if a Spinoza were to write his works in Hebrew, a Meyerbeer compose his operas on strictly Jewish themes, and Ahad Ha-am create a wonderful museum of Jewish antiquities in Jerusalem. . . . Sometimes [I] . . . am seized by the urge to hate Palestine when [I] meet with those among its advocates who, whether fastidiously or ecstatically, push aside all thought for the people and its needs in order to devote themselves fully to some kind of national essence.[14]

Despite the opposition of Borochov and his faction, this national "essence" remained a central concern for Jewish nationalists in Russia. Most of the debates concerning Jewish culture revolved around this undefined essence, which was to be deciphered and reconstructed out of the cultural shards and artifacts that the members of the Jewish intelligentsia started to collect toward the end of the nineteenth century.

### CULTURAL REVIVAL AT WORK

The rapid spread of Jewish cultural societies in Russia in the first decade of the twentieth century was not only a sign of an increasing national orientation among the Jewish intelligentsia but also one of political frustration. From the time of Alexander II (1855–81) until the Bolshevik Revolution in 1917, the history of Russian Jewry consisted of a sequence of hopeful signs indicating the government's willingness to improve the situation of the Jews. Such promises, however, went unfulfilled, leaving behind the sobering reality of a fundamentally anti-Jewish tsarist agenda. After the assassination of Alexander II in 1881, his reforms were abolished and new anti-Jewish legislation introduced.[15] The attempted democratization of tsarist Russia following the 1905 Revolution had a similarly devastating effect on the Jewish population. The tsar's manifesto of 17 October 1905, which contained a declaration of civic equality and thus implied the abolition of restrictive laws against the Jews, instigated a wave of pogroms throughout the Pale of Settlement. Costing numerous lives and much material damage, the pogroms also served as a pretext for the tsar not to apply the new law of equality to Jews.[16] Partially out of political frustration Jews turned inward and started to mobilize their economic, educational, social and cultural resources toward the modernization of Jewish life.

In 1882 Dubnov and political activist Maksim Vinaver (1862–1926) founded the Historical-Ethnographic Commission (Istoriko-etnograficheskaya komissiya), which served as a framework for historical research. Since state archives were closed to Jews, Dubnov's only means for conducting historical research was collecting Jewish source material. In 1891, while working on a monumental history of the Jews in Eastern Europe, Dubnov had circulated a pamphlet calling for the collection of Jewish historical documents. Dubnov and Vinaver's findings appeared in a two-volume study and in supplements to *Yevreyskaya starina* (Jewish antiquity).[17] Several articles about folk songs were published in the early volumes of *Yevreyskaya starina*.[18] In 1898 historians Saul Ginzburg (1866–1940) and Pesach Marek (1862–1920) called for collecting Jewish folk songs. Their collection, *Yevreyskiye narodnïye pesni v Rossii* (Jewish folk songs in Russia), appeared in 1901 as a supplement to *Voskhod*. Like other contemporaneous folk-song collections, it contained only the texts of the songs, grouped into eleven thematic categories.[19]

With Dubnov as its vice-chair, the Jewish Historical-Ethnographic Society (Yevreyskoye Istoriko-Etnograficheskoye Obshchestvo) achieved independence from the ORP in 1908.[20] Between 1912 and 1914, under the leadership of writer and folklorist Shlomo Zanvil Rappoport, better known by his penname Semyon An-sky (1863–1920), this society organized major ethnographic expeditions for the systematic collection of Jewish ethnographic material in the centers of Hasidism, in the Ukrainian districts of Volhynia and Podolia. An assimilated Jew who published in both Russian and Yiddish, An-sky was a socialist who turned to Jewish folk art only after returning to Russia to participate in the 1905 Revolution. Giving up political activity for a while, An-sky focused his energies on the "systematic and comprehensive collection of objects representing every aspect of folk art, treasures of Jewish heritage, descriptions of every facet of daily Jewish life,"[21] which seemed to be perishing before his eyes. An-sky was determined to dedicate the rest of his life to this project. His mission was not without a political agenda. Demonstrating that Jews had an indigenous culture of their own, An-sky also wanted to justify their right to autonomy and to counter the common assumption that Jews simply borrowed the cultural artifacts of others. With the financial support of Vladimir Gintzburg, two expeditions took place, one in 1912, the other in 1913. The expedition lasted two years, during which An-sky and his team collected, among other documents of

Jewish culture, one thousand melodies.[22] Members of An-sky's team included Moscow critic and composer Yoel (Yuliy) Engel (1868–1927) and
ethnographer Zusman (Zinovy) Kiselgof (1878–1939),[23] both prominent
figures in the OYNM. Many of the songs appeared in OYNM collections and
in arrangements by OYNM composers.[24]

After 1905 numerous Jewish societies were founded both in St. Petersburg, then the center of Jewish activities, and in the provinces.[25] The programs of these societies, many of which functioned as substitutes for the
schools that were closing their doors to Jewish students, were very similar:
they offered courses for adults, set up libraries, and organized popular lectures and professional discussions. On 16 November 1908 the founding
meeting of the Jewish Historical-Ethnographic Society took place in St. Petersburg. Activities surrounding this society might have been a factor in the
foundation of the OYNM, which also came into being in 1908, approximately
at the same time as Betsalel, a society for Jewish art, was founded.[26]

THE SOCIETY FOR JEWISH FOLK MUSIC

At its inception, the OYNM had aims very close to those of the Jewish Historical Ethnographic Society: the collection, preservation, and cultivation
of Jewish cultural artifacts—in this case, primarily Jewish folk music. According to chroniclers of the OYNM the founding members had to accept
the specification "folk music" in the OYNM's name, since folk music was the
only kind of music Russian authorities were willing to recognize as a basis
for a Jewish musical society. The name "Society for Jewish Folk Music" was,
however, not a complete misnomer. When in the 1940s one of the founding members, Solomon Rosovsky (1878–1962), recounted the foundation
of the OYNM, he still described Jewish music as folk and synagogue music.
As examples of Jewish art music Rosovsky referred to compositions by
Glinka, Balakirev, and Musorgsky. Here is how Israel Rabinovitch retold
Rosovsky's account:

> When we entered the bureaucrat's sanctum, we saw before us twelve forbid-
> ding-looking officials who regarded us with considerable suspicion. Nisviszki
> explained our mission: we were interested in founding a society for Jewish mu-
> sic. "Jewish music?" The ejaculation came from Drachevski.[27] "What is *that*?"
> Tomars nudged Rosovsky to jump into the breach; as advocate, Rosovsky could
> now show his talents; the reception was going to be definitely unsympathetic.
> Rosovsky did not require to be coaxed; forthwith he launched into a lecture
> on the history and the nature of "Jewish music"; the purport of which was that
> Jewish music had always existed and that its development had never been in-
> terrupted. The impromptu lecture adduced the example of synagogal music
> and did not fail to mention songs vernacular and typical of the daily mode of
> Jewish life. He alluded to the music of Chassidim, he spoke of Jewish instru-

mental music. Finally, by way of peroration, and as clinching argument, Rosovsky referred to the fact that the Russian composers Glinka, Balakirev, and Moussorgsky, had in their own music made use of Jewish melodies. Upon Moussorgsky's tomb, Rosovsky added, joining pathos to reason, there was engraved an aria from his oratorio *Joshua-ben-Nun,* the melody for which had been borrowed from the synagogue.[28]

Drachevski began to display some interest, he stroked his mustache, he reminisced. Yes, he had himself heard some Jewish music, at a Jewish wedding it was, but that was folk-music. Certainly not music as it was understood today. Not Jewish music as such. Folk-music, yes. He was of the opinion that the society should be called "The Society for Jewish Folk-Music."[29]

The participants of this interview, Solomon Rosovsky, the pianist Leo Nisvitzky (later Arie Abilea, 1887–1959), and the singer Joseph Tomars (professional name of Iosif Beer, 1864–1934), were all devoted Zionists. Six of the seven members of the first music committee of the OYNM—Efraim Shklyar (1871–1943?), Rosovsky, Mikhail Gnesin (1883–1957), Pesach Lvov (1881–1913), Alexander Zhitomirsky (1881–1937), and Lazar Saminsky (1882–1959)— were students of Rimsky-Korsakov. Later other musicians joined the OYNM, among them composers such as Lev Mordukhov Tseitlin (1884–1930),[30] Moses Milner (1886–1953), and Joseph Achron (1886–1943). In 1914 the board of directors included such prominent figures as An-sky and dilettante art critic Maximilian Sïrkin (1858–?).[31] In 1913 pianist David Schorr (1867–1942), Yoel Engel (1868–1927), Jacob Weinberg (1879–1956), and Alexander Krein (1883–1951) founded a separate Moscow branch. Other branches were soon founded in Kiev, Kharkov, Ekaterinoslav, Riga, Simferopol, Rostov-on-the-Don, Baku, and Odessa.[32]

The OYNM's activities included the organization of public lectures and concerts of Jewish music, the collection of folk music, and the publication of compositions by OYNM composers. The first concerts were modeled on Engel's concert in Moscow in November 1900, which was regarded as the first concert of Jewish music. Engel, whom historian Pesach Marek asked to review the musical material of *Jewish Folk Songs in Russia,* organized the concert as part of the series of folk music of different ethnicities sponsored by Russia's first ethnomusicological organization, the Musico-Ethnographic Commission of the Imperial Society of Friends of Natural History, Anthropology, and Ethnography (MEK for short).[33] Lectures by Marek about the texts and by Engel about the music of folk songs preceded the concert. Prayer songs, love songs, family songs, and comic songs appeared in Engel's simple, strophic settings on the program. Yet despite Engel's pride in keeping the tunes intact, he could not resist building drama when called for by the text. At the end of "Das kind liegt" he thickened the piano texture, raised the dynamic level, and emphasized the rhythm suggestive of a funeral march to convey the tragic death of the child's mother implied in the text (ex. 1).

Example 1. Ending of Engel's "Das kind liegt" *(Yidishe folkslieder)*, mm. 25–33. Lyrics originally in Yiddish, Russian, and German.

([Who would] take you to school [my child]? There is no mother here, there is no consolation.)

A few months later Engel repeated the concert in St. Petersburg, where it drew a significant number of students from the Conservatory—at that time the only institution of higher education in Russia in which the number of Jewish students seems not to have been strictly regulated by quota.[34] The memory of this concert must have lingered on, for at the second meeting of the OYNM on 19 December 1908 the board invited Engel to organize a similar event.[35] The Conservatory hosted Engel's concert on 12 April 1909. Another concert had taken place three months earlier in the concert hall of the Society of Civil Engineers. The program was similar to Engel's, except that most arrangements were by Shklyar and that they also performed Jewish songs by two idols of Russian music, Rimsky-Korsakov and Musorgsky.[36]

Following Engel's model most concerts opened with preconcert lectures on topics related to Jewish music.[37] Beginning in 1913 Rosovsky also organized courses with the aim of making performers familiar with the style of Jewish music.[38] The Jewish music to be performed was provided by OYNM members, who, like Engel, arranged folk songs that they had either collected themselves or, in most cases, borrowed from the transcriptions of folklorist Zusman Kiselgof.

The OYNM published Jewish music in easily performable arrangements. The most user-friendly publication was Kiselgof's 1912 anthology *Lieder-Zamelbukh far der yidishe shul un familie* (Collection of songs for the Jewish school and family).[39] Pesach Lvov's and Alexander Zhitomirsky's simplified arrangements were wholly utilitarian. The volume contained twelve *skarbove* or sacred songs, forty-five secular folk songs, five *niggunim* or "songs without words,"[40] and seven unaccompanied cantillation melodies, called *trop* in Yiddish (see table 1). As in most of the OYNM's early concerts, art music was represented in Kiselgof's volume by twenty-three works by well-known Western or Russian composers, among them Orientalizing ones excerpted from Anton Rubinstein's operas, choruses by Musorgsky, and Glinka's "Yevreyskaya pesnya" (Hebrew song), mixed with vocal pieces by Mendelssohn, Beethoven, Mozart, and Saint-Saëns, arranged for three- or four-part a cappella chorus, for duets with piano accompaniment or, in a few cases, for solo voice and piano.

The mixture of sacred and secular, folk and art music, Russian and non-Russian, Jewish and non-Jewish composers shows that Kiselgof adhered to no particular nationalist bias. He included favorite melodies most commonly used in Jewish households without forcing any specific ideological purpose on the users of his *Zamelbukh*. While ideologically neutral, his selection reflected the taste of Russian Jews, who eagerly embraced the stereotype of Jews as Orientals. Of the sixty-two folk melodies in the *Zamelbukh,* thirty are in minor and twenty-five in the exotic-sounding altered Phrygian, also called *frigish,* a mode distinguished by the half-step between its first and second and the augmented second between its second and third degrees.[41]

TABLE 1. Table of Contents of Kiselgof's *Lieder-Zamelbukh far der yidishe shul un familie* (Collection of Songs for the Jewish School and Family, 1913)

*I. Skarbowe Volks-Nigunim*[a]

| 1 | Scholojm aleichem! (Peace be with you!) |
|---|---|
| 2 | Adir bimlucho (Mighty is His kingdom) |
| 3 | Zur mischeloj ochalnu (The rock from which we have eaten) |
| 4 | Jojm schabos kojdesch hu (The Sabbath day is holy) |
| 5 | Mnucho w'simcho (Rest and happiness) |
| 6 | Eli Zijojn w'oreho (God of Zion and its cities)[b] |
| 7 | Ejlijohu hanowi (Elijah the prophet) |
| 8 | Ism'chu w'malchuscho (The Heavens will rejoice) |
| 9 | Ogil w'esmach b'simchas tojro (I will rejoice and be happy on Simkhat Torah) |
| 10 | Sissu w'simchu (Rejoice on Simkhat Torah) |
| 11 | Hamawdil bein kojdesch l'chojl (He who distinguished between the sacred and the weekday) |
| 12 | Ejlijohu hanowi, Ejlijohu hatischbi (Elijah, the prophet, Elijah the Tishibite) |

*II. Weltliche Folks-Lieder*

| 13 | Der alef-beis (The alphabet) |
|---|---|
| 14 | Oder Iden sajnen mir (But we are Jews) |
| 15 | Helf uns Gottenju (Help us, our God) |
| 16 | G'wald že Brider (Oy, brothers) |
| 17 | Amol is gewen a majse (Once upon a time) |
| 18 | Hot Haschem isborach arob geschickt (God, blessed be His name, sent down) |
| 19 | Ale-lu-le, schlof majn gdule (Ayle-lyu-le, sleep, my glory) |
| 20 | Schön bin ich, schön (I'm really pretty) |
| 21 | Gej majn Kind in chejder (Go to school, my child) |
| 22 | Schlof majn Tochter (Sleep, my daughter) |
| 23 | Zehn Brider (Ten brothers) |
| 24 | Oj, chanuke (Oh, Chanukah) |
| 25 | Zint on lichtlech (Light candles) |
| 26 | A Purim-lied (A Purim song) |
| 27 | Hob ich a por Oksen (I have a pair of oxen) |
| 28 | Hob ich a klejnem Michalku (I have a little Mikhalko) |
| 29 | Bulbe (Potatoes) |
| 30 | A gnejwe (A theft) |
| 31 | A retenisch (A secret)[c] |
| 32 | Schlof, schlof, schlof (Sleep, sleep, sleep) |
| 33 | Di gilderne Pawe (The golden peacock)[d] |
| 34 | Der Ejberster is der mchuten (God is the father-in-law)[e] |
| 35 | L'chaim, rebe! (Cheers, rabbi!) |
| 36 | As ich wolt gehat (If I had)[f] |
| 37 | Die Mesinke ojsgegeben (Giving away the youngest daughter)[g] |
| 38 | Chazkele[h] |
| 39 | Schlof, majn Kind (Sleep, my child)[i] |
| 40 | Ich bin mir a chossid'l (I am a little khosid) |

TABLE 1 *(continued)*

41  Sitzen, sitzen sieben Kinder (Seven children are sitting)
42  Schlof, majn Kind, majn Krejn (Sleep my child, my crown)[j]
43  Kinder, kumt, der Friling ruft (Children, come, the spring calls)
44  Unter dem Kinds Wiegele (Beneath the child's cradle)
45  Ich bin a bal-agole (I am a coachman)
46  Saj že mir gesund (Fare thee well)
47  Sejt gesunter-hejt (Bless you)
48  Omar Adojnon l'jakojw (God said to Jacob)
49  Schir eres (Lullaby)
50  Alte Kasche (The eternal question)[k]
51  Unser Rebeniu (Our rabbi)
52  Mejerke, majn sun (Little Mejer, my son)[l]
53  Wos wet sajn, as Moschiach wet kumen? (What will be when the Messiah comes?)
54  Zindt on di hawdole (Light the habdalah candle)[m]
55  Welcher jojm-tojw is der bester? (Which holiday is the best?)
56  O, Bruder, sog (Ah, brother, tell me)
57  A gute Woch (A good week)

*III. Lieder ohne Werter*

58  A redl, wie men sing si: Stiller—wejnt sich, gicher—wilt sich tanzen—(A little round, how people sing it: Quietly, it weeps, faster, so you want to dance)
59  A Nigun on a sof (A niggun without end)
60  A Nigun
61  A redel fun Lubawižer rebe (Round of the Lubavitcher Rebe)
62  A Ljadier chabadnize (A "chabad" song from Ladi)

*IV. Kinstlerische Lieder [translated into Yiddish by M. Riwesman, into Hebrew by S. Tchernikovsky]*

63  Alz git a schewach dem bojre (Everything praises the creator) (Betchowen)
64  Di Frejd (The joy) (Betchowen)[n]
65  Du, finstere nechtele (You, dark little night) (Rubinstejn)
66  Zu dem silber-kloren tajchel (To the silver-clear little stream) (Rubinstejn)
67  Der Chor fun bnej-Schejm (The chorus of the sons of Shem) (Rubinstejn)
68  Der Chor fun bnej Chom (The chorus of the sons of Ham) (Rubinstejn)
69  Die Frejd fun jagd (The joy of the hunt) (Rubinstejn)
70  Jhojschua-bin-Nun (Joshua the son of the Nun) (Musorgski)
71  Der Persische Chor (The Persian chorus) (Glinka)
72  Herbstlied (Autumn song) (Mendelsohn)
73  Der Wald (The forest) (Mendelsohn)
74  A Gruss (The greeting) (Mendelsohn)
75  A Winterlied (A winter song) (Mendelsohn)
76  Ot is der jojm tow gekumen (Holiday has just arrived) (Mendelsohn)
77  Es falt a thoj (Dew is falling) (Mendelsohn)
78  Schejn Fejgele, du sing (Song, beautiful bird) (Mendelsohn)
79  Das gesegenen sich fun a jeger (The goodbye of a hunter) (Mendelsohn)
80  Die Feldblumen (The wildflowers) (Mendelsohn)

TABLE 1 *(continued)*

81    Der Chor fun di Plischtim (The chorus of the Philistines) (Sen Sans)
82    A Owendlied (An evening song) (Mozart)
83    Lejas Gesang (Lea's song) (Rubinstejn)
84    Der hejliger Schabbes (The sacred Shabbat) (Rubinstejn)
85    A Jüdisch-Lied (A Jewish song) (Glinka)

*V. Trop (Tajmej honginejs)*

86    Batojro (The Torah)
87    B'haftejro (The Haftarah)
88    B'jomim nojroim (The High Holidays)
89    Mgilas Estejr (Esther)
90    Mgilas Ejcho (Lamentations)
91    Schir haschirim, Rus, Kejheles (Song of Songs, Ruth, Ecclesiastes)
92    Akdomojs (Hymn recited by Ashkenazik Jews on the first day of Shavuous)

[a] Transliteration follows Kiselgof's original.
[b] Arranged also by Tseitlin (1914, OYNM, number 45).
[c] A different version is arranged by Pesach Lvov (1912, number 26).
[d] Arranged also by Efraim Shklyar (1909, OYNM, number 1).
[e] Arranged also by Zhitomirsky (1911, OYNM, number 21).
[f] Arranged also by Zhitomirsky (1910, OYNM, number 10).
[g] Song by Varshavsky, arranged also by H. Kopït (1912, OYNM, number 29).
[h] Arranged also by Shklyar (1909, OYNM, number 4).
[i] Arranged also by Zhitomirsky (1912, OYNM, number 24).
[j] Arranged also by I. Schumann (1912, OYNM, number 33).
[k] Arranged also by Shklyar (1909, OYNM, number 2). The same song was set also by Maurice Ravel, as one of his *Deux mélodies hébraiques* (1914).
[l] Set also by Maurice Ravel as "Chanson hébraique" (1910).
[m] Habdalah is the ceremony performed at the close of the Sabbath.
[n] Yiddish translation of the *Ode to Joy* of Beethoven's Ninth Symphony.

Because of the Orientalizing effect of the augmented second, the scale came to be considered the "most Jewish" in the public mind. It appears in the *Zamelbukh* not only in Jewish folk tunes but also in the excerpts from Anton Rubinstein's *The Demon, The Tower of Babel,* and *The Maccabees,* in which augmented seconds represent Georgians, Philistines, and Syrians, respectively. In some of these examples the augmented second occurs also in the upper register of the scale, producing an even more exotic scale, the so-called "Gypsy" scale (ex. 2).

FROM JEWISH FOLK MUSIC TO RUSSIAN ART SONG

In addition to Kiselgof's *Zamelbukh,* the OYNM published a series of sheet music. The cover page for the third series captured perfectly what the OYNM stood for: based on Jewish folk art that mixed Jewish symbols with elements borrowed

Example 2. Excerpt from Anton Rubinstein's *The Tower of Babel* in Kiselgof's *Lieder Zamelbukh*, no. 67, mm. 21–26 (piano part only).

from other folk traditions, the cover design was the work of an assimilated Jewish artist, Moisei Lvovich Maimon (1860–1924), whose 1893 painting *The Marranos and the Inquisition in Spain* earned him a membership in the Russian Academy of the Arts (fig. 1).[42] The figures on the cover were typical images of Jewish folk art, familiar from An-sky's collection. The columns as a frame represented the columns of the Temple in Jerusalem, while the harp of King David was a clear reference to the musical content of the publication. Because of the appellation of Judah in Genesis 49:9 as "a lion's whelp," images of lion abound in Jewish folk art. In Maimon's illustration, however, the lion has wings, which relates Maimon's lion to that of the Divine Chariot in Ezekiel's vision (Ezekiel 1:10). The wings might also have musical significance, referring to the seraphim, the winged creatures with undefined shape that sing the praise of God. More unusual, though, is the pairing of the lion with a winged stag.[43] Stags or deer are not uncommon in Jewish folk art, although they are more typically Ukrainian. Here on the cover of a musical publication it is tempting to associate the stag with Jacob's blessing of Naphtali as a "hind let loose" (Gen. 49). The antlers allude to the name Naphtali, which means wrestled or twisted.[44] Naphtali has a specific musical association: Deborah, known from the "Song of Deborah," supposedly came from Naphtali's tribe. "Awake, awake, Deborah," says the Bible in Judges 5:12, "awake, awake, utter a song."

While Kiselgof's *Zamelbukh* was intended for use at home and in schools, the series of sheet music the OYNM published was designed for more trained musicians. Most compositions were arranged for voice and piano, but musicians could find any variety of ensembles (see table 2): voice and string quartet; voice and string quintet; vocal duet and piano; voice, violin, and piano; solo and chorus; four-part chorus and piano; piano; English horn; violin and

Figure 1. Moisei Maimon's cover page for the 1913 OYNM sheet music series (Saminsky, "Ani hadal"). The Wallersteiner Collection of Jewish Music, Irving S. Gilmore Music Library, Yale University.

TABLE 2. List of Publications of the OYNM in St. Petersburg

| | Composer | Title | Date | Description | Notes |
|---|---|---|---|---|---|
| 1 | Shklyar | Di gilderne pave (The golden peacock) | 1910 | S, A, T, B (pf) | "Volkslied" [arrangement] |
| 2 | Shklyar | Alte kashe (Eternal question) | 1910 | S, A, T, B (pf) | "Volkslied" [arrangement] |
| 3 | Shklyar | Faryomert, farklogt (Depressed, dejected) | 1910 | S, A, T, B (pf) | [arrangement] |
| 4 | Shklyar | Khatskele | 1910 | S, A, T, B (pf) | [arrangement] |
| 5 | Shklyar | Hatikvah (The hope) | 1910 | S, A, T, B (pf) | [arrangement] Text and music by Imber |
| 6 | Shklyar | Shtey oyf mayn folk (Arise, my people) | 1910 | S, A, T, B (pf) | [arrangement] |
| 7 | Zhitomirsky | Dem rebns nign (The rebbe's niggun), op. 3 | 1910 | 2 vl, vla, vc, cb | [arrangement] |
| 8 | Saminsky | Unter soreles vigele ('Neath little Sarah's cradle) | 1910[a] | 1 v, 2 vl, vla, vc | [arrangement] |
| 9 | Saminsky | Khsidish (Hasidic dance) | 1910[b] | vl, pf | "Volksmelodie" [arrangement] |
| 10 | Zhitomirsky | Az ikh volt gehat (If only I had), op. 4, no. 2 | 1910 | 1 v, vl, pf | "Volkslied" [arrangement] |
| 11 | Zhitomirsky | Du meydele, du sheyns (You pretty girl), op. 4, no. 1 | 1910[a] | 1 v, pf | [arrangement] |
| 12 | Lvov | Zog mir du sheyn meydele (Tell me, pretty maid) | 1910[a] | 1 v, pf | [arrangement] |
| 13 | Shalit | Eli, Eli (My God, my God) | 1910[a] | 1 v, pf | [arrangement] |
| 14 | Shklyar | Der parom (The ferry) | 1910 | 1 v, pf | "Volkslied" [arrangement] |
| 15 | Shklyar | Yerusholayim, Yerusholayim (Heb. Jerusalem, Jerusalem) | 1910 | 1 v, pf | Text by Halevi, music by Shklyar [arrangement] |
| 16 | Kopït | Freylekhs | 1912 | pf | [arrangement] |
| 17 | Kaplan | Yidishe melodye (Yiddish melody) | 1912 | harp[c] | [arrangement] |

*(continued)*

TABLE 2 *(continued)*

| | Composer | Title | Date | Description | Notes |
|---|---|---|---|---|---|
| 18 | Tseitlin | Reb Nachmons nign (Nachmons's niggun) | 1912 | 2 vl, 2 vla, vc | "arrangiert" |
| 19 | Zhitomirsky | Dem rebns nign (The rebbe's niggun), op. 3 | 1912[a] | vl, pf | Transcr. by Kiselgof |
| 20 | Lvov | Volokhl | 1912 | vl, pf | [arrangement] |
| 21 | Zhitomirsky | Der eybershter iz der mekhutn (God is the father-in-law), op. 5, no. 1 | 1912 | Solo, S, A, T, B, pf | Transcr. by Kiselgof |
| 22 | Gurovitch | Riboyne shel oylem (Lord of the world)[d] | 1912 | Solo, S, A, T, B, pf | "arrangiert" |
| 23 | Potoker/ Tseitlin | Zogzhe rebenyu (Tell me, oh rebe) | 1912 | Bar, T, pf | Transcr. by Kiselgof |
| 24 | Zhitomirsky | Shlof, mayn kind (Sleep, my child), op. 5, no. 2 | 1912 | 1 v, vl/vla, pf | Transcr. by Kiselgof |
| 25 | Lvov | Vos vet zayn mikoyekh burikes (What will be about the beets) | 1912 | 1 v, pf | Transcr. by Kiselgof |
| 26 | Lvov | A retenish (A riddle) | 1912 | S, Bar, pf | Transcr. by Kiselgof |
| 27 | Kaplan | N'umo ferakh (Heb. Sleep, flower) | 1912 | 1 v, pf | "Volkslied," transcr. by Kiselgof, text by A. D. Lifshits |
| 28 | Kopït | Der filozof (The philosopher) | 1912 | 1 v, pf | "Volkslied," transcr. by Kiselgof |
| 29 | Kopït | Di mezinke oysgegebn (The youngest betrothed) | 1912 | 1 v, pf | Text and music by Varshavsky |
| 30 | Shalit | A lid fun a feygele (Bird's song) | 1912 | 1 v, pf | [arrangement] |
| 31 | Shalit | Mlave malke (The close of Sabbath) | 1912 | 1 v, pf | [arrangement] tune from "Ost & West" |
| 32 | Schumann | Bayse Malke, efn mir (Bayse Malke, open up) | 1912 | 1 v, pf | [arrangement] |
| 33 | Schumann | Shlof, mayn kind, | 1912 | 1 v, pf | [arrangement] |

TABLE 2 *(continued)*

| | Composer | Title | Date | Description | Notes |
|---|---|---|---|---|---|
| | | mayn kroyn (Sleep, my child, my crown) | | | |
| 34 | Rosovsky | A viglid (A lullaby) | 1912 | 1 v, pf | |
| 35 | Achron | Hebreyish melodye (Hebrew melody) | 1914 | vl, pf | |
| 36 | Achron | Hebreyish tants (Hebrew dance) | 1914 | vl, pf | |
| 37 | Achron | Hebreyish viglid (Hebrew lullaby) | 1914 | vl, pf | Hebraische Volksmelodie, transcr. by Kiselgof |
| 38 | Tseitlin/ Achron | Eli Tsion (Wail, o Zion) | 1914 | vl, pf | (see no. 45) |
| 39 | Saminsky | Kleyne rapsodye (Little rhapsody) | 1914 | vl, pf | |
| 40 | Saminsky | Lid fun Esterke (Song of little Esther) | 1914 | 1 v, pf | "Im Volkston," text by Imber |
| 41 | Saminsky | Lid fun a yesoyme (Song of an orphan) | 1914 | 1 v, pf | "Volksmelodie," transcr. by Kiselgof |
| 42 | Saminsky | Unter soreles vigele ('Neath little Sarah's cradle) | 1914 | 1 v, pf | "Volkslied" |
| 43 | Saminsky | El yivne hagalil (Heb. God will rebuild Galil) | 1913 | S, A, T, B, pf | [arrangement] |
| 44 | Saminsky | Ani hadal (Heb. Poor as I am) | 1913 | S, A, T, B | "Melodie der Jemeniten" (orig. Ben Jehuda "Luach erez Izrael) |
| 45 | Tseitlin | Eli Tsion (Wail, oh Zion) | 1914 | vc, pf | "Fantasie über eine Volksmelodie und Trop" |
| 46 | Gnesin | A nign fun Shyke Fayfer (Shyke Fyfer's tune) | 1914 | vl, pf | |
| 47 | Rosovsky | Fantastisher tants (Fantastic dance) | 1914 | vl, vc, pf | |
| 48 | Rosovsky | Lomir zikh iberbetn (Let's cease our quarreling) | 1914 | 1 v, pf | [arrangement] |

*(continued)*

TABLE 2 *(continued)*

| | Composer | Title | Date | Description | Notes |
|---|---|---|---|---|---|
| 49 | Rosovsky | Ikh bin a balegole (I am a coachman) | 1914 | Bar, pf | |
| 50 | Kopït | Vos vet zayn mit reb Yisroel dem frumen (What will become of pious reb Israel) | 1914 | 1 v, vl, pf | "Volksmelodie," text by Rivesman |
| 51 | Kopït | Oy, efen mir (Oh, please open to me) | 1914 | Bar, T, pf | "Volkslied" |
| 52 | Milner | Baym rebn tsu mlave malke (With the rabbi at the close of the Sabbath) | 1914 | pf | Folk tune recorded by N. Jasnogrodsky |
| 53 | Milner | In kheyder (At school) | 1914 | 1 v, pf | "Worte und Musik von Milner" |
| 54 | Milner | Unsane Toykef, op. 2, no. 5 (Traditional Yom Kippur prayer) | 1913 | Solo, S, A, T, B | |
| 55 | Milner | Iber di hoyfn (Over the heap) | 1914 | Bar, T, pf | Folk tune "Idel mit'n fiedel" |
| 56 | Milner | Unter di grininke beymelack (Under the green trees) | 1914 | 1 v, pf | |
| 57 | Shklyar | Farn opshid (Before parting) | 1914 | 1 v, pf | Text by L. Jaffe, transcr. by Rivesman |
| 58 | Streicher | Fun Shir Hashirim (From the Song of Songs) | 1914 | 1 v, pf | |
| 59 | Achron | Tants improvizatsyon (Dance improvisation) | 1914 | vl, pf | |
| 60 | Kaplan | Danse hébraïque | 1917 | 2 vl | Transcr. by Kiselgof |
| 61 | Aisberg | A khasene lid (A Hasidic song) | 1917 | pf | On two folk tunes, transcr. by Engel |
| 62 | Aisberg | Reb Shmul's nign (Samuel rebbe's niggun) | 1917 | pf | Transcr. by Kiselgof |
| 63 | Kopït | Freylekhs No. 2 | 1917 | pf | |
| 64 | Levinson | Umetum finster, shtum (All dark and silent) | 1917 | 1 v, pf | Text by Rivesman |

TABLE 2 *(continued)*

| | Composer | Title | Date | Description | Notes |
|---|---|---|---|---|---|
| 65 | Tseitlin | Shabes lid (Song of Sabbath) | 1918 | T, T, B, B | |
| 66 | Saminsky | Shlof, mayn zun (Sleep, my son), op. 11, no. 2 | 1917 | 1 v, 2 vl, vla, vc | |
| 67 | Saminsky | Gebeyt fun reb Levi Yitskhok, op. 12, no. 3 ("Di dudkele") (Levi Yitskhok's prayer) | 1917 | 1 v, pf | Transcr. by Kiselgof |
| 68 | Saminsky | Un reb Elyezer hot gezogt ("Omar fun Elosor") (And Eliezar told us), op. 12, no. 4 | 1917 | 1 v, pf | |
| 69 | Saminsky | Patsh, patsh kikhelakh (Patty cake, patty cake) | 1918 | 1 v, pf | "Kinderlied," transcr. by Kiselgof |
| 70 | Saminsky | Di nakht (The night), op. 12, no. 2 | 1917 | 1 v, pf | Text by Ansky |
| 71 | Achron | Variations sur le thème hébraïque, "Eil ivne hagalil," op. 34 | 1917 | pf | |
| 72 | Shalit | Shoyn nito der nekhtn (Yesterday is no more) | 1917 | 1 v, pf | [arrangement] |
| 73 | Shalit | Klesmorimlech majne libinke (My dear little klezmer players) | 1917 | 1 v, pf | [arrangement] |
| 74 | Levinson | Yidishe viglid, op. 28, no. 1 (Jewish cradle song) | 1917 | vc, pf | |
| 75 | Levinson | Opshids lid, op. 28. no. 2 (Farewell song) | 1917 | vc, pf | |
| 76 | Levinson | Freyecker tants, op. 28, no. 3 (A merry dance) | 1917 | vc, pf | |
| 77 | Rosovsky | Der shuster Moyshe (Moyshe the cobbler) | 1917 | woodwind quintet | |
| 78 | Rosovsky | Nign on a sof (Song without end) | 1917 | woodwind quintet | |

*(continued)*

TABLE 2 *(continued)*

| | Composer | Title | Date | Description | Notes |
|---|---|---|---|---|---|
| 79 | Rosovsky | Chassidic nign (Hasidic niggun), op. 8, no. 1 | 1917 | English horn | |
| 80 | Saminsky | Shchav, bni (Viglied fun dem Apten Row) (Sleep, my child [Lullaby for the Apten rabbi]), op. 11, no. 2 | 1917 | 1 v, pf | Transcr. by Kiselgof |
| 81 | Rosovsky | Chassidic nign (Hasidic niggun) | 1917 | vc, pf | |

[a] Reprinted in 1917.
[b] Reprinted in 1918.
[c] Or violin and harmonium.
[d] The melody is the same as in "Eli, Eli."

piano; violin duets; cello and piano; violin, cello, and piano; piano trio; harp, flute, and harmonium; string quartet; string quintet; and woodwind quintet. Some pieces appeared in different arrangements in different editions. The first thirty-three compositions were all arrangements of *frigish* and minor folk tunes or popular Jewish songs. The two categories were not sharply divided. I. Kaplan's "N'umo ferakh" (OYNM no. 27) appeared as "folk song, transcribed by Kiselgof," but the publication also named the author of the text (A. D. Lifshits). Songs by Abraham Goldfaden ("Faryomert, farklogt," no. 3 and "Shtey oyf mayn folk," no. 6) or Mark Varshavsky[45] ("Di mezinke oysgegebn," no. 29) passed easily as "folk songs." Instrumental pieces, such as H. Kopït's "Freylekhs No. 2" (no. 16), even if they do not specify the original melody, were usually free arrangements of instrumental folk tunes. Sometimes even pieces that are not labeled "arrangement" and thus suggest original compositions, still name Kiselgof as the transcriber of the original melody.[46]

The arrangements, though most kept the original melody unchanged, were more ambitious than those in the *Zamelbukh*. The effort to elevate the arrangements into the sphere of art music occasionally resulted in pieces that were more artificial than artful, such as Zhitomorsky's 1911 folk-song setting "Der eybershter iz der mekhutn" (God is the father-in-law),[47] which he also arranged for Kiselgof's *Zamelbukh*. In the OYNM publication Zhitomorsky set three strophes, instead of just one, harmonizing each differently and providing the last with a running bass line in double octaves. He set the third refrain in imitative texture, adding a realistic touch at the end by depicting the guests shouting, "Mazel tov" (ex. 3).

Signs, or one might even say posters, of academic training abound in the OYNM arrangements: elaborate instrumental introductions and postludes,

Example 3. Zhitomirsky, "Der eybershter iz der mekhutn."

a. Arrangement in Kiselgof's *Zamelbukh,* no. 34, mm. 1–8.

(God is the groom, the Torah is the bride, Moses our teacher is the matchmaker.)

b. Arrangement of the third strophe in the OYNM series (no. 21), mm. 51–58.
Lyrics originally also in Hebrew characters.

(continued)

Example 3 *(continued)*

o - rent - lich    un    fajn___    si   is   be - sser   wi   alz

(A bride, a pure one, she is rich and beautiful, honest and refined, she is better
than . . . )

c. Imitative ending, mm. 67–75 (text missing from some parts in the OYMN
publication).

Sop.    Es   fli  –  en    i - de - lech    sin – gen    lid – lech

Alto    Es   fli  –  en    i - de - lech

Ten.    Es   fli  –  en    i - de - lech    sin – gen

Bass    Es   fli  –  en

Example 3 *(continued)*

(Twirling Jews are singing songs, each shouts, the groom's side and the bride's side: good luck.)

Example 4. Piano introduction to P. Lvov's "A retenish" (OYNM no. 26), mm. 1–4.

some featuring chromatic voice leading (ex. 4); sections of contrapuntal texture in choral music or string ensembles (ex. 5) as well as in songs, such as
Kaplan's "N'umo ferakh" (no. 27), in which the composer layered different
lines of the melody above each other (ex. 6). To lend the arrangements the
appearance of lied, OYNM composers, like Engel before them, often dramatized folk songs by the use of extreme dynamics (see the *ff* outburst in
Shklyar's "Der parom," no. 14, in ex. 7). It was also common to highlight
specific words with unusual harmonic juxtapositions, as in Saminsky's choral
"Ani hadal" (no. 44), in which the word "Adonay" (Lord) starts on a minor
dominant (ex. 8). But Conservatory training manifested itself most obviously
in the harmonization of songs: augmented sixth chords, chromatic harmonic
sequences, and modulation to distant keys (e.g., from F♯ minor to the
Neapolitan G minor in Kopït's "Vos vet zayn mit reb Yisroel dem frumen"
[no. 50] [ex. 9]), also occur.

OYNM arrangements overflow with descending chromatic scale segments à la Borodin, sometimes stretching, like in Shklyar's "Der parom,"
to almost two octaves (ex. 10). Descending chromatic bass lines occasionally result in strange harmonic sequences, such as the one in a piano interlude of Shklyar's "Yerusholayim, Yerusholayim" (no. 15), in which the harmonic progression can be best explained as the consequence of chromatic
voice leading (ex. 11). The sequence of mainly half-diminished chords in P.
Lvov's "Vos vet zayn mikoyekh burikes" (no. 25) is also built on a chromati-
cally descending bass line, accompanying, in this case, a same-note recitation in the vocal part (ex. 12).

Descending chromaticism, though, was not only a sign of composerly arti-
fice. Chromaticism was also one of the infallible marks of Orientalism in Russian
music, characterizing Jews, Georgians, Arabs, or Polovtsians, in other words
any people living—geographically or imaginatively—east of Russia. One of the
musical signs by which these "others" were distinguished has been associated
by Richard Taruskin with the strongly erotic "sweet bliss," or *nega* in Russian.[48]
The musical characteristics of *nega* include syncopated undulation, a drone,
and, most important, a chromatic accompanying line, the most characteristic
turn of which is the sixth degree descending via flat sixth to the dominant,

Example 5. Contrapuntal texture in Tseitlin's string quintet arrangement of "Reb Nachmons nign" (OYNM no. 18), mm. 10–13.

Example 6. Contrapuntal combination of different thematic lines in J. Kaplan's "N'umo ferakh" (OYNM no. 27), mm. 10–12. Lyrics originally in Yiddish.

Example 7. *Fortissimo* outburst in E. Shklyar's "Der parom," mm. 19–23.
Lyrics originally also in Hebrew characters.

( . . . racing they are escaping. All the people pray and wish a happy crossing of the river.)

Example 8. E♭-minor dominant chord at the word "Adonay" in Saminsky's
"Ani hadal" (OYNM no. 44), mm. 15–16 (piano part only).

(the name of the Lord)

Example 9. Modulation from F♯ minor to G minor in H. Kopit's "Vos vet zayn mit reb Yisroel dem frumen" (OYNM no. 50), mm. 18–21.

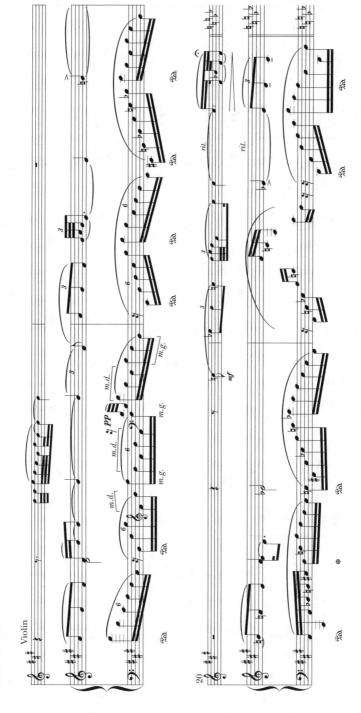

Example 10. Descending chromatic bass line in Shklyar's "Der parom" (OYNM no. 14), mm. 13–18. Lyrics originally also in Hebrew characters.

( . . . on both banks people, horses, and wagons are racing as they flee.)

Example 11. Harmonic sequence in Shklyar's "Yerusholayim, Yerusholayim" (OYNM no. 15), mm. 68–73.

Example 12. Sequence of inverted half-diminished chords in P. Lvov's "Vos vet zayn mikoyekh burikes" (OYNM no. 25), mm. 8–9. Lyrics originally also in Hebrew characters.

( . . . till Passover there are still three weeks. We will borrow beets from the neighbor)

or ascending from the dominant via the same chromatic route (ex. 13). In Balakirev's "Yevreyskaya melodiya" (1859), a setting of one of Byron's "Hebrew Melodies" in M. Lermotov's translation, the occasional flat sixths in D♭ major and flat seconds in B♭ minor lend a hint of sensuality to Balakirev's otherwise stark representation of Byron's romanticized Hebrews (ex. 14).

But Jews were characterized as Oriental "others" not only by Russians. Yoel Engel's setting of the Yiddish folk song "Di sheyne Rochele" (The beautiful Rachel) displays the same Orientalizing characteristics as its Russian counterparts. There is nothing in the simple four-line song in G natural minor, printed separately after the setting in the score, that would call for a harmonically adventurous accompaniment. The extreme chromaticism with which Engel surrounded the melody is a badge of the East. With the sinuously chromatic lines and sensuously arpeggiated harmonies Engel turned the song's Jewish heroine into an exotically desirable woman (ex. 15).

An explicit sixth–flat sixth–fifth descent in a major key rarely appears in

Example 13. *Nega* in Borodin's *Prince Igor,* no. 7, mm. 33–38 (from Taruskin's *Defining Russia Musically,* p. 69) (piano part only).

Example 14. Flat sixths in D♭ major and flat seconds in B♭ minor in Balakirev's "Yevreyskaya melodiya" (1859).

a. Mm. 1–4.

(My soul is dark. Hurry, singer, hurry!)

b. Mm. 70–75.

Example 15. *Nega* in Engel's "Di sheyne Rochele," *Yidishe folkslieder,* no. 5, mm. 1–8. Lyrics originally in Yiddish, Russian, and German.

*(continued)*

Example 15 *(continued)*

(She combs her hair by the window, her fine hair; for everyone she is a loose woman, for me she is honest. Oh, misery, what a shame, oy wey, what agony.)

songs by the composers of the OYNM, which, like Engel's original, are mainly in minor. More fittingly for the minor, the chromatic descent became a sharp sixth–natural sixth–fifth sequence, as in Zhitomirsky's setting of "Az ikh volt gehat" (no. 10) (ex. 16).

There are only a few genuine art songs among the OYNM's publications. The most famous among them is Moses Milner's "In kheyder" (1914, no. 53), the title page of which proudly states: "words and music by Milner." Moses Milner (originally Mikhail Melnikov) was widely regarded as one of the most significant composers of Jewish art music. Yoel Engel held him in such high regard that he applied an old Jewish figure of speech ("one page of the Talmud is worth all your Tolstoy and Dostoyevsky") to Milner's song by claiming that even one page of Milner's "In kheyder" proved the existence of Jewish art music. Ironically, what made Milner's song a beacon of Jewish art music was his painstaking imitation of Musorgsky's technique of realistically reproducing the rhythm and inflection of the text. The imitation garnered for Milner the nickname the "Jewish Musorgsky" (ex. 17).[49]

Another genuine art song among OYNM publications is Shklyar's "Farn opshid" (Before parting, no. 57), which further illustrates the adherence of OYNM composers to their Russian idols. Shklyar's song is an example of the Orientalizing exotic song that was Rimsky-Korsakov's specialty. "Farn opshid" seems to be inspired specifically by Rimsky's "Yevreyskaya pesnya" (Op. 7, no. 2), a 1867 setting of words from the Song of Songs in Lev Alexandrovich Mey's translation. Rimsky's song is dedicated to Musorgsky, who also set a section from Mey's translation in the same year. A typical example of dreamy musical Orientalism, Rimsky's "Yevreyskaya pesnya" starts with long, sustained half-diminished harmonies built over a C♯ that accompanies the entire song as a pedal. The vocal line enters in the middle register with a long solo, replete

Example 16. VI♯–vi–V progression in minor in Zhitomirsky's "Ak ikh volt gehat" (OYNM no. 10), mm. 66–68.

Example 17. Beginning of M. Milner's "In kheyder" (OYNM no. 53), mm. 1–12. Lyrics originally also in Hebrew characters.

Kum a-her, in-ge-le ne-hen-ter zu mir un thu a-kuk in di klej-ne ei-ssi-lach

taj - e-re ej - sse-lach gil - der-ne ej - sse - lach

*(continued)*

Example 17 *(continued)*

gi-cher, gi-cher kum— a - her.

*p dolce*

(Come here, little one, come nearer to me and look at the scroll letters, dear letters, golden letters. Quick, come here.)

with augmented seconds and graceful embellishments. Although the melody ends on c♯¹, the song is in altered F♯ Phrygian. Only three harmonies alternate in the accompaniment of the sensuously meandering vocal line. There is no modulation, and although the C♯ dominant pedal finally resolves to F♯, for most of its duration the song feels suspended rather than driven toward its final cadence. Rimsky complements the text with music in which life stands still and gives way to a world of dreams (ex. 18).

Shklyar used the same altered F♯ Phrygian scale in "Farn opshid," a setting of Zionist poet Leib Jaffe's poem. Like Rimsky, Shklyar ends the song on an F♯-major chord, but, unlike his teacher, he reaches F♯ via G, thus emphasizing the Phrygian character of the tonality. Besides their common tonality and abundant use of augmented seconds, Shklyar's and Rimsky's songs also have melodic affinities (ex. 19). But while the text of Rimsky-Korsakov's "Yevreyskaya pesnya" justifies his choice of Oriental musical idiom, the heroic tone and the topic of longed-for freedom and rebirth of Jaffe's Zionist poem do not obviously call for sensuous grace notes and augmented seconds.

Shklyar's song is more dramatic than Rimsky's. It modulates to D major for its middle section and, unlike Rimsky's setting that fluctuates between *piano* and *pianissimo* to enhance the sensuous effect, uses the whole range of dynamics between *piano* and *fortissimo*. Rimsky-Korsakov's song ends in a low register, which is a common mark of sensuous Oriental women. Shklyar's singer finishes an octave higher, which, especially after the heroic, *fortissimo* a² that preceded it, projects more energy as a final note. Shklyar's piano postlude, however, brings back the embellished, augmented-second-ridden, soft Oriental tone, a gesture that ultimately undermines the poem's heroic subject matter. The traditional characterization of Jews as dreamy Orientals was a stronger impulse for Shklyar than the optimistic Zionist message of the text (ex. 20).

Example 18. Rimsky-Korsakov's "Yevreyskaya pesnya," op. 7, no. 2.

a. Beginning, mm. 1–12.

(I sleep, but my sensitive heart is not sleeping.)

b. Ending, mm. 45–50.

(Open to me, you beautiful girl.)

Example 19. Melodic similarities between Shklyar's "Farn opshid" (OYNM no. 57) (mm. 13–16) and Rimsky-Korsakov's "Yevreyskaya pesna" (mm. 16–18).

Example 20. Ending of Shklyar's "Farn opshid," mm. 37–47. Original lyrics in Russian and Yiddish in Hebrew characters.

Example 20 *(continued)*

(Wonderful links connected us, our ideal brings us together. And the reflection of the dawn of rebirth set fire in both of our souls.)

It is not only the musical idiom that brings this song into contact with Rimsky-Korsakov. In later accounts "Farn opshid" was regarded as a breakthrough in the history of Jewish music. As the proponents of Jewish music recounted, when Shklyar brought it to a composition class, Rimsky-Korsakov, like Sabaneyev twenty or so years later, had prophesied the coming of a Jewish Glinka: "Well, write another thirty such things and you will found a new school . . ." Then turning to his Jewish students he said, "Why do you imitate European and Russian composers? The Jews possess tremendous folk treasures. I myself have heard your religious songs, and they have made a deep impression upon me. Think about it. Yes, Jewish music awaits her Jewish Glinka."[50]

However flattering for Jewish composers, Rimsky's comment was self–contradictory. While rebuking his Jewish students for imitating Russian composers, he encouraged them to follow the Russian *kuchka* model for creating national music. It is doubly ironic, of course, that the piece that supposedly elicited Rimsky's enthusiasm was indebted to his own Orientalizing musical idiom.

## A NEW AGENDA

It may be that Rimsky's comment was not inspired by "Farn obsheid" but by another piece by Shklyar. Saminsky and Rosovsky, whose accounts seem to be the main source of the story, had their own agendas. They made sure that Rimsky's remark, which would have more easily fit a folk-song arrangement, became associated with an original composition. There are several divergences between the various versions of the story. Rosovsky described Shklyar's piece as "a Yiddish song" (despite the fact that the song's original language was most likely Russian);[51] Lazare Saminsky remembered it as "a firm song built on an old Hebraic chant,"[52] while Mikhail Gnesin, in all probability the most reliable source, recalled the title of Shklyar's legendary piece as "Eastern Melodies." Although Yiddish folk songs, Hebrew liturgical music, and Eastern melodies (a designation that usually referred to Hasidic tunes) were not as generically distinct in practice as was often claimed, their use as designations seems to indicate the storytellers' own preferences in Jewish music. Moreover, in Gnesin's story there is no mention of the future Jewish Glinka; Rimsky-Korsakov's comment, in Gnesin's telling, was confined to surprise at Shklyar's calling what Rimsky-Korsakov regarded as a typically Jewish melody "Eastern" *(vostochnaya)* instead of "Jewish."[53] The part about Glinka seems to have originated with Lazare Saminsky, who attended the St. Petersburg Conservatory with Rosovsky years after Shkylar's studies with Rimsky-Korsakov ended.[54] It is unlikely, then, that Saminsky or Rosovsky were present when Shklyar presented his "Eastern" piece.

Lazare Saminsky played a crucial role in shaping the image of the OYNM. A founding member and the group's first secretary, Saminsky, at least in his later account, became a major force in the OYNM between 1909 and 1916 while chairing its Art and Publication Committee.[55] In his autobiographical notes Saminsky recalled recruiting twenty-five composers to serve on the Music Committee.[56] Despite Saminsky's emphasis on the creation of art music, as late as 1914 an OYNM pamphlet still identified Jewish music mainly with secular and religious folk music:

*From the Protocols of the Society for Jewish Folk Music*[57]

I. The Goal and the Rights of the Society
   1. The Society for Folk Music has as its goal to cooperate in the learning and development of Jewish folk music (synagogal and secular) through collecting examples of folk creations, reworking them artistically and disseminating them among the Society, also to support Jewish composers and other musicians.
   2. In order to achieve the stated goals, the Society has the right:
      a) To publish and help publish music and theoretical works on Jewish musical topics;

b) To organize musical gatherings, concerts, operatic performances, lectures, etc.;

c) To have its own chorus and orchestra;

d) To have a library of sheet music and books about the question of musical art;

e) To publish a journal dedicated to Jewish music; and

f) To hold competitions for better musical works by Jewish composers.

3. In addition, the Society has the right to open branches in various cities of the country, in accordance with local laws.

4. The activities of the Society will be spread over all of Russia.

For Saminsky, as for the historiographers of Jewish music, point 2f was the most important goal of the OYNM. In the English translation of this text both Weisser and Rosovsky replaced the phrase "musical works by Jewish composers" with "musical compositions of a Jewish character."[58] The change in meaning is significant. While the original text refers to any compositions by Jewish composers, the translation suggests the prior notion of specifically Jewish art music.

Art music indeed became central after the 1917 Revolution when, instead of the St. Petersburg OYNM, the reorganized Moscow branch (founded on 8 October 1923) became the main institution of Jewish music in Russia.[59] The omission of "folk" from the name of the Moscow Society (Obshchestvo Yevreyskoy Muzïki, henceforth OYM) not only marked the difference from the St. Petersburg branch, but now represented a new attitude toward the society's function. In a revolutionary spirit the brochure of the OYM announced that it was "no longer sufficient to restrict [the society] to the Jewish music of the past—the task of the hour is to create actively new musical treasures reflecting the contemporary life of the Jewish people."[60] Unlike the OYNM, the OYM planned "to create a fund . . . to award prizes for the best works of Jewish music in an effort to stimulate creative work." By 1926 the brochure could proudly assume that the "young school of Jewish music" was on its way to joining "the mainstream of European music."

The list of compositions the OYM advertised shows the efforts to be part of the "mainstream."[61] Thus while at the first concerts of the OYNM most works performed were arrangements of folk tunes, the OYM concerts presented mainly original compositions that fit the expectations of a general audience of classical music. In Joachim Braun's comparison of the OYNM's first concert and the OYM's fourth concert the change is clear. While in 1909 there were five folk-song arrangements on the program, in 1926 there were none. As genuine "art music" in 1909 three pieces on Jewish subjects by non-Jewish composers were played. On the 1926 concert all four composers presented (Achron, Bloch, Gnesin, and Milner) were Jewish. Even more significant is that most compositions on the 1926 concert used synagogue music instead of folk music as their basis—a sure sign, in Saminsky's opinion, of composerly sophistication.[62]

As Sabaneyev's article demonstrates, in the historiography of Jewish music the story of the OYNM and OYM merged into a heroic narrative of the development of Jewish art music. The more recent the accounts of the societies' developments, the more they have tended to reflect views first introduced by Saminsky. Joseph Yasser (1893–1981), who as a student of Moscow composer Jacob Weinberg started to popularize the ideas of the OYNM in the United States after his 1923 emigration, went so far as to describe unconscious ideologies underlying the aims of the OYNM. These ideologies, even he had to admit, were "rather vague at the outstart and have been brought to a fuller understanding at a much later date." The key concept in Yasser's presentation of the OYNM's latent ideology was the combination of modern achievements with ancient glory, the task "to lift the present status of Jewish music to a degree that may render it just as eminent, relatively speaking, as it used to be in the biblical times."[63] Only folk music—the original raison d'être of the OYNM—failed to find a place in Yasser's elaborate ideology. The same assumption, originating from Saminsky, about the priority of an ancient tradition over the folklore of the present and the focus on modern art music set the tone for the infighting that plagued the OYNM during its short existence.

Saminsky's emphasis on ancient music and his selective amnesia concerning the musical culture of the Jews in the Diaspora reflected the ongoing political debate represented by Ahad Ha'am's purist and Dubnov's Diaspora-oriented vision of Jewish culture. Like Ahad Ha'am's spiritual nationalism, the Jewish art music Saminsky envisioned severed its ties with its cultural environment. This loss of ties, however, was not an automatic process. It needed to be orchestrated, both through institutions and through the aggressive rhetoric that characterized Saminsky's polemical writings on the subject. Like Ahad Ha'am, Saminsky and his followers advocated a process of purification that would detach Jewish art from its Diaspora associations and, as Saminsky hoped, would elevate it to the concert podium as part of the "classical" mainstream. Detachment, however, came at a heavy price, for "purification" of Jewish music resulted in its almost complete assimilation to its Russian models.

# Chapter 2

# *Zhidï* and *Yevrei* in a
# Neonationalist Context

*Every nation in the course of its historical life is subjected to a great number of dif-
ferent influences; it is surrounded by other peoples, lives among them, its folk-music
absorbs with a varying degree of eagerness — according to the qualities of the nation —
all these external influences which, being deposited in layers, deform its musical phys-
iognomy. The creative work of a people is in itself an impure product as yet; that we
may judge of its artistic value it must be purged of its alloys.*

LEONID SABANEYEV, "The Jewish National School in Music" (1924)

In an essay entitled "Aladdin's Lamp" and published on the occasion of the
edition of An-sky's *The Jewish Artistic Heritage*, Abram Markovich Efros (1888–
1954), a leading Russian art critic, declared that the Jewish artistic renaissance could flourish only "on the twin roots which underpin all contemporary world art—modernism and folk arts." He did not endorse the imitation
of Russian art in the 1890s (mockingly referred to as "the golden cockerel
style" or "the balalaika period"),[1] because, he wrote, it drew upon the surface of the folk art instead of its "internal laws and inner structure of its
forms." By 1918, when Efros published his article, "the golden cockerel style"
had been long out of fashion. For Jewish art a more modernist approach was
needed, which, Efros believed, would help artists recognize the "pure essence
of Jewishness" in the "scrappy and garish patchwork of alien elements" that
constituted Jewish folk art. Relying on that essence "folk art will become a
vitalizing and miraculous source for us," Efros professed, but "only when it
is *creatively re-fashioned not imitatively adopted.*"[2] What Efros described was
neonationalism, a creative combination of folk art and modernism in which
the supposed authenticity of folk art lent stylistic credentials to modernist
art. By 1918, neonational, or neo-Russian, aesthetics had been present in
Russian art for more than a decade and had been the mainspring of the success of Sergey Diaghilev's artistic enterprise in the West.

In Russia neonationalists considered the Europeanized styles that came
into fashion with the Westernizing efforts of Peter the Great as nationally insignificant, while they valued peasant antiquities as "the real art of Russia."[3]
In the debates about the sources of Jewish art music an opposition was sim-

ilarly constructed between the near past and ancient times, between the "contaminated," Oriental-sounding Yiddish folk music and the less Orientally colored sacred music that, many believed, was historically traceable to Biblical times. For composers on the modernist side of the polemic, representation of Jews as Orientals by nineteenth-century musical idioms became progressively more embarrassing. More appealing to the nationalistic imagination were the Biblical Hebrews, whose triumphant image was recalled by all European nationalist movements, even by those with anti-Semitic agendas.[4] To replace the feminine, Oriental image of the Jews with the strong, male portrait of Biblical Hebrews was the goal of OYNM composer Lazare Saminsky. Although they never invoked politics, the opposing factions in the Saminsky-initiated polemic among OYNM composers about Jewish music used a rhetoric that strongly resonated with the political debates between advocates of Dubnov's Diaspora-centered nationalism and Ahad Ha'am's purist cultural Zionism. Even more crucially, Saminsky's modernist approach mirrored Russian models just as OYNM composers' early compositions imitated those of their Russian teachers. In this new phase of Jewish art music, *kuchkist* preoccupation with folk music as an expression of national identity was replaced with a neonationalist orientation, in which national musical sources were abstracted, or, as Efros put it, "creatively re-fashioned," until their national character became well-nigh undistinguishable from their modernist context.

## RUSSIAN MODELS

But how could the Biblical Hebrews, whose music was not as readily available as folk music, be represented in music? The task was difficult, as Alexander Serov's opera *Judith* (1863) amply demonstrates. On Stasov's advice, Serov engaged the well-known archeologist Nikolai Veniaminovich Nabokov to design historically accurate costumes for the Jews and Assyrians.[5] Yet Serov seems to have been at a loss when he tried to characterize musically the opposing forces in the opera. For the Assyrians he drew on stock Oriental idioms, borrowed, as César Cui observed, from Glinka's *Ruslan and Ludmila*. To portray the spiritual greatness of the Jews, Serov relied on what Musorgsky heard as Catholic and Protestant church music. "It's about time to stop converting Jews to Christianity," Musorgsky wrote to Balakirev in his 1863 report on Serov's opera. As the prototype of Serov's Hebrew music, where it does not recall Christian music, Cui identified Glinka's "Yevreyskaya pesnya" in the incidental music to *Prince Kholmsky*.[6]

Glinka's 1840 "Yevreyskaya pesnya" is indeed the archetype of the musical representation of the Biblical Hebrews. Although the song is not free of Orientalizing characteristics, such as the grace notes in the vocal part and the undulating chromatic middle parts in the piano postlude (including, typically, the *nega* progression of $\sharp\hat{6}-\hat{6}-\hat{5}$), Glinka's Jewish song is a far cry from

Rimsky-Korsakov's Oriental fantasy. The steady march rhythm, the archaizing plagal progressions, the chorale-like homophonic arrangement of chords, and the exultant arrival on A major at the end lend nobility to the Jewish heroine longing for Palestine (ex. 21).

But the Russian composer who most definitively defined the musical image of the Biblical Hebrews was Modest Musorgsky. Musorgsky's most famous piece written in his personal Jewish idiom was the chorus *Iisus Navin* (known also as "Joshua," 1877), most cherished by Russian Jews because, in true *kuchkist* fashion, it relied on a traditional Jewish melody as its model. Since historical accuracy was important for Musorgsky, he proudly marked the manuscript of his Jewish chorus "based on Israelite folk songs."[7] The tune that he designated as an Israelite folk song was in fact a Hasidic *niggun* attributed to Rabbi Abraham ha-Mal'akh (1741–81). As Rimsky-Korsakov and Stasov remembered, Musorgsky heard it during Sukkot from Jewish neighbors (ex. 22).[8] Though the tune itself lacked the most typical Oriental characteristics, Musorgsky further reduced its Eastern associations. He set the beginning of the minor tune in A-flat major, turning to F-minor harmonies only at the end of phrases. The tonic potential of the F-minor chord is further lessened by the preceding minor dominant on C. Musorgsky's omission of the dramatic leap to the upper tonic in the second phrase also serves to detonicize F. The most obvious change he made, though, was to strip the original tune of its grace notes, which, again, helps turn the melody into a firm march, appropriate for Musorgsky's dark biblical text (ex. 23).

Musorgsky's "Yevreyskaya pesnya" (1867), which is, like Rimsky-Korsakov's, a setting from Mey's translation of the Song of Songs, displays further characteristics of Musorgsky's stark biblical tone (ex. 24). The rhythm and the meter of the song are reminiscent of Glinka's "Yevreyskaya pesnya," as is Musorgsky's constant use of an unstable sixth degree, which appeared only in Glinka's postlude, but permeates Musorgsky's entire song. As in Rimsky-Korsakov's setting, the sensuous text evokes grace notes and chromatic harmonies. Musorgsky's chromaticism, however, does not serve to enhance tonal relations. The tonality of the song is ambiguous because of the fluctuating major and minor sixths, which keep the song between G♯ minor and G♯ Dorian, the open fifths with which the song starts and ends, and Musorgsky's regular avoidance of leading tones. Even when the leading tone appears (mm. 11, 20), it fails to lead to the tonic. The unstable seventh helps keep the song free from the most hackneyed Orientalizing device, the augmented second. Despite its coloristic chromaticism, then, the song maintains an archaic modal character that lends Musorgsky's Jewish music the ancient patina needed for the representation of the virile Biblical Hebrews.

In his "Yevreyskaya pesnya" Musorgsky did not indeed convert the Jews to Christianity (as he blamed Serov of doing), but he assimilated them into his own Russian nationalist idiom. Because of Musorgsky's practice, this Russian

Example 21. Second strophe of Glinka's "Yevreyskaya pesnya," mm. 12–28.

(The light of dawn will shine, will glisten, and we'll carry organ, and timbrel, and pipe and silver, and goods, and a sacred object to the old house, to Palestine!)

Example 22. Rabbi Abraham ha-Mal'akh's *niggun* (from Schwarz, "Musorgsky's Interest in Judaica," 91).

Example 23. Musorgsky's "Joshua" as published in Kiselgof's *Zamelbukh*, no. 70, mm. 1–9. Original in transliterated Hebrew and Yiddish.

*(continued)*

Example 23 (continued)

ki___misch - po - taj___ loj jo - do - u

p cresc.

chasak

p cresc.

(So said the Lord: destroy the Emorites, you will command them with the sword, because they don't know my laws.)

Example 24. Musorgsky's "Yevreyskaya pesnya," mm. 1–13.

Andante, con passione

pp    p    p    pp

"Ya, tsve - tok po - le - voy, Ya, li - le - ya do - lin."

p    mf

Example 24 *(continued)*

("I am the flower of the field, I am the lily of the valley." "My white-bosom dove, among the young girls you are almost like a lily among thorns, my white-bosom dove.")

idiom became associated with the music of the Biblical Jews or *yevrei*. Musorgsky also depicted contemporary Jews, commonly referred to in the anti-Semitic climate of Russia as *zhidï*. Used interchangeably with *yevrei* until the end of the eighteenth century, *zhid* became an insulting designation in Russia, employed as a synonym for huckster and usurer.[9] Although less specifically, the distinction between *yevrey* and *zhidï* existed in music, too. As Musorgsky's

"'Samuel' Goldenburg and 'Schmuÿle'" in his *Pictures at an Exhibition* and the opening market scene in *Sorochintsï Fair* demonstrate, Musorgsky used all the augmented seconds for the representation of *zhidï* he spared in his music for *yevrei*.[10] No wonder Jewish composers were eager to see and to represent themselves as Musorgsky's *yevrei* rather than his *zhidï*. Jewish neonationalism, like its Russian model, had its own *kuchkist* inspiration.[11]

STASOV'S CONVERT: YOEL ENGEL

In January 1915 Saminsky evaluated the compositional activity of the OYNM in the Zionist Russian weekly *Razsvet* (Dawn). Although he mentioned no names, Saminsky's evaluation was a blunt attack on the OYNM's early, populist ideas represented by the society's most prominent member, Yoel Engel. More than Rimsky-Korsakov, Engel was considered the founding father of nationally inspired Jewish musical activities. A product of *haskalah,* Engel had been able to assimilate so thoroughly that under the name of Juliy ( Julius) Dimitrievich Engel he became a respected music critic in the Russian-language press. As staff music critic for the *Russkiye vedomosti* (Russian news), he exerted significant influence on Moscow's musical life.[12]

Engel came into contact with Zionist ideas in a group known as Za-kharyevka during his studies at the Moscow Conservatory, which he entered in 1893. Zakharyevka was the name of a boarding house, a gathering place for Jewish students and other intellectuals. Folk songs played an integral part in shaping the Zakharyevka group. It was through this circle that Pesach Marek engaged Engel to investigate the melodies he and Saul Ginzburg received for their collection. The group also inspired Engel to string together folk songs learned from his father into the first act of a Purim skit, *Esther.*

But casual singing of Jewish folk songs did not awaken Engel's Jewish identity. He recalled that although *Esther*'s success raised the esteem of Jewish music in their group, none of them recognized the national significance of folk music. "Jewish melodies appealed to me," Engel confessed in his memoirs, "not because I was a Jew, but for the very opposite reason, that is to say, because I wasn't enough of a Jew." And indeed, for the fully Russified Engel, who learned Yiddish only through his involvement with folk songs and Hebrew while working on the incidental music to An-sky's *Dybuk,*[13] Jewish folk music must have sounded more like an exotic curiosity than his native musical language. Engel's Jewish inspiration came not from his encounter with Jewish folk music but from an important Russian, Vladimir Stasov.

Chief ideologue of Russian nationalism in the arts and an adherent of radical literary critic Vissarion Belinsky's notions of the necessary social commitment of the artist, Stasov was always ready to provide artists with a rationale. Stasov's definition of genuine art was a nationalist cliché. "What the artist is born with," Stasov preached, "the impressions and images that surround him, among which he grew to manhood, to which his eye and soul were riveted, only that can be rendered with deep expression, with truth and genuine force."[14]

National expression meant difference, and for Stasov marking the difference of the new Russian art from the European mainstream carried special weight. Resentment played no small part in Stasov's urge to detach Russian art from Western Europe. The rejection of the West also brought about a growing interest in the East, especially in Asia: Stasov believed that Russia showed Asian influence in its "language, clothing, customs, buildings, furnishing, items of daily use, ornaments, melodies and harmonies, and fairy-tales."[15]

Because he saw Russia as an integral part of the East, Stasov developed an exceptional interest in Jewish culture. He was attracted to everything Eastern and ancient, and saw in Jewish culture a noble, pure, non-European culture that was waiting for representation in high art. He eagerly followed archeological discoveries that proved the existence of Jewish art since antiquity.[16] His encouragement of Jewish artists earned him a relatively long entry by Ilya Gintsburg in the 1906–13 *Yevreyskaya entsiklopediya* (Jewish Encyclopedia).[17] Baron David Gintsburg (1857–1910), with whom Stasov published a book on Hebrew ornaments in 1905 (a companion to his 1872 *Russian Folk Ornament*), remembered Stasov's reproach of "the Jewish nation for its complete indifference regarding the products of its national genius." Overzealous as he was, Stasov "discussed, commented, and stirred minds," David Gintsburg wrote, and thus became a major instigator of Jewish art.[18]

Like Gintsburg, Jewish sculptor Mark Antokolsky (1843–1902) saw only the liberal side of Stasov's stubborn passion for national art. "He was a patriot to the bottom of his heart," he remembered, but not "a narrow one, not a fanatic, and even less a calculating patriot." Antokolsky believed that Stasov "loved passionately all of Russia, not differentiating people by classes or religion. He wanted only that everyone keep his individuality and would perfect it for the common good and progress."[19]

Stasov's ideas about national art must have been familiar to Engel, who, as a music critic, had intimate knowledge of *kuchkist* aesthetics. What was new to him was Stasov's conviction that the *kuchka* model applied also to Jewish artists. Stasov argued that since art was rooted in the people and not in the individual and hence artists were obliged to express their ethnic group identity, Antokolsky the sculptor or Engel the musician could create true art only if they immersed themselves in their Jewish background. Stasov took it upon himself "to concern [himself] with the rights and obligations of the Jewish people." "Someone from among the Gentiles should occupy himself with it," Stasov wrote, "at a time when Jews themselves do not do what they should."[20] These "rights" and "obligations" could be liberating or restrictive, depending on what the individual Jewish artist wanted to do. Stasov's attitude was certainly not laissez-faire, for he assigned tasks to artists according to what he considered inescapable national or, in the case of Jews, racial categories.

For Engel, Stasov's prompting was a revelation. The epiphany occurred at their first meeting, when in Engel's presence Stasov confronted Antokolsky with the question of national obligation:

> "How is it," [Stasov] asked, "that Antokolsky is blind to the great field for art, the extraordinary possibilities for sculpture, within the life of his own Jewish people? Tell me"—he exclaimed turning to Antokolsky—"what manner of a Russian are you? What, for instance, is your name?"
>
> "My name," murmured Antokolsky in confusion, "is Mark."
>
> "Mark! What kind of an appellation is that? It's not even a Slavic name, it's Latin! You're Mordecai! What a noble and resounding name! Mordecai! Power! Inspiration! But Mark! Really what kind of a Mark are you?"[21]

Antokolsky, who in an effort to ensure success abandoned Jewish subjects after 1871 and turned to Russian historical themes, also earned the scorn of Ahad Ha'am, who accused him of denying his Jewishness.[22] Stasov was no less fervent a nationalist than Ahad Ha'am and was convinced that Jewish artists like Antokolsky should explicitly identify themselves as Jews in their art. But neither his good intentions nor the fact that Jewish artists greeted his behavior toward them as revelatory mitigated the dangers inherent in the ethnic determinism Stasov advanced.

According to Weinberg the episode between Stasov and Antokolsky that Engel witnessed occurred in 1897. In 1907 Engel himself described his first meeting with Stasov as occurring in 1901 at his second concert in St. Petersburg.[23] Although Engel had started to organize concerts of Jewish folk music in 1900, he did seem to have started his big project of actively participating in the collection and publication of folk songs only in 1904. Like Antokolsky, Engel received repeated encouragement from Stasov, who "always felt that it has been long overdue to introduce some Jewish seed-money into the history . . . of modern (Christian) European music." He believed that "a good half and perhaps more of all Gregorian, Ambrosian, and other Christian melodies have Jewish roots." Jewish music, in Stasov's naïve theory, was one component in a vast ocean of universal world music, consisting of folk and liturgical songs that, he assumed, were, at least at their roots, "of similar constitution, essence, character and form." The study of Jewish melodies, Stasov hoped, would "become one of the first foundation stones in the studies of contemporary, new European music."[24]

Engel never subscribed completely to this universalizing concept of Jewish music. What he sought in folk music was not the roots of Christian music but a musical expression of contemporary Russian Jewry. His response to Stasov reveals both the superficiality of his acquaintance with the different types of Jewish music and his devotion to a populist program. He collected secular, and not liturgical, melodies, he wrote to Stasov, because many of the religious tunes had already been published. But, according to Engel, nobody had published Jewish folk songs. With the publication of folk songs Engel's goals were much more modest than what Stasov suggested:

> At this point I do not set broad goals such as comparing Jewish themes with other [folk music] and do not dare to draw any general conclusions because I do not feel I am qualified to do that. For now my goal is to acquaint our musicians and singers with material that is evidently very worthy of their acquaintance. At the same time I plan to publish some melodies (by fall), and if they are well received, they will influence people positively (of course, intellectual Jews first of all) who live surrounded by Jewish folk songs but never pay any attention to them and never write them down.[25]

Engel's program thus expressed what the OYNM originally stood for: politically uncommitted, populist nationalism. It was a tolerant, artistically unambitious version of *kuchkism,* which—despite Stasov's coaching and Saminsky's later attack—Engel was reluctant to turn into a broader artistic mission.

### POLITICAL OVERTONES: THE SAMINSKY-ENGEL DEBATE

While the initial enthusiasm for the collection of Jewish folk music united the members of the OYNM, questions surrounding the creation of art music soon broke the unity. The first disagreement among the composer members concerned the question of publishing their own compositions. Even the common national cause could not have silenced divergences between the stereotypes of St. Petersburg's "intellectual" and "pedantic" and Moscow's "over-emotional" and "hysterical" composers. Led by Saminsky, the Art and Publication Committee of the St. Petersburg section refused to publish works by Moscow composers because of "aesthetic considerations." In response, the Moscow composers established their own branch of the society in 1913.[26] This separation signaled an ideological conflict, especially between the two most distinguished members, Petersburg Conservatory graduate Lazare Saminsky and Moscow Conservatory graduate Yoel Engel.

In addition to their different institutional backgrounds, Saminsky and Engel represented different attitudes in musical nationalism: their confrontation reflected the discrepancy between Romantic and modernist notions of the relationship between folk music and art music. Their argument about the national value of Yiddish folk songs had strong political overtones, reverberating the bitter polemics among Eastern European Jews before the 1917 Bolshevik coup.[27]

Saminsky questioned the national value of Yiddish folk songs, or "domestic songs," and Hasidic music, both cherished by other members of the OYNM, because, according to Saminsky, they bore "the fatal imprint of alien influence." He recommended the use of "old traditional sacred melos," superior because of, as he put it, "its racial purity."[28] Engel had a different hierarchy of Jewish music. Instead of "racial purity," his guiding principle, or so he thought, was authenticity. He fought with Yiddish writer Sholom Aleichem (1859–1916) about whether the songs by popular singer Mark Varshavsky could be considered "true" folk songs.

Engel initiated the debate when in 1901 he came across Sholom Aleichem's enthusiastic introduction to Varshavsky's collection of Jewish folk songs. Engel, who around the same time started to arrange folk songs himself, gave vent to his wrath in *Voskhod*. He criticized Varshavsky's songs for their primitive arrangements in which the piano right hand played along with the voice, accompanied by simple harmonies in the left hand. What angered Engel was Varshavsky's unsophisticated technique, which, as Varshavsky pointed out to Engel in self-defense, was all one could have expected from a dilettante folk singer. That Engel indeed mistook the subject of his criticism as art music was demonstrated by his requirements of sophisticated harmonic language and strong interrelationship between text and music, which, he thought, Varshavsky ignored when setting the serious words of his song "Di shif" (The ship) to music of merry character (ex. 25).[29] Although in his exchange with Sholom Aleichem Engel insisted that his objections were raised by Varshavsky's calling the songs in his collection "folk songs," the details of his critique reveal that he confused professional quality with authenticity.

The issues raised by Saminsky's attack on Engel repeated the same confusion, although on a different level. The new debate also changed Engel's position, for now it was Engel who was accused of questionable professional quality. Despite Saminsky's claim, however, his concerns were not exclusively aesthetic and cannot be detached from the Russian Jewish cultural and political milieu that had shaped his views.[30]

Like Sabaneyev, Saminsky believed that music could be considered national only when a deliberate effort to purify its sources had taken place. "National music is that stage in the musical creation of a race or a people," Saminsky wrote, "when the *conscious* work of clearing the original culture-substance from alien accretion is already achieved."[31] What Saminsky advocated was a sanitizing process for the sources of Jewish art music in order to create the basis for a "racially pure" art. In composition this purification meant the elimination of most folk and Hasidic music because of what Saminsky called their "racial contamination." In contrast, Engel argued that no folk music had ever been devoid of foreign influence, and that the presence of folk music in the everyday life of the people, not its abstract origin, made it valuable for the nation: "Is it not sufficient that Jewish folk song has an unmistakably Jewish cast of face? . . . For insofar as borrowed music was changed and altered by Jews to their taste and manner—by that much was it definitely Judaized. In its secular music, too, the Jewish soul finds expression; perhaps not to the same

Example 25. Varshavsky's "Di shif," from *Muzïka k yevreyskim narodnïm pesnyam. Notn tsu di yidishe folkslieder* (c. 1900).

Andante e dolce

Dort wait ojf dem Jam ojf dem groj - ssen steht grojss wie a Moj - jer a Schif_____ m'seht Men-schen fun in - nen fun oj - ssen gehn loj-fen a roup un a - rif_____ Ihr wet sej a - wa - di der - ken - nen. Ihr hot sej - er Un - glik ge - hert_____ Sej klou-gen wie e - lend sej sen - nen dous Pou - nim is schwartz wie die Erd._____

(There, on the large sea stands a ship. We see people inside and outside going hither and thither. You'll probably recognize them, you heard about their misfortune. They complain about their misery. Their face is as black as the earth.)

fulsome extent as in its religious music, since that harks back to the ancient time, but certainly with a diverse and many-sided exuberance."[32] In Saminsky's view this was a loose and impermissible attitude, "a policy [that was] already responsible for the mire of assimilation and neutralizing in which Jewish musical creation is sunk." Saminsky insisted that the "essence and power of national gravity in art" could be achieved only through "clearing of every channel of the national spirit from worthless alien sediment, from borrowed *pasticcio* that distorts the growth of the golden wheat of racial creation." He drew a parallel between the nation and the human body, and compared foreign elements in music to threatening ailments:

> In the present organic period, demolition is . . . just as important and valuable as is building up. My whole being, that of a worker in the Jewish musical field, revolts against the plea that in this domain "a place should be granted to everything and everybody."
> The banal, the racially neutral, the muddy and rickety, the flagrantly borrowed element of our music, should be weeded out mercilessly from the cycle of means in use by our young creators. Otherwise this element is a source of feebleness and instability in our budding national-musical organism. And our young composition is doomed to a work nationally insignificant.[33]

Although eccentric metaphors and racist clichés were characteristic of the writing style of the time, it is hard not to hear sinister political overtones in Saminsky's obsession with purity. But one should not too hastily place Saminsky's ideas in a proto-fascist context. Rather, the context that shaped his rhetoric was the debate surrounding Jewish nationalism in Russia in the 1910s. When he had first raised his voice in protest to Engel in 1915 nobody could have missed the political message he was communicating. Folk music was a metaphor for Yiddish culture, while the "pure" religious melodies Saminsky propagated stood for a revival of a purified Hebrew culture. The debate over their primacy is closely related to the polemic between Dubnov and Ahad Ha'am over the primacy of Diaspora culture or a Hebrew culture in a future Jewish state.

There was also a related debate, initiated by Zionists for the acceptance of Hebrew as the national language of the Jews and, concomitantly, for the elimination of Yiddish, equally despised by both assimilated Jews and anti-Semites. Called *zhidovskiy zhargon* ( Jewish jargon) in Russian, Yiddish, as its designation indicates, was considered corrupt, a contaminated German used as the lingua franca of the uneducated Jewish masses. Although the "racial purity" of Yiddish was not discussed per se, its mixture of German, Hebrew, and other local languages could only have rendered it suspect in the eyes of purist fanatics. Yiddish distinguished Eastern from Western Jews and became the linguistic marker of the Diaspora, which Zionists wanted to eliminate. Hebrew, on the other hand, was the language of the Bible and liturgy, understood primarily by the educated layer of the Jewish community. With the declaration of Hebrew as a national language, Russian Zionists hoped not only to connect the masses of Russian Jews to their ancient past, but also to make them acceptable by European standards.

The opposition between the Yiddishists and Hebraists gathered steam around 1910 in connection with debates about a projected reform of Jewish schools, wherein it was revealed that despite Zionist efforts, Yiddish was the only language of effective propaganda among the Jewish masses. The disappointment of Zionists close to Ahad Ha'am's ideals was aggravated by the Chernowitz Yiddish Conference in 1908, at which Yiddishists pressed for a declaration of Yiddish as the national language of Russian Jews. "We no longer want to be fragmented, and to render to every Moloch nation-state its tributes," Yiddish writer Isaac Leib Peretz (1852–1915) announced in his emotionally charged speech. "There is one people—Jews, and its language is—Yiddish."[34]

Under Zionist pressure the conference concluded that Yiddish was not "the" but "a" national language of the Jews. This modification did not lessen the triumph of the Yiddishists. Yiddishists, who in political terms were equated with socialists, and who gradually became the dominant group in Jewish politics in Russia, openly criticized Zionists for their utopianism. "Before you Zionists—whether of the spiritual or the material school—take it upon yourselves to demand something from the Jewish masses," An-sky, a future member of the OYNM, wrote in 1906, "it is permissible to ask whether you have fulfilled any kind of duty to those masses."[35] An-sky was not the only populist member of the OYNM. The secretary Israel Okun was active in the *Bund,* and it was probably through his instigation that the *Bund* provided considerable financial support for the OYNM.

Neither Engel nor Saminsky had direct associations with socialist circles or the Zionist party. Ironically it was Engel who, although admittedly not a Zionist, had Zionist leanings in politics and finally moved to Palestine, while Saminsky, much as he was supported by Zionists, especially after he left Russia following the 1917 coup, was never directly involved in Zionist activities.[36] Still, the striking parallel between the musical and political rhetoric of the time demonstrates how close the rhetoric of modernist musical aesthetics can come to that of political nationalism.

### THE MUSIC OF *YEVREI*

The rejection of the music of the Diaspora, apparent in Saminsky's refusal to accept Jewish music that showed signs of foreign influence, would have left him with little choice had he not turned—as Zionists did before their first world congress—to the religious aspects of Judaism. But even in religious music Saminsky had to sift carefully to find material he was willing to accept, for even religious music carried the imprint of the music of other ethnicities. It was heavily influenced, for instance, by Arabic music, from which Saminsky most wanted to dissociate Jewish music.

The detachment, however, was not easy, for in the arts the use of Oriental features was the main characteristic associated with Jews. Though an enthusiast of Biblical Hebrews, Stasov advised St. Petersburg's Jews to build their synagogue in an Arab-Moorish style, much in vogue for Jewish architecture in Western Europe at the time. Completed in 1893, the St. Petersburg Choral Synagogue openly displayed its "Jewish" features, just as the St. Petersburg Church of Resurrection, built in Russian neonationalist style between 1883 and 1907, exhibited characteristics of seventeenth-century Muscovite architecture. In Stasov's spirit both indicated non-European, Eastern origins.[37]

But while Stasov valued Oriental characteristics because they could function as a distinctive mark for Jews as well as Russians, for Saminsky Orientalism represented the "emasculation and de-hebraization" of the Hebrew melos.[38] Saminsky tried to establish an opposition between the "elevated, original, well crystallized" Hebrew and the "lowly, vagabond, common Oriental pattern to which Hasidic melodies so often belong." What makes Saminsky's rhetoric so unsettling is that his strong adjectives reflect hatred toward the kind of music cherished by many Jews as "Jewish." Significantly, he switched to offensive anti-Semitic figures of speech when he argued against the "bad kind" of Jewish music, just as Jewish publicists willingly employed the word *zhid* when denouncing negative traits of their coreligionists.[39] In Saminsky's discourse, Jewish music became a metaphor for the Jewish people: folk music standing for the despised masses of the ghetto, sacred music for the elevated noble characters in the Bible. "The worthlessness of the melody of the vagabond type, of the lowly kind of domestic and chassidic music," Saminsky stated, "lies in its basic melodic neutrality: this music does not arrive anywhere because melodically it comes from 'nowhere,' as far as the Jewish racial taste and folk-creation perceive it."

According to Saminsky there were two types of influences that contaminated the music of the ghetto: the "highway-begotten, flat Orientalism," and the "near-by Aryan culture." But none of these could destroy the true Hebrew taste, because, he argued, "the root-character of Jewish music harbors no exotic and expressive platitude; it bears a mark of poise, austerity and majesty, all the traits of cultural greatness."

The belief that the noble and great music of the Bible was preserved in certain types of Jewish music was shared by many and was the basis of Abraham Zvi Idelsohn's ethnomusicological project that he began while residing in Palestine between 1907 and 1921.[40] In *The Music of the Ghetto and the Bible* Saminsky repeatedly referred to Idelsohn when he wanted to back up his theory about the "contaminated" nature of Jewish folk song or about "the historic continuity of Hebrew melos."[41] But he deliberately ignored Idelsohn's basic assumption that "as the Jew, being of Semitic stock, is a part of the Oriental world, so Jewish music—coming to life in the Near East—is, generally speaking, of one piece with the music of the Orient."[42]

In contrast, Saminsky regarded Orientalism in Jewish music as unacceptable. He gave many reasons for trying to detach Jewish music from the Orient. One, he argued, was a common prejudice that "Jewish music as such does not really exist, that it is but a slightly modified common Oriental melos."[43] Thus while for Stasov marking Russian music meant to connect it to the East, for Saminsky creating a specifically Jewish idiom in music meant to sever Jewish music from an Oriental musical style that could block its way into the European mainstream.

Saminsky's dislike of Oriental-sounding Jewish folk music not only reveals his anti-Diaspora attitude, but also shows the reverse side of the myth that in the process of seeking their roots members of the Jewish intelligentsia instinctively recognized Jewish music as their own. Israel Rabinovitch, the only author on Jewish music who has unequivocally sided with Engel in the debate over folk music versus Biblical chant, explained Saminsky's stance as a mixture of Saminsky's support of musical modernism—"a revolt against the banal, a rejection of the hackneyed"—and his detachment from his own religious background as the main factors influencing his rejection of folk songs. "Were these musicians Jews of the orthodox persuasion, who pray thrice a day, who do hear throughout the months and seasons the varied synagogal cantillations, no doubt these, too, would appear banal and hackneyed to them, a synagogal routine," Rabinovich wrote. "These men, however, are far removed from the precincts of the synagogue, at best they remember it with the same nostalgia which one entertains for one's childhood; they have surrounded it, therefore, with romantic associations, and, as [a] natural consequence, the old Hebraic melos appears to them in a new and artistic metamorphosis."[44]

Indeed, Saminsky's familiarity with Moldavian, Jewish, Ukrainian, Polish, and Bulgarian folk songs, heard in his native Russian Romanian village, made him look for the "purest strata of Hebrew music" far away from that all-too-familiar mixture, among Georgian Jews in the Caucasus, where he went in 1913 under the auspices of the Jewish Historical-Ethnographic Society. One suspects that the choice of location was deliberate, for some legends claim that the Jews of Georgia were descended from the Ten Tribes exiled by Shalmaneser, or that they were the exiles from Judah under Nebuchadnezzar[45]—in other words, that they belong to the most ancient Jewish communities. There Saminsky found what he was looking for, namely, that this "typically *Oriental branch* of Israel *knows of no song built on the favorite Oriental scale* seemingly inherent in the domestic song of Jewry-at-large."[46] He used his new findings to justify his campaign against what he called a prejudiced and "harmful idea that the Jewish song built in major or in ordinary minor, in the Aeolian or Dorian mode, is not as typically Jewish, as melody molded in the common Oriental vein."

Saminsky related these modes to the *magen-avot* (Aeolian, with Phrygian cadence) and *adonai-malach* (Mixolydian) modes of Biblical cantillation. He rejected the *ahavah-rabbah* mode (Phrygian with raised third scale degree) because of its Oriental character. Tracing it to Arabic and Moorish sources, Saminsky blamed this mode for deflating and neutralizing "the melodical Jewish trend." Although Saminsky would later support a more modernistic approach to Jewish music, for the time being he was satisfied with the elimination of augmented seconds and with the restoration of the Aeolian, Mixolydian, and Dorian modes.

One suspects that behind Saminsky's differentiation between the national significance of different types of Jewish music lay as well Musorgsky's example of representing *yevrei* with modal music and the *zhidï* with Orientalizing augmented seconds. Saminsky's splitting of Jewish music into a glorified and a debased branch is very similar to the psychological mechanism called Jewish self-hatred, defined as Jews' acceptance of anti-Semitic accusations as true. The construction and then rejection of an unacceptable Jewish "other" (in Saminsky's case the Orientalizing music associated with *zhidï*), which carried all the negative attributes created by anti-Semites, helped purge the positive side of Jewish identity of the burden of otherness.[47] And, indeed, instead of representing "otherness," the music thus created displayed an increasing resemblance to that of the dominant culture.

FROM "VAGABOND ORIENTALISM" TO "HEBRAIC POISE"

In publications before 1914 Saminsky did not yet try to select songs displaying features that he called "Hebraic" as opposed to "Judaic." "Unter soreles vigele" ('Neath little Sarah's cradle, no. 42) is an arrangement based on a folk song transcribed by Z. Kiselgof.[48] The folk tune is in the Oriental-sounding *frigish* mode, which Saminsky emphasizes by adding a piano interlude that revels in augmented seconds (ex. 26).

The change in Saminsky's attitude is signaled by his arrangement of a Yemenite tune, published by the champion of modern Hebrew Eliezer Ben-Jehuda (1858–1927) in the literary almanac *Lu'ah Erez Isroel*. While the first forty-two pieces in the OYNM series were in minor or *frigish*, "Ani hadal" (Poor as I am, no. 44) is in major, a mode that, according to Idelsohn, appears only infrequently in Jewish folk music.[49] No wonder Saminsky had to rely on Yemenite sources to come up with a melody in major.[50] He underlines the purity of the major melody by the accidental-free, simple harmonization of the first verset (ex. 27). Only the name "Adonay" (Lord) seems to necessitate the introduction of chromatic harmony. The second part of the setting (a varied arrangement of the same versets) uses chromatic voice leading with less restriction, as if the divine name had liberated the musical language.

"Patsh, patsh kikhelakh" (Patty cake, patty cake, no. 69), an arrangement Saminsky finished in Tiflis in 1914, marked his new "Hebraic" period. The tune is an almost purely pentatonic children's song in Kiselgof's transcrip-

Example 26. The end of Saminsky's "Unter soreles vigele" (OYNM no. 42), mm. 21–32. Lyrics originally also in Hebrew characters.

Zi-ge-le wet foh-ren hand - len    Ro - sin - kes mit Mand - len.

(The goat will go trade raisins and almonds.)

Example 27. Beginning of Saminsky's "Ani hadal" (OYNM no. 44), mm. 1–7. Lyrics originally also in Hebrew characters.

Soprano

A - ni    ha-dal w'o-si    ir u-mig-dal,

Harmonium
oder Piano
ad libitum

*(continued)*

Example 27 *(continued)*

(I am poor, but my strength is the city and the tower)

tion. Saminsky emphasizes the supposedly archaic character of the mode with open fifths at the beginning and at the end of the song (ex. 28).

In 1915, only two months after Saminsky had launched his first attack on "contaminated" Yiddish folk songs, he finished the Hebrew song "Shchav, bni," op. 11, no. 2 (Sleep, my child, no. 80), and dedicated it to Engel. The original melody, attributed to "Alter Rov" (the old rabbi),[51] was collected by Kiselgof. To demonstrate to Engel that he was not against the use of folk song in general, Saminsky pointed to "Shchav, bni" as one of the rare examples of folk song "of the elevated type" that displayed "the highest, truly national melodic type."[52] The melody moves in a range of a fifth between A and E, with occasional touches on the subtonic G. To emphasize the simplicity of the song, Saminsky sets its first part without using accidentals. Although the sixth scale degree is missing from the melody, it appears later in the piano accompaniment, alternating, as in Glinka's and Musorgsky's "Yevreyskaya pesnya," between natural and raised sixth degrees. By inserting a middle section in F♯ natural minor and replacing F with F♯ at the end of the song, Saminsky seems to highlight the Dorian character of the mode. Despite the B♭ that occurs at the vocal cadence and lends the melody's ending a Phrygian color, the closing measures of the piano settle in A-Dorian (ex. 29).

Example 28. Saminsky, "Patsh, patsh kikhelakh" (OYNM no. 69).

a. The folk tune, transcribed by Kiselgof, printed before Saminsky's arrangement, and the beginning of the arrangement, mm. 1–5.

Di Volksmelodie in Original farschriben fun S. Kisselhof

Patch,___ patch   ki - che - lach,   der Ta - te   t'kei - fen   schi - che - lach,

schi - che - lach   wet   er___   kei - fen   un in Chej - der   wet dos kind___ lei - fen.

Tranquillo (M. M. ♩ = 60)

Canto

Patch,___ patch

Piano

(Patty cake, patty cake, the father will buy shoes, and the child will run to *shul.*)

b. Open fifths at the end of Saminsky's arrangement, mm. 43–46.

Example 29. Saminsky's "Shchav, bni" (OYNM no. 80).

a. Beginning of Saminsky's "Shchav, bni," mm. 1–12.

(Under my tree, my son, stands a little goat, my son.)

b. End of Saminksy's "Shchav, bni," mm. 49–76.

Example 29 *(continued)*

(Study to become learned and to make wonders, hush, sleep, lie down.)

In his collection of Eastern European folk songs, Idelsohn has only a handful of songs in minor with alternating major and minor sixth scale degrees.[53] Yet while Dorian was a rare mode in Jewish folk music, in Russian folk tunes it appears so frequently that Balakirev called it the "Russian minor." Jewish folk music had its own special variant of Dorian. Idelsohn described it as "Ukrainian Dorian," a scale with a raised fourth degree that resulted in an augmented second between the third and fourth degrees. Beregovski calls the scale "altered Dorian" and points to its use in creating the impression of lamentation for humorous purposes.[54] As its name indicates, this scale would hardly fit Saminsky's definition of a "racially pure" mode. He advocated in its stead an unaltered Dorian, ignoring, in this case, its Russian connotations. Curiously, then, the Hebrew music he envisioned could resemble Russian; only Ukrainian, Romanian, Moldavian, Hungarian, Polish, Bulgarian, and, most crucially, Arabic influences had to be repressed.

Even more pointed is Saminsky's setting of An-sky's poem "Di nakht" (The Night, no. 70), composed in April 1915 in St. Petersburg and published in 1917, in which musical representation of *yevrei* and *zhidï* appears side by side. "Di nakht" is a generic Romantic poem in which the poet, after describing the nature that surrounds him, puts the majesty of God and the miserable loneliness of the individual into sharp contrast. Saminsky began the song with archaic-sounding open fifths. At the *fortissimo* cry "Oh mighty God" the song changes its modal orientation from G natural minor to G Dorian, and for a climax peaks on the dominant of C major. The dotted rhythms and the Musorgskyan unison melody in the piano underline the protagonist's address to God in the poem. To illustrate the contrasting misery of the human condition in the text, Saminsky brings back the E♭ in the music and introduces an augmented second (C♯-B♭), turning, for a moment, to the Ukrainian Dorian as the mode of lamentation (ex. 30). While perhaps not the subtlest musical image, it certainly drives home Saminsky's creed in a purified, noble melos, unhampered by an augmented second–ridden musical style.

The piece Saminsky praised as one representing a new, promising current in the OYNM's output was Lev Mordukhov Tseitlin's *Eli Tsion*, published in 1914 for cello and piano, and in the same year in Joseph Achron's arrangement for violin and piano.[55] What accounted for the popularity of *Eli Tsion*, evident by its frequent performance at the OYNM concerts, was Tseitlin's use of the well-known melody "Eli Tsion ve'areha" (Wail, Oh Zion and thy cities), an anonymous dirge inherited from the Middle Ages. The song was recited at Tishah be-Av, the traditional day of mourning and fasting for the destruction of the First and Second Temples in Jerusalem. Published in various Jewish song collections, *Eli Tsion* became the symbol for the persecution of Jews in exile. Tseitlin relied on the version of the melody Kiselgof published among the *skarbove* songs in his *Zamelbukh*.[56] Although the song was quite well known

Example 30. Saminsky's "Di nakht" (OYNM no. 70), mm. 28–56.

(continued)

Example 30 *(continued)*

(Oh mighty God! Your world is as beautiful as a diamond in the tsar's crown. And I, your son, as if of stone, am poor and lonely, poor and alone!)

Example 31. The Eli Tsion melody as published by Kiselgof and set by Tseitlin.

Example 32. Comparison of the original cantillation motive, Tseitlin's version of it, and the Eli Tsion melody.

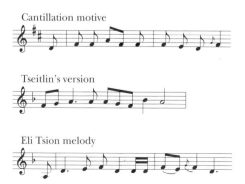

to Jews, Tseitlin marked it as "Jewish" for gentile audiences by introducing a gratuitous augmented second into the melody (ex. 31).

The respect Tseitlin's *Eli Tsion* gained in Saminsky's judgment was due to Tseitlin's effort to combine the melody of this well-known song with motives from a cantillation melody, or *trop*, used for the singing of Shir hashirim (Song of Songs), which Tseitlin took from the appendix to Kiselgof's *Zamelbukh*. From a liturgical point of view Eli Tsion and the Shir hashirim *trop* are incompatible, as the first is linked to the commemoration of the destruction of the Temple, the second to the reading of Shir hashirim on the Shabbat of Passover, the remembrance of the Jews' exodus from Egypt. Indeed, had Tseitlin had liturgical considerations in mind, he could have picked another *trop* from Kiselgof's appendix, the one used for the reading of the Book of Lamentations, a Biblical text read during the synagogue services for Tishah be-Av. As it stands, Tseitlin's decision can be interpreted either as religious ignorance or as compositional sophistication. It was the latter that Saminsky celebrated in the piece; he especially appreciated the use of cantillation motives and Tseitlin's primarily motivic approach that allowed him the subtle combination of the two musical themes.

In Tseitlin's version the cantillation melody does not reach its fifth degree at its first appearance. With this modification Tseitlin's melodies of Shir hashirim and Eli Tsion both start with a motive rising to the third and touching the fourth degree as their highest note (ex. 32). Thus when in the second part of the piece Tseitlin introduces the cantillation motive, it first sounds like a major variation of the Eli Tsion melody. Only at the very end of *Eli Tsion* does Tseitlin bring the original version of the cantillation melody back to its original key, D major, thus ending the piece on a note of hope (ex. 33). In this respect *Eli Tsion*, although its combination of traditional tunes is liturgically incongruous, conveys a Zionist program; the melody expressing the sorrows of the exile is superseded by one associated with the Exodus from the land of slavery.

Example 33. The end of Tseitlin's *Eli Tsion* (ORNM no. 45), mm. 62–71.

*(continued)*

Example 33 *(continued)*

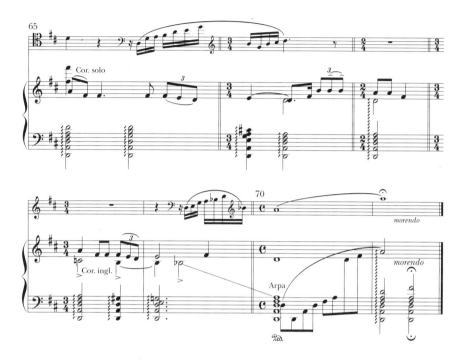

### FROM NATIONALISM TO NEONATIONALISM: ALEXANDER KREIN

Tseitlin's treatment of the two traditional motives in his *Eli Tsion* already shows a compositional approach that goes far beyond the simple settings in the OYNM's early publications. Moscow composer Alexander Abramovich Krein (1883–1951) went even further on the path toward a modernist interpretation of Jewish music. Krein was one of the Russian Jewish composers whom Saminsky described as a representative of "the true musical Israel." Sabaneyev, who considered Krein to be the most prominent member of the OYM, saw Krein's compositions as the markers of "the *birth of Hebraism in the musical world.*"[57] Krein was a perfect candidate to fuse traditional elements and modernist techniques in his compositions. His father, Abraham Krein, was a klezmer violinist; seven of his ten sons became professional musicians. Alexander was trained at the Moscow Conservatory and moved in the circles of Alexander Skryabin, whose theosophy-inspired compositions represented the most modernist, and most technically advanced, tendencies in Russian music.[58]

Krein's first explicitly Jewish composition was his 1910 *Jewish Sketches*. Its success inspired him to write a second set. The ensemble of string quartet and clarinet, familiar to listeners of classical music mainly because of Mozart's and Brahms's famous clarinet quintets, was also an art music rendition of a klezmer band, which frequently employed the clarinet and violin as solo instruments. Neither of the two movements of Krein's second *Jewish Sketches* moves away from the home key, G minor. The melodies he uses are filled with augmented seconds, the tritest Orientalist marker of Jewish art music. Although Krein's sensitivity to color and his careful handling of balance display his thorough conservatory training, nothing in his *Jewish Sketches* indicates his future willingness to combine folk music with modernist sound.

In 1913, around the time Krein joined the Moscow branch of the OYNM, he became fascinated with Hebrew liturgical music. Sabaneyev, who knew Krein personally, greeted the new interest with great enthusiasm. Krein's gaze, he wrote, "penetrates . . . back into the epoch when, in his opinion, the race was purer and the melody mirrored more exactly the psychic essence of [the Jewish] race."[59] While no Biblical account justifies the assumption of racial purity in ancient Judaism, purity was a central concept in modernist aesthetics. What Sabaneyev called the "essence of race" was very close to the purified, abstracted essence of Jewish folk art that Efros advocated as a desirable basis for a true Jewish art that could match its Western counterparts.

In his compositions Krein indeed relied on increasingly more abstracted elements of Jewish music. Abstract techniques govern his 1919 setting of Chaim Nachman Bialik's Hebrew poem "Natof natfah hadim'ah" (The tear has indeed dropped).[60] The song, published in the Moscow series of Jewish music, appeared with a cover page designed by Eliezer (El) Lissitzky (1890–1941). The design was fitting, for it was created by a Russian Jewish artist who, after his initial fascination with the combination of Jewish folk art and Western modernist styles, turned to abstraction and constructivism (fig. 2).

Krein builds the entire song on a short motive, the four notes of which (A♯–B–C♯–D) indicate minor (or *frigish*) mode, common in Eastern European Jewish folk music. The melodic shape of Krein's motive, however, is strange. Its most characteristic interval, the diminished fourth, is usually avoided in folk music, although it appears occasionally in liturgical chant (ex. 34). Krein transposes the motive along an A♯–C♯–E–G axis, thus mapping the tonal space of the song in Lisztian (or Rimsky-Korsakovian) fashion. The only transposition that does not fit this scheme is the fourth one on D♯, which, in Krein's system, provides the song with its tonally far-out point. The four notes of the motive form an octatonic tetrachord, which together with its transposition at the tritone create a complete octatonic scale, a marker of evil magic in nineteenth-century Russian operas.[61]

It is by no accident, then, that the first transposition occurs on E, a tritone away from the original A♯. Yet despite passages that are saturated with octatonic sounds, Krein's song is not primarily octatonic in tonality. Because of the stable role of the F♯ dominant, the song's B minor tonal center remains

Figure 2. Cover design by El Lissitzky for the OYM sheet music series (Alexander Krein, "Natof natfah hadim'ah"). Amherst College Russian Culture Center, used by permission, © 2006 Artists Rights Society (ARS), New York/VG Bild-Kunst, Bonn.

Example 34. Diminished fourth in Eastern European synagogue music (Idelsohn, *Der Synagogengesang der Osteuropäischen Juden* [Leipzig: Hofmeister, 1932], no. 125, p. 37).

(Exalted be the Living God and praised. He exists unbounded by time in His existence. He is One, and there is no unity like His Oneness.)

intact. Nevertheless, structuring the song around a diminished seventh axis of octatonic tetrachords shows Krein's awareness of octatonic possibilities.

Krein's fascination with ninths and even occasional thirteenth chords, his urge to create new chords such as combinations of French and German sixth chords, French sixth and half-diminished seventh chords, or ninth chords with augmented fifths (the latter being an extension of what is often referred to as the "Skryabin sixth"), and his ability to expand the dominant function (as in m. 5, where he combines the dominant with a German sixth chord, both potentially resolving to the tonic) show him to be an expert in Skryabinesque harmony. As in Skryabin's music, the source of this harmonic complexity is revealed by Krein's signal use of a half-diminished seventh chord in the piano introduction of "Natof natfah hadim'ah." The sixth degree in the bass, the emphatic presence of the augmented sixth in the middle parts, and the short appearance of B that for a moment turns the harmony into a French sixth right before its resolution to the dominant make the *Tristan* association unmistakable (ex. 35).[62]

Despite its abstract features, "Natof natfah hadim'ah" still keeps characteristics such as augmented seconds and rich ornamentation close to the surface so that the music remains easily identifiable as Oriental, or Jewish. In

Example 35. The beginning of Krein's "Natof natfah hadim'ah," mm. 1–10.

Na-ver-nu-las' sle - za… Raz-dro-bil ye-yo svet za-mer -tsav - shiy…

(A tear welled up . . . the light, which began to glimmer, shattered it . . . )

Example 36. Beginning of Krein's Sonata for Piano, mm. 1–6.

Example 37. *Revia* cantillation *trope* (a) compared to the theme of Krein's Sonata for Piano, mm. 17–20 (b).

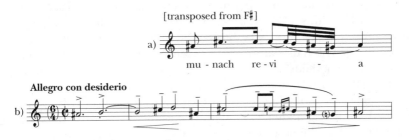

Krein's 1922 Piano Sonata the Jewish melody that serves as the main theme of the composition is hidden amid dense, dissonant harmonies. The introduction, as in the previous song, presents a short, octatonic motive that sums up Krein's melodic language (ex. 36). Sabaneyev claimed that Krein borrowed his main theme from one of the Eastern European cantillation versions of the Song of Songs. The last six notes of Krein's theme are indeed almost identical with the *revia* cantillation *trope*.[63] Krein altered the original pattern by the addition of an augmented second and thus gave the motive a more distinctly Jewish character. The alteration also resulted in the octatonic transformation of the theme, enforced by the addition of the inverted version of the initial motive to the theme (ex. 37).

Unlike Krein's early *Jewish Sketches*, the Sonata is packed with references to prestigious Western art music. Its one movement, which includes slow sections and a fugato passage, and thus incorporates elements of a four-movement form, is built on constant transformations of the same thematic material. Krein's model was unquestionably Franz Liszt's B-minor Sonata. To make this reference unmistakable, Krein, like Liszt, uses the key signature of B minor at the beginning, and B major at the end of his Sonata. While the structure is Lisztian, Krein's harmonic language derives from Skryabin, whose innovative chords, some of them dubbed "ecstasy," "mystic," or "pleroma" (plentitude), were manifestations of Skryabin's constant striving to transcendental heights. Ironically, Sabaneyev, who as the first biographer of Skryabin recognized the Russian composer's strong influence on his Jewish contemporary, still celebrated Krein for discovering the appropriate "harmonic environment" for the Jewish national melos. In Krein's erotic inclinations, manifested in Skryabinesque performance instructions in the Piano Sonata like *con desiderio* (with desire), *amoroso* (tenderly, or lovingly), and *con fuoco* (with fire), Sabaneyev was unwilling to recognize the emulation of Skryabin's erotic ecstasy. Instead, he identified Krein's inspiration with "the spirit of Hebraism which," he wrote, "in the continual seductions of its environment was allured by the bloody and sensual cults of the orgiastic East."[64]

There is no way to measure the proportion between modernistic tendencies (octatonic potential and harmonic complexity) and the Jewish characteristics (present mainly in the uninhibited use of augmented seconds) in Krein's music. Is this a "Hebraization" of Western art music, along lines Saminsky prophesied, or the "Skryabinization" of Jewish music, a musical assimilation that Jewish nationalists, among them Saminsky, fought against in theory even as they yielded to it in practice? As Jewish music seemed to be approaching the modernist mainstream, it was rapidly losing its specific Jewish characteristics. Not the least of these characteristics was the accessibility that helped the Jewish audience to identify it as their own musical expression at the time Engel had started his missionary work.

·   ·   ·

Ultimately, then, the "Hebraic" trend in art propagated so aggressively by Saminsky became almost indistinguishable from mainstream modernism. By refusing Orientalism, exoticism, Yiddishism—all of which would have rendered Jewish music marginal by Western standards—and by subjecting it to abstract artistic techniques, Jewish composers gained entry for Jewish music into high art at the price of redefining its audience. Recapitulating again the dominant culture's dilemma of an elite art claiming to represent the whole nation, Jewish art music was gradually leaving behind the Jews of Eastern Europe, whose culture served as the inspiration for the Jewish cultural renaissance. The process of secularization that spurred artists to build a secular but specifically Jewish art that would inherit the status formerly held by religion was now driving the same artists past their nationalist phase. Many

of the most talented joined the rising European avant-garde—a melting pot
if ever there was one.

Analyzing the process in his 1918 essay "Aladdin's Lamp," Abram Efros
still cherished the illusion that Jewish artists would sacrifice their individual
ambitions to their nationalist obligations:

> Truly, we lag behind and are the last to arrive at the aesthetic of folk art. It's
> also true that we feel considerable awkwardness in front of the assembled gen-
> tiles, for our popular-art enthusiasm has come very late, and in the world art
> market, apologetics on behalf of folk arts are obviously already becoming dé-
> modé. But therein lies the difference . . . between us as recent followers of fash-
> ion, tricked-out in the latest style, and us as present-day old clothes dealers
> clutching our rags tightly to our breasts, like that old lamp which seems like
> Aladdin's to us. . . . [W]e say that we respectfully hand back our admission ticket
> into good society, if keeping it means giving up our tears and raptures over the
> humble aesthetic, a pinkas [record book] blossoming with patterns, or the as-
> tonishing swirling spiral of a tombstone; we say that . . . there is no price we
> would not pay, so long as we can cling on avidly, fiercely tenacious, to the world
> of national beauty that has been revealed to us. And if there is one thing more
> than another that we fear, it is that Jewish artistic thought, in its innocence,
> might, on hearing the inevitable street cry: "Who will exchange old lamps for
> new?" give up the precious old junk of Aladdin in exchange for some glitter-
> ing fashionable utensil.[65]

As Saminsky's ardent polemic demonstrates, "junk" was indeed thrown away,
although ideas about what was considered "junk" kept changing according
to political currents and artists' agendas. Efros himself, who considered folk
art only a source for modern art, might be found guilty of putting modernist
art above the "junk" of folk creation. Unwilling to remain in a ghetto, most
Jewish artists, as Efros feared, left folk "junk" behind in an effort to assimilate their art into European modernism that in its quest for new forms and
expressions favored, at least for a while, the folkloric and primitive. With the
new tendencies in art Jewish artists were no longer considered outcasts but,
in Efros's words, "equals among equals."[66] It was no surprise, Seth Wolitz explains, that as the talents and efforts of Jewish artists "had brought them up
to the cutting edge of Russian avant-garde art," their enthusiasm about the
quest for a Jewish style lessened. "Their devotion to purely artistic concerns
was always a basic premise in their national artistic experiments," Wolitz in-
sists, and "therefore, it was natural that they should abandon ethnic concerns
in the face of such exciting abstract challenges when their national identity
was no longer a hindrance."[67] There is some truth to Wolitz's suggestion that
national identity matters most when it also appears as a hindrance. But his
emphasis on "purely artistic concerns" is an anachronistic overstatement intended to justify these artists' later personal decisions. For what the career

of these Jewish artists ultimately demonstrates is how an artistically periph-
eral, politically populist national movement in art became an elitist movement under the influence of a neonationalist combination of modernism
and nationalism.

What Wolitz called "purely artistic concern" was in fact a tendency among
Jewish artists to turn to abstraction. In an article about Jewish painting Issachar
Ryback (1897–1934) and Boris Aronson (1898–1980) announced that abstraction and nationalism are not exclusive terms. On the contrary, their combination was claimed to be the only possible way for Jewish artists. "Only
through the principle of abstract painting, which is free from any literary aspects, can one achieve the expression of one's own national form," sounded
Ryback and Aronson's neonationalist creed. Yet despite their modernist
stance, Ryback and Aronson maintained the belief in the existence of an ethnic essence in art created by Jewish artists. "However much the artist may strive
to be international in his work," they declared, "his painterly feelings, when
expressed in the abstract, will be national because the spiritual character of
the artist always grows from the accumulated feelings of his environment."[68]

Was the attraction of Jewish artists to abstraction only a reaction to current artistic movements, a sort of zeitgeist, or was it related, as many assumed,
to the Second Commandment, which forbids the creation of images?[69] Ryback and Aronson certainly did not recall the Second Commandment to defend their abstract aspirations. Instead, they referred to the cerebral mind
of the Jews as a reason for their interest in abstraction.[70] A safe place to hide
in the midst of politically tumultuous times (or so they hoped in 1919), abstraction also seemed to be a solution for Jewish art, caught, as debates surrounding the OYNM demonstrate, between the desire to enter the mainstream of Western modernism and to maintain a distinctive Jewish identity
based on traditional sources.

Neither Krein nor the others (Gnesin, Milner, or Achron) listed by Saminsky as nominees for representatives of "the true musical Israel" could achieve
the status of a "Jewish Glinka." Achron, who emigrated to the United States
and had a considerable reputation for a while, never became a central figure
in Jewish music. Krein, Gnesin, and Milner, who stayed in Russia after the
Revolution and for a short period were able to continue their work in the
field of Jewish music, were obliged to turn to compositional styles required
by the Soviet Communist Party in the 1930s. In an ironic twist they had to
abandon their abstract tendencies and revert to folk music as an expression
of "proletarian culture." In keeping with Soviet Russia's ambiguous politics
regarding its Jewish population, most Jewish composers did not feel comfortable incorporating Jewish folk music into their work and thus used the
music of other minorities.

It is no accident that the two composers most prominently marked as "Jewish" in the West had little if any relation to living Jewish traditions or Jewish

national movements. Neither Ernest Bloch nor Arnold Schoenberg relied on specific Jewish sources (or acknowledged their reliance) to create what they, or their critics, conceived as Jewish music. Their Jewish identity, if at all present in their music, is far more abstract than that of the OYNM composers. Yet the issues raised by their music and aesthetic convictions bring the tension between representing the "Oriental" (Diaspora) or the "Biblical" Jews, and that between Romantic musical nationalism and modernism, into sharp focus.

# PART II

# Man's Most Dangerous Myth

*Ernest Bloch and Racial Thought*

# Chapter 3

# Racial Mystique

## Anti-Semitism and Ernest Bloch's Theories of Art

*Of all vulgar modes of escaping from the consideration of the effect of social and moral influences on the human mind, the most vulgar is that of attributing the diversities of conduct and character to inherent natural differences.*

JOHN STUART MILL, *Principles of Political Economy* (1848)

Physical anthropologist Ashley Montagu (1905–99) started his 1942 study on race by calling his subject one of the greatest and most tragic errors of his time.[1] As a scientist, Montagu felt the need to disprove scientifically what he considered "man's most dangerous myth." By 1942 the dangers of racial theories had become obvious in Nazi Germany, where racial dogmas were exploited to justify genocide. After World War II racial thinking became taboo in Europe. Replaced by "ethnicity" or banned altogether, the word *race* seems to have disappeared from discussions of European history, culture, and the arts after the war. Yet it is hard to gain perspective on the attitudes of intellectuals in the first half of the twentieth century if one ignores the significance of racial concepts that had permeated cultural discourses for more than a century.

What Montagu attacked as a politically dangerous myth, Jacques Barzun ridiculed as a "modern superstition." Working from the same perspective as Montagu, although perhaps less given to alarm, Barzun presented a cultural-historical analysis of European racial thinking in his *Race: A Study in Modern Superstition* (1938). His detailed analysis amply demonstrated the pervasive presence of racial thought in almost all layers of culture. He recognized that the scientific and cultural vagueness of the concept, which Montagu criticized, was precisely what provided race with its "protean power." Notwithstanding its scientific untenability, Barzun argued, the "facts of race" remain "scientific truth" for both the racialist and his object.

For its advocates, however, race is more than "scientific truth." It is also a belief that satisfies, in Barzun's words, "deep mystical impulses."[2] Barzun found the source of man's need for the race concept in the desire for a "small, simple, and complete cause for a great variety of large and complex events." The ulterior motive behind racial theories is to gain access to "a literally infinite series of possible systems," which, according to Barzun, are "more and more complex as civilization expands, more and more abstract as the changing standards of morality demand an ever more intellectual rationalization for the concealment of primitive aggressiveness and snobbery." Intertwined with modern European culture to such an extent that it came to constitute "an ingrained superstition," race by the 1930s seemed to have provided the answer to most social and cultural questions. Echoing philosopher John Stuart Mill (1806–73), Barzun concludes that using race to explain complex human characters, social differences, and events is "a vulgar error, not only because it thrives and is abroad among people, often unaware of itself, but always charged with hatred and hypocrisy," but also "because it denies individual diversity, scouts the complexity of cause and effect, scorns the intellect, and ultimately bars Mind from the universe of created things."

After the Nazis' rise to power in 1933 it was easy to see the devastating social consequences of racial theories. But few, if any, had recognized the conceptual absurdity or the potential political danger of racial thinking at the beginning of the twentieth century, when the new biological category of race had started to be used interchangeably with the historical sociopolitical concept of nation. This interchangeability further complicated the issue of race, for although the term supposedly referred to genealogically continuous groups, it was simultaneously used to distinguish what in today's parlance would be called ethnic groups, and hence also accounted for cultural difference. Modern anti-Semitism was in fact the prototype of this early "culturalist" racism, which, while it theoretically considered Jews to constitute a biological unit, maintained cultural difference as its liminal test.[3]

"Culturalist" racism was prevalent in the arts mainly because, as Barzun observes, racial theories provided the simplest and most common way to cover up critics' ignorance concerning artistic genius and its transmission.[4] Criticism of art was frequently reduced to the description of racial characteristics, flexibly adapted to the critics' needs. In music, grouping composers according to their race instead of their nationality was a well-established habit, the most notorious example of which was Richard Wagner's *Judaism in Music* (1850). An exception at the time of its publication, Wagner's racial approach to music became pervasive by the early twentieth century.

Perhaps the first and certainly the most successful composer to define his art as racially Jewish was the Swiss Ernest Bloch. Bloch's willingness to see his artistic personality as racially determined should be understood in the context of a cultural environment saturated with racism. In the aftermath of the Dreyfus affair, which was one of the first manifestations of the new race hysteria, it was not difficult for Bloch, who was of Jewish heritage, to recognize that he was expected to identify himself artistically as a Jew.

This chapter relates the story of the formation of Bloch's racially specific artistic personality by investigating how Bloch, with the help of his friend

the playwright Edmond Fleg (1874–1963), began his quest for a Jewish identity, and how specific concepts of race determined Bloch's artistic vision, self-
identity, and reception. I trace these concepts from Wagner to Bloch by way
of Bayreuth ideologue Houston Stewart Chamberlain (1855–1927) and
Bloch's friend Robert Godet (1866–1950), the French translator of Chamberlain's viciously anti-Semitic book *The Foundations of the Nineteenth Century*
(1899). The outcome of Bloch's tale is bitterly ironic. Like many other Jewish intellectuals who came to accept their Jewish identity as the basis of their
character and creative output, Bloch also subscribed to a wide variety of anti-
Semitic beliefs. The presence of these beliefs in Bloch's conception of Jewishness might be explained as another aspect of what Theodor Lessing
dubbed "Jewish self-hatred," but only if one is willing to subscribe to racial
determinism implied by a term that indicates a belief in a Jewish essence
present in every person of Jewish descent, an essence against which hatred
is directed.

## AN IMPROBABLE PAIR: DISRAELI AND WAGNER

For most who argued against racism immediately before and during World
War II, the most urgent question to answer was whether Jews constituted a
race. Montagu maintained that Jews could not be distinguished as a group
upon physical grounds, hence they could not be considered a race.[5] This
did not disturb most racial thinkers, however, because they considered vague
cultural characteristics more important than empirically observed ones. The
power of racial mystique linked anti- and philo-Semites; for, with few exceptions (including Montagu himself, who was of Jewish origin), Jews readily adopted race as a new basis for their secular identity.[6]

A striking example of race consciousness was British prime minister and
author Benjamin Disraeli (1804–81), who made race the central underlying theme in his novels. His character Sidonia—an idealized Rothschild from
the 1844 novel *Coningsby*—explains the indestructible character of Jews as
a result of their racial purity. As is often the case when racial purity is used
in an argument, Sidonia takes it as a proof of racial superiority. "No penal
laws, no physical tortures, can effect that a superior race should be absorbed
in an inferior, or be destroyed by it," he states. "The mixed persecuting races
disappear; the pure persecuted race remains."

But there is more at stake than the survival of a race. In Sidonia's opinion
a superior race, even if it is a minority, has a great effect on its environment.
Despite centuries of degradation, Sidonia declares, "the Jewish mind exercises a vast influence on the affairs of Europe." When Coningsby asks Sidonia about the lack of creative minds among Jews—a question that shows that
the stereotype of the uncreative Jew was established well before Richard Wagner's notorious words on the subject—Sidonia proclaims that, on the con-

trary, the "passionate and creative genius" is in fact the Jews' most precious possession. The Jews preserved a fervent imagination, which endowed them, Sidonia tells Coningsby, "with almost the exclusive privilege of MUSIC." "At this moment," Sidonia boasts, "musical Europe is ours. There is not a company of singers, not an orchestra in a single capital, that is not crowded with our children under the feigned names which they adopt to conciliate the dark aversion which your posterity will some day disclaim with shame and disgust. Almost every great composer, skilled musician, almost every voice that ravishes you with its transporting strains, springs from our tribes." [7] The exaggerated claim that Jews were ubiquitous in the arts was repeated ad nauseam during the course of the nineteenth century. While Disraeli exaggerated out of pride, others distorted reality out of an anti-Semitic bias that was spreading in countries where political and economical instability helped develop a suspicious attitude toward the effects of assimilation. Disraeli, preoccupied as he was with his own position in English high society, seemed to be blissfully unaware that what his imaginary Jewish characters like Sidonia proudly asserted could be easily turned into a weapon against real Jews.

Six years after Disraeli's *Coningsby,* Wagner publicly displayed his anti-Jewish paranoia in his infamous *Judaism in Music.* The essay, in which Wagner denigrated all art produced by Jews, was the result of Wagner's irrational fear of Jewish dominance in the arts. Wagner argued that Jews had no art of their own, as he put it, no "artistic utterance of [their inner] essence." Neither could they participate genuinely in the artistic life of other peoples, whose language and culture, according to Wagner, "have remained to the Jews a foreign tongue." Language is "not the work of scattered units," Wagner maintained, "but of a historical community," and thus "only he who has unconsciously grown up within the bond of this community, takes any share in its creation." Wagner used this imagined Jewish "speech impediment" to support his claim that Jews lack the ability to use spoken words for artistic expression of feelings. Since he believed that music was "the speech of Passion," Wagner argued that the linguistic barrier that separated Jews and Germans also prevented Jews from creating genuine German music. Whether in speech or music, Wagner asserted, Jews can only imitate.[8]

He cited two of his famous rivals, Felix Mendelssohn and Giacomo Meyerbeer, as casualties of a conflict between the composers' Jewish ethnicity and their profession as composers of Western art music. While Disraeli described these two composers as "great creative minds" whose "exquisite inventions" influenced all of Europe,[9] Wagner dismissed their music completely, condemning Mendelssohn's as superficial and Meyerbeer's as commercial. For Wagner the successful Meyerbeer was the chief representative of what he described as the Jewish commercial attitude of converting art into what he called *Kunstwaarenwechsel,* approximately translated as "article of exchange."[10]

While their conclusions were diametrically opposed, Disraeli's and Wagner's assumptions exemplified a common deterministic obsession with race that by the end of the nineteenth century became central in the struggle of nations toward self-definition. Since racial theory often helped nations rise from the degrading feeling of political and economic inferiority to a sense of racial superiority, it rapidly became the basis of popular pseudo-science and pseudo-religion. Bloch was only one of many artists and critics who had been trapped in the seductive discourse of race.

## THE QUEST FOR NATIONAL IDENTITY

In 1903 Bloch showed his Symphony in C-sharp Minor to Max von Schillings (1868–1933), professor at the Königliche Musikschule in Munich, a city where since 1901 Bloch had been immersing himself in Wagner's music. Schillings faulted the symphony for its lack of an identifiable national character; as he told Bloch, it was fundamentally German, but with French rhythm, and with themes of a melancholic gaiety.[11]

Growing up in Geneva, Switzerland, Bloch developed little sense of national belonging. Nor did his nationally mixed musical training serve to clarify a national orientation for his artistic expression. In Geneva he studied with Émile Jaques-Dalcroze (1865–1950), in Brussels with Eugène Ysaÿe (1858–1931) and François Rasse (1873–1955); in Frankfurt he took private lessons with Iwan Knorr (1853–1916); and in Munich he finished his compositional training through occasional consultations with Ludwig Thuille (1861–1907) and Schillings. This diversity of educational influences left Bloch adrift between French and German aesthetics. Essentializing national characteristics, he complained that the Germans were too regular, too dispassionate, while the French—whose "mediocrity" made him "suffer less than German coarseness"—lacked "grandeur."[12] The young Bloch was at loose ends, disturbed by what he saw as instability in the world around him and a state of lawlessness in the arts.

The critical reception of his symphony (the two middle movements of which were performed at a 1903 Festival of Swiss and German Music in Basel) confirmed Schillings's criticism of Bloch's wavering between national idioms. French critic Robert Godet heard overtones of Chabrier in the symphony; others identified Wagner, Bruckner, and Strauss as Bloch's models. Although negative reviews focused mainly on the high level of dissonance in Bloch's movements, behind the complaints lurked the critics' irritation at Bloch's effort to combine what were considered to be incompatible French and German styles. A German reviewer criticized Bloch's grandiose orchestration as unsuited for the composer's thematic ideas, which, he wrote, were too insignificant.[13] Though it is not stated specifically, it seems that for many of his critics (just as for Schillings) the lack of a focused national identity was the most important and most troubling characteristic of Bloch's music.

In Bloch's next major undertaking, the opera *Macbeth* (1910), which he wrote with Fleg, such stylistic elements as Debussyan whole-tone scales, augmented chords, and parallel motion predominate. Yet the result differs greatly from *Pelléas et Mélisande.* In Debussy's opera, the absence of tonal tension, nondiatonic scales, and soft dissonances help create an obscure atmosphere in which the story and the characters' feelings remain vague. In *Macbeth,* Bloch combined elements of Debussyan technique with a plot that the French audience regarded as "a hideous melodrama, a dark butchery."[14] The opera presents murder, guilt, and revenge with shrieking dissonances, nervous tremolos, and harmonies saturated with augmented triads (ex. 38). Where Debussy affected his audience through understatement, Bloch shocked his with expressive excess, creating an atmosphere closer to that of Strauss's bloodthirsty *Salome* or the psychological torture in Musorgsky's *Boris Godunov* than to Debussy's world of shadows.[15] The result was meant to be a Debussyan opera ennobled by German "grandeur" à la Beethoven, a grandeur that Bloch felt was lacking even in Debussy, whose music he admired and whom he fancied to be his friend.[16]

But while *Pelléas* seemed quintessentially French, Bloch's music was again considered a national hodgepodge—as a contemporaneous cartoonist put it, "a potion composed of Debussyan dissonances and Wagnerian cacophonies."[17] Even positive reviews emphasized Bloch's suspicious capability to assimilate the diverse styles of Wagner, Strauss, Debussy, and the Russians, a capability that for most was related to the composer's Jewish origin. For Henry Prunières (1886–1942), author of a belated positive evaluation of *Macbeth,* and for Romain Rolland (1866–1944), the most influential supporter of Bloch, the composer represented "the great wandering Jew of music."[18]

*Macbeth* did not realize Bloch's dreams for success. After thirteen performances that met with mixed reviews, the opera was shelved because, after a negative review, prima donna Lucienne Bréval (1869–1935) withdrew from the production.[19] Disillusioned with Parisian musical life, Bloch went back to Geneva, his quest for artistic identity more desperate than ever.

Like many who searched for national identity in music, Bloch turned to Wagner, whom he had designated as his Messiah as early as 1901.[20] In 1911, a year after the failure of *Macbeth,* he visited Munich to immerse himself again in Wagner's music, to experience, through Wagner, the sensation of belonging to a nation, "to plunge [his] roots deeply into a sacred soil." He described his entranced experience of a performance of *Die Meistersinger* to his librettist and friend Edmond Fleg: "For the first time, and with an incredible intensity," he confessed, "I understood what Wagner meant by *deutsche Kunst* [German art] and *Kunst im Allgemeinen* [art in general]." Embittered by his Parisian failure, Bloch grew closer to German music. While French music now appeared superficial, Wagner's *deutsche Kunst* seemed even more profound to him than during his first stay in Germany. Compared to Wag-

Example 38. Bloch's *Macbeth,* act 1, scene 2, Macbeth's monologue (Edizioni Suivi Zerboni), mm. 125–34.

(continued)

Example 38 *(continued)*

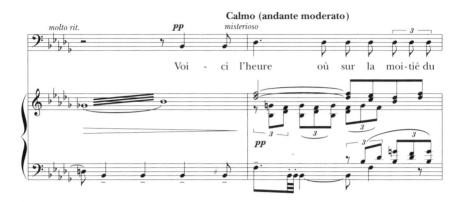

(Ah! I see you again! And now I see the drops of blood on your blade, which were not there before! . . . Behold the hour when in half of the [world nature will die.])

ner's, Debussy's art looked no more significant for Bloch than an *objet de vitrine,* "the expression of *one* sensibility, a small corner of the human soul, stylized, refined, very pretty." Music's role, Bloch claimed, was to unite people, and this, he thought, was fulfilled only by German music. French music was amusement, a mere luxury item.[21]

Bloch drew his naïvely generalized statements about the genius of nations from a common stockpile of pre–World War I music criticism. Even Romain Rolland, who was repelled by the narrow nationalism of his time and who moved to Switzerland to escape it, built his novel *Jean-Christophe* around a set of national stereotypes, dulling their potentially political edges by including the positive sides of both the German and the French national genius. But just as Rolland's political neutrality was frowned upon by French and German nationalists alike, so Bloch's amalgam of French and German aesthetics was considered unacceptable in an era so preoccupied with national and racial essences in music.

### CONSTRUCTION OF RACIAL IDENTITY: EDMOND FLEG

Caught between French and German models, Bloch had turned his quest in a new direction. Behind his enthusiasm for Wagner's strong national expression lurked a dispiriting recognition that, as he explained it to Fleg, they were neither French nor Germans but Jews.[22] Like many others, Bloch agreed with Wagner that Jews were deceiving themselves when they believed that they could easily assimilate to the people among whom they resided. Echoing Wagner, Bloch saw the Jews as misled by their ability to adapt, by their capacity to seem German in Germany and French in France.[23] Yet contrary to Wagner's belief that for a Jew to become "man" and especially to become German meant first of all the total renunciation of being a Jew, Bloch believed that Jews should embrace their racial identity to "become completely human."[24]

For Bloch as for Wagner true humanity was represented by German culture, specifically by German music ("all in depth"), which Bloch felt was closer to the realization of the *rein menschlich* (purely human) values than the "pretty musical forms of the French" ("all on the surface"). Wagner inspired Bloch to declare a union between the Jews and the Germans. Jewish art, like German, "has to be human," and what the Jews "proclaim should speak to all." But Bloch was also convinced that before Jewish artists like Fleg and himself could communicate the *rein menschlich* to all peoples, they first had to find their own voice, and pursue their own way.[25]

Fleg, for one, emphasized the universal mission of the Jews. In his memoir *Pourquoi je suis juif* (Why I Am a Jew) he related how he had turned away from the Orthodox Jewish milieu of his parents.[26] He listed as reasons for his disillusionment atheist rabbis and members of a congregation who regularly read the newspaper during synagogue services. He had finally found his way to a new concept of Judaism that, although it accepted religion as part of Jewish tradition, concentrated on secular national identity and, more crucially, on a universal mission for this newly recovered Jewish nationhood. Fleg's vision was one of peace for all mankind, a peace communicated to all peoples by the Jews, the "most human of all races." This pipe dream of embracing universal humanity through Jewishness was part of a defense mechanism that a psychologist might call reaction formation, in which an objectionable, repressed impulse is replaced by its opposite; in Fleg's vision, centuries of Jewish isolation turned into a universal mission.

The viciously nationalistic and anti-Semitic atmosphere of post-Dreyfus Paris paved Fleg's road to Zionism. Reading the proto-fascist *L'Action Française* about the Jews' political situation aroused his Jewish self-awareness. Affected by Zionist ideology Fleg admitted that the anti-Semitic accusation that Jews constitute "a nation within the nation" had finally come true.[27] Fleg's best friend, journalist polemicist Lucien Moreau (1875–1932), was an outspoken anti-Dreyfusard and a regular contributor to *L'Action Française*.[28] Fleg adopted Moreau's anti-assimilationist sentiments, and let his friend guide him back to his long-abandoned Jewish ideals. Jewish and French nationalisms, Fleg and Moreau agreed, "traveled in parallel lines," making them both leave behind "the vision of humanity for that of country," which, for Fleg, became a Jewish land.[29]

Bloch's perception of Judaism differed from Fleg's. The Jewish religion, at least as Bloch judged it from his experiences in the Jewish community of

Geneva (where the local rabbi, Bloch reported to Fleg, "did not believe in anything" and was the "worst anti-Semite"),[30] did not attract him. His family did not help preserve respect for the Jewish faith. His father was an atheist, and even his mother, although attached to what Bloch saw as remnants of her Jewish education, lacked religious belief. No wonder that as early as 1902 Bloch declared himself an "atheist, convinced materialist."[31] As he later wrote, he saw in institutionalized religion "a dogmatic and desiccated form, remote from nature, morbid, lifeless, a fairy-tale that has lost all its meaning."[32] For Bloch religion in general represented either prejudice tied to dysfunctional, hypocritical institutions, or abstract, pure belief in some supernatural force that determines human destiny. The less he knew about a particular religion, the more he was willing to let himself be impressed by its "pure forms."[33] Jewish religion could have little place in this lofty spirituality.

Fleg argued in vain that the religious customs of the Jews were still the core of a living Jewish tradition, however imperfect. Bloch resisted joining a religious community of which he had humiliating memories:

> For a long time I have wanted to go to the Synagogue, but the memory of the fellow who read the *Tribune* at Yom Kippur—a memory from when I was 10—is still with me. It seems that this has not changed. Perhaps I will go all the same; but if I see this spectacle again, I will make a scandal, that's for sure. The Jews have not changed, since Biblical times; more than ¾ of them are nasty Jews. . . . I would like to be part of the community but I am afraid that I will find that it lacks spirit. Will I have to go, like my sister, and look for this spirit among the Goyim?[34]

Fleg was shocked by Bloch's proposition and defended the "Jewish spirit" that he felt might still triumph, if not immediately, then in a later generation:

> As far as I am concerned, I also recall thousands of details that shocked me in my childhood. Yet in spite of it all, it is this imperfect cult that maintained the tradition! There is something inexplicably touching in the feeling that, in spite of the loud conversations, the newspaper-reading during prayers, the swindlings of the *shammash* [sexton], and the skepticism of the rabbi, all of the people who come together there feel themselves Jewish in some way; and because of their imperfect reunion, Judaism perseveres and triumphs. Think about the son of Perlemann who is doctor Perlemann, and that among the sons of those who chat there or read their newspaper, some great spirit could arise, which would revive all the genius of the race! If you don't accept a religion the way it is, with its moving and ridiculous imperfections, don't be part of it; you are not yet Jewish enough![35]

In this respect Bloch never became Jewish enough. But he too believed in the existence of an unspoiled "Jewish spirit." While Fleg sought it among outstanding Jewish personalities, Bloch located it in an idealized vision of the poor Jews:

You talked to me a lot about the Jewish spirit, and as an example you referred to the "successful" men. . . . But if it is so, then woe to the *Jewish spirit!* I myself admire the Jewish spirit more in the poor, starving peddler who goes from one town to another and refuses the meat offered to him by the goyim! ; . . . If I were alone, without wife, without children, do you know what I would do? I would go to live in a poor community of old Jews who are pure and strict, in Turkey, anywhere! And there I would do my work.[36]

Idealizing a community with which he had no real contact came easily to Bloch. As with a number of Bloch's other grand plans, such as using his art to aid Soviet Russia or moving to a Gauguinesque seclusion in Tahiti, Bloch never tried to fulfill his idealized vision of life among poor Jews.

Fleg was more realistic than Bloch and sought out contact with "living Judaism," in cultural as well as in political spheres. By contrast, Bloch stubbornly concentrated his energies on his art. Still, Bloch was not entirely blind to the gap between his artistic ideals and reality. After professing his profound faith in race, he sounded a word of caution. One cannot live outside of the race, he wrote to Fleg,

and nonetheless neither you nor I can live in a fictitious milieu, created by our imagination. . . . There are few true Jews these days, alas. . . . I only think that the clash between our imagination and the present reality is particularly jarring. In what Jewish milieu can we live *sincerely?* ; . . . The lack of individuality exasperates me. Where are the Jews who correspond to our Judaism? I really think that the majority of Jews will be our *worst* enemies. But we don't work for the "majority."[37]

Bloch could find his ideal Judaism nowhere in the real world. It had to be constructed in his art.

### EPIPHANY: ROBERT GODET

Like Fleg, Bloch also had an anti-Semitic friend who spurred him on in his quest for his Jewish identity. In the margin of William Lawson's 1941 type-script biography of Bloch, in which Lawson suggested that Bloch's interest in Judaism coincided with the composing of the first piece in his "Jewish Cycle,"[38] the composer commented: "I am not sure of this . . . [it] seems very superficial to me. . . . [I]n 1895–6 I composed a Symphony on 'Jewish motifs'—then an 'Oriental' one. It is the article of *Robert Godet,* about my C♯ minor Symph. ('Le Temps,' Paris, 1903)—and a *few antisemitic criticisms* which, I think, made me *conscious* of what was or could be 'Jewish' in my background."[39] In a 1954 letter to his supporter and friend Olin Downes (1886–1955) Bloch made the same claim in more definitive terms. Reacting to Godet's unsigned positive review of the 1903 Basel premiere of two movements of his Symphony in C-sharp Minor, Bloch wrote, desperately, a letter to the anonymous author of this article. . . . This man was Robert Godet, "the only friend I ever had," Debussy told me in 1907. He was the man who translated the book that made Hitler, by H. S. Chamberlain, "The Foundations of the 19th Century." When the book was published in French, in 1913, we broke our relations. Godet was the most extraordinary man I ever met, and I did not realize, during the ten years of our profound and intimate friendship, that he was the worst anti-semite that ever existed. It is this man, in his article of *Le Temps,* that attracted my attention to what could be Jewish in me.[40]

Anticipating Downes's stupefaction at the suggestion that his Jewish music was inspired by an anti-Semite, Bloch himself asked: "How can anyone, who wants to write the history of my life, reconcile such a contradiction?"[41]

Today Godet is remembered as Debussy's friend and one of the earliest Musorgsky enthusiasts in the West. His friendship with Bloch is little known, and his major work, the French translation of Chamberlain's *The Foundations of the Nineteenth Century,* is long forgotten. As Bloch recalled, Godet won the composer's sympathy by praising him as a composer whose music "can hold its rank in the world." The following year Bloch took Godet as his pupil in composition.[42] Soon, however, the pupil became the spiritual guide of the teacher. Godet converted Bloch to the "true" art of Musorgsky by writing him long letters about Musorgsky's significance, and sending him lists of pieces Bloch should learn—lists on which Godet carefully pointed out Musorgsky's "Jewish" pieces, such as the chorus *Iisus Navin,* the setting from the "Song of Songs" ("Yevreyskaya pesnya"), and "Samuel Goldenberg and Schmuÿle" from *Pictures at an Exhibition.*[43]

In Godet, Bloch found the spiritual partner for whom he longed. Bloch's first visit to the Godets in 1906 resulted in an epiphany:

> Finally I was able to see myself without a veil, and this awakening of all the past that I feel to be rooted very far away and long ago in the race itself, gave me the intense joy that one might also get from the spontaneous yet painful creation of a work of art. How this happened I cannot tell. Godet is a soul who communicates without the slightest jargon, there is no facade in him. . . . For Godet the conception of art, like that of life, has dignity, a superb height. It is the opposite of materialism but it is not attached to other doctrines either. He searches for the truth of life and not for its superficial representation. He prefers the gesture to the word, the repressed accent to its exteriorization, in sum all that originates in the most sacred *instinct* and not in convention or moreover in privilege.[44]

Bloch welcomed Godet's interpretation of "true" art as coming from the instinctive layers of human consciousness. Following French philosopher Hippolyte Taine (1828–1893), both Bloch and Godet identified these deep strata with race.[45] "From the moment when a demon of truth, defined by the possibilities of the race, speaks in us," Godet wrote to Bloch, "we must depend on our sincerity and courage in order to serve it faithfully."[46] "Profoundly moved" by Bloch's and Fleg's intentions to create a specifically Jewish art, Godet started to take an active part in the project by providing Bloch with readings about various Jewish subjects. [47]

Reading about the prophets guided Bloch back to the Bible. There at last he found the long-awaited inspiration. "Who knows?" he wrote to Fleg,

> Perhaps you and I will find there [in the Bible] the liberation from our time, the Liberation! This music is in us. We must make people hear the Jewish spirit, the greatness and the destiny of this race. It should inspire confidence in the future, and the Jews should be ashamed of what they are now and of the false path they have taken . . . and there should be an awakening among them. . . . Reading certain passages I almost regret that I have nothing but music for communication; but the Jews listen to music.[48]

Years later, when Bloch summarized his artistic development he called this time of biblical inspiration the period of his "first liberation."[49] What brought about this sense of liberation was not merely the inspiration of the Bible, nor the decision to assume a Jewish identity, but Bloch's passionate assumption of a prophetic role. Once he assumed this role, he never abandoned it— even in later years, when his Jewish identity had begun to wane.

Bloch's prophetic posture kept him outside the confines of any existing Jewish community. Prophets were outsiders among the people whom they instructed, led, scorned, and cursed. They stood apart as representatives of God rather than of the people. The Hebrew prophets were equally revered by Jews and Christians, although for different reasons. Their negative proclamations about their own people played into the hands of modern anti-Semites. A most outspoken one, Houston Stewart Chamberlain, analyzed in detail the prophets' characters and their fight for "true morality" as opposed to that of the "Jewish cult."[50]

Bloch envisioned a scenario in which he himself would undergo the isolation, sufferings, and final triumph of a prophet. This role coincided with the Romantic, Beethovenian image of the composer as a creative genius who, in tragic isolation, leads his people even against their will. The prophetic role also allowed Bloch to assimilate Godet's anti-Semitic convictions about contemporary Jews and to justify his voluntary detachment from the religion and culture of the people whose "race" he claimed his music represented. A critical view of the Jews was almost indispensable for Bloch to substantiate his prophetic mission of making the Jews recognize "the false path they had taken."

### THE REAL INSPIRATION: H. S. CHAMBERLAIN

Godet supported Bloch in his new prophetic role. Yet it was not the Bible that provided Godet's primary inspiration; it was Chamberlain's *The Foun-*

*dations of the Nineteenth Century,* on whose French translation (published in 1913) Godet was working at the time. Chamberlain, the son of an English admiral who transformed himself into a prophet of the Teutonic race (gaining admittance into the Teutonic pantheon through marriage to Wagner's daughter Eva), intended his 1899 book as the first part of a three-volume study celebrating the century that was coming to its end. Despite its title, what Chamberlain presented in his book was not the foundations of the nineteenth century but of Nazi ideology. His plan was to turn human history into the history of the Teutonic race, culminating, as Cosima Wagner anticipated, with "the towering genius of the century," Wagner, the artist who, in Chamberlain's view, most truly fulfilled the racial mission of the Teutons.[51] Chamberlain never completed the projected three-volume study and thus never penned its Wagnerian climax. Still, his enterprise was a fully Wagnerian project that was meant to purify and thus elevate the Teutonic race just as Wagner hoped his music would.

Most Wagnerian was Chamberlain's anti-Semitic passion. Shrewdly disguised behind pseudoscientific analyses, Chamberlain presented European history as the struggle of racial forces, from which the pure Teutons and the Jews stood out as the most antagonistic. Like most anti-Semites, Chamberlain could never make up his mind whether to consider the Jews a pure race (the anti-race of the Teutons), whose supposed sacred attachment to the "purity of inherited blood" deserved his admiration, or a mongrel race. In opposition to Count Arthur de Gobineau, who in his *Essai sur l'inégalité des races humaines* (1853–55) pessimistically maintained that human races were rapidly declining, Chamberlain argued that "the sound and normal evolution of man is . . . not from race to racelessness, but, on the contrary, to an ever clearer distinction of race." This confused logic led him to claim that "even if it were proved that there had never been an Aryan race in the past, we will have one in the future; for men of action this is the decisive point of view."[52]

The paranoid hatred of the Jews that governed Chamberlain's entire project so strongly distorted his vision that his *Foundations* could be considered one of the most anti-Semitic writings of his time. Indeed, rising anti-Semitism strongly contributed to the book's immense success, which made its author a celebrity overnight. Although criticized for its often incorrect details and falsified data, the *Foundations* quickly became required reading for European intellectuals.

Robert Godet prefaced his 1913 French translation with a sixty-three-page essay in which he provided a French context for Chamberlain's theories. Godet downplayed the book's anti-Jewish argument, dedicating to it only two-and-a-half pages. Yet he seems to have agreed with Chamberlain's major premise about the "Jewish question." "If Chamberlain is right," he concluded "it is we who have created the Jewish peril by accepting in our organism an element that it could not assimilate. . . . We must therefore free ourselves from the Jewish yoke by spiritual means of our own."⁵³

For a time Bloch seems to have ignored the sinister side of Godet's views. He readily accepted most of Godet's anti-Semitic views since he was convinced that they applied only to the "bad" contemporary Jews. Moreover, he shared Godet's conviction that, instead of assimilation (which he believed could never eradicate the fundamental differences between races), Jews should pursue their own racial destiny. In 1911, already deep in his work on Chamberlain, Godet called Bloch's attention to the separatist "truth," proclaimed in Deuteronomy (11:26), that Jews were blessed if they followed God's commandments, and cursed if they turned away from them. Through their apostasy the modern Jews had brought suffering on themselves. "Is it not because you served other gods," Godet asked Bloch, "and have flirted with too much gold and money that you met the curse?" Ultimately, Godet assured Bloch, the curse—the suffering that had come from the scattering of the Jews— would pay off: it would lead them back to their God.⁵⁴ Godet also quoted the commandment to kill whoever tried to seduce Jews into serving other gods (Deut. 13:6). It was a cruel law, Godet asserted, but justified "because of the saintly task of the race." He cited the razing of Carthage and Jerusalem under the Romans, which might be considered barbarous crimes, but which, he insisted, were "beneficial as well as terrible" for the sake of humanity.

Godet's examples all came from Chamberlain's *Foundations*. What Godet did not reveal to Bloch was that Chamberlain justified the destruction of Jerusalem because it spared Christianity from becoming a mere sect of Judaism.⁵⁵ Crueler than the destruction of harmful civilizations, Godet explained to Bloch, were the deceitful philanthropic pretensions that objected to such destruction, pretensions that were the "awful consequences of humanitarian ideology (the rights of man = The Terror) and *Menschheitswahn* [illusion of humanity]". Godet's antidemocratic assertions reverberated in Bloch's elitist political opinions throughout his life.

Bloch himself had no better opinion of his fellow Jews, who "run after the Golden Calf" and "could not remain true to their God."⁵⁶ Although only a few of Bloch's letters to Godet survive, his correspondence with Fleg demonstrates how deeply he absorbed Godet's ideas. Worried about Fleg, who, according to Bloch, had been too much influenced by his Parisian surroundings, Bloch quoted the same passage from Deuteronomy as had Godet about the necessary separation of the Jews from their neighbors. The laws of separation described in the Bible are not restrictions, he explained to Fleg. The Biblical laws of separation, just like the laws of natural organisms, are inescapable and ensure the body's vitality. Quoting another favorite dictum of Chamberlain's, Bloch referred to Goethe's declaration that the individual should be "externally limited" in order to be "internally limitless."⁵⁷

It is eerie to see Godet luring Bloch into discussions, the underlying purpose of which he kept hidden. On 8 February 1912, Godet asked his friend to look up an expression for him in the French translation of Heinrich Graetz's *History of the Jews*, a book he assumed Bloch as a Jew would own. With feigned naïveté he urged Bloch to find an appropriate translation for Graetz's description of Christ as "die Neugeburt mit der Totenmaske" (the newborn with the death mask), which, he wrote, he could not understand. In his next letter he asked Bloch to interpret for him Graetz's strange comment about the cross: "the Jews do not need this convulsive emotion for their spiritual improvement, *particularly not among the middle-class city dwellers!!!*"[58] Bloch apparently looked up the requested passage but failed to explain it to Godet's satisfaction. In fact, Godet did not need Bloch's explanation. He was satisfied with Chamberlain's, from whose *Foundations* his quotation came, and who, in his usual fashion, quoted Graetz out of context to prove that Jews were genuinely disposed against Christianity and incapable of grasping the "greatness of the suffering Savior."[59]

## FALLING-OUT

Godet must have been fully aware of the offensive anti-Semitic aspects of Chamberlain's argument, for during the many years he devoted to the translation of the *Foundations* he kept his work hidden from Bloch. Bloch knew only that his friend was involved in an immense collaborative project, which used up all his energies, and, Bloch noticed, turned him into an old, exhausted man.[60] When in 1913 Godet presented the composer with the completed volume, he did it with a certain sense of guilt. Bloch took offense, to which Godet responded with feigned surprise. However phony, Godet's reaction indicates his hope that Bloch, who shared many of his friend's anti-Semitic ideas, would not be scandalized by the book's anti-Jewish stance. Seeing Bloch's irritation upon reading the book, he admitted that giving the book to Bloch had been a mistake. But, he argued, "I believed that it would not hurt you."[61]

Godet thought that Bloch's negative reaction to Chamberlain's *Foundations* came from reading only portions of the book and thus missing essential points.[62] His argument was the same as that of Chamberlain and his advocates who defended the book against the charges of factual and logical errors by claiming, as one reviewer did, that since the book is "not a mechanical aggregate of assertions and opinions, but rather a living organism . . . , it is not to be read as a scholarly argument, but as a deep-moving, dramatic and lively monologue."[63] Trying to diminish the book's potentially dangerous effect, Godet reassured Bloch: "what offends you today was written 15 years ago, and during this period nobody has died of it."[64]

Godet's claim, which was likely formulated to calm his friend's "overreaction," intensified rather than diminished Bloch's suspicions. Yet Bloch's emotional response to Godet's present was not caused solely by the content of Chamberlain's argument. Bloch and Godet's exchange came at a time when they were having a personal quarrel, caused by Bloch's interfering in an argument between Godet and Matthias Morhardt (1863–c. 1940), a symbolist poet and editor of *Le temps* in Paris.[65] In the heat of their quarrel Bloch could not repress the fear that there was something else behind Godet's irritation and, to Godet's surprise, found the explanation for Godet's behavior in his friend's involvement with Chamberlain's anti-Semitic book.[66]

Godet reacted to Bloch's emotional outburst by putting an end to their communication, which, he maintained, had become impossible. "The words we exchange do not mean the same thing to the one and to the other," he explained to Bloch.[67] Godet wrote of a personal offense, but, as his reference to their "different languages" indicates, behind the demise of their friendship there lurked his continuing belief in irreconcilable racial differences.

Despite their emotionally charged quarrel, Bloch's ties to Godet were not severed in 1913, as Bloch later claimed, but only after Bloch left Europe in 1916. Even from the United States, the composer attempted to reestablish their old, intense friendship. "Do you still love me?" he began his confessional letter, which he sent to Godet after much hesitation in November 1920. The loss of the man who, as Bloch declared, understood him best, was the greatest tragedy of his life.[68] Yet, Bloch admitted, in comparison to the horrors of the war their argument seemed to be a trifle. Distanced from their emotional breakup, Bloch was less adamant about the anti-Semitic implications of Godet's work. "You would laugh if you knew," Bloch wrote to his onetime friend, "that it happened to me more than once here that I had to defend that poor Chamberlain, whom I had accused of having separated us!"[69]

Godet never answered Bloch's letter. His reviews in *La revue musicale* of Bloch's First String Quartet and *Schelomo*, however, can be read as an irritated reaction to Bloch's attempt to renew their friendship. While Godet's critique of Bloch's string quartet, although negative, addresses the music,[70] his commentary on *Schelomo* sounds like a coded personal attack. The offensive tone of the writing still adheres to the emotional rhetoric of Bloch and Godet's 1913 tumultuous exchange. But the anti-Semitic clichés with which Godet packs his critique demonstrate not only his irritation with Bloch but also the extent of his absorption of Chamberlain's ideology. It would be hard to compose a more cumbersome and more charged sentence than the following: "If the Jews would in fact listen," Godet wrote in reference to Fleg's collection of poems *Écoute Israel* and the protagonist of Bloch's *Schelomo*, "while groaning like in the synagogue, and mewing like in the Stock Exchange, and would raise their stiff neck or knock their heads against the walls, the Oriental Wise Man's proclamation of faith in divine election were dignified." He finished his strange critique with venomous rhetorical questions, addressed again more to Bloch than to the reader: "Why does it have to be that the pilgrim, having just reached a sacred summit, tumbles down, full of spite or nostalgia, toward his ghetto?" he asks. "And what does it mean exactly, this constant, masochist need to show himself grinding his teeth once more while pondering his grievances?"[71] Shaken by the overt animosity of the review, Bloch wrote to Fleg: "I believe that the 'masochist' is not Solomon (or Ernest Bloch, rather), but him, Robert Godet, who no doubt finds a certain joy in trampling under foot the one he had loved."[72]

Despite Godet's public hostility, Bloch could not give up their friendship. In 1925, when his Symphony in C-sharp Minor was published in Munich, Bloch dedicated it to his former friend. To this gesture Godet finally responded in a letter that Bloch read, in tears, to his family. "What can I add?" he replied to Godet on 21 July 1925. "This dedication explains all and I am happy that you could understand. Nothing has changed in me, and this past is still dear to me."[73]

Reverberations of Bloch's relationship with Godet were still felt in the 1930s. In 1934, detached from the emotional disturbance it had caused when he had received it from his one-time best friend, Bloch belatedly took Godet's advice and reread Chamberlain's *Foundations* in its entirety. "He was a Prophet," he reported to his lover Winifred Howe. Chamberlain's theories, Bloch claimed, were "based on *real, sound, biological facts.*" Biological processes, "growth, races" are *"brutal facts,"* Bloch declared, and had nothing to do with *"thought, ethics, justice,* or beauty." "There is but *one,* one terrible *logic,"* he summed up his reading, "whether we *rebel* or not, against it."[74] Although he recognized how the German government could exploit Chamberlain's ideology for its purposes, Bloch maintained that "in spite of its fanaticism and hypothesis—like Darwin or Marx after all—the book is a great book." Bloch argued that it was not the ideas but their practical application by "smaller minds" that could turn Chamberlain's ideology into a "terrible weapon."[75] Ultimately, Bloch's opinion did not differ much from that of Godet. He seems to have admitted Chamberlain into the pantheon of great thinkers and used Chamberlain's theory to justify his own aversion to a certain intellectualism both he and Chamberlain associated with Jews:

> Very strange that *both* [Sigmund] Freud and [Alfred] Adler are Jews! They represent and embody the *two* different kinds of "mental" Jews—the prophetic one—and the Talmudic one. The last one is the type so common amidst Jewish scientists or scholars, which Chamberlain hates so much—with reason! And he, Chamberlain, makes a generality of it. . . . And does not want to *admit* the existence of another Jewish spirit. This Adler is just the kind of very intelligent—too intelligent!—Jew, who, at the end, is always "à côté"—and misses everything—makes false theories—based on false premises—and then has an atrocious influence on contemporaries (I think a little of Schönberg . . . and a few others).[76]

Uncritical acceptance of anti-Semitic clichés thus prevented Bloch from refuting completely Chamberlain's ideology. Reacting to the performance of his *Sacred Service* by the "Jüdische Kulturbund" in Berlin and Leipzig in 1934 and to the segregation of Jews and Aryans in Germany, Bloch again referred to Chamberlain as the originator of Nazi ideas: "I think they [the Jews] can do what they want, between themselves, provided it remains 'Jewish' and no 'Aryans' are allowed! I heard that even they are encouraged to do 'things Jewish,' and are not hampered, provided they do not mix with 'Germans'— a queer situation, absolutely *understandable*—though I do not approve it of course!—if one reads the Chamberlain, on which all their ideas—political, religious, racial—are based." Bloch disagreed with Chamberlain, yet he could not repress a malicious remark about his fellow Jews. "The attitude of certain Jews—in Italy!—and especially here [New York], towards me—and towards everything—seems to justify in a good degree the actual mentality and revolt of the leaders of Germany."[77]

Personal resentment fueled other similarly disturbing remarks by Bloch. He was particularly sensitive about Jewish audiences who, as the reception of the first performance of his *Three Jewish Poems* showed, could react critically to his self-created Jewish style.[78] Bloch tended to essentialize audiences and critics alike, pointing at their Jewish ethnicity as if it were the reason behind their attitude toward his music. An outsider among both Jews and gentiles, Bloch easily fell prey to Godet's anti-Semitic ideology, which, even after the bitter end of their friendship, remained central in his conception of Jews and Judaism.

## DESCENT TO THE ROOTS

On 28 February 1914, at the composer's invitation, Godet went to hear the premiere of Bloch's *Three Jewish Poems*, the first work performed publicly from the "Jewish Cycle." On 6 March 1914 he sent Bloch a detailed description of his impressions of the piece. The problem of speaking different languages, a metaphor for racial difference in their personal quarrel, now reappeared in the context of music. Like some of Musorgsky's works that remained alien to Godet because of Musorgsky's too specifically Russian language, Bloch's *Three Jewish Poems* also used a foreign language, which Godet believed was Hebrew.[79] This was a necessary phase, he assured Bloch, preceding the ultimate liberation of the personality:

> In order to descend to the roots of pure humanity, where a given race communicates with all other races, one should follow doubtless one by one the inflexions of one's own stem *[tige]*, one shouldn't believe that it's possible to reach that layer if one skips any of the particular stages. Ah well, if I rely on my purely musical, immediate and spontaneous impressions, I have the feeling that your *Fêtes juives* is one of the stages of the particular that, if everything

goes well, will lead you to the depths of a more general reality. This is why, perhaps, the emotion that they stimulate does not completely communicate to
someone, who, like myself, comes from a different stem.[80]

Godet convinced Bloch that the particular (in this case the expression of a
particular race) would lead to the universal, to some shared human reality.
What Godet presented was a Wagnerian vision of reaching the eternally human through the descent to humanity's common roots via race.

Wagner found this instinctive, purely human layer in myth, which allowed
him, he believed, to reach the foundation of human relations and to identify "the human shape itself."[81] For Bloch it was the barbaric that reached
this universal human condition. Bloch's attraction to the barbaric coincided
with the modernist vogue of primitivism, exemplified by Stravinsky's *Rite of
Spring*. Bloch's barbaric mode was different, however. It expressed his attachment to the image of a romanticized Biblical past, which, though similar to Saminsky's nostalgia for the imagined purity of the Biblical Jews, centered more around the Jews as a barbarian tribe of ancient times, with savage
rites and a savage God. In the *Three Jewish Poems,* hoarse brass fanfares, shrieking woodwinds, and pounding timpani announce the manifestation of Jehovah in his "terrible grandeur" (3 mm. after rehearsal number 3). In the
*Israel Symphony* the arrival of Jehovah is signaled by similarly barbaric instrumental calls (rehearsal number 4). In "Yom Kippur," the second section
of the *Israel Symphony,* the barbaric music characterizes not Jehovah but his
people. As the program note describes, "irregular, savage rhythms, fanatic
Hebrew motives express the exalted gestures of the people falling down, piti-
lessly weighted by their sins" (rehearsal number 17).[82] Hackneyed as these
images seem, one might recognize in them a barbaric expression that Bloch
used in his search for the universally human behind the racially specific. While
Wagner plunged into myth to reach a prenational human condition, Bloch
descended to the biological roots of humanity, to a communal past preceding racial division, to a time when men communicated with universal gestures
unrestrained by the incomprehensibility of different languages.

Godet's belief that racial particularity was not an end in itself but a path
to the universal resonated with Bloch's ambitions. In 1913 he repeated to
Fleg his universalistic credo: "We have to be Jewish, not in order to separate
ourselves from the 'others,' but to be more human. In searching for our roots
we will also find those of the others for they plunge into the same ground.
The more M. Musorgsky is Russian, the more he also becomes human and
universal. It is there [in the realm of the universal] that I foresee a new music, which will be neither French, nor German, but which all who listen to it
will understand."[83]

In a letter to Romain Rolland, Bloch's formulation of the same idea is
even closer to Godet's. His Jewish works, he explained to Rolland, are "hu-

man more than anything; but to pronounce the truth, its truth, one has to plunge one's roots into the more profound layers of one's race, into oneself . . . and there one finds the common ground of all people."[84]

.    .    .    .

The Wagnerian belief in the possibility of reaching the universally human through the racially particular stayed with Bloch for the rest of his life. So did the disappointment and the bitterness that would follow when he recognized that Godet had misled him yet again, for Bloch's racially specific expression did not serve as a transitional stage leading to a universal language. For the musical expression of the barbaric, prelinguistic condition that Bloch envisioned as a shared memory of humanity was received by his critics not as a universal but as a specifically Hebrew racial expression. Increasingly race was used more to divide than to unify humanity. As Montagu recognized, racial thought came to justify wars, racial discrimination, ethnic cleansing, and eugenics. Anti-Semites, like Chamberlain, welcomed racial theory because it provided them with a system for anti-Jewish assumptions. Yet the concept, as Bloch's example demonstrates, was embraced by Jews too, who, in their modern, secular condition were in need of finding a new sense of identity.

With its pseudo-scientific pretenses the racial discourse about art provided a way station between individualistic Romantic expression and modernist "objectivity." It shielded artists like Bloch from the charge of outmoded Romanticism, for, as Bloch kept emphasizing, his personal expression sprang from the instinctive, and was thus the artistic utterance of a racial essence. In Bloch's vision, by relying on racial instinct he could create art that was the expression of a community but was free of social or political commitments.

More crucially, like Disraeli, Bloch could turn his Jewishness from a social handicap into an attractive, powerful, Romantic posture. Bloch's racial aesthetics of music, like Disraeli's Jewish pose, was the expression of what Hannah Arendt called "a very real Jewish chauvinism" that characterized the secularized, assimilated layers of Jewish society.[85] But as Bloch's inflated racial rhetoric assured the initial success of his Romantic Oriental music, the emphasis on his Jewish voice ultimately prevented him from entering the pantheon of universally acknowledged composers. Once he declared himself a Jewish composer, Bloch would be permanently confined to the ghetto he had constructed for himself on a foundation of racial theory.

## Chapter 4

# Denied and Accepted Stereotypes

## From *Jézabel* to *Schelomo*

*When Jehu was on his way back to Jezreel, Jezebel was informed. She made up her eyes with mascara, adorned her head and then appeared at the window. As Jehu came through the gateway she said, "How did Zimri get on after killing his master?" Jehu looked up to the window and said, "who is on my side? Who?" And two or three officials looked down at him. "Throw her down," he said. They threw her down and her blood spattered the walls and the horses; and Jehu rode over her. He went in and ate and drank, then said, "See to this accursed woman, and give her burial; after all, she was a king's daughter." But when they went to bury her, they found nothing but her skull, feet and hands. They came back and told Jehu, who said, "This is the word of Yahweh which he spoke through his servant Elijah the Tishbite, 'The dogs will eat the flesh of Jezebel in the field of Jezreel; the corpse of Jezebel will be like dung spread on the fields, so that no one will be able to say: This was Jezebel.'"*

2 Kings 9:30–37

The story of Jezebel's violent death belongs among the cold accounts of bloody wars, battles, and massacres in the Old Testament. Despite the frequency of similar stories, there is something especially disturbing about Jezebel's slaughter by men who then "eat and drink," thereby treating her murder as a routine task that does not involve emotion. Bloch, who was attracted to the savagery of some Old Testament stories and who, as his opera *Macbeth* reveals, did not shrink from setting bloodshed to music, chose Jezebel as the heroine of his projected Jewish opera. The opera stage required some leavening of the plot's Biblical grimness, which Bloch achieved by turning Jehu into Jezebel's lover (a strange modification, considering the Biblical precedent) and by introducing moral and emotional ambiguities that transformed the characters into human beings with moral choices. Despite these drastic changes, the basic message of the tale, the Biblical obligation, quoted by Godet and then by Bloch from Deuteronomy, of "killing whoever lures you into adoring different gods," remained true to the spirit of the Bible.

As the preservation of Judaism's purity required sacrifices in the Bible, so Bloch's assumption of a Jewish artistic identity called for purifying his style of what Sabaneyev, referring to the music of the Russian Jewish composers, called "foreign alloys." But, as in the case of the Russian composers, deciding which musical style symbolized "foreignness" and which "purity" was more dependent on stereotypes (whether accepted or rejected) than on musical characteristics of traditional Jewish music. Like Saminsky before him, Bloch chose Orientalism as a sign of foreignness. For Bloch, however, Orientalizing music did not symbolize the Diaspora but a physical sensuousness that endangered spiritual ideals.

Bloch first articulated what he conceived as a purified Jewish identity in the sketches for his projected opera *Jézabel* (1911–18). Several years later Bloch transformed his Jewish style into a more conventional, Orientally colored Jewish idiom in *Schelomo* (1916), the last piece of his so-called Jewish Cycle. The difference between what constituted "Jewish" in the style of the opera and in *Schelomo* demonstrates the flexibility of the conception of Jewish art music. Like Bloch's Jewish identity, his Jewish musical style also kept changing, manifesting, as theories of social identity would have it, a process rather than an unchangeable essence.[1] Focusing on changes rather than on constant components in Bloch's Jewish identity presents an anti-essentialist argument that goes against anti-Semitic assumptions of Jewishness and at the same time contradicts Bloch's own belief in racial essences. The change of focus that occurred between *Jézabel* and *Schelomo* also demonstrates the bitter irony of Bloch's tale: despite the composer's wish to create a Jewish style that would purify Judaism through the force of art, in his most widely acclaimed Jewish compositions his style confirmed anti-Semitic stereotypes.

## JEZEBEL: THE SENSUOUS ORIENTAL

Before leaving Europe in 1916 Bloch focused his energies on writing music that would express what he then believed was the most important component of his personality: his Jewish race. He was opposed to deliberately integrating traditional Jewish music into his musical style because he feared that a conscious effort would inhibit precisely those instinctive layers from which he expected the emergence of a racially determined creative impulse. In letters to Fleg, Bloch repeatedly hinted at his passive role in the fermenting of this new musical style. He allowed God to dictate to him by leading his fingers on the piano in order to find "a superb cry of suffering," which, Bloch believed, would be representative of "the entire Jewish soul."[2] Describing his compositional process as occurring "despite himself," Bloch suggested the linked roles of the Biblical prophet and the modern genius.[3] Bloch believed his passivity was proof that the new style he was developing truly came from the unconscious, racially defined layers of his personality. "I feel an entire prayer germinating within me," he wrote to Fleg. "I don't force it, I don't *produce* anything, and for the moment I am not trying to give a form to these sketchy ideas." Form will come later, Bloch assured his friend: "I feel that the hour will come and I wait for it in confidence, respecting the present silence imposed upon me by the laws of nature, which know better than I do." With nature's help he would create "new forms" that would be "free and clear at the same time, clear and sumptuous; I feel them without seeing them in front of me." To further emphasize his divine calling, Bloch pointed to his outsider status in Judaism. "It is quite strange that all this emerges so slowly, and that this impulse chose me, since I am such a stranger in all my *exterior* life to everything that is Jewish," he wrote to Fleg.[4]

To help find this new musical style, Bloch needed a topic on which he could concentrate his musical imagination. He found it in the Biblical story of Jezebel. Although Bloch never completed his opera *Jézabel*, some musical themes and, more generally, the style Bloch developed for it lived on in his later compositions. *Jézabel* served as a touchstone for Bloch, and thus it is indispensable for understanding the formation of his Jewish style.

The idea of writing an opera about the infamous queen of Israel first occurred to Bloch in 1904 when he and Fleg were looking for potential topics for a *drame lyrique*. In spite of Bloch's complaints about the overwhelming fashion for medieval Christian themes in the arts, he began his research by looking at books about medieval French legends, flipping through Anatole le Braz's *La légende de la mort en Basse-Bretagne: croyances, traditions et usages des Bretons armoricains* (1893), Edouard Schuré's *Les grandes légendes de France* (1895), and Paul Sebillot's *Légendes, croyances et superstitions de la mer* (1886).[5] In May 1904 he came across the one-act play *Jézabel* by English writer William Rutherford Hayes Trowbridge (1866–1938). He was captivated immediately.

Dedicated to Sarah Bernhardt, Trowbridge's play was published only in French in 1903. Half gossipmonger, half historian, Trowbridge thrived on the scandals surrounding famous women like Catherine the Great, who appears with six other aristocratic femmes fatales in his *Seven Splendid Sinners* (1909). Trowbridge's only Biblical character, Jezebel shares a noble birth, dangerous ambition, morally suspect conduct, and insatiable sexual appetite with his other heroines, thus fitting the fashion for turn-of-the-century misogynist representations of women in art.[6] Yet unlike contemporary artistic depictions of Judith, Herodias, or Salome, Trowbridge's Jezebel is not demonized. He even blunts the misogynist edge of the story by introducing the female prophetess Séphorah as Jezebel's moral counterpart.

While Bloch commented on the Maeterlinckian symbolism of Trowbridge's *Jézabel*,[7] he never seems to have acknowledged the most obvious model for the play, Oscar Wilde's *Salome* (1893)—also published in French and dedicated to Sarah Bernhardt.[8] The parallel between the two is so obvious that one suspects deliberate modeling.[9] The subject matters were indeed related. Jezebel's name was so strongly associated with female corruption that in Flaubert's *Herodias,* one of the numerous plays inspired by Gustave Moreau's *Salome* (1876), Jokanaan addresses Herodias as "Jezebel."[10] Simi-

larities between Wilde's and Trowbridge's plays go even further. Like *Salome,*
at least half of *Jézabel* consists of disjunct conversations between secondary
figures contemplating Jezebel's astonishing beauty from afar. Jezebel's most
ardent follower is the former prophet Abner, who abandoned his faith under the magic spell of the pagan Jezebel. Abner shows both his devotion and
the power of Jezebel's enchanting physical appearance by killing himself—
just as Narraboth does early in Strauss's *Salome*—to assure the queen, waiting for her enemy Jehu, that she will have power over him as well.

The most Wildean scene is the appearance of Jehu, visible to Jezebel but
not to the audience. The dialogue between Jezebel and Jehu that follows is
clearly inspired by the dialogue between Salome and Jokanaan: both women
try to seduce their interlocutors by giving a sensual account of the body of
a man whose interest lies exclusively in the spiritual. As in *Salome,* a conflict
is set up between sight and sound.[11] For a long time Jehu refuses to look at
Jezebel in fear that what he sees might distract him from hearing the voice
of God. Jezebel describes in great detail the beauty of Jehu's hair, his eyes,
his body, and then attempts to turn Jehu's attention to her own beauty. Jehu,
like Jokanaan, is blind to corporeal beauty ("Seul Iaveh est beau! Seul le
Seigneur Dieu est désirable!")[12] and orders her execution. Thus the prophecy, announced in Trowbdrige's *Jézabel* by Séphorah (not by Elijah as in the
Bible), is fulfilled because the queen's beauty has failed her. The violent ending, just as in Wilde's *Salome,* is not displayed on stage. In Trowbridge's play
the curtain falls as the eunuchs, commissioned to murder her, approach their
queen.

Despite Bloch's initial fascination with Jezebel, he soon grew tired of Trowbridge's verbose symbolism and for a time gave up the idea of reworking
*Jézabel* as a libretto. Yet he maintained his faith that the subject had the qualities of a modern *drame lyrique.* Among these were the "philosophical ideas"
and "intense psychology" that Bloch hoped would lend universal validity to
the opera. Most important, the subject had an appealing Oriental color. The
Oriental milieu inspired Bloch to create "new tonalities à la Gustave Moreau,"
a painter whom Bloch considered to be an *"immense* genius," and whose
paintings, as he wrote to his wife after visiting the Gustave Moreau Museum
in Paris, made his head "swarm" with music.[13] Moreau's *Salome* was surely
in his mind when he imagined his voluptuous opera heroine. Not surprisingly, Bloch's conception of Jezebel shared many features with Wilde's and
Strauss's *Salome,* and with so many other dangerous women in the arts of the
early twentieth century whose sweet and sensuous appearance hid the instinct of a serpent and the destructive force of a beast.[14]

Bloch's initial enthusiasm for Jezebel as a potential subject for an opera was
thus typical of the times, fitting perfectly with contemporaneous operatic
trends. Nothing yet indicated that *Jézabel* would turn into Bloch's most ambi-

tious Jewish project, the incompleteness of which would haunt him for almost twenty years. In 1904 the choice of a Biblical topic for an opera amounted to no more than another experiment in effective Oriental *couleur locale.*

At the end of 1908 Jezebel still appeared as only one of several possible topics for Bloch and Fleg's next operatic project, the only woman in the company of other potential opera heroes such as Moses, Job, Saul, and Gargantua.[15] Gargantua and Saul were never seriously considered, and Moses and Job were soon dismissed, for, as Bloch explained to Fleg, Job called more for an oratorio than an opera, and as far as Moses was concerned, he felt that they were too young to do it. "It should be one's *Parsifal*," he wrote to Fleg.[16]

Bloch resolved to set *Jézabel*, yet he transformed it to incorporate the moral concerns of the rejected subjects. He dropped Trowbridge's version in order to turn the story into a drama about "the opposition of two moralities, of two conceptions of life," which Bloch interpreted as the contrast between the Jewish and the pagan worlds.[17]

### VILIFYING THE VILE

In the Bible, Jezebel promotes the worship of two Canaanite fertility gods, Baal and his consort Astarte. Daughter of the pagan King Ethbaal of Sidon, Jezebel married King Ahab of Israel and introduced him and his people to the orgiastic rites of her country, thereby arousing the fury of the prophet Elijah. The two episodes connected with her are chronicled in 1 Kings (21:23–24) and 2 Kings (9:36–37). One is the murder of Naboth, which she arranged to acquire his vineyard for Ahab, and which provoked Elijah's curse. The other, quoted at the beginning of this chapter, is her assassination, on orders from Jehu, the new king of Israel.

Bloch and Fleg used these two episodes from the Bible and added a third, a scene on Mount Carmel, which concerns Jezebel only indirectly. In the years of a great famine Elijah ordered the prophets of Baal to come to Mount Carmel and call to Baal for rain. When they failed, Elijah appealed to Jehovah, and the drought came to an end (1 Kings 18:20–46). Elijah then had all the prophets of Baal killed and ordered Ahab to abandon worshiping Baal. Jezebel was not won over by the miracle on Mount Carmel. Upon hearing of the murder of her prophets, she threatened to do to Elijah what he had done to the servants of Baal, and Elijah was forced into exile once again. In the Bible Elijah's triumph on Mount Carmel is followed by Naboth's murder, but Fleg changed the order of events into a sequence that would be more effective dramatically. In the libretto Naboth's death comes before the Carmel episode, so that Jezebel's sin of causing his death is followed by the triumph of the righteous Elijah and then by Jehu's punishment of Jezebel.

As the subtitle of the printed version indicates, Fleg's libretto is a "midrash," a parable that reveals new meanings by rearranging or even distorting Biblical events.[18] The most striking distortion was Fleg's complete elimination of Jezebel's husband Ahab from the story.[19] From a midrashic standpoint the elimination served Fleg's purposes: it liberated Jezebel's erotic sensuousness from marital control, and, more crucially, it turned Jezebel into the single culprit of the Biblical parable. While in the Bible Jezebel arranges the murder of Naboth as a favor for her corrupt husband, in Fleg's version she wishes Naboth's death out of her own desire to possess his vineyard. Naboth had refused to give it up out of respect for the Torah, which decreed that it was unlawful to sell land that had been given to its owners by God. Naboth's disobedience to Jezebel confirmed the eternal link between the God of the covenant and the Jews. Bloch further vilified Jezebel by insisting that instead of simply ordering Naboth's death, she should murder him herself on stage. This cruel action, Bloch argued, would demonstrate the unbridgeable divide between pagan and Jewish moralities, one denying, the other affirming the significance of the life of the individual: "[Jezebel] says: 'a man? What does it matter?' Israel says: 'a human being.'"[20]

Fleg obeyed Bloch's wish. In his libretto, during a feast in honor of Baal, Jezebel reads aloud the Sixth Commandment ("Thou shall not kill") from the tablets that she had ordered to be carried to the scene of Baal worship. She then orders the servants to throw Naboth on the tablets of the law and murders him while crying out: "Well, where is he, Jehovah? What does he do? What does he say, the invisible Elohim?"[21] In his prose scenario Bloch made the scene crueler still:

> At the culmination of the dance they bring in Naboth. His young son follows him, crying and beseeching. Jezebel has him brought in front of the tablets of law. With a torch, she shows Jehu the place where God wrote with his hand: "You shall not kill" and raises her arm to strike him. The son of Naboth asks to die in his father's place! "No, you, you are young and beautiful, you are worthy to serve Baal," and she stabs Naboth. "Throw his corpse to the dogs! And now, what does he do? What does he say, where is he? Your God is dead, your sad God, your invisible God!"[22]

This gruesome spectacle was to be performed before Jehu, commander of Ahab's army, who in the Bible has no connection to Jezebel before ordering her execution. In Bloch and Fleg's version of the story, Jehu is infatuated with Jezebel and is thus torn between his sensuous desire and his conscience. Jezebel lures him into her plot against Naboth, but when Jehu is about to kill Naboth the prophet Elijah appears and stops him. Elijah reveals to Jehu that in spite of his sins, Jehovah chose him to be king of Israel and the foe of Jezebel, one who will drive the queen to her shameful end. Torn between moral obligation and love, Jehu became the central figure of the opera. "It is basically Jehu's drama," Bloch explained to Fleg, for the drama revolves around him more than around Jezebel.[23]

In the libretto Fleg softened the violent ending of the Biblical story. Jehu does not order Jezebel's death as in the Bible. After her attempt to seduce him fails, Jehu calls Elijah, who commands that she be removed from the palace. Jezebel is taken away, accompanied by the mob's excited cries: "To the dogs! To the dogs! Death to Jezebel! Throw her down! To the dogs!" Torn, Jehu falls on his knees, but his cry is silenced as the sun suddenly appears from behind the clouds. In contrast to the Bible, where Jehu is anointed by Elisha (2 Kings 9), in the opera Elijah takes the crown and puts it on Jehu's head, praising "Him who shines in the light."[24]

In his prose scenario Bloch again lends his own touch to the ending. In Bloch's rendition Jehu's refusal of Jezebel was more complete than in Fleg's libretto. And Jezebel, hardened even in the moment before her death, cannot admit the fatal failure of her seductive powers. She is unwilling to yield. Her last words confirm her belief in the joys of Baal:

> JEHU:   "I see only the Eternal God, I don't see your beauty
> any more, I see only your crimes. Under the paint
> of your face I see already old age and death. . . .
> Executioner, do your job!"
>
> JEZEBEL, *standing up:* "No, not by the executioner. Jezebel will not survive the
> first defeat of her beauty! My God is still the true God.
> Joy survives all deaths. I die for Baal!"
>
> *She stabs herself . . .*
>
> *Emotions of Jehu . . .*
>
> *Elijah enters with the crowd.*
>
> ELIJAH:   "Carry this woman to the dogs!"
>
> THE CROWD:   "Long live Jehu, long live the king of Israel!"

In Bloch's scenario Elijah thus enters only after Jezebel has stabbed herself, and he orders her corpse to be thrown to the dogs—a distortion of the Biblical story, in which Elijah does not carry out his own prophecies.

Bloch's version of Jezebel's death negates any sympathy that one might feel for her when reading the Bible or even Fleg's libretto, in which she throws herself on her knees in front of Jehu begging for pity. Jezebel's egotistic cruelty and preoccupation with her erotic charms, together with the sexual explicitness of many scenes of the opera, made her abhorrent to a degree rarely encountered even on opera stages routinely populated by evil and seductive sorceresses. Vilifying the already disreputable Jezebel—whose name has been used for centuries to epitomize lust, promiscuity, and political intrigue—was a task Bloch pursued passionately. Symbolically, Jezebel fulfilled for him the role of a sacrificial animal. Her inevitable fall purged God's people of their sins—as Jehu in the Bible had purged Israel of Baal by slaying all of his worshipers (2 Kings 10). By maligning Jezebel, Bloch portrayed the antipode of the ideal Jew he wanted to create through the purifying force of his art. The attempted purge is even more striking since many of the exaggerated features of Jezebel—such as her Oriental "otherness," sensuousness, materialism, and complete lack of morals—were common traits of anti-Semitic clichés.

### THE OPPOSING WORLDS OF BAAL AND JEHOVAH

The musical sketches for *Jézabel* belong to two different chronological layers.[25] The one bound sketchbook from 1911 ("Esquisses & Notes") contains a thematic index, listing "Jézabel, Jéhu, Elie (Israel), Dances, Naboth," and "thèmes païens." This sketchbook can serve as a guide to Bloch's early conception of the musical characters in the opera. Resuming work on *Jézabel* in New York in 1918, Bloch wrote a new thematic index, now listing the characters in the new order of importance as "Iéhou, Elijahou, Naboth, Danses païennes/Astarté, Danses de Baal (et thèmes divers de Baal), Iézabel." In this new index the first page of some thematic groups also contains descriptions of the scenes and broader ideas corresponding to the motives. Naboth's themes, for instance, were connected to all the other musical materials in the opera that "symbolize the Jewish spirit" (fig. 3).

As the thematic sketches reveal, in the opera Bloch attempted to contrast an ideal, pure Judaism with corrupted paganism. He accomplished the polarization of Jehovah's world (represented by Naboth) and Baal's (represented by Jezebel) by sharply differentiating the kinds of music attached to them. Music for Jezebel and the cult of Astarte and Baal was to portray, in Bloch's words, the "great pagan stream, the exterior, joy and fatal sensuality, pomp and color"; while music for the Jews was to capture "the moral force and justice, the battle against human nature . . . law and order, interior joy."[26]

Bloch believed that his treatment of leitmotifs in *Jézabel* differed significantly from Wagner's, Debussy's, and Strauss's. Although he never explained the difference in relation to *Jézabel*, he described his music in *Macbeth* as depicting not characters (like he claimed Debussy did) or silhouettes (which, according to Bloch, was Strauss's custom) but "destiny, power, ambition, justice," in other words, "the forces that made the characters act."[27] In *Jézabel* Bloch polarized these forces as moral right and wrong (the latter characterized, in a simplistic fashion, by sexual misconduct).

As Bloch marked them in the sketches, Jezebel's themes are "seductive, languishing, voluptuous, and perfidious." Many are chromatic, with occasional augmented seconds, and tend to move either in a narrow range, repeatedly falling back to the same note, or to descend slowly but ineluctably as if obeying the law of gravity (ex. 39a–b). Jezebel also has themes that show her power, such as the one Bloch intended to use as a pagan theme in opposition to Elijah. The sharper rhythm and the aggressively rising fifths of this motive depict a Jezebel who can be a forceful antagonist to Elijah (ex. 39c).

Figure 3. Facsimile page of Naboth's themes from the 1918 New York thematic index. Ernest Bloch Collection, Library of Congress, Washington DC, folder 6 (used by permission).

Example 39. Themes associated with Jezebel.

a. "Seduction (sacred grove)" (1911).

b. "Languishing" (1911 and 1918).

c. "Pagan theme opposing Elijah" (1911).

The themes labeled "dances" and "pagan themes" are also intimately connected with Jezebel. Like her themes, the musical images of Astarte and Baal are marked by Orientalist clichés. "There is no theme for Baal, the music is vague, not exact," Bloch wrote to Fleg. He meant to depict this pagan world with "some ardent or voluptuous, languorous, perfidious, and capricious phrases."[28] This amorphousness fits precisely a broad stereotype of musical Orientalism. In the music for Baal, Astarte, and Jezebel static ostinatos, grace notes, a narrow range, an abundance of augmented seconds and tritones, and the occasional use of the octatonic scale (one of the Russians' signs for the fantastic, or for the inhuman) display Bloch's rich Orientalizing arsenal (ex. 40). Thus in *Jézabel,* as in Alexander Serov's *Judith* or Saint-Saëns's *Samson et Dalila,* the Orientalizing themes, frequently associ-

Example 40. Themes associated with Baal and Astarte (1911).

a. Augmented seconds, grace notes, and tritones in the theme of Astarte and Baal (1911).

b. Static ostinato in the theme of Astarte and Baal (1911).

c. Ostinato and octatonic melody in the theme of Baal and Astarte (1911).

ated with Jews in art music, represent instead the antipode of Judaism, the pagan world.[29]

In the opera the music of the Jews centers around the figure of Naboth. Writing to Fleg, Bloch described Naboth's themes as "very melodious, even sentimental."[30] In sharp contrast to Jezebel's music, Bloch intended to depict Naboth's pure world with diatonic, sometimes even pentatonic motives (ex. 41). As early as 1911 Bloch decided to introduce some traditional Jew-

Example 41. Themes associated with Naboth.

a. "Calm" (1911).

b. "Prelude to Naboth(?), atmosphere II" (1918).

c. "Jewish (calm and serene joy)" (1911).

d. "Character" (1911).

ish themes in association with Naboth.[31] The presence of these themes undermines Bloch's later statements about never relying on traditional melodies to give Jewish character to his work.[32] His selection of traditional themes was scarcely random. He preferred diatonically simple motives that matched the style of his other Jewish themes in the opera, and excluded those that might share some of the Oriental features of the pagan themes.

In its first version Bloch might have notated the theme he labeled "profession of faith" from memory, recalling it from his childhood. Some years later in 1918, when at Fleg's instigation he was searching for his musical roots in the *Jewish Encyclopedia* in the New York Public Library,[33] Bloch located this motive among the melodies associated with the Ne'ilah service.[34] The melody of the "profession of faith" (or *Shemot*) closes the service of Ne'ilah (the last service on Yom Kippur) with the reader and congregation's seven-fold proclamation of "The Lord is God."[35] When Bloch decided to use the melody in 1911,[36] he was likely to have been aware that this part of the ceremony refers to Elijah's invocation on Mount Carmel and is therefore thematically connected to the subject of the opera (ex. 42). Bloch planned to use other traditional melodies for the scenes that include Naboth, but the only motive he specified as being borrowed from Jewish liturgy besides the motive of the "profession of faith" is the first part of a prayer-mode melody for the Sabbath morning service ("Ki el melekh gadol" [For God is a great king]), which he also found in the *Jewish Encyclopedia* in 1918 (ex. 43). This motive accompanies Naboth's entrance to Jezebel's palace in act 1.[37]

Bloch never identified the main motive he used to represent "true" Judaism in *Jézabel* as borrowed from a specific source. The motive had already appeared in connection with Naboth in the first draft of act 1, and it became the marker of Naboth's world in the 1918 revised version. Providing a peaceful ending, the same motive appears in Bloch's *Israel Symphony* (1912–16). Because of its programmatic associations with Judaism in these works, Bloch scholars have assumed that the motive has traditional Jewish roots. While David Kushner connects it to a Passover Seder song, Alexander Knapp traces it to a cantillation motive used for the Blessing over the Bible (ex. 44).[38] The diatonic purity of both these melodies is characteristic of Bloch's musical representation of the idealized Jews in his opera.

More central to the thematic material of *Jézabel* is the music of act 2, the motives for which Bloch associated in his 1918 thematic index with the "Festival of Sukkot, prayers and psalmody." Sukkot (Tabernacles) is one of the three pilgrim festivals preceding the Simhat Torah in the tradition of the Diaspora. Sukkot is also known as the festival of harvest *(hag ha-asiph)*, and it is in this sense that Bloch included it in act 2, where it is linked to the grape harvest in Naboth's vineyard. The music associated with the festival of Sukkot stands in sharp contrast to the other feast in the opera, the orgiastic night dedicated to Baal, a scene that was to follow the Sukkot scene in act 2.

Example 42. The melody of the "Profession of Faith" *(Shemot).*

a. In the *Jewish Encyclopedia* (1905).

1. She - ma'_____ Yis - ra - el, A - do - nai E - lo_____
he - nu, A - do - nai_____ e - had 1, 2, & 3. Ba -
ruk_____ Shem_____ ke - bod_____ mal - ka - to_____ le 'o_____
lam_____ wa ʼed. 1. to 6. A - do - nai,_____ Hu ha - E - lo-
him._____ 7. A - do - nai._____ Hu_____ ha - E - lo - him._____

(Hear, Israel, the Lord is our God, the Lord is One. Blessed be the Name of His glorious kingdom forever and ever. The Lord is God, the Lord is God.)

b. In act 1, scene 4 of *Jézabel* (first version).

Example 43. The melody of "Ki el melekh gadol."

a. Prayer motive for Sabbath morning service in the entry "Music" in the *Jewish Encyclopedia* (1905).

Ki El Me-lek ga-dol we-ka - dosh_____ At - tah. Ba -

ruk At-tah A-do - nai_____ ha - El_____ ha - ka - dosh.

(For you are God, the great and holy king. Blessed are You Lord, the holy God.)

b. At the moment of Naboth's arrival in act 1, scene 4 (second version).

Example 44. The motive of Sukkot in *Jézabel* and its sources.

a. The main motive of Sukkot in act 2.

b. A Passover Seder song (Kushner, "The 'Jewish' Works of Ernest Bloch," 31).

E - chad mi - yo - de -          a

c. A cantillation motive (Knapp, "The Jewishness of Bloch," 107).

Bor' - chu    es A - do - noy . . .    no - sein ha-to-roh_____

Example 45. Four motives for the "Fête de Soukkoth" (1918).

Like his main Sukkot motive, the other motives Bloch indexed under the label "Fête de Soukkoth" are also diatonic, meant to depict the purity of the
heart (ex. 45). Their rhythms (most typically triplets alternating with pairs
of eighth notes) lack the kinetic energy of Jezebel's dance-inspired music.
By purposefully avoiding corporeal associations, the music of Naboth's
scenes sets up a contrast between the sensuous music of Baal/Astarte and
the seraphic music of the faithful Jews.

## THE FIGHT BETWEEN GOOD AND EVIL:
### THE MUSICAL GESTURES OF JEHU AND ELIJAH

Bloch himself felt distant from both the Orientalism of Jezebel and the
purified simplicity of Naboth. His personal concerns brought him closer to
the figures of Jehu and the prophet Elijah. In the opera's microcosmic Jewish world, Jehu represents the fight between good and evil, between ideal
and corrupted Jews, while Elijah is the adamant messenger of God, the
prophet whose role Bloch himself assumed with increasing conviction.

Corrupted by his love for Jezebel, Jehu shares some of her chromatic motives (ex. 46). He has his own music, though, which differs significantly from
Jezebel's. In contrast to Jezebel's meandering motives (representing femi-
ninity), Jehu's music is passionate and dynamic, characterized by large ascending leaps that then often fall back by step (ex. 47). Jehu's double bind
is demonstrated by motives that Bloch identified as "Jewish." The dropping
fourth and undulating chromaticism of the motive Bloch labeled "Jewish cry"
and conceived as "a truthful national cry" represent Jewish suffering (ex.
48).[39] Falling fourths seem to have carried some Jewish association for Bloch,
as they mark both the "pain of Jehu (Jewish)" and the "to Carmel" motives
(ex. 49).

Despite Bloch's designation of Jehu as the complicated central character
of the opera, he was musically more inspired by the figure of Elijah, whom
he associated with "violence, ardor, vision, and pride." The prophet appears
in only one scene in the completed portion of act 2 and not at all in act 1;

Example 46. Themes associated with Jehu (1918).

Example 47. Passionate gestures of Jehu.

a. "Cry of passion and pain (one Jewish, one pagan)" (1911).

b. "Feverish and distressed" (1911 and 1918).

Example 48. Theme of "Jewish cry."

Example 49. Motives with falling fourths.

  a. "Pain of Jehu ( Jewish)."

  b. "To Carmel."

and yet the seven pages of thematic sketches Bloch wrote in 1918 related to the dramatic situations that include Elijah far exceed in number all the musical materials for the other characters in the opera. Most of the music for Elijah in act 2 comes from the end of the Baal feast and is associated with Elijah's prophetic declaration of God's decision to close the skies and impose famine, and with the prophet's curse on Jezebel. The undrafted act 3 was to have contained the central event in Elijah's prophetic mission, the triumph over the priests of Baal on Mount Carmel.

Unlike the motives surrounding the figure of Naboth or the ones representing the contrasting world of Jezebel, Elijah's music eludes characterization as simply diatonic or chromatic. It is not so much the technical details of the music that unify this group of motives as their intensity of utterance. In the 1918 thematic sketches the motives are alternatively labeled as representing "character" or "declamation," but Bloch collected similarly forceful musical gestures under both categories.

Example 50. Belligerent motives associated with Elijah.

a. Motive associated with Elijah, "declamation and character" (1918).

b. "Law" (1918).

c. Motive associated with Elijah (1911).

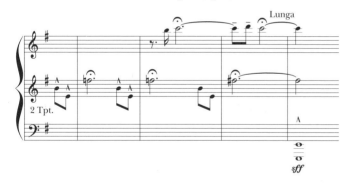

d–e. Motives of Elijah labeled as "declamation" (1918).

Example 50 *(continued)*

f. "Savage (like a cry of nature)" (1911).

The vehemence of most of these motives is manifest in rhythmic contrasts and frequent use of accents—often underlining the end of the motives with gestures that function like the exclamation points Bloch used so frequently in his own prose (ex. 50a). The motive of the "Law" is recognizable in the draft of act 2 not only by its rising melodic line, but also by its accented ending (ex. 50b). Elijah's music is further characterized by aggressively ascending melodic shapes, idiomatic brass figures (arpeggios or repeated notes), and an abundance of perfect fourths, fifths, and tritones (ex. 50c). The belligerent, barbarous character of these motives presents a prophet who communicates with forceful gestures more than with speech. Here even his motives described as "declamation" have an instrumental rather than a vocal character (ex. 50a and d–e). In the 1911 thematic sketches Bloch included a motive among Elijah's musical material that he labeled "savage (like a cry of nature)" (ex. 50f). Like all of Elijah's music, this savage motive is also instrumental in character, orchestrated for oboe, horn, violas, and cello in a further sketch.

The mouthpiece for Bloch's judgment of the Jews, Elijah seems to be in a constant state of fury, trying to break through the deafness of his people with piercing sounds. Elijah's intense and aggressive instrumental gestures reinforce a sense that his music carries the weighty proclamation of some eternal truth—be it the unity of the universe and the eternal laws of nature (both fundamental in Bloch's pantheistic belief) or, less broadly, the composer's own prophetic mission. Bloch's previous opera, *Macbeth,* was full of intense utterances and violent musical gestures. But in *Macbeth* human emotions lay behind the violence, which manifested itself in crime and in psychological torture. In other words, the dramatic situation called for the musical expression of violence and not, as in the case of Elijah's music in *Jézabel,* the unshakable belief in one's mission.

Of Elijah's motives only the "mission of Israel" and the "Israel" motives partake of the idealized Jewish world of Naboth, and thus lack the belligerence of the other motives associated with the prophet (ex. 51). Both motives reappear later among the sketches of the projected *Jeremiah Symphony.* They also return in the fifth part of the *Sacred Service* (1930–33), the piece that

Example 51. Motives associated with Israel.

a. Theme of "mission of Israel" (1911 and 1918).

b. Theme of "Israel" (1918).

Bloch intended to fulfill the "mission of Israel" by uniting all humanity through its supposedly ecumenical musical style.

In addition to these two motives and the exotic style associated with Jezebel and her pagan court, the musical gestures related to Jehu and Elijah also reappear in Bloch's later compositions. Even after Bloch's enthusiasm for creating a Jewish musical style had faded, a continued personal interest in these two characters kept their musical expressions alive. Jehu's struggle between religious obligations and sensuous yearnings reflected the unbridgeable gap between Bloch's ardent desire to take up the role of the prophet of humanity at large and his real-life personality, which—as is abundantly evident from his correspondence—was perennially caught between extramarital love affairs and a self-image of moral rectitude.[40] No wonder Bloch transformed Jehu from the politically minded, goal-oriented leader of the Bible into a self-doubting, suffering man trapped in a schizophrenic personality. Surrounded by an artificially Oriental dramatic setting that helped present his own desire (and its object) as part of an alien world, Jehu personified Bloch's divided personality. Elijah represented another desire, Bloch's quest for an ascetic spirituality. What lay between these two opposing desires was an unresolved tension that characterized both Bloch's personality and his music. But the widely publicized Jewish associations of Bloch's belligerent, somewhat didactic musical rhetoric have subordinated personal interpretations of his music to racial-cultural ones.

### THE ORIENTAL CLAIMS ITS DUE: *SCHELOMO*

*Jézabel* remained unfinished, and thus Bloch's original musical image of an ideal, purified Judaism never reached the public. What survived were the works constituting his "Jewish Cycle," pieces that are intimately connected to *Jézabel* because they utilize themes and musical gestures that Bloch had conceived while working on the opera. The declamatory intensity of their musical language, even their bombast, assured Bloch's later public success. Thanks to this success, the stylistic characteristics of these pieces became tokens of a generalized Jewish expression in music.

Bloch's rhapsody for cello and orchestra, *Schelomo*, the last and most popular piece in the cycle, has come to be the chief representative of Bloch's Jewish voice. Reading *Schelomo* in the context of *Jézabel* reveals a considerable change in Bloch's perception of his Jewish style. In *Schelomo* the Orientalizing music—a traditional stylistic referent that Bloch had used in *Jézabel* to represent the opponents of the Jews—reclaimed its Jewish associations. Yet in *Schelomo* musical Orientalism was not a mere rehashing of Jezebel's luscious eroticism. In the rhapsody Bloch's Jewish style achieved a synthesis by turning Elijah's God-driven hardness and Jehu's voluptuous side into dual characteristics of King Solomon, the title figure of *Schelomo*. The combination of musical gestures representing Elijah's stubborn prophetic utterances and Jezebel's Oriental sensuousness resulted in a significant conceptual difference that distinguished the styles of *Schelomo* and *Jézabel*. Instead of the sharply differentiated musical styles depicting moral conflict in *Jézabel*, in *Schelomo* the style is more unified and at the same time corresponds more to the most commonly accepted stereotypical representation of the Jews as Orientals. This radical conceptual change may have been one of the reasons why Bloch could not complete the opera.[41]

Although searching for inspiration in the Bible had become a compositional routine for Bloch, the primary stimulus for *Schelomo* was not the Bible but a wax statuette of King Solomon made by Katherina Barjansky, wife of Bloch's friend, cellist Alexander Barjansky (1883–1961). The Russian-Jewish couple were among the first people who recognized the potential for success in Bloch's Jewish compositions. Listening to his *Psalms* in Bloch's home, Katherina Barjansky "was so moved," Bloch reported to Fleg's wife, "that she

asked my wife for paper and pencil, and . . . said: 'I will thank you in wax.'"
Katherina Barjansky's artistic response to Bloch's explicitly Jewish works,
which Bloch saw as an "amazing artistic revelation," offers a visual expression of what Bloch's audience expected from and consequently heard in a
music labeled "Jewish": heavy Orientalism, black and golden colors, and a
sensuous, peremptory expression (fig. 4). Bloch's description of the wax statuette suggests that he saw a combination of Elijah's and Jehu's traits in Katherina Barjansky's creation:

> The King is sitting on a black velvet throne, he is dressed in an ample, black
> and golden gown; the head, the hands and the feet are painted wax, decorated
> with gold, rings and oriental sumptuousness, which is both sober and severe.
>     The hands and the feet have admirable expressiveness. The head is one of
> the most beautiful things I have seen, with a rarely-attained complexity of ex-
> pression. The forehead is immense, the eyes investigating and profound; the
> lips are both sensuous and bitter, dominating and resigned. All this is marked
> by the sign of a genius, and by a Jewish genius.[42]

The "oriental sumptuousness" of the statuette's decoration, combined with
the "profound" expression of its face, reconciled what were irreconcilable
in the opera: sensual and spiritual intensity.

*Schelomo's* subtitle "rhapsody" refers not only to the genre associated with
a deliberately free musical form, but also to the role of the ancient Greek singer
of epic tales, the rhapsodist, taken here by the solo cello. As his program notes
indicate, Bloch attempted to separate the voices of the soloist and the orchestra, characterizing one as an individual or the main character and the
other as a collective voice or the atmosphere surrounding the hero. Like
Richard Strauss in *Don Quixote*, he assigned almost precise verbal expressions
to the cello, while he described the orchestra as reflecting the hero's ideas.

In 1932 Bloch wrote a detailed a posteriori program for *Schelomo*. He "psy-
choanalyzed" the work to emphasize his unconscious creative process. Despite its tedious overabundance of details, Bloch's program note deserves
our attention both because it has determined nearly all attempts to explain
the work, and because it demonstrates how Bloch struggled to resolve inconsistencies in his vision of the piece:

> I had no descriptive intention. I was saturated by the Biblical text and most of
> all by the miseries of the world to which I was always sensitive. Now I had the
> idea of "psychoanalyzing" my work: and these notes are the result. And so I
> have written a program "after the fact," "ex post facto," following the music.
>     It's possible, if one wishes, to imagine—as so it seems, indeed—that the vio-
> loncello in Schelomo is the incarnation of King Solomon and that the orches-
> tra, a more collective voice, represents the World around him and his experi-
> ences of Life, although sometimes it is the orchestra that seems to reflect the
> thoughts of Solomon while the solo instrument expresses his words.

Figure 4. Bloch's photograph of Katherina Barjansky's statuette of King Solomon.
Ernest Bloch Archive, Center for Creative Photography, The University of
Arizona, used by permission.

The Introduction, which contains the germ of most of the essential motifs, laments the vanity of things—"Nothing is worth the pain it causes." "All is vanity;" but up until the violoncello cadenza it seems that this is a sentimental, almost physical reaction. At the cadenza, the pessimist philosophy is formulated and expressed in words. This beginning is evidently a soliloquy.

A new and very important motif appears in the violas and the atmosphere changes: although it remains impregnated with pessimism and sometimes with desperation, it seems now to depict the World, now the experiences of Life, as if a rhapsodist—Schelomo himself—recounts what has led him to his sad conclusions, to his hopeless pessimism. One hears the rhythms of lugubrious dances: are they symbolic of the passions? The rhapsodist seems to say: "I have tasted all of this, but all is vanity!"

The orchestra picks up the same theme, now more accented, richer, more tentative. One might say that the wives of Solomon, his concubines attempt to tear him away from his thoughts. The lascivious dance continues, and he seems to join in ; . . . Then, for the third time, the orchestra intones the theme. Here is all the royal pomp, the treasures, the riches, the power, the women, all that a man could desire on earth amidst the barbarous colors of an Oriental world. "I am the King! the entire earth belongs to me!"

And suddenly, revulsion: "Why is all this? Vanity!"

The rhapsodist continues his comments, more gently, but yet more desolately, and expressing without doubt the "Sehnsucht," the wounded and painful idealism of Schelomo, who dreams that "it would be possible if; . . . " The lascivious dance returns: Schelomo resists and the orchestra interrupts it. In this grand tutti there is the upheaval of the multicolored and barbarous world of that time. The comments, the rhapsodic motives also express Majesty, Power, Might, earthly Goods; and in a refulgent orchestral cadenza all of the splendors of Wealth appear.

Schelomo: "And this is all? Nothing! Nothing!"

There follows an episode that I cannot describe, for I myself would not know how to define it in words. It is a motive that my father often sang in Hebrew; I myself don't know the significance of the words. Is this strange motive of the bassoon, which much later assumes great importance and which I created completely, the call of the "muezzin"? Or are they the priests perhaps? I don't know. At first Schelomo seems to contradict them, then he joins in, but only externally, it seems, for soon, above the voices of the crowd—or are they prayers?—one hears his laments again. His agitation grows; a feverish anxiety attacks him. And there is another Tutti. Is this Schelomo? Or is this the crowd, the maddened people, who, now conscious of their misery and who, bewildered, hurl blasphemies against God? "Vanity of vanities, all is vanity! Nothing!" The tumult calms down, gradually recedes into the distance ; . . .

Schelomo remains alone and meditates. A grimace of bitter pain; then: "I have seen so many things, lived so much, seen the wasted effort, the triumph of wicked: I too knew hope like others; I have seen the vanity of things . . ." A desolate gesture: "All is Vanity."

The orchestra then seems to leave this world of Nothing and to fly far into a Dream: into a vision of a better world, an earthly world where peace, justice and love would reign . . . and Schelomo lets himself be carried by the dream; . . . But then he leaves it aside quickly. Veiled, obscure and far away are the splendors of the throne, of power—but like old spent gold pieces—ruins. And here Schelomo seems to think through the orchestra, while his voice, the solo cello, cries: "Ah! the World! Power! Wealth!" And again he agitates himself and utters his curses. The orchestra continues and seems to magnify his thought: but this time the cadenza is not more intense: it is a downfall, a wearing out that produces the tired, discouraged epilogue. With a sudden start, Schelomo rebels again; then he collapses in silence: "Vanity of Vanities, all is Nothingness!"

Almost all of my works, however dark, end with optimistic conclusions, or at least with a hope. This is the only one to end thus, with an absolute negation. The only passage of light and hope is the one I already pointed out, which comes after the meditation of Schelomo. Nor have I discovered its true meaning . . . only fifteen years after I wrote it ; . . . And I used this fragment to illustrate a page of my Hebrew Oratory, where the words express the hope, the ardent prayer that one day Men will at last recognize their brotherhood, and learn to live in harmony, in peace.[43]

The contrast Bloch posited in *Schelomo* between solo and orchestra is not simply a division of roles but also a conflict—similar to the one in *Jézabel*— between the physical and the spiritual, the Oriental sumptuousness of the external world (depicted by the orchestra) and the verbally expressive, spiritual inward voice of the solo instrument. But while in *Jézabel* Jehu's inward calling triumphs forcefully over Jezebel's sensuous temptation, in his agonizingly torn condition the hero of *Schelomo* can offer only bitter resignation. However effective this last, Don Quixotesque moment is in the music, it does not neutralize the luxurious sensuality of the score. Despite its putative secondary position in Bloch's description, the music depicting the Oriental atmosphere remains as characteristic of *Schelomo* as the one portraying the hero's magnificent effort to tear himself away from the lascivious dances.

The conceptual contrast set up in Bloch's program notes is already displayed in the introduction where the rhythmically free, descending theme of lamentation (with which the cello starts off the piece "very freely, like a cadenza") is juxtaposed with a rhythmically more regular passage, the sinuous melodic line and rhythm of which are reminiscent of Jezebel's sensuous dance (ex. 52). In fact, this first dance-inspired music in *Schelomo* might even be seen as an Orientalized version of one of Jehu's motives in the opera (ex. 53).

Despite the concertato interplay between cello and orchestra, their narrative roles are inseparable: solo and accompaniment share all the important themes Bloch listed in the program note. Even their contrasting materials are related. The two themes of the introduction, which express two sides of a single personality (one yielding to desperation, the other becoming lost in sensuous pleasures), have important musical characteristics in common. Descending minor seconds govern the melodic line in both, lending them

Example 52. Contrast in *Schelomo* between themes of lamentation and of dance.

a. Theme of lamentation, mm. 1–3.

b. Theme of dance, mm. 6–7.

Example 53. Motive associated with Jehu ("espressivo doloroso, Juif") (1911 and 1918).

a claustrophobically narrow range. The difference lies in their contour: while the first theme lacks interior repetition and descends to outline a dominant triad, the second theme, like Jezebel's music, lingers around the same notes, falling back on repetitions in a manner that recalls musical images of languid, sensuous Orientals.

Even the cadenza that Bloch identified most closely with the personal voice of the cello is related to a group of Oriental themes (ex. 54) that share musical features with the two themes of the introduction. As if the initial occurrence of the cadenza were the first time the cello formulated the pessimistic message of the piece, its melodic gestures suggest a desperate effort to give utterance to something significant. Repeating the initial motive, the solo cello climbs three octaves with an immense effort, only to fall back again to the low D from which it began (ex. 54e). Bloch uses this cadenza to interrupt the flow of the piece three times, as if he wanted to rebut the luxurious colors of the orchestra with this gesture of denial. He also placed it at

Example 54. "Oriental" motives in *Schelomo.*

a. Oriental motive in the viola, *con sord.,* mm. 16–17.

b. Oriental motive in the solo cello, mm. 25–27.

c. Oriental motive in the solo cello, mm. 31–35.

d. Oriental motive in the orchestra, mm. 55–56.

e. Oriental cello cadenza, mm. 13–15.

the end of the piece, where (à la Strauss's *Don Quixote*) it gives voice to a final resignation. Yet the strong motivic relationship between the cadenza and the Oriental group of themes in *Schelomo* makes it difficult to hear the cadenza as an expression of denial. The cello's musical vocabulary is of a piece with its surroundings. Instead of its purported separation from the orchestral material, it underscores the protagonist's unbreakable bond with his ostensibly rejected milieu.

The relationship between the solo instrument and the orchestra is, however, not always peaceful. A serious conflict breaks out when in the middle section the cello resists picking up the melody so persuasively presented by the orchestra (m. 144) and instead repeats the cadenza. When the melody of the cadenza appears for the third time, Bloch puts it in counterpoint against the orchestra's melody, which is now hammered out in barbarous fifths (ex. 55). This aggressive presentation of the orchestral theme forces the cello to yield and to repeat the orchestra's tune in an even faster tempo (m. 156).

Significantly, the orchestral theme first rejected and then accepted by the cello is a melody that Bloch claimed to have heard his father reciting in the mornings. Leaving tempting Freudian interpretations aside,[44] it is important to note that this melody is the only traditional Jewish theme in *Schelomo*, identified by Alexander Knapp as related to two cantorial extracts in the *magen avot* mode (ex. 56).[45] Both the quotation and its first refutation by the cello remained unexplained in Bloch's program. This is the only part of the piece that Bloch admitted he was not able (or willing) to "define in words."

Bloch's rare lack of explanation only enhances our interpretative curiosity. For the presence and, even more crucially, the transformation of the prayer melody into barbarous melodic fragments trigger hermeneutical questions. The words of the original tune and their meaning got lost in Bloch's memory; only the gesture of singing remained. Deprived of its verbal specificity, the traditional melody turns into a mechanical rhythmic figure that aggressively intrudes several times to impede the cello's gestures of expressive singing. At the climax of the piece the rhythmically tight variation of the Oriental theme of the introduction is interrupted by and then fused with a mechanical brass motive, contrived as a savage rendition of the prayer melody (ex. 57).

In addition to the traditional prayer melody, Bloch also quotes a motive from *Jézabel*, which he labeled "Passover" in the 1918 thematic index. Although it is related to the first motive of lamentation, the motive transcends sorrow, especially in its climactic manifestation (ex. 58). Its spacious opening fifths and melodic line, which after a short descent returns to its starting note, signal relief, a possibility to escape to a less tortured existence. This moment of hope reappears later in *Schelomo* in the form of another motive, marking, as Bloch put it in the program note, "a vision of a better world, an earthly world where peace, justice and love would reign" (ex. 59). As a welcome relief the

Example 55. Cello cadenza in counterpoint with the orchestra's melody in *Schelomo,* mm. 144–50.

Example 56. Prayer melody from two cantorial extracts ([a1] Blessed are You, O Lord our God, King of the universe; [a2] For You are God, the great and holy king) as related to the "prayer" motive in *Schelomo*, mm. 132–43 (b). (From Knapp, "The Jewishness of Bloch," 104.)

Example 57. The Oriental dance motive is interrupted by the barbarous variation of the traditional Jewish theme in *Schelomo*, mm. 228–33.

Example 58. Motive of Passover in *Jézabel* and in *Schelomo*.

a. Motive of Passover from the music of Sukkot in *Jézabel* (1918).

b. Climactic motive of lamentation in *Schelomo*, mm. 72–73.

c. Motive of Passover as it appears in *Schelomo*, mm. 80–82.

Example 59. The "vision of a better world" in *Schelomo*, mm. 292–96.

new theme finally presents melodic major seconds, which, for a moment, release the tension of intense chromaticism that saturates most of the score. This is the only theme in *Schelomo* that remains unaffected by its surroundings and does not undergo motivic transformation. Years later in the pages of the *Sacred Service* the same music stands for Bloch's longing for universal brotherhood, delivered to humanity (as Fleg predicted) by the Jews. In *Schelomo*, as in the *Sacred Service*, this longing remains a dream; Bloch did not even attempt to present it as anything more than a passing moment of illusion, the fleeting presence of which highlights rather than counterbalances the otherwise heavy Oriental atmosphere of the music of *Schelomo*. No other piece in Bloch's oeuvre shows so clearly that Bloch's idealized Jewish world was destined to remain an unrealized dream.

Since no sharp distinction is made in the music of *Schelomo* between the disillusioned, morally distraught hero and the barbarous Oriental milieu that torments him, Jews again became marked for Bloch's audience as Oriental "others," as alternately sensuous, barbarous, and miserable. Bloch's obsession with the barbarous was an aspect of his music that his reviewers often greeted with satisfaction because it cast the Jews thus portrayed into a comfortably distant time. While the Oriental colors that most forcefully connoted Jewish character to the audience distanced the Jews geographically by placing them East, the primitive, barbarous ostinati that govern the music of *Schelomo* located the Jews in a historically distant past, thus identifying them with the ancient Hebrews. It was a Romantic image, yet as Godet's vicious criticism shows, it coincided with many hackneyed anti-Semitic clichés of Jewishness. The coincidence of audience expectations and Bloch's assumptions about Jews—both conditioned by widely accepted social anti-Semitism—ensured Bloch's success.

Bloch himself might have been unaware of the difference in meaning that distinguished the music of *Jézabel* and of *Schelomo*. As his program note shows, he still seemed to be convinced that interior and exterior, hero and milieu, are as radically different in his music as Naboth's fervent spirituality was from Jezebel's nihilistic sensuality. Ironically enough, it was precisely the sonic representation of what in his program note Bloch called "the barbarous colors of an Oriental world" that made Bloch's music appealing to audiences with widely varying perceptions of Jews and "Jewish music." Even Saminsky embraced Bloch's *Schelomo* because, although in its "melancholy and contemplative parts" he heard the "slightly vulgar Orientalism" of the "Hebrew domestic melody," in its "superior passages" he recognized "the real Hebrew and ancient element," which Saminsky identified with "the old liturgical melody."[46] In *Schelomo*, instead of representing a struggle between the Biblical and the Oriental, Bloch achieved a combination of the two, which, as Downes later wrote, lent the music "the warmth, the melancholy, the sensuality, the prophetic fervor of Hebraic literature."[47] Trite and clichéd as Saminsky's and Downes's descriptions may sound, they signal a successful fusion of the two most commonly evoked Jewish stereotypes: that of the strong, "barbarous" ancient Hebrews of the Bible, and that of the Orientally colored, weak, and victimized Jews of the Diaspora.

· · ·

Bloch's emphasis on the barbarous and the Oriental confirmed, albeit involuntarily, the anti-Semitic conviction that Jews differ essentially from the main population, no matter where they reside. As Godet's essentialized image of the Jewish Bloch had led the composer to accept himself as different from his milieu, so Bloch's music ultimately reinforced an image of stereotyped Jewish difference. I stress the word "stereotyped" here, for although by the turn of the twenty-first century it has become fashionable to tolerate and even celebrate difference, history has taught us to fear the process of stereotyping that forces minority groups into rigid, essentialized identities, which are easily available for political manipulation.

It is striking to observe the extent to which the commonest "Jewish" clichés in music (all at one time or another participating in anti-Semitic stereotyping) corresponded with elements of Bloch's music. Although Bloch did not react directly to anti-Semitic criticism of his music (never consciously affirming as positive traits those attributes of his music that were ridiculed as "Jewish" by hostile critics), the anti-Semitic clichés of Jewish music can fit music such as *Schelomo* all too easily. The "characteristically Jewish" features Erich Müller enumerated in his 1932 "Das Judentum in der Musik" might be taken as describing *Schelomo:* erotic sensuousness (defined by Müller as a distinctive feature of the Jewish Minnesinger Süsskind von Trimberg); subjectivity (characterizing, according to Müller, Salomone Rossi's music); melodiousness, mosaic-like form, and sentimentality (for which he condemned Mendelssohn's music); the tempo changes freely indulged by Jewish performers; and the supposedly damaging introduction of quarter tones into Western music.[48] This is not to say that, despite anti-Semitic stereotyping, such features cannot be part of a legitimate Jewish style. Still, Bloch's initial refutation of these stereotypical features and his eventual yielding to many of the same conventions illustrate the difficulty of creating a musical representation of Jewishness that would be recognizable without recourse to stereotypes, including the most hackneyed and abusive ones.

Ultimately, it would be hard to deny that the clichés of Jewish music, as variously formulated by anti- or philo-Semites, helped popularize Bloch as the first and, in the words of his Italian apologist Guido Gatti, the only truly "creative" Jewish composer.[49] The ease with which Bloch slipped from his initial ideal of a universal Jewish music, as embodied in the aborted opera

*Jézabel,* to the commonly accepted clichés of the Jews is a perverse tribute to the insidious power of stereotypes. It was the novel remanipulation of these clichés, and not (as Godet would have argued) a hidden Jewish essence, that made Bloch's music, in Wagner's terms, both "creative" and "racially iden-tifiable." Bloch's absorption of these implicitly anti-Semitic stereotypes in his music demonstrates Hannah Arendt's theory that "in a society on the whole hostile to the Jews . . . it is possible to assimilate only by assimilating to anti-Semitism also."[50] Bloch's most overtly Jewish music was a manifestation of just such an assimilation.

## Chapter 5

# The Confines of Judaism and the Elusiveness of Universality

## The *Sacred Service*

*For 15 years in my studio there has been an immense Christ from the 16th century!!! I also have a Buddha who meditates in his own language on the same problems, and a Confucius, a Lao Tsé, who dominates the Jeremy of Michelangelo! And all under-stand each other because they come from the same, unique family! Here is my "Ju-daism"! It is all too natural that the Jews don't understand it at all.*
Bloch to Lucien Haudebert, 4 June 1924

*My children did not receive any religious education and our life is not Jewish. She [Suzanne] has simply lived in the atmosphere of my books, my Christ, my Buddha, a "Confucius" and Jeremy that I have around me—one religion! And my only religion!*
Bloch to Romain Rolland, 18 May 1925

Edmond Dantes, the narrator of Italo Calvino's short story "The Count of Monte Cristo," shares the fate of the story's original protagonist in Dumas's novel of the same title. Calvino's story of the Château d'If that imprisons Dantes is a parable of human existence. As Calvino puts it, the "fortress . . . grows around us, and the longer we remain shut in it the more it removes us from the outside." Paradoxically, by working out the possibilities for es-cape, Dantes is compelled to mentally construct the perfect fortress from which there would be no departure. If the real prison proves to be less per-fect than the conceived fortress, Dantes argues, this will be "a sign that here an opportunity of escape exists": he has only "to identify the point where the imagined fortress does not coincide with the real one and then find it."[1]

Calvino remains silent about the outcome of Dantes's experiment. Yet im-plied in the existential problem posed by his version of the story is that, un-like Dumas's hero who finally escapes, Calvino's protagonist remains trapped in the complex maze of his imagined prison. Calvino's main theme is not the fate of Edmond Dantes but the interchangeability of the real and the imaginary and, even more crucially, the dangerous potential of mental processes. The parable frightens in its proposal that intellectual constructions can confine one even more than almost perfectly built prisons. The trapped existence of Calvino's protagonist parallels Bloch's confinement in his intellectually constructed racial self-image. One can argue, as I have in chapter 3, that Bloch's racial self-definition was an attempt to escape constraining social prejudice. But as in Calvino's story, attempted escape fortified rather than weakened prison walls. Bloch's image of himself as a racially determined Jewish composer, though conceived as a refutation of Wagner's accusation that Jews are creatively impotent, ultimately remained true to Wagnerian principles. It accepted Wagner's first premise, namely, that art can be genuine only if based on an indefinable, mysterious racial essence.

Bloch's first years in the United States proved his racial theories immensely appealing and seemed to ensure a brilliant future for the composer. His success was short-lived, however, and the disappointment that followed left Bloch bitter for the rest of his life. Reality did not measure up to Bloch's hopes, and thus the composer, abandoning his lofty Jewish aspirations, turned to racially neutral projects. Yet audiences and critics insisted on keeping him in a Jewish ghetto. The debate, still ongoing, about the extent to which Bloch was a "Jewish" or a "universalistic" composer intensified as a response to Bloch's *Sacred Service*. Paradoxically, it was the *Sacred Service*, the only composition Bloch wrote to a Jewish liturgical text, that represented most intensely the composer's aspirations to universality. But this universalistic aspect of the *Sacred Service* triggered rather than silenced race-inspired criticism of Bloch's music. Considered by both Jews and non-Jews as deeply flawed for what was seen as a diluted racial expression, the *Sacred Service* demonstrated that however scientifically untenable, race remained a strong enough cultural factor to hinder Bloch's universal claims.

### THE PROMISED LAND

The failure of Maud Allan's dance group, with which Bloch arrived in the United States in 1916, bitterly disappointed Bloch, who had hoped that he would be able to establish himself in the New World. Unknown and penniless, Bloch contacted people in the artistic world of New York to whom he had been introduced by Romain Rolland. Through Rolland he met the young writer Waldo Frank (1889–1967), founder and associate editor of the *Seven Arts* (1916–17), a short-lived art journal that expressed a novel nationalist spirit awakened by World War I.

In a 1917 editorial James Oppenheim, vice president and editor of the journal, expressed the country's need to become "a great nation." The fires of the Great War, Oppenheim wrote, "show us to be thin silhouettes moving about without real purposes and meanings." Americans should fight against

commercialism, the "ennui of a colorless social life," and should find a unifying experience not in religion, social upheavals, or common heritage but
in the idea of nation. Most important for the contributing artists of the *Seven
Arts* was the conviction that this new national experience was to be created
through art, for, as Oppenheim argued, a "nation finds itself when it creates
a great book, a great architecture, a great music."[2]

Since Frank believed that the "kinship of the Puritan and the Jew, as they
appear on the American scene, is close,"[3] Bloch was welcomed into the nationally inspired group of artists associated with the *Seven Arts*. Bloch's contribution to the March issue of the first volume (1917), "Man and Music,"
fit the group's anticommercialist and anticosmopolitan stance. Bloch saw the
problem of contemporaneous art as consisting in burgeoning industrialism
and "acute intellectualism," the consequence of which he registered as the
"schism between life and art." Bloch's solution was simple. Art "must have
its roots deep within the soil that brings it forth," he declared. "Needless to
say," he added, art "cannot be the direct output of crowds, but however indirectly, they must have contributed to its substance." Bloch's definition of
art was a combination of racial theories and Romantic notions of the genius:
"A work of art is the soul of a race speaking through the voice of the prophet
in whom it has become incarnate," he claimed. "Art is the outlet of the mystical, emotional need of the human spirit." To reach the soul of the race,
Bloch wrote, art should be "created rather by instinct than by intelligence;
rather by intuition than by will." Bloch's emphasis on the intuitive side of
artistic creation was a Romantic bromide. His replacement of the social concept of nation with that of the biological category of race as the mandatory
basis of musical composition was not entirely new either, yet it represented
a new pervasiveness of racial concepts in art.

During the war Bloch felt justified in his conviction that the arts that aimed
increasingly to achieve "individualistic, non-representative and non-racial expression" were incapable of reacting to the "tragic upheaval" of the war, a
failure that Bloch believed contributed to the loss of music's communal role.
"Music was no longer the emanation of a race and a people, a spontaneous
birth out of life," he argued. "It was a music of musicians."[4] There is some
truth to Bloch's analysis of the artistic tendencies of the war period. Yet his
proposition that *l'art pour l'art* music should be replaced with the communal expression of racial art was too close to racialist propaganda to provide
a liberating solution.

Bloch had been introduced to readers of the *Seven Arts* in February by
critic Paul Rosenfeld (1890–1946). One of the first propagators of modernism in America, Rosenfeld was cofounder of the journal.[5] At the time a
private student of Bloch's, he had first-hand information about the composer.
In the spirit of the journal's nationalist orientation, Rosenfeld presented

Bloch's music in racial terms, describing it as "a large, a poignant, an authentic expression of what is racial in the Jew." Echoing the composer's own theories, Rosenfeld distinguished between the "theatric orientalism of Rimsky-Korsakov and Balakirev" and the "barbaric and ritual" sound of Bloch's music, the former producing a merely coloristic effect, the latter resulting in the authentic expression of the race. For Rosenfeld the essence of this Jewish musical expression was based on "the harsh and haughty accents of the Hebrew tongue" and on the "abrupt and passionate gestures of the Hebrew soul."[6] The fact that Bloch himself did not speak Hebrew would hardly have fazed Rosenfeld.[7] Like many others he assumed that race contained an essence deeper and more constant than language, "an element that has remained unchanged throughout all the ages, an element that is in every Jew, an element by which every Jew must know himself and his descent."[8]

Rosenfeld's presentation of Bloch as a Jewish composer again raised the specter of Wagner's theory about the creative impotence of Jewish composers. And again, the enthusiastic publicity surrounding Bloch seemed to confirm all of Wagner's assumptions. Even the ethnically Jewish Rosenfeld corroborated Wagner's anti-Jewish judgment. For him Bloch's success proved Wagner's point. Next to the achievement of Bloch, "who has opened himself to the genius of his race," the works of Meyerbeer, Mendelssohn, Rubinstein, and Karl Goldmark—composers "who have hitherto represented 'Judaism in Music,'"—seemed "futile" and "barren" to Rosenfeld: "After all, Wagner's stricture was just. . . . They had but to face themselves. They had but to say: 'We are what we have ever been,' and the way to freedom, and certitude, and self-possession would have been theirs. A mighty ore lay buried within them. They could have refined it. But they turned shamedly [sic] away, and donned their flimsy masquerades to hide it further. They wanted courage and humility. And so they arrived at nothing. The lordly gold that lay concealed within the race was not for them." Expressions like "flimsy masquerade," which could have been borrowed from Wagner, and "lordly gold," a modest version of Saminsky's "golden wheat of racial creation," demonstrate not only Rosenfeld's flaccid and vacuous style, but also the omnipresence of clichés about Jewish musicians in the musical writings of the time.[9]

Rosenfeld closed his essay by asserting that in Bloch's music "the ancient spirit had attained rebirth" because Bloch, unlike other Jewish composers before him, did not "inhibit any portion of his impulse," and thus revealed his racial heritage in his compositions. Later critics echoed Rosenfeld's views, pointing at Bloch as "a living refutation of the anti-Semitic assertion that the Jew is never creative, never anything more than a brilliant and flexible imitator."[10] Being situated in a Wagnerian context worked initially to Bloch's advantage. The constant reference to Wagner in the early reviews of Bloch's music was symptomatic of critics' effort to market the Jewish Bloch to a gentile audience.

## A JEWISH COMPOSER FOR GENTILES

Thanks to critics' enthusiastic embrace of Bloch's Jewish cause, within a year Bloch became accepted as the epitome of a Jewish composer. "They start to publish articles and studies about me almost everywhere, placing me very high and boldly declaring me the first great Jewish composer," Bloch wrote proudly to his mother in February 1918. "A rabbi visited me, and cantors, delighted to see finally a Jewish artist who does not hide his race but affirms it publicly with honor! This is an unprecedented fact," Bloch added. "Here where many artists are Jewish, but try . . . to apologize for it!"[11]

Despite his delight in being praised by cantors and rabbis, Bloch seems to have been more eager to please his gentile audience. Both his frequent sanctioning of anti-Semitic clichés in music and his often repeated statements about his detachment from existing Jewish musical styles served to ease his relationship with an audience unfamiliar with Jewish music and suspicious of Jewish composers. Bloch went even further than Rosenfeld in his willing affirmation of Wagner's anti-Semitic assumptions about Jewish music and Jewish musicians. In an interview with Siegmund Spaeth in April 1917, Bloch publicly endorsed Wagner's assertion about Jews' lack of creative potential:

> The Jewish people have always been remarkable for their faculty of assimilation. . . . Is it not after all the mechanical side of music that finds its greatest exponent in the Jew? He is by nature a materialist, and in this age of commercialism, when the interpreter is hysterically glorified beyond the composer (a sure sign of artistic decadence, by the way), he naturally takes the quickest and easiest way to fame and fortune.
>
> Some of the best writers of ragtime are Jews. But their creative work is a trick, or a spontaneous expression of self. Your Jew is a wonderful psychologist and a wonderful imitator. He can be more Parisian than a real Parisian and more German than a real German. And because he has always been willing to ape that which is popular, he has produced no characteristic secular music of his own.

Echoing Rosenfeld, Bloch portrayed himself as the exception. He composed "sincerely and from the heart." The result showed "strongly Jewish characteristics" despite the fact that he had "not written consciously as a Jew, but only as a human being."[12]

Bloch's self-aggrandizement was sincere. He was convinced that he was the only Jewish composer worthy of the name. He even deprecated Mahler (whom he otherwise admired) because, like so many others, he had also failed to proclaim his Jewish self in his art:

> I think the principal reason that Jewish composers have never as yet attained the first rank in musical composition is that, consciously or unconsciously, through fear or a lack of self-knowledge, they failed to proclaim themselves in their art.

> I think the great shortcoming of Mahler as a composer was that he failed
> to realize this. So he built with idioms that were outworn and inadequate to
> the things he wished to say and the manner in which he would have said them.
> If, in his restless searching for "the word" he could have linked himself to the
> genius of his race, what might he not have accomplished? As it is, we listen to
> Mahler's great symphonies that tower so high, and aspire so much higher, and
> realize with sorrow that for all their spirituality their musical material is too
> conventional, too certain to crumble with the passage of time.[13]

Wagnerian as Bloch's judgment on Jewish composers sounds, his proposed
solution shows that, like Rosenfeld, he also misread Wagner's stricture when
he assumed that the curse of creative impotence could be lifted from the
Jewish composer if he turned to his own race for inspiration. Synagogue
music, in Wagner's judgment, was "the travesty of a divine service of song,"
a "sense-and-sound-confounding gurgle, jodel and cackle." What for other
nations was a "genuine fount of Life amid the Folk," for Jews was only the
"mirror" of "intellectual efforts." Only if the Jewish composer would find
the "instinctive" and not the "reflected," which Wagner indicated was contrary to the Jews' artificial, intellectual disposition, would his art gain genuine racial quality.[14] What Wagner offered the Jews was no solution, then,
but a dead end.

Avoiding the complex problem of sources, Bloch made sure that his music could not be easily associated with any specific type of Jewish music. He
frequently emphasized the abstract nature of his Jewish inspiration, as if knowing that his vague references to the presence of a Jewish essence in his music
could assure his Jewish status more effectively than relying on traditional Jewish music. Vagueness also helped critics with no knowledge of traditional
Jewish music to assess Bloch's Jewish inspiration. The first notice on Bloch's
Jewish style by his American apologist Olin Downes (1886–1955), at that
time music critic of the *Boston Post,* was based on an interview with Bloch.
"[I] found it extraordinary," Bloch wrote to Downes after reading his review
in the *Post,* "that you were able, without knowing one note of my music, to
relate it so exactly and in so striking a manner after our short interview."[15]
Downes's example demonstrates the extent to which critics relied on Bloch's
earnest self-description rather than on his music.

Downes inspired Bloch to formulate his ideas about the influence of race
in composition. In their second interview Bloch carefully separated nationalism and what he called "racial consciousness" in music ("Nationalism is not
essential in music, but I think that racial consciousness is"). His own racial
expression, Bloch was at great pains to emphasize, did not come from the
use of Jewish folk melodies, which, he found, "on some occasions limits and
constrains a composer instead of inspiring him to write more freely and personally than would otherwise be the case." Racial quality "is not only in folk
themes," Bloch explained to Downes,

it is in myself! If not folk-themes, you might ask, then what would be the signs of Jewish music? Well, I admit that scientific analysis of what constitutes the racial element in music is difficult. But it would be unscientific to deny the existence of such elements. Racial feeling is certainly a quality of all great music, which must be an essential expression of the people as well as the individual. Does any man think he is only himself? Far from it. He is thousands of his ancestors. If he writes as he feels, no matter how exceptional his point of view, his expression will be basically that of his forefathers.[16]

Proclaiming "thousands of his ancestors" as an integral part of his own individuality, Bloch could create racially determined music without relying on the traditional music of his forefathers. The Jewish quality, he announced, "must be the mind, the emotion, the inner part" of his music.[17] In anticipated self-defense Bloch warned that Jews "learned in their lore" might not recognize this Jewish quality of his music. Emphasizing his detachment from previous conceptions of Jewish music he declared: "It is my conception of Jewish music, *my* interpretation, and because I felt it deep within me clamoring for release, I expressed it. Artistic affiliations I have none, I hope."[18] Expressing the "Hebrew spirit" left Bloch free in terms of musical specifics:

I do not propose or desire to attempt a reconstruction of the music of the Jews, and to base my works on melodies more or less authentic. I am no archeologist. I believe that the most important thing is to write good and sincere music—*my own music.* It is rather the Hebrew spirit that interests me—the complex, ardent, agitated soul that vibrates for me in the Bible; the vigor and ingenuousness of the Patriarchs, the violence that finds expression in the books of the Prophets, the burning love of justice, the desperation of the preachers of Jerusalem, the sorrow and grandeur of the book of Job, the sensuality of the Song of Songs. All this is in us, all this is in me, and is the better part of me. This is what I seek to feel within me and to translate in my music—the sacred race-emotion that lies dormant in our souls.[19]

Bloch believed in the moral obligation to express one's own race in music; in the possibility of presenting race without specific reference to traditional music; in the spiritual force of such an expression; and in the individuality of the composer who let his forefathers' ancient voice permeate his own personal idiom.

## "AGGRESSIVE JEWISHNESS"

Bloch's views were widely publicized, and thus discussion of his racially inspired compositional style soon occupied a large portion of the reviews of his music. German conductor Karl Muck's initial unwillingness to perform the *Three Jewish Poems* in Boston unless the composer changed the title enabled Bloch to again obscure the line between personal and racial expression: "Dr. M[uck] you speak exactly like my Jewish friends, who advised me to change the title for obvious reasons," Bloch supposedly responded to Muck. "My music is not as much Jewish," he then declared, "as it is Ernest Bloch's expression. But as long as there are prejudices against the Jews, I will not put my flag in my pocket, and the title shall remain." Bloch's open embrace of his Jewishness, so the story goes, converted Muck to his cause. "Dr. Muck came over [to] me, shook hands, saying: 'If there were more Jews like you, there would be less anti-Semitism. I will fight *myself* for this title if necessary!'"[20] Suggesting that it was the Jews' behavior and not social prejudice that produced anti-Semitism, Bloch unintentionally confirmed anti-Semitic arguments. Yet as a letter to his wife demonstrates, he was not deceived by Muck's favorable response: "Muck performed on 17 February. I will return to hunt him down, this old humbug; he will certainly play my work, but one has to create trouble for him. Did I tell you that in Boston I played a piano on which the autographed photos of the Kaiser, of that pig Ferdinand of Bulgaria and of Bethmann-Hollweg sit as if on a throne . . . from the time when the Pangermanist Muck was in Berlin? . . . That fierce anti-Semite, nourished in Bayreuth, was happy, I believe, to see how my *aggressive Jewishness* confronted him."[21]

Muck's anti-Semitism did not hurt Bloch. Neither did Bloch's "aggressive Jewishness" harm the American reception of his works. On 24 March 1917 the Boston Symphony premiered the *Three Jewish Poems* with Bloch conducting. The headline for Henry Taylor Parker's review in the *Boston Evening Transcript* reads: "Strange and Signal Music of Ernest Bloch—Three Jewish Poems That Evoke a Composer of Remarkable Idiom and Procedure, Invention, Imagination and Power—Pieces of a Stinging Vehemence."[22] No less enthusiasm characterized Olin Downes's review in the *Boston Post,* in which Downes, like Rosenfeld before him, celebrated Bloch's inwardly inspired Oriental style. Bloch's Orientalism, Downes wrote, "comes from the inside out, rather than from outside in. The composer has not found these rich and fascinating idioms because of a deliberate search for that which would be externally indicative of his quest, but because such forms of expression were forced into existence by the driving power of his own emotions and ideas, and by the birth-right inherited from his forefathers."[23]

As these reviews show, the Oriental flavor as well as the "passionate intensity," now considered characteristic of Hebraic expression, were not only acceptable in a Jewish composer but welcomed as an appealing novelty. The openly Jewish title *(Three Jewish Poems)* contributed to the positive reception in no small degree. Soon more pieces from Bloch's "Jewish cycle" were programmed. On 3 May 1917 the Society of Friends of Music featured a whole concert of the composer's Jewish music at Carnegie Hall. The concert that took place thanks to the enthusiastic support of the president of the society, J. F. D. Lanier, was one of Bloch's greatest triumphs. Moved almost to tears he wrote to his mother:

They really understand me! They understand the message that I want to deliver to the entire Humanity through music! They understand that it is a brother who addresses his brothers and wants to seek to unite them with a bit of love and faith, that deep down I am a priest in my own way and my art is a religion. Many people cried! And many told me that I helped them live! And what is amazing that I myself was moved . . . it did not seem to me that I am the author of these works, but that I am a small instrument that served to make them. *And this is the only truth in art.*[24]

After the Carnegie Hall concert Bloch was called upon to write more program notes and give more interviews, in short, to propagate his racial aesthetic principles. His commentary captured the imagination of the critics. A few titles of the reviews of the Carnegie Hall concert demonstrate the effect of Bloch's racial rhetoric: "Ernest Bloch Experiment in the Music of Jewry" *(New York Times)*; "Unique Music by Ernest Bloch Receives Notable Exposition (Music of Great Power and Sincerity Designed as an Expression of the Jewish Race)" *(Musical America)*; "Jewish Music Played in Modern Style at Concert" *(New York Herald)*; "Jewish Music Concert Arouses Enthusiasm" *(World)*; "Music and Drama: Jewish Music Up to Date" *(Evening Post)*; "Music of Ernest Bloch Is Splendid Expression of Jewish Idealism" *(Call)*. Although some reviewers complained about the "sameness of mood," and the "virtual identity of emotional direction and intent,"[25] popular success was unquestionable.

In no more than a year the idea that Bloch's music expressed his racial heritage had become a solid foundation for what promised to be a great career. As Bloch's daughter, Suzanne, remembered, "Bloch's rhapsodic statements about his music were printed everywhere, and unfortunately created the impression that he specialized only in Hebraic music." According to Suzanne, "Bloch did not foresee these misconceptions until after his return from Europe with his family to settle in New York in the fall of 1917."[26] Resentment about critics' "misconceptions," however, came only later. Bloch's initial statements show how deeply he believed that his much-publicized Jewish expression would indeed liberate rather than constrain him.

REALITY CHECK

In his first years in the New World Bloch truly believed that he had found artistic freedom, success, and more. In New York, for the first time in his life, he came into contact with a Jewish community that seemed to be close to his ideals of ancient traditions combined with religious sincerity. Soon after his arrival in the city he visited the Jewish ghetto on New York's Lower East Side: "What savour! What activity, also!" he exclaimed in his report to Fleg. "All of the billboards were written in *Hebrew letters,* everywhere. And this jargon, and these types! And what noise! Ah! They don't have 'cold blood' there." The exotic scene appealed to Bloch's Romantic imagination: "Here a fellow with his hands behind his back, long frock-coat; yellow hat, long beard; familiar gestures! They are like family! Here an old woman who could be *my* aunt or *yours*. I am moved by the children whose eyes are both lively and profound. And the old men! What gazes! If I hadn't been so sick to my stomach—their icy water is terrible—I would have bought some sausages (kosher) or smoked meat."

He was, nevertheless, confused. "I could not go there again," he confessed to Fleg. "I had such mixed impressions. What sadness and what disgrace at times. A lot of these people are complete strangers to us. Others very close."[27] Like his mother whom in 1920 Bloch took to the ghetto "where a million of Russian, Polish, Romanian and Oriental Jews swarmed," he felt a stranger among these Jews.[28]

In April 1918 Rosenfeld introduced Bloch to Judah Leon Magnes (1877–1948), a Reform rabbi active in Jewish culture and politics. In the spring of 1918 Magnes took Bloch to a Hasidic Passover service. Bloch's experience there was so far removed from his childhood memories of Geneva that Judaism finally became part of his spiritual fantasy. The three hours he spent amid the Hasidim he counted as one of his most profound religious experiences. (The other experiences were the singing of Benedictine nuns in a Paris church, the dance of Hopi Indians in New Mexico, a funeral service in Châtel, and a synagogue performance of his *Sacred Service* in Paris.)[29] The poverty of the Hasidic Jews, the intense religious life that permeated their everyday existence, their fanaticism and joy, the sense of community that still allowed individual expressions of worship, and the feeling of participating in something truly ancient, even timeless, touched Bloch deeply. "How far we are from all this!" he wrote to Fleg. "Here, this is the nomad, primitive tribe, the desert, the orient, three thousand years ago!" The music that accompanied the Passover service had an "extraordinary effect" on Bloch:

> There are short melodies that are repeated to the point of dizziness; then the painful cantillations that come from so far away; afterwards other songs, rugged like the rocks of Sinai. These are probably the most striking. *Songs* borrowed from here and there throughout the ages. Here is Spain, without doubt. Everybody plays his part. One hears guitars, castanets. People strike the tables, murmur the "tra la la dzing and the brrr" and above that others sing real Spanish dances! Then there is Turkey! Arabia! Poland! Greece also, with its modes, and Russia too. And modern times, represented by the most vulgar street songs, aggravated, orientalized, Judaized, *wildly* frenetic, a round of joy, which is naive and barbaric. Strange that everything that seems to me inevitably Jewish is sad and melancholic or harsh. The songs of joy are almost always borrowed.[30]

He even tried to transcribe a short melody that the rebbe recited and the community repeated endlessly with its variants:

In front of the "Saint of Saints" the officiating ministers, rising their tallithim about their heads and covering almost their entire face . . . sang a short melody, and repeated it about a hundred times; all the community joined in. A transcription can never render the impression of the incredible *tumult* of fifty or sixty simultaneous variants that infringed on each other. The intervals did not correspond to those of our scale either.

* quarter tone

Suddenly a *solo voice* burst out in this strange symphony, with very different notes, fast, with no connection to the rest, a sort of formidable incantation, as if they wanted to scare the old Jehovah into showing himself. Moreover, there was some unnamable intimacy with the old Eternal Father, a tête à tête, almost a dialogue. . . . I don't think that any religion permits such an intimacy, such audacity in the address of their God.[31]

Inspiring as this experience was for Bloch, however, he also realized how far removed he was from that community. These were not the ancient Jews from Biblical times whose music Bloch believed he could capture through listening to an inner voice. After leaving the Hasidic Jews, Bloch admitted that his music was "quite small" compared to what he had heard.[32]

Despite this momentary sense of humility in the face of traditional Hasidic music, Bloch felt he had a better chance of succeeding as a Jewish than as a Swiss composer. His new friends encouraged his hopes. Conductor Kurt Schindler (1882–1935), who, like Bloch, was "obsessed" with his race, promised to find people who could finance Bloch's project of living in the ghetto "for two or three months and work on [his] Hebrew with an old rabbi."[33] Schindler played Russian Jewish songs for Bloch and encouraged Bloch's search for Jewish melodies in the New York Public Library. Bloch bought recordings of cantor Joseph Rosenblatt (1880–1933), whose voice contained, the composer said, "all the distress, hope and faith of Israel." "How I would like to write a piece, a psalm for this admirable man," Bloch wrote enthusiastically to Fleg.[34]

To further Bloch's promotion of Fleg's work, Magnes introduced Bloch to Yiddish dramatist and novelist David Pinsky (1872–1959). Like his visit to the Hasidic service, the evening with the Pinskys made Bloch see the contrast between his ideals and his "compromised and rotten" life. "It is hard to repress the voice brooding in me and telling me to send everything to hell, and to isolate myself for ever and write my oeuvre," he wrote to Fleg after his visit.[35]

Even more disturbing for Bloch was a 1919 concert organized under the patronage of the American Zionist Association for the erection of a "Temple of Arts" in Jerusalem. "The said concert was a farce of the worst taste," Bloch wrote to Fleg. The performers were graduates of the St. Petersburg Conservatory and members of the chamber ensemble "Zimro" (Song), which clarinetist Simeon Bellison (1883–1953) founded in 1918.[36] They played arrangements of Jewish folk music, probably many by OYNM composers. Bloch's reaction to this music sharply contradicts assumptions about his spiritual or stylistic association with the Russian Jewish composers.[37] "This was neither music, nor Jewish, nor Jewish music!" Bloch protested. "Or if this is Jewish music, oh well, all the worse! A series of plagiarisms, badly digested, badly assimilated, half Russian, half Rumanian, half Gypsy . . . a bickering orientalism!" Bloch was "disgusted" and thought the concert was "anti-Semitic" because it presented music that, he wrote to Fleg, gave "Chamberlain reason a hundredfold" to despise Jews. Bloch was especially discouraged to see that "the Jewish masses that fill Carnegie Hall appreciate this! Once more I am convinced," he exclaimed, "that only the elite counts, among all peoples, all races."[38]

It is hard to say what dragged Bloch further and further away from his original grandiose plans concerning Jewish music. Disappointment in the lack of support from the "rich Jews," a complaint Bloch often repeated in his correspondence, was unquestionably an important factor. His failure to recruit New York's Jewish financial elite to sponsor his work heightened his suspicions about the Jewish reception of his music. Contrary to Schindler's and Bloch's hopes, the main proponents of his Jewish music remained non-Jews like Lanier, Downes, and Muck. Reporting to Romain Rolland about his Carnegie Hall concert and the support of Mrs. Lanier, Bloch bitterly wrote: "Of course she is not Jewish: the Jews here—the rich ones—are skeptical and reserved about me! *As I've always foreseen!*"[39] His meetings with wealthy Jews only reinforced his misgivings. During an "ultra-fancy" dinner at the Laniers Bloch met philanthropist Felix Warburg and his wife who, Bloch reported, "have millions and millions!" and who, Bloch realized, were unsympathetic to his music. "It seems to me that the Warburgs did not understand it at all, despite their compliments; no doubt it is too Jewish for them. They don't like it when one reminds them of that!" Only non-Jews (mainly women) were enthusiastic: "Mrs. Bodanzky and Mrs. Stokowski were agitated. And after the smart set left at midnight, Mrs. Lanier and Mrs. Stokowski asked me again to play my music for them."[40]

The lack of wealthy Jews' support left such a sour taste in Bloch's mouth that as late as 1954 he still became enraged when he recalled his disappointment:

In New York in 1917 the eminent *Jews* refused Dr. *Schiller,* husband of Yvette Guilbert, who knew that I was in a distressing situation and hopeless, and *wrote to them.* Two of their great good men refused to take even the slightest interest in a "Suisse in need"—I have their letters! One of them, son of a *multimillionaire* from Lengnau whom my father saved several times from dying of hunger!! It is only after my *success* that I achieved through my music and with the support of *Mrs. Lanier* and the *Friends of Music* (non-Jews!) that the Jews— at least some of them—boasted of me.[41]

## TESTING THE LIMITS

Gradually Bloch turned away from his grandiose Jewish projects and from establishing himself as an exclusively Jewish composer. In addition to his disappointment at the willingness of Jews to finance his enterprise was perhaps also the realization that his artistic goals were indeed more universal than he had initially presented them in the United States. Whatever the cause, Bloch increasingly began to emphasize the universal side of his artistic mission, which, while it had always been present behind his idea of a specifically Jewish musical idiom, had been less prominent during his first successful years in America.

The first piece Bloch wrote after the "Jewish Cycle" was the Suite for Viola and Piano (1919). It was decidedly non-Jewish in character. It is "probably Far-East," Bloch wrote to Fleg after its completion, and "certainly by the good Ernest Bloch."[42] Although Bloch won the Coolidge Prize with it, critical reception of its orchestral version, premiered by the National Symphony Orchestra under Artur Bodanzky on 5 November 1920, was poor. Bloch wrote to his mother disappointedly about the "strange impression" the piece produced. "Criticism was furious, terrible, violent, insulting!!!" Bloch complained. "The public was cold, smiling, hostile; some more enthusiastic than ever; they argued, they almost insulted each other!"[43]

H. E. Krehbiel, who had previously greeted Bloch's Jewish works with such enthusiasm, was now openly hostile. The piercing cries reminded him of "a Chinese clarinet" or "a pig under a gate." The piece, he wrote, "begins with the hanging of Till Eulenspiegel in the Orient, and ends with a movement which . . . is a riot of cacophonous colors—lurid, pitiless, penetrating, nerve-rasping—scraped off the palette of Stravinsky." Since Krehbiel insisted that, contrary to Bloch's statement that the suite did "not belong to his so-called 'Jewish works,'" there were "spots in it suggestive of 'a certain Jewish inspiration,'" his antimodernist rhetoric also resonates with Wagner's description of the defective speech of the Jews. "There is scarcely a moment in which the instruments speak the language native to them," Krehbiel characterized Bloch's orchestration. "Every brass instrument has a plug thrust down its throat and croaks, whines, wheezes, gibbers, cackles and cachinnates in musical polyglot." "We are told that there are Chinese Jews," Krehbiel concluded his hostile review, "but we hope that Mr. Bloch did not think them capable of making music like his or suggesting any of its elements.

The worst we can think of them is that they might appreciate the grotesqueness of his last movement."[44]

Krehbiel's hostile criticism of the universal Bloch was not unique. But what consisted initially of a few anti-Semitic remarks by some of Bloch's critics[45] turned into a blatant anti-Semitic attack when Bloch's *America*, an "Epic Rhapsody" for chorus and orchestra, won first prize in a competition sponsored by *Musical America*. The prize, announced in June 1928, earned Bloch simultaneous performances with the most important orchestras in the United States.[46] This was the greatest triumph in Bloch's career. Critical reception, however, was not unanimously enthusiastic. While Americans applauded when Bloch declared that his Jewish works expressed the Hebrew soul, they felt much less comfortable with the idea that Bloch's *America* reflected the spirit of the American nation. The concluding hymn, conceived by Bloch as a new national anthem, was dismissed as commonplace. The whole composition, so self-consciously unified by foreshadowings of the hymn, was criticized for "doubtful cohesion and unity" and for "ranging from the sublime to the ignoble."[47] Disappointed with the work's racial neutrality, Downes called *America* "second-class Bloch and superficial" in comparison with Bloch's Jewish works that Downes claimed "stem equally from his own creative essence and that of his race." Paul Rosenfeld's opinion was just as dismissive. For him, "the prophetic gesture of *America* was pretty thoroughly belied by the slackness of its aesthetic quality." In other words, Bloch's "elaborately manufactured Americanism"[48] was considered unconvincing in large part because it was seen as inauthentic.

No doubt offended national pride had an important role in the inimical critical reception of Bloch's prize-winning *America*. But Bloch's status as a racially defined composer was equally responsible for the mixed reception of the work. In a 1947 essay on Bloch, Dika Newlin explained the failure of Bloch's noble intent in *America* on the basis of Bloch's own statements. In *America*, Newlin argued, Bloch was unfaithful to his own principles by trying to reconstruct the music of a nation, in other words by becoming an "archeologist." His style succumbed to "specific citations, which are meant to illustrate specific life-situations."[49] Specificity, especially regarding another "race" than his own, was not acceptable from the composer of the Jewish racial spirit. A work intended to be nationalistic with respect to an actual country could not free Bloch of the Jewish label.

In fact, just the opposite occurred. The label proved to be not only eradicable, but also damaging. Discussing the harmful effects of Jewish influence on American music, composer and critic Daniel Gregory Mason (1873–1953) communicated most clearly the anti-Semitic sentiment spurred by the success of Bloch's *America*. Bloch, Mason wrote, who had been "long the chief minister of that [Jewish] intoxication to our public, capped his dealing with us by the grim jest of presenting to us a long, brilliant, megalomaniac, and," Mason added maliciously, "thoroughly Jewish symphony." Here and elsewhere Mason pressed the point that his warning had nothing to do with anti-Semitism, for he did not want to judge "the intrinsic value of the Jewish element in American art in general."[50] Yet Mason was ready to exclude Bloch from American music the moment Bloch dared break out of his self-constructed, but nevertheless constraining Jewish idiom.

As Mason pointed out in 1930, he had already warned American musicians ten years earlier against "the insidiousness of the Jewish menace to our artistic integrity," which, according to Mason, was attractive because of "the speciousness, the superficial charm and persuasiveness of Hebrew art, its violently juxtaposed extremes of passion, its poignant eroticism and pessimism." The description, as expected, fits Bloch's overpublicized Jewish works. In this recollection of his 1920 prophecy Mason failed to mention that he did not mind this "extreme passion" and "poignant eroticism" as long as it was safely confined to "Jewish music." He acknowledged the superiority and sincerity of Bloch's earlier Jewish works, especially in comparison to, as he wrote, the "pompous rhodomontade of Bloch's *America*."[51]

Bloch "the Jew" did not seem to disturb Mason, but Bloch "the American patriot" did. He criticized *America* not on the basis of the work's artistic qualities or persuasiveness (with which critics might find fault regardless of the composer's nationality or ethnicity), but on the basis of racial prejudice, which excluded Bloch from American musical culture. This exclusion is demonstrated in John Tasker Howard's 1946 book *Our American Music*, in which the author felt he needed to justify Bloch's presence in the volume: "If for no other motive than hospitality," he wrote, "we may place [Bloch] here at the end of this chapter, separate from our other composers, and the reader may choose whether or not he will call him an American."[52] Howard's ambiguous attitude toward Bloch was widespread. Just as Mason refused to accept Bloch's more universal aspirations, let alone his claims of Americanness, so too enthusiasts of Bloch's racially expressive style were reluctant to change their perspective on the composer. With the firm approval of Saminsky, American critic William James Henderson (1855–1937) stated that the "creations of Jewish musicians in this country are Jewish music." To drive his point home he added: "Even Ernest Bloch's *America* sat down by the waters of Babylon."[53]

Bloch tried in vain to gain universal acceptance not only for *America* but also for his earlier Jewish pieces. *America*, Bloch insisted, "is not different in its impulse and necessity from all I have done. It is part of my *Weltanschauung*—only the form and cadre [frame] are different." That *America* was "not different" from Bloch's Jewish works was readily accepted, but the continuation of Bloch's explanation, namely, that in *America* he tried to "give a message of hope and faith" to "poor struggling humanity" in "America's own language," was carefully ignored by many. In *America*, Bloch declared, he acted "no more [as] a Jew (though all my Jewish works are written rather by a man with Jewish roots than by a limited Hebrew), but as a man alone."[54]

David Ewen (1907–85), who championed Bloch's ideas about race-conscious music in a monograph on Jewish music,[55] willingly repeated Mason's ideas about the eternally Jewish qualities of Bloch's music in his entry on Bloch in *The Universal Jewish Encyclopedia.* Describing works such as *America, Helvetia* (1928), *Evocations* (1938), the Violin Concerto (1938), and the Piano Quintet (1923), Ewen boldly stated:

> In many of these works, Bloch may seem to have digressed from his Hebraic path. . . . And yet, even in these works, Bloch remains always a Hebrew composer. It is the opinion of some critics, including this writer, that his most successful religious work is, in fact, the Piano Quintet. Though it is not programmatic, this work remains a profound religious document, touched with Hasidic mysticism, dramatic with Hebraic suffering, made sublime by Hebraic resignation. Thus, even when he makes no attempt to write of the Jew in his music, Bloch continues to write music that is Jewish in character and spirit. It has been the penetrating commentary of one writer that the Indians in the America symphony dance with Hasidic feet. Though Bloch may, on occasion, abandon Hebrew music, it is obvious that Hebrew music will not abandon him.[56]

In a letter to Nicolas Slonimsky, written just before *America*'s premiere, Bloch reacted angrily to these limiting views: "Why should I be bottled, labeled, compelled to eat kosher all my life? I have more personalities than one. I have not said my last word."[57] But Bloch in fact did not have multiple personalities. Nor did he have completely distinguishable "Jewish" and "universal" musical voices. And since it was less the musical style than its description that had changed, Bloch's critics, conditioned to identify the composer's individual expression with a specific, instinctive racial utterance, kept hearing the Jewish voice in Bloch's music.

### UNIVERSAL MASS

More than in works like the nationally specific *America* or *Helvetia,* or the nationally unspecific Suite for Viola, Sonata for Violin, or Piano Quintet, Bloch's universalistic aspirations came to the fore in the proposed ending of his *Israel Symphony.* Bloch saw the story of the composition of the work as a tragic parable that symbolized his miserable situation as a great composer who, lacking the necessary support, was never allowed to accomplish the great work that would save humanity. "As nobody is helping me—they finance little Jewish violinists, but never a creative man!! . . . I have to struggle to liberate [myself] alone!" he complained bitterly to two faithful confidants, Ada Clement (1878–1952) and Lillian Hodgehead (1886–1972), founders of the San Francisco Conservatory, which Bloch directed at their invitation from 1925 to 1930. "Perhaps I may do it, in 3, 4, 5 years [of] hard work. Then I will be 50, old, worn out, disgusted, or dead, or insane." But he would not be the loser, Bloch declared. "Humanity will be. Not my fault. But they are too stupid to understand!"[58]

What Bloch had in store for humanity was a new conception of Judaism, which, as he explained to Fleg, would allow him to "surpass the nation Israel," and to project "the eternal thought—the eternal hope of the Prophets in the future." The new ending would represent Bloch's own version of Zionism, next to which the original one now seemed to be "a stopping point, in time and space."[59] Compared to this new music that he imagined as "strange, clear and mysterious," "both primitive and refined, naturally savage and exotic, with elemental forces, a music that comes from farther away than Palestine, a music of the beginnings that surpasses Judaism," his former pieces seemed "dull and limited."[60]

Bloch's conception of this new, universal musical expression found a supporter in Rabbi Stephen Wise (1874–1949), whom Bloch saw as a kindred spirit because he was, like Bloch, "an ardent *Jew*, proud of his race," and had, like Bloch, a crucifix in his salon. Bloch's idea of the conclusion of the *Israel Symphony* "seized him [Wise]," as it did Dr. Schiller and David Mannes, who "*cried* when [Bloch] told them that at the end of [his] symphony the singer will turn in silence toward the audience and sing the 'Shema Israel.'" The conclusion of this tragic work, Bloch announced, will be "a musical *sermon*" about "the idea of justice, brotherhood, peace between men."[61] In a 1925 letter to Clement and Hodgehead, Bloch provided more details about his new vision of the projected second part of the *Israel Symphony:*

Israel?
A sad story.
I started [it] in *1912*. I wanted to write a *synthesis* of the Jewish soul. I thought first of characterizing it with *Jewish festivities,* the great religious Feasts, embodying all the souls of Israel . . .
This was meant to be the *1st part of Israel* . . .
The *second Part* has *not* been written.
There was going to be a kind of *Scherzo,* showing the "sales juifs" [nasty Jews], the renegades, the parvenus, the disgrace of Israel, the ones who have sacrificed to *False Gods.* The last movement (conceived in 1912–1914) and of which I have sketches, was meant to signify: "next year in Jerusalem"—but in a *Symbolic* sense. The triumph of Truth and *Justice* and *Peace on Earth.* At the end, the Bass would . . . proclaim a *Credo* embodying my ideas of Judaism, of Humanity: "Here ends Israel . . . but here *begins* the realization of its *ideals* which are those of *all humanity,* according to the great prophets!" proclaiming the *Unity* of Humanity, and a chorus would have sung a hymn of Peace and Love.
In *1914*, I *could* not write these words! The tragedy was too terrible. All faith in Humanity was gone. The War! I thought, *after* the war.
Alas! After the war came the *Peace,* fifty times worse than the War. . . .

Then, slowly came [an] idea, for the *end*. And it is going to be . . . a Mass.
Yes a Catholic, but symbolic, universal *Mass!*
    . . . This *Mass,* which would bring my excommunication from among the
Jews, the Protestants, the Catholics, would be a tremendous thing. The *text of
the Mass* combines the whole philosophy of Life. The *Kyrie* would embody all
the sufferings of man, since the beginning of the world. The struggles in the
Darkness! The appeals to God. . . . I would use *Jewish* motives, *Protestant Chorales,
Gregorian chant!* The *Crucifixus* will not mean Christ only, but *all* those who have
suffered and been crucified by man's insanity, stupidity, cruelty. And the *Resur-
rexit!* and the Dona nobis Pacem!
    Then I could realize my whole Philosophy of Life and Thought.
    Shall I ever be able to do it?[62]

The idea of writing a Catholic Mass that, as Bloch wrote to Fleg, would incorporate "Gregorian themes, Lutheran chorales, and motives from [his]
Jewish works" also appears independently of the *Israel Symphony.* This universal mixture, for which Bloch already sketched a Kyrie in 1922 and which
he envisioned to be a "Credo 'in unam cath[olicam] ecclesiam' in the widest
sense of the word,"[63] would finally shake off the "Jewish" label, which by 1925
had become a stigma that hampered Bloch's desire to achieve the status of
a universal composer. Bloch hoped that with the help of his universal Mass
he would finally be "excommunicated from everywhere."[64]

    Bloch never composed his universal Mass.[65] Instead he set the Jewish Sab-
bath Morning Service, the text of which he understood as being an expression of the unity of humanity and nature. However obviously tied to a Jewish liturgical context, Bloch's *Sacred Service* thus served as a perfect substitute
for his projected universal Mass. His most ambitious work since his incomplete opera *Jézabel,* the *Sacred Service* was Bloch's *Parsifal,* a religious drama
that propagated a pagan worship of nature and depicted the unsettling anxiety of human existence.

### TRANSCENDING RACIAL BOUNDARIES

Addressing mankind is difficult. It is especially difficult to do so in a Jewish
liturgical work, in other words, a liturgical work central to the religion of a
minority that had been persecuted for centuries and whose annihilation
was already being contemplated at the time of the work's premiere in countries whose cultural values had been equated with those of "mankind." Yet
this was the task Bloch set for himself in his *Avodath Hakodesh* (*Sacred Service,*
1930–33).

    The idea for the commission of the *Sacred Service* came from Reuben R.
Rinder (1887–1966), cantor of Temple Emanu-El in San Francisco and
founder of the Society for the Advancement of Synagogue Music.[66] Rinder
asked Daniel Koshland to raise three thousand dollars for the commission,

a sum that Gerald Warburg (1901–71), cellist, founder of the Stradivarius Quartet, and son of banker-philanthropist Felix M. Warburg, found too small an honorarium to draw "one of the greatest musical geniuses of our time into the field of liturgical music." Backed by his family's wealth, Warburg offered ten thousand dollars.[67]

Bloch accepted the commission and in July 1930, with a two thousand dollar advance in hand, moved to the mountains on the Swiss-Italian border to devote himself to the project. He sent long, regular reports about his progress to Rinder, letters that Rinder had typed and later used in his lectures on the composer. Under Rinder's guidance Bloch immersed himself in the text of the Sabbath Morning Service as given in the *Union Prayerbook for Jewish Worship,* the official prayer book of North American Reform Synagogues. He patiently memorized the Hebrew text and its English translation, reciting it until the words of the service were transformed for him into what he had "always wanted to express, since [his] youth." He changed "idolatry" to "fetishism" in the text, for, he explained to Rinder, "fetishism is much *stronger* and more general—and truer—for it contains all *forms* of false gods men adore (Law! Money! beliefs in cure-alls, *isms* of all kinds!)."[68] Gradually the task of writing a Jewish service melded with Bloch's dream of the universal Mass that he had wanted to write as the conclusion of the *Israel Symphony.* "Of course, I will write a Service, as I said, for a Reform Synagogue Service," Bloch assured Rinder, but he also felt that "such a text [was] too big for one conception." He wanted "to give such [a] Poem a larger and still more elaborate Form." The *Service,* Bloch announced, "will become a huge *Cosmic Poem* for Orchestra, Cantor, and chorus." Bloch imagined the *Service* to be only the first in a series of Hebrew and Latin works that will be "more primitive still, like *rock,* and *sand,* and *sky* above."[69]

In his program note for the first American performance (New York, 11 April 1934) Bloch explained in more detail his cosmic interpretation of the liturgical text. Its different parts expressed "the feeling of nature" (in the initial Meditation, Mah Tovu, Vechavto), "the cosmic element" (Shema Yisroel, Echod hu Elohenu, Adon Olom), "the necessity of order" (Vechavto), "the exultation of man" (Mi Chomocho, Echod hu Elohenu, Adonoy Yimloch, Lecho Adonoy, Hodo al Eretz, Etz Chayim), "the dramatic, tragic side" (Tzur Yisroel), "the mystic and ethereal element" (Kedusha), and "the philosophical side" (Adon Olom).[70] But besides its universal dimensions, the five parts of Bloch's service also paralleled unmistakably the five parts of the Catholic Mass Ordinary, creating the clearest counterparts between the Shema and the Credo, and the Kedusha and the Sanctus.[71] Pantheism and ecumenical religiosity were both integral parts of Bloch's universalistic vision.

Bloch's critics reinforced the composer's belief in the universality of his *Service.* Bloch "approaches the liturgical text from the point of view of its universal religious and ethical significance," Alfred Frankenstein wrote in his review of the San Francisco premiere in 1938, "and therefore composes for it a music that transcends purely racial considerations."[72] Repeating Bloch's own statements, Downes greeted the *Service* as a work that was "far broader than . . . dogmatic or ceremonial expression."[73]

Downes's reaction, however, changed somewhat after hearing the New York premiere. The universal conception of the *Service* resulted in, as Downes put it, "pages which in the racial sense are neutral in idiom." These pages did not satisfy the audience that had been "most deeply moved by the fire and exoticism of earlier scores," and that found the composer's new, universal music "tame, if not denatured."[74]

Paul Rosenfeld's reaction was even more negative than Downes's. He dismissed the *Service* completely, seeing in it signs of an "alarming progress of a spiritual decline." The work is "passionless, and tiresome and old-fashioned as are all things that have little or nothing to say," he wrote in his brutally short review.[75] In a 1936 collection of essays Rosenfeld repeated that Bloch's *Service* was "appallingly tame, resembling [a] work one might have expected of an English Victorian." For Rosenfeld, as for Downes, racial specificity showed itself, by its absence, to be indispensable. "The 'universal' style was hybrid," Rosenfeld wrote, "chiefly a dilution of the earlier Bloch; and the bland forms and expressions had all the old-fashioned character of things felt without warmth and intensity." Bloch suspected that Rosenfeld's negative opinion signaled a change of allegiance.[76] Yet it seems that, like in the case of *America,* Bloch's former proponents all felt uncertain about how to react to the new, racially neutral voice presented in the *Service*. Most equated the lack of strong racial characteristics with the exhaustion of the aging composer's creative energies.

The English critic and devoted Bloch enthusiast Ernest Newman (1868– 1959) did not express his dissatisfaction in such strong terms. Instead he revived the Jewish Bloch by giving a Jewish touch to everything Bloch meant to be universal: "Universal as I believe the appeal of the work to be, it is of course Jewish at heart: Bloch may mourn the sufferings that the modern world has brought on itself by its blindness and its cruelty, but he obviously suffers in the first place as a Jew. His aspiration for a better world in which hatred and division shall have made way for human brotherhood is universal in its scope, but even for the non-Jewish listener what gives the music its peculiarly moving quality is the cry throughout it all of a sorely persecuted race."[77]

Newman could have added that it was precisely because he was listening to the *Service* as a concert piece and not as a religious ritual that he was so easily convinced of the work's "Jewish quality." To the religious members of the Jewish audience, as Bloch feared, the universalistic aspirations of the *Service* seemed not only religiously unspecific but downright offensive.[78]

## THE LIMITS OF THE UNIVERSAL

The harshest review of Bloch's *Service* appeared in the Italian Jewish periodical *Israel* following the work's Turin premiere and radio broadcast (16 January 1934). Bloch never got over it. Sixteen years later the bitterness still cut through his words in a letter to Samuel Ladermann:

> In *Torino*, at the premiere of this same work, the only *Jewish* paper "Israel" wrote pages of *insults*, and it was the prominent Jew,—with an Oxford accent!— Cecil Roth, who gave me the article, at a reception in London (1934) at Mme Sieff. When I read it, a few hours later, in our little suite, with Mme Bloch . . . she said I grew pale . . . and I told her: "In *Switzerland,* they say I am a Swiss renegade—In America: a Swiss expatriate who steals the prizes from *our* native composers (L. Gilman!). In Germany, I am a "Frenchman" because I fought for Debussy!—in France, I am a "German" because I defended G. Mahler— and now . . . the *Jews* put me "out," say I am not a "Jew" . . . *where* must I go to live and to belong! In the Moon?!!⁷⁹

The long article in *Israel* included Mary Tibaldi Chiesa's introductory essay on Bloch, "The Master," a discussion of "Jewish Music in the Sacred Service" by Jewish ethnographer Leo Levi (1912–82), an interview with Bloch, and the overview of Bloch's music by musicologist Massimo Mila. The insulting part of the article was the analysis of the *Service*'s Jewish aspects by Levi, who, already at the beginning of his essay, declared that he found nothing in Bloch's conception that "would not offend the sensibility of a Jew." ⁸⁰

Levi's review is a manifestation of the gap that separated Bloch's conception of Judaism from the religious practice of observant Jews. Levi had mixed feelings about the Turin performance that took place under Catholic auspices in a theater that, as Levi pointed out, had previously been owned by the city's anti-Semitic aristocracy. Levi also objected that the organizers scheduled the concert and its radio broadcast for Friday evening without any consideration of observant Jewish audiences.

The question of intended audience became even more acute when, soon after its New York premiere, the *Sacred Service* was performed in Nazi Germany (by the Jüdische Kulturbund), where, as Bloch proudly reported to his friends, "there were Nazis in the orchestra and in the audience," and "even the Nazi 'Berliner Tageblatt' had a little, shy and short notice about it!"⁸¹ In his enthusiasm about the work's positive reception Bloch was obviously unwilling to acknowledge the limits to his universal acclaim.

The Berlin performance of Bloch's *Service* elicited what may have been the most embarrassing comment the composer ever made in public. When in a *New York Times* interview Bloch's interlocutor expressed his surprise about the performance of a Jewish work in Nazi Germany, Bloch responded:

> The phenomenon of Germany is bigger than the treatment of the Jews. A movement as profound as the Lutheran Reformation is taking place. I greatly re-

spect Hitler's sincerity. He believes wholly and disinterestedly in what he is doing. He is a fanatic, if you will, on fire with his cause, but certainly not an opportunist making political capital. I do not think he is right. But to label him and his movement merely as anti-Jewish is inaccurate. The movement goes much further back; its Jewish aspect is discernible in H. S. Chamberlain's "Genesis of the Nineteenth Century."[82]

Although Bloch's correspondence shows that his political sensitivity was in fact quite acute, he never acknowledged the offensiveness of his remarks:

> The Jews have persecuted me here—because I said *Hitler* was not a "madman" nor a "fool," but a terribly *serious* and *sincere* fanatic, he and his associates—It is rapidly spreading *all over the world*. And the *nervous* and *dishonest* Jews here make "mock trials" and other *farces*, to advertise themselves, which *hurt* and *do not help* the poor Jews in Europe—They forget too that Hitler persecutes not only the Jews, but all liberal minded people—But *who* wants the Truth! Who wants common sense, and thought, nowadays *here*, in this land of no culture, no background, no honesty??—people do not realize the seriousness of the situation.[83]

Although Bloch's fears about the possible harmful effects of American Jewish protests on German Jews might have been justified, his complaints about the behavior of the "nervous and dishonest Jews" reveals his anti-Jewish bias more than his political foresight. His comments also demonstrate that Bloch was confident that his intimate knowledge of Chamberlain's *Foundations* entitled him to pass judgments on the situation of the Jews worldwide. But, as Levi's negative reaction indicates, for many Bloch's universal message in the *Service,* which meant to prove that the Jews were part of universal brotherhood (and hence innocent of the crimes of which they were accused), seemed inapposite at a time when irrational anti-Semitism was becoming a viable political program in Europe.

For Levi, this universalizing tendency was the most irritating aspect of Bloch's *Service.* He criticized Bloch's Hebrew title *Avodath Hakodesh* (literally "The service of the sacred"), which, as he accurately observed, had no basis in Jewish tradition: the term *avodah* (work, worship, service) can refer either to the Temple sacrificial service or to the Day of Atonement ritual of the high priest entering the Holy of Holies, but not to the contemporary synagogue service. For Levi, Bloch's title sounded like the composer's Hebrew rendering of the Catholic "Missa solemnis" and hence seemed to be proof of Bloch's effort to turn the Jewish service into a Christian rite.

Bloch's use of texts from the *Union Prayerbook* (performed in Italy in Mary Tibaldi Chiesa's Italian translation) also met with opposition. In the opinion of the journal's editor, the American Reform text was "already detached from the eternal and vivid inspiration of the people" and "reduced for the consumption of the already anemic taste of a paltry Western Jewish audience in the disgraceful process of assimilation."[84] Levi was equally harsh in his criticism of Bloch's text. After patronizingly congratulating Bloch for his efforts to incorporate Judaism in his music, Levi reprimanded the composer for wasting his energies on ideas borrowed from American Reform Judaism, which Levi, like his editor, equated with "the ideology of emancipation and assimilation."

Bloch's origin in Geneva's Jewish milieu likewise failed to earn the composer better marks from Levi, who disapproved of Bloch's paraphrasing Israel as "mankind." What the Swiss-American Bloch found in the Bible, Levi wrote, was "a universal religion, which is between Calvinist Puritanism and Anglican Pietism," combined with a "Romantic nostalgia toward primitivism and barbarism, which represents a state between Rousseau and Negro dance." In Bloch's *Service*, Levi complained, Judaism "is reduced . . . to a race that has a religion like all others." For Levi the religion Bloch presented seemed like a mixture of "contemporary messianic aspirations after some sort of social justice and universal fraternity, located between the International Labor Bureau, and exercise of salvation." In Levi's analysis it was a religion that combined strong racist assumptions about irreconcilable racial differences on the one hand, and on the other, universalistic aspirations that ultimately deny difference altogether.

Levi did not dismiss completely Bloch's symbolic use of the Hebrew text in his cosmic drama. The *Service* was not Jewish enough, Levi concluded, but it was truly Ernest Bloch. He welcomed the fact that the composer, instead of writing a Mass, turned to his own religious tradition. Ultimately, he thought, the work might communicate something about Judaism to the Christians, as well as to assimilated Jews alienated from their tradition. It might even have brought Bloch closer to Judaism, Levi suggested, for the composer "started to study Hebrew and demonstrated an interest in the Jewish world, which, although he does not know, he claims to love." Levi ended his review by turning back to the original meaning of the Hebrew word *avodah* (work): if the *Service* is the means that brings Bloch closer to his own Jewish tradition, he concluded, the *Avodath Hakodesh* is indeed a "sacred work."

## THE *SACRED SERVICE* AS METAPHOR FOR UNITY

Bloch's first concern when he started work on the *Service* was the lack of unity he found in the musical settings Rinder had shown him as models. "They were only small fragments, unrelated, arias, recitations, choirs," he complained, "with no connection, no nervous system, no circulatory system, no directing brains in them." Rinder approved the unity Bloch wanted to achieve in his *Service*, seeing it not as a composerly requirement, but as the basis of Jewish religion. In the margin of Bloch's letter Rinder put an explanatory note: the "central theme [is] Monotheism."[85]

Yet Bloch's "central theme" was not tightly bound to any religion. In letters to friends Bloch downplayed the religious orientation of the work that, he declared, "is more than Jewish," more than "a Service. It is the craving of my soul for a higher plane." "I do not write it for the Jews—who probably will fight it—nor [for] the critics!" he wrote to Hodgehead. The work, Bloch explained, "has become a 'private affair' between God and me."[86]

When Warburg postponed payment for the *Service* because of financial difficulties, Bloch interpreted his hesitation as justification of his misgivings about future Jewish reception of the work. Infuriated, he declared: "If the *Jews* do not *pay* for it, as they promised, *they* shall *not* have it. *Humanity, yes.* They deserve a little lesson, anyhow, the Jews." To show that his anger was not caused by financial disappointment, he assured his friends that he would give the work free to Soviet Russia if he were living there. "Only they would have to change *the words!*" and replace them with "all what was *inside* of me, the real, true, deep human philosophy—much greater than a 'Jewish service.'"[87]

As Bloch himself soon realized,[88] Soviet Russia in the 1930s would hardly have provided the best pulpit from which to preach the universal, "deep human philosophy" of the *Service*. It would also have been hard to fit another text to the tight structure Bloch constructed around the text of his religious service. As table 3 demonstrates, recurring words or ideas are consistently bound to a particular type of musical material and thus create a text-inspired musical structure. For example, Bloch brings back the music of Shema Yisroel (Hear, O Israel) from part one with the Shema of part three; he recalls the mechanical ostinato figure that accompanies Adonoy Yimloch (the Lord shall reign) in the first part when the text Yimloch Adonoy leolom (Thou shalt reign, Lord, evermore) appears as the closing section of part two; and in the proem to the Kaddish of part five he recapitulates the melody and the text of Tzur Yisroel (Rock of Israel) from the conclusion of part one. References to the Law in the text—Toroh Tzivoh in the third and Toras Adonoy in the fourth parts—are also musically related.

Structural ties inspired by the text, however, did not fully satisfy Bloch's desire to transform the *Service* into an organic unit. To give musical as well as spiritual unity to the *Service,* Bloch built the whole work on a single motive. A seeming revival of the old cantus firmus practice, Bloch's idea is also both a maximalization and an oversimplification of the Wagnerian leitmotif technique, for to express in music an unadulterated ideal, an "essence" that permeates the entire composition, Bloch made the presence of his single motive didactically obvious in the *Service*. There are hardly any portions of this fifty-minute composition in which Bloch relieves his listeners from this mark of enforced unity.

Indeed, Bloch's leitmotif is of such calculated universality that one is tempted to call it a musical *locus communis,* or, to maintain a connection with religious topoi, a *locus oecumenicus.* It is a common Fuxian cantus firmus, which

TABLE 3. Structure of words and music in Bloch's *Sacred Service*

| | Textural/musical links | Musical links |
|---|---|---|

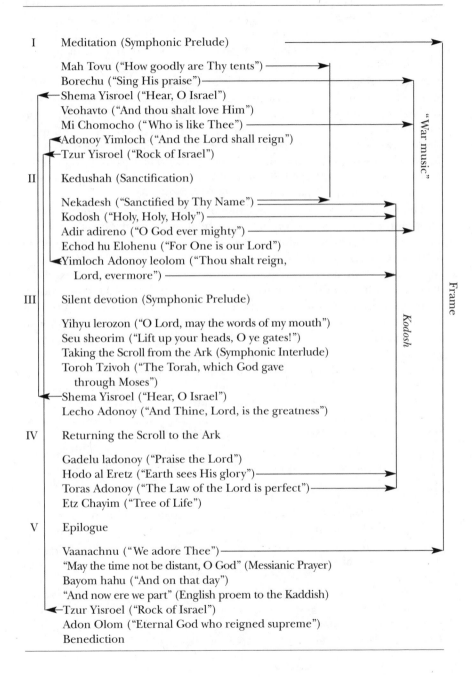

I   Meditation (Symphonic Prelude)

Mah Tovu ("How goodly are Thy tents")
Borechu ("Sing His praise")
Shema Yisroel ("Hear, O Israel")
Veohavto ("And thou shalt love Him")
Mi Chomocho ("Who is like Thee")
Adonoy Yimloch ("And the Lord shall reign")
Tzur Yisroel ("Rock of Israel")

II   Kedushah (Sanctification)

Nekadesh ("Sanctified by Thy Name")
Kodosh ("Holy, Holy, Holy")
Adir adireno ("O God ever mighty")
Echod hu Elohenu ("For One is our Lord")
Yimloch Adonoy leolom ("Thou shalt reign,
    Lord, evermore")

III   Silent devotion (Symphonic Prelude)

Yihyu lerozon ("O Lord, may the words of my mouth")
Seu sheorim ("Lift up your heads, O ye gates!")
Taking the Scroll from the Ark (Symphonic Interlude)
Toroh Tzivoh ("The Torah, which God gave
    through Moses")
Shema Yisroel ("Hear, O Israel")
Lecho Adonoy ("And Thine, Lord, is the greatness")

IV   Returning the Scroll to the Ark

Gadelu ladonoy ("Praise the Lord")
Hodo al Eretz ("Earth sees His glory")
Toras Adonoy ("The Law of the Lord is perfect")
Etz Chayim ("Tree of Life")

V   Epilogue

Vaanachnu ("We adore Thee")
"May the time not be distant, O God" (Messianic Prayer)
Bayom hahu ("And on that day")
"And now ere we part" (English proem to the Kaddish)
Tzur Yisroel ("Rock of Israel")
Adon Olom ("Eternal God who reigned supreme")
Benediction

"War music"   Kodosh   Frame

Bloch's daughter found in one of her father's counterpoint exercises,[89] and which had figured conspicuously in many classical works (most notably in the finale of Mozart's "Jupiter" Symphony). It is also a simplified version of the beginning of the mode eight Gregorian Magnificat melody, an association Bloch justified by speculatively relocating the Gregorian melody's origin in the old synagogue in Jerusalem (ex. 60a–b).[90] As Bloch later confirmed, he did not believe that traditional synagogue melodies, coming mainly from Poland and Russia, had anything to do with the ancient music of the Temple. It was Gregorian chant, he insisted, that contained "whatever seeds survive of the temple songs."[91] Bloch's motive has nineteenth-century associations as well. It recalls the "Grail" motive and, with the omission of its second note, the motive of "faith" in Wagner's *Parsifal,* reminiscences of which lend the *Service* its air of grandiose mysticism (ex. 60c–d).[92] The first four notes of the *Parsifal* version, highlighted by the first horn and second trumpet, appear most explicitly at the final "Amen" of the *Service* (ex. 60e).

The Gregorian connotations of Bloch's leitmotif were mentioned in almost all the reviews of the *Service.* As the relationship with Gregorian chant provided a ticket of admission for Jewish liturgical music into musicological studies, so did the resemblance between Bloch's motive and the Gregorian Magnificat create a connecting link between Bloch's Jewish *Service* and the Western tradition of sacred music. Because of the Gregorian connotation Saminsky could celebrate the work as being cleansed "from much of that well known plaintive and insipid Oriental *melopoeïa* which passes for Jewish music, and which marred Bloch's former Hebraic style." Tellingly Saminsky compared parts of the *Service* to the "stillness, the delicate glow of pathos that reminds one of the hymn of the early Christian hermits."[93]

Bloch's universal motive pervades the *Service* in several guises. Its contrapuntal elaboration in the symphonic prelude at the beginning of the *Service* establishes the modal character of the composition. Its appearance also functions as a structural device: framing sections, as, for example, in Mah Tovu (How goodly are Thy tents), helping to effect transitions, or fulfilling both roles at once as in the symphonic interlude that accompanies the "Taking the Scroll from the Ark" (part three, m. 79). The motive permeates the vocal and instrumental parts, as both fragmentary references (part one, mm. 182–84) and forceful *cantus firmi* in the bass (part three, mm. 57–58). Its recognizable fragments appear as ornamentation (part one, mm. 92–93), and threateningly mechanical ostinatos (part two, mm. 85–87). Its authoritative voice dominates both peaceful and triumphant endings (part four, mm 122–25).

Besides its Mixolydian, Dorian, and Phrygian incarnations, the *Service*'s leitmotif also has a form that Bloch called "Oriental."[94] This chromatic version accompanies the English proem to the Kaddish, the mourners' prayer near the end of the service that Bloch omitted from his Jewish oratorio.[95]

Example 60. The leitmotif of the *Sacred Service* and its associations.

a. The leitmotif of the *Sacred Service.*

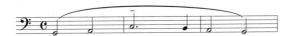

b. The first line of the Gregorian Magnificat.

Mag - ni - fi - cat    a - ni - ma  me - a    Do - mi - num.

(My soul doth magnify the Lord.)

c. The "Grail" motive in Wagner's *Parsifal.*

d. The motive of "faith" in Wagner's *Parsifal.*

e. The Wagnerian version of the motive at the final "Amen" of the *Sacred Service,* Benediction, mm. 15–20.

Example 61. The "Oriental" version of the motive (with tritone transposition), part five, mm. 95–98.

The transposition of the motive by a tritone results in an octatonic set (ex. 61). This Oriental motive foreshadows the return of the Tzur Yisroel melody that Bloch brings back in the last part to accompany, in the form designed for the synagogue, the recitation of the Kaddish prayer in its original Aramaic.

## PERSONAL MARKS

Tzur Yisroel is the only traditional melody in the *Service*. Bloch received it from Rinder, who had set it himself in the *ahavah-rabbah* mode. The presence of Rinder's setting of Tzur Yisroel in Bloch's *Service* was taken as proof of the authenticity of the composer's Jewish inspiration: "When the critics first heard it," Rinder's wife remembered, "they said, 'By this you can tell that Ernest Bloch has a fine Jewish background, a real understanding of Jewish music.'"[96] Often expressing agitated emotions in the practice of Eastern *hazzanim*, the *ahavah-rabbah* mode had the most Oriental flavor of all the synagogue modes.[97]

Because of its Orientalizing tone, the Tzur Yisroel melody resists assimilation to the modal language of the rest of Bloch's *Service*. At its two appearances Bloch suspends harmonic motion by sustaining one chord, built on A in the first appearance (ex. 62) and on B♭ in the second, for the duration of the melody (part five, mm. 108–14). The melody thus seems to stand apart from the universal aspirations of Bloch's message. It functions as a reference to something outside of the composition, a quotation that is not integrated into the fusion of styles that embodied Bloch's universalistic intent. Coupled with the Kaddish at its second appearance and thus associated with the service for the dead, the melody of Tzur Yisroel also leaves the present tense to reach, in Godet's spirit, an undefinable past that would neutralize its Jewish specificity; hence Bloch's instruction that, if performed with the Kaddish, the performers must sing it *"da lontano,"* and *"ppp* as a *far distant lamentation of all mankind."*[98]

The Messianic Prayer in part five ("May the time not be distant"), which Bloch included in his *Service* at the suggestion of Rinder, and in which he later recognized the "key to the whole service," was also addressed to mankind. The text expressed, as Bloch declared, "the deepest part of [his] own philosophy of Life, and which *permeates all my works,* whether Jewish or not! a Human *Credo!* The Faith that 'it can be done' on *Earth*—as opposed to Christianity 'in the other world' (!!)." Because of this revelation, Bloch decided to salvage his abandoned plan for the *Israel Symphony* and end the *Service* with "a proclamation in the deepest, clearest, most *universal* way of the *true ideals of Israel,* of our great Prophets." As at the projected end of the symphony, "[a] preacher was to come, and before the final chorus, proclaim to the *world* these same hopes, and truth, about the *Unity* (again! Again!) of man, of the Universe!" To express this universal message the words needed to be translated into the language of the country where the work was to be

Example 62. Tzur Yisroel in the first part of the *Service,* mm. 223–29.

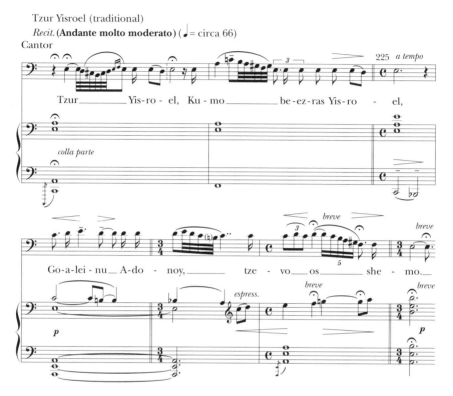

(Rock of Israel, arise to the help of Israel! Our deliverer, Adonoy, oh bless and praise His Name.)

performed, into "French, German, Italian etc.," Bloch wrote, anticipating a worldwide interest in his composition. The change of language, he explained enthusiastically to Rinder, would be "striking and symbolic!"[99]

The music of the Messianic Prayer bore Bloch's personal interpretative mark. At "O may all men recognize that they are brethren" Bloch used "one of the most beautiful motives of *Schelomo.*" At "Then, shall *Thine Kingdom,*" he quoted a motive from his unfinished *Jeremiah,* which originally appeared as the motive of "Mission of Israel" in *Jézabel* (part five, mm. 56–70). But why do quotations from Bloch's Jewish works appear in the part of the *Service* that strives most ardently for a Beethovenian, all-inclusive brotherhood? Seen in view of Bloch's conception of the text, one is tempted to see these quotations as an attempt to wash off the Jewish stigma by reinterpreting his earlier, insular Jewish works in light of his new, universalizing human creed.

## THE DIVINE OTHER

Just as the universal solvent of Bloch's new style proved incapable of absorbing the traditional melody of Tzur Yisroel, other Jewish elements in the *Service* remained unadaptable to an all-embracing universality. The most strikingly insoluble element is Bloch's image of God. Within the expressive traditions of Western musical practice, Bloch's portrayal of God is remarkably unconventional. Little wonder that in reviewing Bloch's *Service* for the journal *Commentary*, critic Kurt List (1913–70) singled it out as the least assimilated feature of the work: "Unlike the God of Catholic liturgy—an alternately benevolent and scolding father—Bloch's is the immutable, strict, avenging Lord of the Old Testament," List remarked. "Where Bloch attempts to express joy, as in Borechu, he succeeds only in expressing stern savagery. 'Sing praise to the Lord' is praise of God the Avenger."[100]

Despite Bloch's strong disapproval of List's review,[101] it is hard to refute List's characterization of the composer's portrayal of God in the *Service*. Bloch frequently referred to this frightening God before whom man is reduced to nothingness. His presence makes man realize his smallness, his ignorance, his nakedness and complete defenselessness. "We do not know anything," Bloch wrote to Rinder, "about Life, Death, Time, Space, Matter, about all what is *important*. And thus, we have to bow humbly and accept," he instructed, "and go on . . . and do our best or what we think deeply, in our conscience, *is* the best . . . but how *lost* we are, in face of that ultimate Truth!"[102]

This fatalistic belief in an impassive God had been part of Bloch's nondenominational conviction since his youth. In 1900, reacting to his mother's outrage at his sister's decision to baptize her daughter, he declared:

> I am certainly not a believer, nor an atheist either. I find it as absurd to want to *prove* there is a God as to prove that there isn't. One will never know except that Man is miserable, full of vanity, wicked and false, who reverts back to the beast when he is let free. . . .
>
> No. I myself believe in a certain fatality, a harmony of the whole *which makes me accept all that happens,* but which will not stop me from recriminating. That's why I am furious when I get upset at the past. What is, is, and was meant to be. To find out if God exists or not is not my business or anybody else's. In any case, if he exists it isn't the fellow that religions portray. He must be great and impassive like Nature and her elements. I become a Pantheist![103]

As zealously as Bloch tried to distance himself from all institutional religions, his representation of God in the *Service* falls very close to the stereotypical picture of the God of the Old Testament. The stereotype appeared most frequently in Christian-Jewish comparisons between the Old and New Testaments. But it was also well established outside of religious polemics. To cite only one example, Romain Rolland, perhaps the most celebrated figure in Bloch's immediate circle, had promoted the stereotype in his novel *Jean-*

*Christophe,* a book Bloch revered after meeting its author in 1911. In the book Rolland contrasts the two ways in which the robust Jean-Christophe and his over-sensitive, poetic French friend Olivier receive the Old Testament. Olivier's portrayal of the Old Testament deity contains many attributes of the stereotypical God of vengeance:

> The God of the Bible is an old Jew, a maniac, a monomaniac, a raging mad-man, who spends his time in growling and hurling threats, and howling like an angry wolf, raving to himself in the confinement of that cloud of his. I don't understand him. I don't love him; his perpetual curses make my head ache, and his savagery fills me with horror. . . .
>
> He is a lunatic who thinks himself judge, public prosecutor, and executioner rolled into one, and, even in the courtyard of his prison, he pronounces sentence of death on the flowers and the pebbles. One is stupefied by the tenacity of his hatred, which fills the book with bloody cries.

In contrast, Christophe, the robust German who despises the French for their sensitivity, attacks the Gospel: "Your religious education in France is reduced to . . . the emasculated Gospel, the tame, boneless New Testament," which, according to Christophe, is "humanitarian claptrap, always tearful." In its stead he recommends that Olivier "take a dose of the full-blooded Old Testament every morning." And this is exactly what Christophe does. Although Christophe, like Bloch, did not read the Bible in a religious spirit, he found in it "a spring in which, in the evenings, he washed his naked soul of the smoke and mud of Paris." He got drunk on the Bible, which is "the very marrow of a race of lions. Stout hearts are those which feed on it. Without the antidote of the Old Testament," Christophe declares, "the Gospel is tasteless and unwholesome fare. The Bible is the bone and sinew of nations with the will to live. A man must fight, and he must hate." Although less cruel, Bloch's God in the *Service* is similarly awe-inspiring. The description of Christophe's God is fully applicable to Bloch's:

> It is the very God, clasping in his terrible, tender arms the poor wretches, weak, ugly, poor, unclean, the poor down-to-heel rascals, the miserable creatures, with twisted haggard faces, thronging outside the window, the apathetic, silent creatures standing in mortal terror, all the pitiful human beings of Rembrandt, the herd of obscure broken creatures who know nothing, can do nothing, only wait, tremble, weep, and pray.—But the Master is there. He will come: it is known that He will come. Not He Himself is seen: only the light that goes before, and the shadow of the light which He casts upon all men.[104]

It is possible to detect familiar anti-Semitic overtones in both Rolland's description of the Old Testament and Bloch's representation of a primitive and frightening God in the *Service.* List noticed the strange implications this presentation could carry and warned that the presence of this God in Bloch's *Service* would undermine the universal acceptability of Bloch's magnum opus. "By depicting the spirit of the Scriptures," List wrote, "Bloch has cre-

Example 63. "War music" announces the arrival of a fearsome God in the Shema, part one, mm. 90–99.

ated such a uniquely separatist and Jewish world that it becomes radically unassimilable for the Western world."[105]

List drew his conclusion from Bloch's music, which has some unexpectedly violent moments. The arrival of God in Shema Yisroel is introduced by bellicose music built on a myriad of repetitions of a Phrygian variant of the leitmotif. The dotted rhythms and the brass announce the proximity of a truly fearsome God (ex. 63). Tellingly, the proclamation of the unity of God

Example 64. The dissonant unity of God in the Shema, part one, mm. 104–6.

(Our God is One!)

*(echod)* provokes a sharp dissonance. An emphatic B-major triad rubs against A minor under the culminating D♯ of the vocal line (ex. 64). The diminished sharp–subdominant seventh combined with the leading tone (ex. 65a) and the mixture of tonic D and dominant A chords (ex. 65b) serve as a musical symbol of the unification of seemingly irreconcilable elements. The recurrence of dissonance whenever the text focuses on unity suggests that this unity is not only absolute but also frightening.

Dissonances and mechanical ostinati are equally connected to the music of Bloch's frightening God. The figure that accompanies the chorus's rigid rhythmic motion in Mi Chomocho is built on a four-note segment of a Phrygian pentachord pattern (B–C–E–F♯) (ex. 66). Another recurrence of a mechanical ostinato based on Phrygian melodic fragments accompanies the Adonoy Yimloch (And the Lord shall reign) section. The fortissimo ending of this part culminates in a dissonant B♭ sharply opposing the perfect fifth A–E (ex. 67). The two-measure orchestral transition that leads to Mi Chomocho (Who is like Thee) brings back the "war music" of the Shema, now transposed a fifth higher (part one, mm. 164–65). The same music comes back before Echod hu Elohenu (For One is our Lord) in the second part of the *Service*. But there its character changes; it comes softly, as a subdued recollection of the God of wars (part two, mm. 54–55).

## HUMAN CONCERNS

And yet Bloch's representation of this strict, avenging God is not devoid of human concerns. What Bloch's music communicates most urgently is anxiety

Example 65. Dissonant unity of God in the *Sacred Service.*

a. Diminished sharp–subdominant seventh combined with the leading tone, part three, mm. 118–20.

(Our God is One!)

b. Tonic D combined with its dominant, part five, mm. 72–74.

(The Lord shall be One, be One, His name be One!)

Example 66. Ostinato figure in Mi Chomocho, part one, mm. 166–68.

(Who is like Thee)

Example 67. B♭ opposed to A–E at the end of Adonoy Yimloch, part one, mm. 211–13.

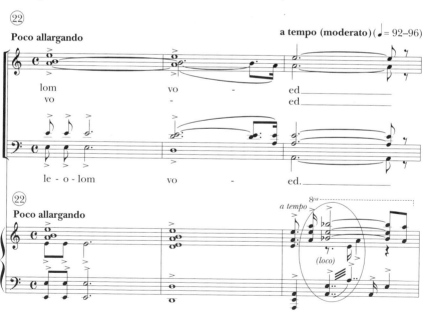

(reign forever.)

in the face of this unknown, terrible thing, be it God, the universe, or any-thing that exists outside of human control and reminds humans of their mortality. That is why the closeness of this God awakens fear. The dissonance in the music signals not only the religious concept of God's unity, but also the contrast between his eternity and human transience.

Bloch's human concerns came to the fore in the fifth part of his *Service*, which carried the heaviest marks of Bloch's reinterpretation of the text. Levi sensed that here, unconstrained by the Hebrew form, Bloch finally felt completely free to express himself.[106] Although the *Service* already contains a reminder of death in the form of the proem to the Kaddish, Bloch gave further emphasis to death at the conclusion of the fifth part, the setting of the medieval poem *Adon Olom*, which in his program note Bloch related to the idea of death:

> I interpreted the last strophe, *"Beyodo afkin ruchi":*
>
>> Into His hand I commit my spirit
>> And with my spirit, my body.
>> The Lord is with me—
>> I shall not fear
>
> by the idea of Death—accepted death—as accepted Life—with serenity, confidence and the conviction that man is too small, too limited, imprisoned in the narrow wall of his senses, to be able to understand the Infinite, the Absolute.[107]

In Bloch's interpretation death and its liberating acceptance are both present in the text of Adon Olom. The music, however, does not expel the fear of death. Along with Tzur Yisroel, Adon Olom is the only part of the *Service* in which the motive that represented the reassuring presence of an undefinable essence of the world is repressed until the very end. In the "primitive, wild, 'primeval'"[108] atmosphere of Adon Olom Bloch attempted to reformulate his ideas about unity, replacing the evocation of God's inhuman otherness with the new image of unity between man and nature. In the two last strophes, Bloch wrote, there is "no more Cosmos, but Earth and Man. The microcosm, after the macrocosm. It is God leaning towards man—as the Jehovah of the Cosmos . . . And in the last strophe, it is man toward God."[109]

But before the music takes its more human shape in the last two strophes, Bloch again invokes the fearsome God of the universe. Here the "war music" that announced the arrival of God before the first Shema and the dissonances that marked God's unity with himself fuse into what Bloch heard as the music of the infinite cosmos, which he described as "hoarse sounds, coming through the Ether, from inhuman voices, thousands of years back . . . before the Earth existed . . . or was only fire—or gas—or nebula!"[110]

Example 68. Pianissimo invocation of the "war music" before the Adon Olom, part five, mm. 122–23, and D–B pedal opposing the E♭-minor chord in the upper strings and woodwinds, mm. 125–28.

Example 69. G in the bass opposing the fifth B–F♯ and the G♯ in the melody, part five, mm. 129–34.

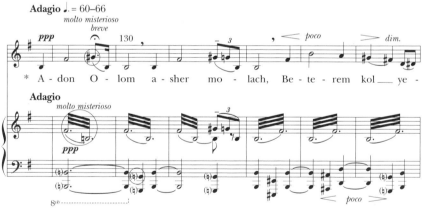

* "Like voices from another world, outside of time, outside of space."

(Eternal God who reigned supreme, while all was yet [a formless void];)

Example 70. Double pedal B–G in conflict with C-minor and F♯-major chords, part
five, mm. 147–55 (piano part only).

The section preceding Adon Olom ends with a pianissimo invocation of
the "war music" (ex. 68). B♭ and then A♭ in the bass grate against the D–A
fifth of the upper voices to recall the dissonant harmonies already familiar
from the chords representing the unity of God. In the instrumental introduction of Adon Olom Bloch uses a similar technique. In the bass a D pedal
generates dissonance against the E♭ minor chord of the upper strings and
woodwinds. When the unison chorus enters, the pedal shifts to B, now alternating mainly with G. This G stands against the accompanying fifth B–F♯.
The melody that is built around the same fifth also includes an emphatic G♯
and thus produces tension between the melody and its bass (ex. 69).

In the corresponding measures that precede the second strophe ( *Veacharey
kichlos* [And after this, if chaos comes]) the basso ostinato B–G stands in conflict first with a pianissimo C-minor triad and then with a climactic F♯-major
chord (ex. 70). The text at the culmination point of this strophe alludes again
to the concept of unity ( *vehu hoveh, vehu yih'yeh* [and One He is, and One shall
be]). At the end of the second strophe the dissonance emphasized by a fer-
mata under the syllable *yeh* ( *yih'yeh* [he will be]) consists of two fifths (D♭–
A♭–E♭) and a B♭♭ in the bass) (ex. 71). Similar combinations of perfect fifths
and a note a half step apart from either component of the fifth characterize Bloch's musical language throughout the five strophes of Adon Olom
(ex. 72). The last dissonance before the final, purified appearance of the
*Service*'s leitmotif is a fifth G–D in the chorus and orchestra opposed by an
A♭-minor triad in the horns (ex. 73).

Example 71. The two fifths (D♭–A♭–E♭) opposing a B♭♭ in the bass, part five, mm. 163–65 (piano part only).

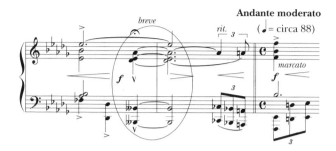

Example 72. Combination of perfect fifths and minor seconds against either component of the fifth in Adon Olom.

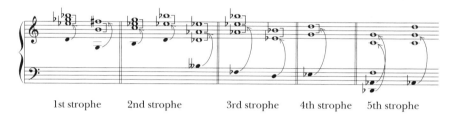

1st strophe    2nd strophe    3rd strophe    4th strophe    5th strophe

Example 73. D–G fifth opposed to an A♭-minor triad, part five, mm. 233–37.

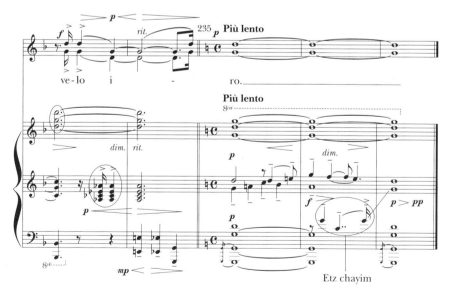

Example 74. Phrygian versions of the leitmotif, part one, mm. 166, 192, 214–15; part two, mm. 54–55.

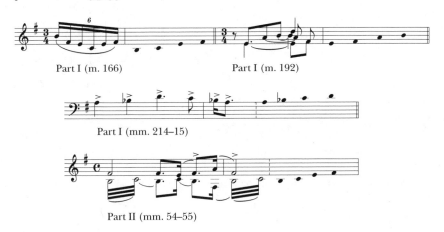

Part I (m. 166)                    Part I (m. 192)

Part I (mm. 214–15)

Part II (mm. 54–55)

But it is not merely the dissonant clashes that create an intimate connection between the harmonies of Adon Olom and the music of the Shema. Laid out horizontally as melodic successions, most of these harmonies turn out to be variants of the Phrygian version of the leitmotif that preceded the Shema and then accompanied Mi Chomocho (part one, mm. 163–64) and Adonoy Yimloch (part one, mm. 192–210), and that emerged several times as a reference to the "war music" (ex. 74). The Phrygian versions of the leitmotif and their related harmonies are connected to the idea of God's otherness, and the fear this otherness awakens in human beings. This fear is what Bloch, in his letter to Rinder, spelled out as the fear of the unknown, "Death, Time, Space and Matter."[111]

### HOPE AND PURIFICATION

To dissolve this fear Bloch attempted to reaffirm life at the end of the fifth strophe of Adon Olom. The shape of motive that starts the Adon Olom section, its rising fifth that, after stepping upwards another major second, falls back to its note of departure, is an inversion of another motive, the one that characterized the "peace song" (Etz Chayim [Tree of Life]) at the end of the fourth part of the *Service* (ex. 75). Its falling then rising fifths appear twice in that movement, first starting from G (part four, m. 76), then from D♭ (part four, m. 104). The same motive permeates the beginning and the ending of the last strophe of Adon Olom. At the end, although contradicted by the horns' A♭-minor triad, the chorus sings it forcefully on the last words "velo

Example 75. The Etz Chayim motive and its inversion: (a) part four, mm. 76–77; (b) part four, mm. 104–5; (c) part five, mm. 129–30; (d) last strophe of *Adon Olom,* part five, mm. 213–15; (e) end of last strophe of *Adon Olom,* part five, mm. 233–35.

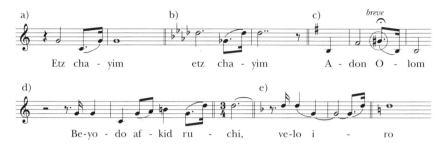

(Tree of life); (Eternal God); (In his hand my soul will rest); (I shall not fear).

iro" (I shall not fear). In the penultimate measure the horns take it over, and combine it with the purified version of the *Service*'s leitmotif (ex. 73). It is no accident that the last melodic gesture of the horns in example 73 that recalls both the Etz Chayim and the beginning of the strophe has G as its point of departure and arrival. Combined with the original form of the leitmotif this G functions as the ultimate liberator that, Bloch imagined, would bring the work to a musical and human redemption.[112] From the beginning of Adon Olom the course of musical events is determined by a desperate search for this place where the leitmotif can be restated reassuringly from G. When we first hear the melody of Adon Olom, the G appears as the dissonant pedal. The same G rubs against the "war music" in the instrumental postlude of the third strophe of Adon Olom, then a few measures later supports a variant, minor-sixth version of the Adon Olom motive now played starting on G by a solo trumpet and then by a solo oboe (part five, mm. 185–86). After Bloch recalls the music from the "Silent Devotion" (part three) at the end of the fourth strophe to invoke the idea of the purification of heart,[113] the violins quote the original form of the Adon Olom motive starting on G (part five, mm. 210–11). The same G remains the central note for the last strophe, the melody of which is built around the axis of fifths C–G–D. Appearing in the bass, a chromatic version of the concluding gesture of the Adon Olom motive falls back to G (part five, m. 234). As the chorus sings the final G–D open fifths, Bloch brings back the *Service*'s leitmotif. In these last three measures Bloch reestablishes the purity of the G-based harmony and at last suppresses the dissonances that signaled disturbance and alarm when facing the God of the universe. With its return to the point of departure this purified ending recalls the utopian vision that inspired Bloch to address the work to all mankind.

Ultimately Bloch renounced the distinction between the specifically Jewish characteristics of his composition and the convictions that Judaism shares with the "universal" concerns of mankind. Inspired by Godet, Bloch maintained that Judaism was simply the beginning: "The more I dwell on this Text—of the Service—the more symbolic it becomes to me, of a philosophy which starts from Israel, but radiates towards the whole world, addresses itself to all mankind (as in America!), a broader 'Zionism,' a bigger 'Fatherland' justified by Science and the latest Philosophy, this little and biggest Truth that Israel proclaimed first to the World."[114]

## OUT OF THE GHETTO

Bloch's effort to accentuate the "universal" qualities in his Jewish service and thereby to bring Judaism out of a perceived ghetto failed. His stereotypical Old Testament representation of God sets his *Service* apart, *cantus firmi* and modal counterpoint notwithstanding. Its intended universalistic, humanitarian message remained occluded behind distracting questions of musical style and representations of Jewishness, which ultimately defeated the composer's purpose of erasing the line dividing Jewish and Christian religious music. Bloch truly believed that he had bridged the two. As he declared to Downes before the New York premiere of the *Service,* he was convinced that his universal Jewish Mass "may be an answer to the accusations of Chamberlain as to the danger of a 'chosen people' seeking to usurp the world." By the same token, Bloch intended "a challenge, too, to those Jews who would limit their faith to their race." The Judaism expressed in his *Service,* Bloch believed, was "not that of the Ghetto but that of the prophets—messianic and universal." Bloch thus turned Saminsky's dichotomy between the ghetto and the Bible (in Saminsky's view pitting the corrupted, impure Jews of today against their pure, ancient counterparts) into a dichotomy between the religion of the ghetto and a universal faith, which, Bloch wrote to Downes, like the *Service,* "though inspired by the ancient service, transcends racial boundaries; the appeal it voices, though rooted in one religion, is to brotherhood. It addresses not Jews alone but mankind."[115] While Saminsky's rejection of the ghetto promoted a narrower view of Judaism, Bloch's inspired a broader perspective, but one in which, as Levi warned, Judaism itself could all too easily disappear.

Instead of strengthening racial expression by turning to the ancient Jews of the Bible (or their imaginary equivalents), as Saminsky advocated and as Bloch attempted to do in the first phase of his career as a Jewish composer, Bloch now wanted to eliminate racial boundaries altogether, trying to reach the universal common language Godet had promised he would through race. Bloch was convinced that in his *Service* he was already speaking that universal language, which, he believed, proved that Jews were able to contribute to humanity's efforts to create a better world. For Bloch the *Service* answered Chamberlain's accusations, for it showed that there were sincere Jews like Bloch who could be respected by everyone (even by the Fascists and by the Nazis). Bloch believed that the *Service* could also demonstrate that Jews were just like other people and there was in fact little difference between a Jewish service and a Catholic Mass (an opinion that Chamberlain might have shared since he despised Catholics almost as much as he hated Jews).

Bloch's own assessment of the significance of his *Service* stemmed from a combination of naïveté and megalomania, both essential parts of the composer's artistic personality. Typical though it was of Bloch's peculiar dual investment in racial determinism and universal brotherhood, the *Service* represented a new phase in Bloch's racial thinking. His experience in the United States, a country where race still had severe social consequences apparent in everyday life, brought about the change. Although anti-Semitism was prevalent in the United States, racial discourse focused on African Americans and other non-Caucasians. Fascinated with everything exotic, Bloch rejected common American prejudice against Native Americans and African Americans.[116] "The Indians and the blacks are the most interesting inhabitants of this country," he wrote to Fleg in 1918. "The so-called inferior races!!" he added as a refutation of Godet's racialist theories.[117]

More significantly, his views of Jews also started to change. His contact with different segments of the Jewish population in the United States threw into doubt the validity of Jewish stereotypes familiar to him from Geneva. Reporting to his sister on his impressions of American Jews, Bloch described his surprise at the unexpected reversal of his old racial prejudices. "Different conditions of life change races with astonishing rapidity," he instructed his sister in a letter sent from the United States. "Your conceptions of the Jews," he wrote, "based mainly on a handful of Alsatian Jews and on the mediocre, ignorant small traders, parvenus and pretentious, of Geneva, would change here quickly." Some Jews he met were "modest, honest and discreet," while some Yankees were brutal and greedy, characteristics he used to associate with Jews in Geneva. The more he looked the less distinction he could make out between the different races in America's melting pot. The Jews, he wrote to his sister, were no better or worse than the rest. In Cleveland they were probably a bit better ("less ostentatious, more generous, discreet, better educated"), while in New York the "rich Jews," whom he frequently blamed for lack of support, were "worse than average."

As an attempt to rewrite his past on the basis of his new experiences, Bloch convinced himself that it was his liberal views that separated him from Godet: "He knew me enough that a simple misunderstanding was not possible [between us]. I've never made myself a champion of any race. I don't believe in the superiority of any. But I don't permit that in the name of any hypothesis they attack any race. My attitude in this matter is such that last spring I offered my resignation [from the Cleveland Institute of Music] because they wanted to discriminate against somebody because the person was Jewish. Of course my attitude cost me the sympathies of our Committee, which does not like Jews at all." The day all prejudices disappear, Bloch reassured his sister, "I will drop my Jewish title and be simply a man; until then I will claim it, as if I would do if I were black." [118]

In a racist framework Bloch's ideas were indeed liberal. His general aversion to political parties, to denominational religions, or to compositorial schools, ultimately made him suspicious even of his own claim to be a Jew. Reversing the "one drop rule" (the theory that one drop of "black blood" makes the person one hundred percent black), Bloch thought it possible to break out of the biological category of race. "I wonder, myself, whether I am 100% Jewish," he wrote to Downes in 1954. "There is no such thing as pure race; having studied genetics for four or five years, I know that one single 'leak' could transform the whole situation." [119] As his statements demonstrate, his racial convictions were so strong that even when in doubt he relied on them. The route of escape was thus built with the stones of the prison. Bloch could never put himself outside of the confines of racial thought altogether. Unlike Montagu or Barzun, he never questioned the validity of the concept of race itself. Ultimately, while Bloch proudly detached himself from the different versions of what he called the "fetishisms" of his time, he remained trapped in "man's most dangerous myth.

# PART III

# Utopias/Dystopias

*Arnold Schoenberg's Spiritual Judaism*

# Chapter 6

# Uneasy Parallels

## From German Nationalism to Jewish Utopia

*The ideal set up by the Party was something huge, terrible, and glittering—a world of steel and concrete, of monstrous machines and terrifying weapons—a nation of warriors and fanatics, marching forward in perfect unity, all thinking the same thoughts and shouting the same slogans, perpetually working, fighting, triumphing, persecuting—300 million people all with the same face.*

GEORGE ORWELL, *Nineteen Eighty-Four* (1949)

*The Jewish United Party stands above all party groupings of the Jews, regardless of their religious, social or other orientation and will fight with all means any attempt to fragment the strength of the Jewish people. . . . The J.U.P. will have to fight to the point of extermination all those parties which—as parties—are opposed to its goals. . . . The members pledge themselves (a) to obey unconditionally all orders of the Party leadership; (b) not to engage, within the Party, in any kind of politics, nor in political or any other kind of propaganda which, in the opinion of the Party leadership, goes against the objectives of the Party and which, in particular, might foment disunity . . . (c) to work for the interests of the Party, in all manner possible (not merely "on behalf of" or "by order of," but voluntarily and continually; the punishment for laxness and apathy may be exclusion); . . . (g) to immediately report to the [Party] authorities any attempt at treason.*

ARNOLD SCHOENBERG, "Jewish United Party Program" (1934)

The word "utopia" was coined by Thomas More, who invented it to describe an ideal society in his *De Optimo Reipublicae Statu deque Nova Insula Utopia* (On the best state of a commonwealth and on the new island of utopia) (1516), the first book in the long series of utopian literature that More's famous work initiated. The complex meaning of the word *utopia* originates from the nomenclature and from the literature with which it has become associated. Composed of the Greek *ou* (written as Latin *u* by More), which describes a negative quality, and the word *topos*, which means place or region, utopia can be simply translated as "nowhere" or "no place." In the preface to his book More declared that his imaginary country can also be called *eu*topia, the Greek *eu* having connotations of good, ideal, prosperous, and perfect.[1] *Ou* and *eu*, prefixes denoting negative and positive attributes, express also humanity's ambiguous attitude toward utopias. For, the more perfect the utopia is—and perfection is one of the main characteristics of utopian sites— the more inhuman it becomes. Perfection is not a human quality. It can be achieved only through inhuman procedures. To create the perfect society of undisturbed satisfaction and happiness in which all men function according to rational principles requires the elimination of messy, uncontrollable emotions and other human qualities that are too closely related to man's instinctive nature. The goal of utopias is total unity, accomplished through total order, which has also been the essential quality of totalitarian political systems in the twentieth century and our own.

Totalitarianism, to quote one definition, is "a society instituted without divisions that assumes command over its organization, is self-reflexive in all its parts, and permeated by the same project throughout."[2] With its undivided totality utopia can be seen as the model for totalitarian societies, and totalitarian societies can be conceived as realizations of utopian dreams. Utopias can thus turn into dystopias and are thus both the ideals and the nightmares of humanity.

Utopias and dystopias have always existed side by side as complementary genres. In the twentieth century, however, dystopias became more prevalent. The horror and devastation of World War I (a war that many utopian thinkers greeted initially as the purification humanity needed to reach a higher reality), the emergence of fascist and then Nazi states in Europe (both built on strongly utopian perceptions), the turn of the communist dream in Soviet Russia into Stalinist totalitarianism, and the failure of capitalism manifested in the Great Depression contributed equally to a new worldview that preferred the satirical and disillusioned mood of dystopia to the naïve idealism of utopia.

The most avid defenders of utopia in the twentieth century, sociologist Karl Mannheim (1893–1947) and philosopher Ernst Bloch (1885–1977) (not to be confused with the subject of the foregoing chapters), still maintained that utopia was essential for humanity because it could influence positive social change. Bloch claimed that utopia allowed men to see the imperfection of the present in the light of utopian perfection and thus spurred humanity to strive for social transformation.[3] True as Bloch's assumption might be, his positive vision of utopia still calls to mind its negative counterpart. For like Edmond Dantes's perfect prison in Calvino's "Count of Monte Cristo," utopia's perfection restrains rather than liberates. It forces its advocates to cut, trim, and purge all that would disturb utopia's wholeness.

Nothing proved utopias' dystopian potential more than the recognition that "ideal" states, as the existence of communist and Nazi states demonstrated, could indeed be realized, and that their realization is horrific. No wonder that although in 1895 Oscar Wilde still thought that "a map of the world that does not include Utopia is not even worth glancing at," by 1933

Russian philosopher Nicholas Berdyaev (1874–1948) pled for a world free of utopian constrains. "Utopias appear much more realizable than anyone used to believe," Berdyaev wrote, and "we now find ourselves facing a most anguishing question: How to avoid their definitive actualization?" Berdyaev hoped that a new age would come "in which the intellectuals and cultivated class will dream of ways to avoid utopias and return to a non-utopian society, less 'perfect' and freer."[4]

Utopian thinking was not limited to social theories and totalitarian political practices. Artists' interest in wholeness, perfection, and progress made them especially susceptible to utopian visions. Avant-garde art at the beginning of the twentieth century was especially utopian. Futurists' celebration of violence as a purifying force, the abstract tendencies in the Russian avant-garde, and the spiritual strivings of some expressionists—all bear the mark of utopia.

### UTOPIA IN MUSIC

The most abstract of the arts, music has long been an expression of utopian dreams. Cultural critic Edward Rothstein goes so far as to claim that music is the primary form of expression associated with utopia. While music cannot describe utopia as literature can, Rothstein writes, it tests "utopian ideas, juxtaposing desire with reality, ideal with the real." Rothstein argues that musical "myths speak with authority about our society, its fragility, its strengths, its desires, and its limits. Music," he concludes, "becomes a wise version of the utopian messenger, pleasing us with his account of an ideal land but also warning us, in his tones, of all the dangers."[5]

Like most observations made about music without historical specificity, Rothstein's claim is too general to help us understand how music can be utopian. Music, however, can carry utopian ideals in a more concrete and historically specific sense. The icon of modernism, Arnold Schoenberg, was one twentieth-century artist with a strong utopian persuasion. His concept of music was closely related to Wassily Kandinsky's utopian vision of spiritual art and Adolf Loos's similarly utopian architectural designs, which were stripped of ornaments so that only "essences" remained.[6] Schoenberg's concept of tonal music reflected totalitarian social order. Tonality, Schoenberg wrote in his *Harmonielehre* (Theory of harmony, 1911), is "the large region in whose outlying districts less dependent forces resist domination by the central power [tonic]. If this central power endures," Schoenberg taught, it "forces the rebels to stay within the circle of its sovereignty." All activity in music, Schoenberg claimed, benefits the "central power."[7] Although *Harmonielehre* represented in part Schoenberg's attempt to fight against this authoritarian system and propagated instead what he called the emancipation of dissonance, by 1921 he argued for "a new form of order," which "soon re-

sembles the old, until it becomes completely equivalent to the old." For order, Schoenberg declared, "is as much of God's will as change, which per-
sistently leads back to order." This new order was Schoenberg's new method
of composition, the principles of which can also be described in utopian
terms, as rules that govern the piece in totalitarian fashion, rendering the
notes into particles in a whole. Schoenberg himself allowed a political explanation of his system. To contradict interpretations of his twelve-tone system as "Bolshevik," the composer proposed another possible reading of his
method: "In a 'fascist' interpretation, the basic set accordingly would represent the leader, the Duce, the Fuehrer, on whom all depends, who dis-
tributes power and function to every note, who also is the originator of all
the three mirror forms, and who is responsible for all the subsequent trans-
positions of the basic set and its derivatives—to function as sub-Fuehrer in
minor affairs."[8] Schoenberg's repulsion of what he conceived as superficiality and virtuosity, and his striving toward some abstract essence, toward the
realization of the "totality of a piece" that he repeatedly tried to describe as
the "idea," can also be seen as utopian. His quest to reach this ideal resulted
in an obsession with unity, which many viewed as evidence of the composer's
application of the Jewish concept of the unity of God to art.[9]

Schoenberg's conception of music has rarely if ever been critiqued from
the angle of its utopian tendencies. Critics have been unwilling to associate
the leading figure of modernism with utopia, which by the middle of the
twentieth century carried too many negative connotations. The association
of utopia with daydreaming may have also seemed to be incongruous with
what a later generation of serialist composers conceived as Schoenberg's rational methods.[10] Yet utopian thinking—notwithstanding its everyday usage
indicating a somewhat naïve, impractical, idealist attitude (which Schoenberg himself ridiculed)[11]—involves much more than striving for an impossible ideal. It is a tendency to build totalities, be it in music, in politics, or in
religion, to prioritize intellectual conceptions as "truth" over reality, and to
relate different aspects of life to a totalizing idea.

Schoenberg's utopian thinking as manifested in his artistic work will be
the topic of chapter 7. Here I discuss a lesser-known aspect of the composer's
utopian inclination: his political vision of a Jewish state, which he created
and re-created in numerous unpublished essays, drafts of speeches, and letters to friends, written in France and in the United States following the composer's escape from Germany in 1933. Few of these writings reached the public in Schoenberg's lifetime. They must therefore be read as Schoenberg's
private reaction to the shock of being deprived of his German identity. Yet
although private, these writings are important documents that cannot be ignored in the study of Schoenberg's Jewish identity.

The following discussion uses 1933, the year of Schoenberg's emigration, as a focal point and, as Schoenberg did himself, interprets earlier works and biographical incidents from that vantage point. But while Schoenberg and others who have emphasized the composer's Jewishness have endeavored to present the development of his ideas about Judaism as a straightforward evolutionary narrative, I shall keep the disruption of 1933 in the foreground and resist the smooth coordination of the chronological sequence of events with the putative evolution of Schoenberg's ideas. It is not the evolution that intrigues the reader of Schoenberg's writings, whether on music, politics, or religion, but the constancy of certain features, such as the obsession with the "idea," unity (of musical space as well as of a future Jewish state), and spirituality, which, especially after World War II, defined his thinking until his death in 1951. Whether we now want to call this obsession "Jewish" or "utopian" is a matter of preference. Both descriptors reveal important aspects of Schoenberg the composer, of his time, and of questions of identity in general.

### DEUTSCHJUDENTUM

In 1937 musicologist Carl Engel (1883–1944), a devoted friend of Schoenberg, characterized the emigrant composer's situation as follows: "Though born, like Fuehrer Hitler, an Austrian, Schoenberg, like the amazing Adolf, is at heart more Teuton than was Hermann, chief of the Cherusci.[12] His dialect may betray the native of the old *Kaiserstadt* on the banks of the Danube; but his musical speech—as his best prose writing—represents . . . the sum total of German logic, German rigor, and, unavoidably, German sentiment. His banishment, therefore, is a piece of the grimmest irony."[13] "Irony," an incongruity between what might be expected and what actually occurs, is a fitting description of the relationship between Schoenberg's self-image as Germany's greatest living composer[14] and his official status as an undesirable element in Hitler's Germany. This irony impelled Schoenberg to assume a new identity that, while focused on Judaism, continued to exhibit unmistakable traits of the old German one. The resulting amalgam was reflected in Schoenberg's political writings from the 1930s and in the handful of late compositions connected with his new commitment to Judaism.

An obsession with Germanness was so typical among German Jews that Gershom Scholem coined the term *Deutschjudentum* to describe it.[15] Yet even among *Deutschjuden,* Schoenberg's nationalist devotion to Germany represented an extreme case. The defeat of Germany in World War I traumatized the composer and transformed his fervent nationalist sentiments into chauvinism. To mend Germany's lost prestige, and to balance his own shaken self-assurance as Germany's greatest composer, Schoenberg became a fanatical advocate of German superiority in music. In a letter sent to Alma Mahler at the beginning of the war Schoenberg the German patriot lashed out at foreign music: "I never had any use for *all* foreign music. It always seemed to me stale, empty, disgusting, cloying, false, and awkward. Without exception. Now I know who the French, English, Russians, Belgians, Americans, and Serbians are: barbarians. . . . For a long time this music has been a declaration of war, an attack on Germany. . . . Now we shall send these mediocre purveyors of kitsch back into slavery, and they shall learn to honor the German spirit and to worship the German God."[16]

In 1919 he made a proposal to the Austrian Ministry of Culture concerning the government's musical policy. "The most important task of the music section," Schoenberg declared, "is to ensure the German nation's superiority in the field of music."[17] Schoenberg's most important contribution to achieving this goal was his twelve-tone method, which, he announced to his student Joseph Rufer, was supposed to "assure the dominance of German music for the next century."[18] In a fragment related to the foreword to his *Three Satires,* op. 28, Schoenberg described criticism of his music as attacks on German culture.[19] In 1931 he still categorically identified German music with his own achievements:

> It is a remarkable thing, yet unnoticed by anyone—although a thousand facts point to it, and although the battle against German music during the war was primarily a battle against my own music, and although (as somebody said recently on the radio, not realizing or understanding what he was saying) nowadays my art has no line of succession abroad (although I was picked to the bones, or to what people take to be the bones); remarkably, nobody has yet appreciated that my music, produced on German soil, without foreign influences, is a living example of an art able most effectively to oppose Latin and Slav hopes of hegemony and derived through and through from the traditions of German music.[20]

This verbose, rhetorically awkward statement was a striking manifestation of Schoenberg's growing anxiety about his position in Germany.

Tragically for Schoenberg, the crisis that followed World War I in Germany increased not only nationalism but also anti-Semitism. Schoenberg's extreme nationalist proclamations about the superiority of German music and about his own indisputable status as Germany's greatest composer covered an increasing sense of insecurity. He became "aware of the shipwreck of assimilationist aspirations" during the war, which, he wrote to musicologist Peter Gradenwitz (1910–2002) after he fled Germany, "was conducted at least as much against the internal foes as against the enemies." The Jews, Schoenberg was shocked to recognize, were considered internal foes, independent of their political position.[21]

For a while he was unwilling to admit that his status as a leading composer was also being questioned in Germany. It is no wonder that when, after long hesitation, he decided to leave his prestigious position at the Prussian Academy of Arts in 1933, it was hard for him to believe that he had indeed been expelled from German culture. Although his flight from Germany bore witness to the fact that not only his artistic achievements but also his life would have been threatened had he not escaped, he later boasted: "When in 1933 I came to America I was a very renowned composer, even so that Mr. Goebbels himself in his 'Der Angriff' reprimanded me for leaving Germany. . . . Even under Hitler, twelve-tone music was not suppressed, as I have learned. On the contrary it was compared to the idea of *Der Führer* by German composer Paul von Klenau, who composed operas in this style."[22] The putative support for dodecaphony in Hitler's Germany was odd evidence for Schoenberg's case against American conductors who were reluctant to program his music in the 1940s. It is indicative of the attitudes this chapter will explore that Schoenberg seems not to have recognized the inappropriateness of his remark in 1949, four years after the end of the war and one year after the first performance of his *A Survivor from Warsaw*.

Schoenberg's identification with German culture was so ineradicable that even after his flight from Berlin in 1933 he interrupted his writings concerning the situation of the Jews in Germany to draft a short commemoration for the fiftieth anniversary of Wagner's death:

> Richard Wagner died in 1883.
> His spirit lived on in a few musicians, but only few *lived* for his principles: "To be German means to do everything for the sake of the cause." Of these I would like to name only two, two who have not achieved more than mere recognition for the honesty of their endeavor: "everything for the sake of the cause"— unfortunately, however, modesty prevents me from [this], so that I can name only one: Gustav Mahler.[23]

In fact, as Schoenberg himself realized, Richard Wagner's spirit did live on. As Schoenberg explained in a speech he gave at a reception of the Jewish musical organization Mailamm[24] in Los Angeles on 29 March 1935, nobody could be a true Wagnerian without believing in Wagner's philosophy, which, as Schoenberg summarized it, consisted of the belief in the "Erlösung durch Liebe" (redemption through love), in *Deutschtum* (Germanness), and in Wagner's anti-Semitic beliefs about Judaism in music.[25] Familiar as he must have been with the ideas Wagner propagated in his *Judaism in Music*, Schoenberg declared Wagner's anti-Semitism "mild" compared to his followers, who, according to Schoenberg, turned Wagner's complaints about the mental and moral achievements of the Jews into racial difference. Wagner, Schoenberg argued, "gave Jewry a chance: 'Out of the ghetto!' he proclaimed, and asked Jews to become true humans, which," Schoenberg believed, "included the promise of having the same rights on German mental culture, the promise of being considered like true citizens." This was a misrepresentation of Wagner's anti-Semitic views. But it gave Schoenberg a chance to blame the Jews, who, unlike Schoenberg's "Aryan" admirers, did not appreciate his music but, discouraged by Wagner's verdict, "turned toward non-Jewish celebrities."[26] By 1933, however, even Schoenberg's "Aryan" supporters could not prevent his banishment from Germany and with it, at least for the time being, from German music history.

### REJECTION OF WESTERN CULTURE

Given Schoenberg's deep belief in the bond between German culture and his art, it is not surprising that the negation of the one—his banishment from Germany—set off his immediate renunciation of the other, composition. The "sacrifice of his art" is a recurring motive in the barrage of letters and propagandistic essays he wrote shortly after his escape from Germany. The letter campaign he began upon his arrival in Paris shows that art was soon replaced by no lesser a cause. In a draft of a speech he announced his decision of giving up all his "previous activities as a composer, writer, music-theoretician, etc., and *to do only one thing from now on:* to work for the salvation of the Jews."[27]

He penned a similar statement in a letter to his former student Anton Webern, in which he now emphasized his final separation from the Occident. "For fourteen years I have been prepared for what has now happened," he informed Webern. "During this long time I have been able to prepare myself for it thoroughly, and have finally cut myself off for good—even though with difficulty, and a good deal of vacillation—from all that tied me to the Occident."[28] The letter shocked Webern, and he passed it on to his fellow student Alban Berg, who responded: "He has shaken me deeply. Even if I regard his departure from the Occident *humanly* as possible (I don't believe it, or at least I don't regard his turning to the *Orient* as possible) there remains for me the unshakeable fact of his musical works, for which there is only one description: German."[29]

For Schoenberg, separation from German culture, which he equated with Western culture, was indeed impossible. In 1939 he admitted: "my heart was bleeding when suddenly the idea struck me: I should not be a German any more."[30] Still, the first shock was followed by a desperate renunciation. "We do not wish to have a part in Western culture," Schoenberg raged in an unpublished political essay in 1934, because that would mean that "we lose the entirety of our native instincts. We will gain insight into ourselves by excluding ourselves from it [Western culture]."[31] In a letter to Jewish philosopher Jakob Klatzkin (1882–1948), editor of the German *Encyclopedia Judaica*, he communicated a similar sentiment. "It is necessary to give up all Western acquisitions," he advised Klatzkin. "We are Asians and nothing essential binds us to the West. We have our [Biblical] promise, and no other temptation can more honor us! . . . [O]ur essence is not Western; the latter is only an external borrowed one."[32]

Despite Schoenberg's determination, Berg's skepticism about his teacher's ability to turn away from Western art was well founded. Uprooted from the culture to which he belonged, Schoenberg's creative energies ceased. What could he have composed that was "separated from the Occident," especially since he was deeply suspicious of the notion of Jewish art music, which, he declared to Albert Einstein in 1924, did not exist? Although he believed that "all Western music points to Jews and even perhaps owes the development of its basic principles to the Jewish essence and spirit," he maintained that "there is only German, Italian, French music, which is written by Jews and which, therefore, certainly contains Jewish traits."[33]

After his expulsion from Germany he was more willing to give at least verbal support to the creation of a national Jewish music, which would prove, he declared in 1934, Jewish "superiority in spiritual matters."[34] He even encouraged the establishment of a national Hebrew Music Academy that should promote, as Schoenberg put it, "a musical culture of a specifically Hebrew character. . . . [I]t is with pleasure," he added, "that I declare my readiness to participate in this project with all the strength at my disposal." Oddly, however, he did not participate and regularly shied away from any activities concerning Jewish music—as he wrote in 1933 in response to an appeal to help found a Music Academy in Tel Aviv, he had "further-reaching plans in Jewish affairs."[35]

In 1934 he talked more openly about these other plans in a letter to Rabbi Stephen Samuel Wise (1874–1949), a prominent figure in Jewish politics whom Schoenberg tried to win over to his political cause during his Paris sojourn. Although he recognized the "agitative value" of the efforts to create "Jewish art music," he wrote to Wise, he was more interested "in militant efforts for solving the Jewish question."[36] The "militant efforts" Schoenberg propagated were intended to abet the founding of a Jewish state, a state that would admit Jews from all over the world, most urgently the German Jews threatened by Germany's anti-Semitic policies. This was not the first time he had fantasized about military action,[37] but never before had political propaganda served as a substitute for artistic creativity. As in music, so in politics Schoenberg assumed the role of the leader whose opinions could not be discussed or criticized, only accepted and acted upon. On 24 April 1923 he wrote to Paul Stefan: "I thoroughly detest criticism (and have only contempt for anyone who finds the slightest faults with anything I publish): this, you see, Herr Bio-Duke, is my rank of nobility: the fact that I believe what I do and only do what I believe; and woe to anyone who lays hands on my faith. Such a man I regard as an enemy, and no quarter given!"[38] While many accepted his authority in music, in politics his leadership remained a fantasy.

UTOPIAN FANTASY 1: THE LEADER

Leaving Germany behind impelled Schoenberg to construct another state that would replace the one he had lost. Considering how rooted he was in German culture, it is no surprise that Schoenberg's utopian state bore a striking resemblance to the one he wanted to eradicate from his background. The most compelling force behind his preoccupation with building a new, imaginary state may have been a wish to replace his lost leadership in the German musical world with an even more dictatorial leadership in Jewish politics. As he explained several times in his propagandistic writings, the realization of this new state that would save world Jewry depended on one man, a man who had the will, the force, and the single-mindedness to force his will upon the others. "Perhaps I will be this man," he wrote in 1933. "I am offering myself. Once before I have forced the world to believe in what I believe! They will have to believe me again, this time."[39] He strongly believed in his leadership qualities, for, he claimed, "as early as 1919, I established the first dictatorship, in deliberate opposition to democracy—even if only in a Music Association—but you have to imagine this: in an association which is the prototype of the democratic way of thinking." In 1934 he expressed the same conviction to Rabbi Wise: "I could point out that even before 1921, long before Mussolini, I had declared that the end of Democracy had arrived; although even before that—at the end of 1918—when democracy broke out everywhere, I founded an artistic group of which I was a dictator, in full consciousness of the value of such a symbol (I called myself then the first dictator of Europe!)."[40] Schoenberg's reckless parallels between himself and the dictators of Europe did not win Wise to his cause. As was frequently the case, the composer was blind to the troubling nature of his rhetoric.

Pleading for positions of leadership is a recurring motive in Schoenberg's political writings. Even where there is no specific reference to his leadership, his ideas depend to a great extent on his being in charge. The sacrifice of his composing career was acceptable to Schoenberg only if he could ensure an even more important role. In the drafts of his propagandistic essays, expressions of personal offenses and frustration frequently permeate political arguments. Sometimes the parallel between his musical and political agendas appears quite explicitly:

> Even though I have remained poor, my work was not without success: those who enriched themselves by it have lived well. And I have achieved one thing: whoever wants to compose modern music today, cannot do so without following my lead. I have prevailed in a struggle against the whole world—no, it was only the professional world—against which I prevailed. Nevertheless, I have the same program here as there: Force and running my head against walls! To be sure, when I used to storm the walls I had an advantage over the profes-

sional world by virtue of having a brain—which the professional world was lacking. . . . Here, in the political arena things will be different: Here, when I say: Force! there will soon be no doubt as to how I mean that.[41]

This was not a very reassuring preposition to anyone who believed in democracy. Even Schoenberg suspected that his belligerent ideas might not prevail if other people had their say.

The dream Schoenberg proposed to realize was an updated version of Herzl's Zionist plans. But, as the composer repeatedly stated, he had little sympathy for Zionism and Herzl, whom he criticized for not being *"strong enough to break the resistance of his opponents,"* a weakness, Schoenberg added, which "might perhaps be ascribed to the soft and humanitarian mentality of the time before the war."[42] As he pointed out in a letter to composer Ernst Toch (1887–1964), a fellow refugee in Paris, a real leader should be a man "who is willing and capable of running his head against walls and who is determined to run over anyone who wishes to merely *discuss,* parley, protest, support and, in one word: weaken." Again, Schoenberg proposed himself as this leader. As he wrote to Toch, "at least everyone knows that I have stormed walls, and it is evident that I have not perished doing it."[43] A typeset draft Schoenberg wrote in France clarifies the role he gave himself in his political plans:

I would prefer to open my campaign with a speech broadcast on the radio. But then I would like to travel—if need be to the smallest places—in order to inflame Jews everywhere. It would be most desirable if I had ample means at my disposal for this purpose. Because those who are aware of the impact of propaganda on the Germans in Germany will not wish to deny themselves this kind of support. I don't think I am completely out of line if I propose:

1. to lease an airplane permitting me to complete as quickly as possible the travels which it would enable me to undertake;

2. if at all possible, also a living van;

3. a special broadcasting staff and, possibly, assuming that the project is generously conceived—

4. disc recordings of my important speeches (which I would compose accordingly)

5. sound-films.

In addition, some assistants would have to be engaged, and I would have to have at my disposal people able to brief me in every instance and in good time concerning special local conditions as well as the prevailing mentality regarding specific points.

Should it be possible to conduct propaganda through the press, then thought might be given to some journalistic assistance (but perhaps only at the later stages—even though I am of the opinion that one cannot begin early enough to shoot sparrows with cannon if one wants to prevent their growing in number and size to the point of invincibility.)

And now in conclusion I must add the following personal observations: I offer the sacrifice of my art to the Jewish cause. And I bring my offer enthusiastically, because for me nothing stands above my people.[44]

UTOPIAN FANTASY 2: ENEMIES

According to Schoenberg the wall against which a leader should run his head was a metaphor not only for political opposition, but also for any kind of criticism. In Schoenberg's ideal state no criticism was allowed. Differences of opinion, he emphasized repeatedly, hampered the Jews even more than other peoples. Jews, especially German Jews, Schoenberg declared, should be "saved against their will: for the sake of the Jewish people!"[45]

The reason why the "truth" of Schoenberg's political convictions had to be "hammered into every Jewish brain"[46] was that Jews had already been corrupted by contemporaneous political evils. Schoenberg listed these evils on many occasions, and one can see how his imagined political system took shape by refusing the models he believed to be corrupting. Schoenberg blamed "the liberal, democratic, pacifist, socialist and otherwise soft, unmanly, undignified actions of un-Jewish weaklings" for the situation European Jewry was facing. Liberalism, Schoenberg argued, did "not suit the Jews. . . . The Jews like orthodoxy—and orthodoxy is conservatism."[47]

Like many disillusioned Germans who witnessed the collapse of the Weimar Republic, Schoenberg had a strong dislike for democracy. Democracy, he insisted, "will never allow the ideas of a truly great man to triumph." Turning from the general to the personal, he admitted that in democracy "*I* will *never* be able to ever give expression to my will, let alone have it prevail."[48] Pacifism was meaningless, for, Schoenberg believed, "war is part of human nature: every slightest difference in opinion, transposed to the international scene, represents itself as a sufficient reason for war." Besides, no people can or should own a country without paying for it with their blood. (The Jews, like their forefathers, have "to fulfill the duty of every nation, to conquer it, to fight for it, to fertilize the soil with their blood.")[49] Schoenberg also opposed the achievements of the Enlightenment, for it allowed "pseudo-intellectuals" to undermine the power of the Church. The knowledge gained by the Enlightenment only damaged the Jewish people because it had led to "quick, albeit cheap success."[50] Socialism was international, and hence threatened national unity. According to Schoenberg the only reason Jews joined socialist parties was that the socialists accepted them more easily than did other political parties. Zionism, like many other Jewish movements, was split according to its members' political and religious orientations.[51] A true utopian, Schoenberg considered any hint of disunity unacceptable.

What, then, did Schoenberg want for his Jewish state? In a letter to Klatzkin he admitted: "If I could have my own preference, and wanted to create a new

Party, a new sect, it would have to be national-chauvinistic to the highest degree, based in the religious sense on the idea of the chosen people, militant, aggressive, opposed to any pacifism, to any internationalism. These are my personal convictions, and I shall not try to deny that I would be strongly engaged in winning sympathizers for these methods, for these very fighting methods."[52] Schoenberg's utopian state was militant indeed. "It is not a shame to have many fiends [enemies] . . . it is an honor!" Schoenberg declared. Nevertheless, the fiend must be "annihilated."[53] The "Jewish United Party," the founding of which Schoenberg considered to be necessary in preparation for the new Jewish state, "will have to fight to the point of extermination all parties which—as parties—are opposed to its goals," or that attempt "to fragment the strength of the Jewish people." Members had to be Jews, a condition Schoenberg defined as either being descendents of Jewish parents, observant of the Mosaic faith, part of Jewish culture, or, if they are "of not purely Jewish descent," people who adhere "to the faith or culture of the Jewish people."[54] All members must obey unconditionally, report attempts at treason, and be punished for laxness and apathy.

### UTOPIAN FANTASY 3: JEWISH SUPERIORITY AND ANTI-SEMITISM

In tribute to Schoenberg's political insight Ringer points to a parallel between "the essentially nineteenth-century racial conceptions" and Schoenberg's attempt "to claim Jewish priority for racial pride." Ringer draws the parallel from Schoenberg's own comment on Germany's racial politics: "except for its specifically German exaggeration," the composer wrote, "racism is an imitation . . . of the faith of the Jews in their own destiny. We Jews call ourselves God's chosen people and are the guardians of the divine promise."[55]

The conviction of personal superiority, heretofore present only in Schoenberg's artistic arguments,[56] became a political issue when applied to an entire people. "Only a fool can deny that average Jewish intelligence, scarcely escaped from the Ghetto, was sufficient for accomplishments for which the host nations require geniuses,"[57] Schoenberg declared. Viewed in this light, Schoenberg kept repeating, anti-Semitism was unavoidable and even justified in that it expressed well-founded jealousy. "Nothing could make us prouder than the global anti-Semitism, which expresses nothing other than what our Promise tells us," Schoenberg announced. "'The Chosen People of God!': which says nothing other than that we are superior to all other people, and that they hate us as 'insolent Jews' because of our pride."[58] To stop the fight against anti-Semitism thus became a central issue in Schoenberg's political propaganda. It was precisely anti-Semitism, he insisted, that would help Jews become a people again. Among Jews the conviction was not uncommon that anti-Semitism had a positive effect in their history, as an obstacle to assimilation. But the aggressive approval of anti-Semitism as proof of Jewish superiority advanced by Schoenberg was rarely if ever so overtly expressed by other anti-assimilationists.

Anti-Semitism, Schoenberg insisted, was a fact. Besides, "the reproaches against the Jews are, by and large, justified." God is also an anti-Semite, Schoenberg wrote, for he punished the Jews for having betrayed him: "He has provided us with special characteristics, but we have used them for wrong and insignificant things."[59] The extent to which Schoenberg was willing to make such sweeping generalizations about all of Jewry is astonishing, considering his confessed ignorance of Jewish history and culture.[60] He used these generalizations to homogenize Jewry, which he believed would again deserve its chosen status after being rid of its bad habits. According to Schoenberg's religious convictions God chose the Jews in order to preserve "the idea of a single, almighty, omnipresent, invisible and unimaginable God."[61] But being chosen also served as justification for the claim of superiority for a people that in practice was being deprived of basic human rights at precisely that historical moment.

UTOPIAN FANTASY 4: UNEASY PARALLELS

Ringer argued that Schoenberg's aggressively militant image of a future Jewish state was modeled on the program of openly militaristic revisionist leader Vladimir Jabotinsky (1880–1940).[62] It is curious, however, that neither Jabotinsky's name nor that of any Jewish politician who played a role in shaping contemporaneous Jewish politics ever comes up in Schoenberg's writings. A more obvious model for Schoenberg was Hitler's Germany, the political aggressiveness of which Schoenberg found attractive despite his opposition to its actual policies, or Mussolini's Italy, the political principles of which he "personally regarded highly."[63]

The affinity of Schoenberg's political views to fascism is one of the most uncomfortable issues in Schoenberg scholarship. In his *Arnold Schönberg und das Judentum,* to date the most detailed account of Schoenberg's involvement with Jewish politics, Michael Mäckelmann goes to great lengths to dispel the notion that Schoenberg's authoritative, militant, antidemocratic, antisocialist, and anticommunist political ideals might have owed anything in concept to the fascist and Nazi ideologies of pre–World War II Europe. Schoenberg's attraction to them does not mean, Mäckelmann writes, that "he was ever a supporter of concrete fascist ideals." What Schoenberg's sympathy shows, rather, is a "conviction that successfully uniting Jewry is possible only through strong, even militant and authoritarian politics." Mäckelmann argues that "Schoenberg saw in fascism an expression of tactical and political means . . . for power, which he also considered to be indispensable for a successful politics of Jewry."[64] This is true. But Schoenberg's statements can nevertheless read as those of a fascist sympathizer, despite his being a victim of persecution—and, I believe, would be read that way were not his reputation as a cultural icon of modernism at stake.

Ringer, for whom Schoenberg's Judaism became a central issue in the celebration of the composer's moral integrity, admits that in some instances Schoenberg's political reasoning "dangerously paralleled that of the enemy, and if there was a tragic flaw in Schoenberg's political activities on behalf of the Jewish people, it was precisely his tendency to castigate both the Nazis bent on genocide and their stunned victims with figures of speech adopted from the totalitarian idiom." Despite this insight, when writing about Schoenberg's planned propaganda campaign Ringer not only accepts but praises the parallel between Schoenberg's intended and the Nazis' actual propaganda methods. "Whatever else might be said about this astonishing proposal," Ringer states, "Schoenberg's grasp of the nature and importance of modern propaganda clearly matched that of the enemy, some of whose most effective procedures he actually anticipated."[65]

Signs of reactionary sympathy with fascism appeared in Schoenberg's writings even before 1933. In 1932, commenting on Erich Krämer's article "Dream and Reality" in the *Vossische Zeitung*, Schoenberg explained that because fascism fights against "the fallacies, mistakes, blunders, and inhumanity of the democratic, and in particular social-democratic theories, and their tactics, propaganda, and organization, [it] provides . . . the one necessary, but inadequate and otherwise futile attempt *at resistance* against the probably inevitable Communism." Ever the modernist, Schoenberg complained that "fascism is—although it pretends to be—not modern enough; not truly new." Arguing against political evils such as democracy and socialism, he announced that the Jews "must turn away from them and endeavor to find new political ideals (they don't have to be fascist ones—but maybe they [the fascists] will prove to be correct)."[66]

One document indicates that sometimes Schoenberg did more than hint at the possibility of a fascist model for a new Jewish state. Ernst Toch's wife, Lilly, remembers that although Schoenberg respected Toch professionally, there were clashes between the two composers over political questions. Once at a meeting in Paris where the situation of emigrants was discussed, one of the speakers warned his fellow emigrants: "You Jews . . . must not behave as if you were fascists." Schoenberg, Lilly Toch recalls, rose and said angrily: "Of course, *jawohl*, we are fascists, and we have to act as such in order to meet the situation." Schoenberg left the meeting and severed contact with Toch for the rest of his stay in Paris because Toch was unwilling to follow his example.[67]

Schoenberg's unbreakable attachment to Germany comes out clearly in his political writings, especially in his discomfort in opposing Germany. He formulated his political slogan "Nothing against Germany! Everything for the Jews!" in 1933, and its variant in 1934: "No fight against Hitler, No fight against fascism."[68] Schoenberg envisioned the mass emigration of German Jews with Germany's help, for what could be more useful for the Germans than getting rid of the Jews? The establishment of the new Jewish state would also help German industry; thus Jewish and German interests would coincide.[69] In a letter (likely never mailed) to conductor Wilhelm Furtwängler, who offered Schoenberg a position in Japan in 1933, Schoenberg depicted the advantages of German-Jewish negotiations: "The Jews put aside all acts of revenge against racially based states," for "racial unity" is also the basis of the Jews' existence. Schoenberg offered furthermore that "international Jewry will help to make peace . . . and clear the Germans [of] evil." Helping the Jews, by giving them a colony, Schoenberg argued, "would be good for German propaganda purposes."[70]

The fundamental contradiction between the two elements of his political slogan ("Nothing against Germany! Everything for the Jews!") led him to go as far as drafting a peace offering to Germany in the name of the German Jews as late as 1939:

> Jewry lost a war and has to stand now the consequences.
>     . . . [The] principal fight of fascism does not show understanding because fascism in its origin was not anti-Semitic and need not be so. On the other hand the affinity of Jews to liberal and radical movements [has been] explained as [being] produced by the idea that they do not persecute the Jews but rather protect them. It would be easily proved that Jews would not consider so much these radical parties if other than these would seem to offer them as much protection.[71]

One of the peculiarities of this draft is that Schoenberg not only fantasized about an imaginary future, but transformed the past into a fantasy by presenting the situation of the Jews in Germany not as the consequence of Nazi politics but as the result of an imaginary, lost Jewish-German war. This shows a disorienting mixture of reality and fantasy, a mixture in line with Schoenberg's persistent refusal to recognize facts that did not conform to his ideas.[72] This tendency enabled him to ignore the similarity between what he wished the new Jewish state to be and what Nazi Germany had already become.

### BETWEEN FANTASY AND REALITY

The meeting Lilly Toch recalled might have been the one at Hans Behr's apartment to which Schoenberg was invited to discuss Zionist issues. Behr included Schoenberg at the suggestion of Jakob Klatzkin, who knew that Schoenberg was interested in Jewish politics. For this occasion Schoenberg drafted a detailed plan about the future Jewish settlement, including its militant organizations and totalitarian political system.[73]

Although Schoenberg's essays and speeches remained unpublished and represented mainly the composer's fantasies about his new surrogate role as a Jewish leader, most documents were written in reaction to concrete events. "Einsteins falsche Politik" (Einstein's mistaken policy), for instance, was a reaction to the scientist's pacifist statements published in newspapers on the occasion of the Disarmament Conference in Geneva in the spring of 1932. In the draft Schoenberg questioned Einstein's openly anti-German campaign.[74] Accusing Einstein of being inconsiderate of Jews still living in Germany, Schoenberg argued against the boycott of German goods that Rabbi Wise (not Einstein) organized in New York to counteract the German boycott of Jewish stores in 1932. Though Schoenberg's fear of the Nazis' retaliation against German Jews in response to international opposition to Germany's anti-Jewish policies is hardly exaggerated, his obsession with the question of boycott also suggests that he was uncomfortable with actions expressing anti-German sentiments.

Another event that affected Schoenberg deeply was the Nazis' burning of books on 10 May 1933, in reaction to which he sketched a proposal in which he requested that "Germany express its regrets for these actions." Furthermore, Schoenberg wrote, "Germany pledges to make known—by means of lists—these authors and works, as well as the number of the destroyed copies, and," he added, "to reproduce the same number of new copies at its own expense."[75] This draft demonstrates that even in the face of Nazi aggression against the Jews, even after he had seen his fears become reality, Schoenberg still could not admit that Germany, his country of high culture, would destroy cultural artifacts in pursuit of racial hatred.

Several drafts and letters that Schoenberg composed during his forced Parisian sojourn and his summer vacation in the French resort town of Arcachon were written in preparation for his planned participation at the Eighteenth Zionist Congress held in Prague between 21 August and 3 September 1933. Yet despite the intense preparation, he did not attend, because, as he wrote to his cousin Hans Nachod, his bank did not return his passport in time.[76] Circumstances, however, point to a more substantial reason for Schoenberg's canceling his trip. Before the congress Schoenberg negotiated with Solomon Rosovsky, a former member of the OYNM, who asked Schoenberg to participate at the conference as "a Jewish composer." Schoenberg did not wish to act as a musician but as a politician whose vision and insight provided, in his opinion, the only solution to the entire Jewish question. As he wrote to the Executive Committee of the World Jewish Congress in August 1933, he hoped that his invitation "as a guest" did not mean a limitation in terms of his involvement ("right to speak, vote, make proposals"). He soon realized that his role would indeed be limited unless he had a mandate, which, as he learned from Klatzkin, he could have obtained "only through election." So instead of "making [himself] ridiculous as an unknown Palestinian musician," Schoenberg withdrew from the congress. As he later declared to Rosovsky, who tried to calm him down by explaining the difficulties of getting mandates, "nobody can insist that I run from one authority to another in Prague like an ambitious beginner."[77]

Schoenberg wrote some of his most extensive drafts on Jewish politics, such as the "Jewish United Party Program," in the United States, where he planned to launch a major campaign, "behind which the purely musical has to retreat," as he wrote to Rosovsky on 23 December 1933. At the time of the letter he could not report anything significant to Rosovsky, and, because of his paranoid habit of making only obscure references to secret plans, it is impossible to tell what, if anything concrete, he had in mind.

Schoenberg's militant political ideas cannot be dismissed by the fact that most of his political writings stayed unpublished in his lifetime and thus remained private documents of personal frustration. He wanted to propagate his ideas, but only after securing the uncritical acceptance of his proposals and his own position as a leader. Yet he knew that neither his leadership nor his ideas would be accepted unconditionally. Even Wise, who he thought would help him realize his political plans, disappointed him. After attending a Good Will Meeting in Boston, he wrote to Rabbi Joseph S. Shubow that although he considered Wise a great man, he himself had quite a different political agenda. "I can't see this meeting as anything but a political gathering. And it would be difficult for me to say anything at this gathering that would be tactful enough not to disrupt the meeting without abandoning my political convictions."[78]

Schoenberg was never tactful. At a public reception given by Mailamm in New York on 29 April 1934 honoring him on the occasion of his arrival in the United States, he shocked an audience expecting to hear only about music with a speech describing his political propositions. The speech, the first Schoenberg had written in English, propagated Jewish unity at all costs: "It is *not* worthy to fight against the hostility, but only worthy to *annihilate the fiend*," Schoenberg declared in his idiosyncratic English. "It is necessary to unify the Jewish people in the same manner, in which other peoples have unified themselves," he proclaimed, "with power, with force, and, if needed, with violence against all those, who oppose themselves to this unity."[79] This was certainly not the speech the organizers, Lazar Saminsky and Joseph Achron among them, anticipated.[80] Beside Cantor Gershon Ephros's recollections, there are no reports on the general reaction to Schoenberg's presentation. But Schoenberg might have sensed some opposition, for, with the exception of two short speeches he gave in California in 1934 and 1935 about his Jewish experience in Europe (none of which mentioned the Jewish Unity Party or the future state of the Jews), he never again addressed Jewish affairs in speeches or published essays.[81]

Nevertheless, Schoenberg's desire to try on the role of a political leader did not disappear. In 1946 he drafted a speech for the imaginary occasion of the foundation of a Jewish government in exile:

> The nth day of the month of March there will be a message broadcast (and re-broadcast at an adequate time) to all countries where Jews are living.
> I will speak to you, saying:
> Here I am Arn[old] Schoenberg, the president of the Go[vernment] in Exile of the Jewish Nation on a ship which I received through the generosity of Pr[esident] Tr[uman], the Am[erican] Government and the Am[erican] People.
> We are standing at the . . . milestone near New York.
> To my right hand I have the honor and privilege to be in the company of the great Powers' [illegible]
> the hundreds of Am[erican]
> the [hundreds] of Eng[lish]
> the [hundreds] of Russia, China
> the [hundreds] of France etc.
> and all the second greatest nations—
> To my left hand are prominent Jews of all kind. Scientists, Artists, merchants etc. But also many notables of non-Jewish race are present there.
> The Government in Exile of the Jewish Nation has thus far been recognized by all great powers and by most of the smaller nations.
> The authority thus bestowed in me enable[s] my collaborators and advisors and me to take the destiny of our nation firmly and consciously in hand and to make such arrangements and agreement with other nations which this government seems suitable for a lucky solution of the 2000 years old Jewish problem.[82]

Schoenberg's plan failed again to find support. Even Klatzkin, who was willing to discuss the composer's ideas with leading Jewish personalities, could not find support for Schoenberg's proposal for a Jewish government in exile. "Leading people in Jewish circles," he wrote to Schoenberg, explained to him:

> 1) that the plan for a Jewish government in exile is not feasible, that it would not be recognized by the leading governments;
>
> 2) that a Jewish government would be best erected in Palestine, which quite probably will soon be the case.
>
> Would you be willing to write an article about your plan and make it available to me? If you wish, I would do my best to have this essay published.[83]

Schoenberg never wrote the article. Instead, he withdrew from politics. His withdrawal, culminating in his oft-quoted statement that he made in 1950 in reaction to the "loyalty oath" controversy at the University of California ("I never made speeches, nor propaganda, nor did I try to convert people"),[84] was not, however, the result of his softening political views, but of his unwillingness to cope with reality and criticism.

.    .    .

Schoenberg's political vision had all the ingredients necessary for a true utopia. It was as complete and total in its details as utopias should be. His imaginary Jewish state was centralized under one strong leader ("thought originates from a *single* brain," he wrote in Arcachon on 2 September 1933).[85] The leader's plans are revealed to the members only partially, as orders to be fulfilled ("My most intimate friends, my most loyal followers will never know more of my plans than is useful for them and than they need for the fulfillment of their task"). The party "exterminates" *(ausrotten)* all opposition and eradicates all attempts to break its unity. Schoenberg insisted that all individuals "capable of developments" should go through "physical and mental retraining" to fit into the new state. He believed that people not only have to obey the party unconditionally, but have to do it with conviction. Citizens are encouraged to denounce each other to the authorities if they notice "any attempt at treason," which, in Schoenberg's utopia, could be the slightest disagreement with party politics. Older people have to accept the new principles, even if they do not agree with them. The leadership, which Schoenberg envisioned as an elite excelling in science, art, economics, athletic accomplishments, organizational skills, teaching ability, talent for propaganda, and power of judgment, was to go through an equally drastic purifying process that was to eliminate "all subjective tendencies, feelings, personal ambition, and striving for individual success." The leader (ostensibly Schoenberg himself) was to possess

> Intelligence, presence of mind, clarity, ability for decision-making; ability for self-sacrifice, unselfishness, selflessness, courage, bravery, bravura; brilliance, élan; effect on the masses; effect on small groups, effect on intellectuals, on schooled- and unschooled individuals, on dull minds; pedagogical talents, "Model" conduct of life, truthfulness, ability to describe, to judge; knowledge of human nature, responsiveness, political acumen; military skills, sports, psychological accomplishments; closeness to life; knowledge, ability, perceptiveness; honesty, firmness, ability to give orders, steadfastness—ability to deal with the principles of the J.U.P. (a) psychologically, (b) intellectually.

Family ties should be broken, for Schoenberg planned to settle initially only combat-ready youth in his new state. Though the religious principle of the chosen people served as a basis for the state, Schoenberg made sure that religion, which could be made personal and thus could potentially endanger unity, was kept under strict state control.

Like most utopias, Schoenberg's was thus also a dystopia. The unlimited control of the party was frightening enough, but the state was also a completely militarized unit in which young people were encouraged to act aggressively. "Strike first," Schoenberg advised them, "there are always reasons for attack." In the spirit of what he called "new *Realpolitik,*" Schoenberg advocated total militarization and bloody battles that would ultimately earn his people the right to their own their country.

Although there is no evidence that anyone in Schoenberg's circles shared his convictions, his writings make constant reference to people working with him. His plan, announced in a speech he imagined he would give to advertise his propaganda tour, "is currently being worked out by specialists."[86] He also acted as if there were a secret party behind him. "For the time being, I do not want to say anything about my ways and means," he wrote to theater director Max Reinhardt (1873–1943) on 24 May 1933. "I would not be allowed to do this!"[87] By whom? one wants to ask. The overwhelming number of these strange, irrational details, most presented as facts, combined with Schoenberg's impressive self-assurance, turn his political fantasy into an eerie copy of the frightening political reality of his time.

Schoenberg's is not a literary utopia, for it survived only in scattered sketchy drafts. Nor was it a utopia of social theory, for even though Schoenberg reacted to current political events, he kept his distance from existing Jewish political movements. Yet it is a utopia, the dystopian features of which are all the more saddening because the man who conceived it had just escaped from a totalitarian state. These documents cannot be simply put aside as irrelevant testimonies of the composer's troubled psychological state at the time of his emigration, not only because they bear too striking a resemblance to the horrific reality of one of the most destructive utopias of the twentieth century, but also because similar utopian tendencies permeate Schoenberg's artistic vision and works.

# Chapter 7

# Torsos and Abstractions
## "Music in Its Promised Land"

*A stadium for festivals and sports events on a mountain in the Alps.*

*A section of the amphitheater-like bleachers is seen on the stage, stretching out in a straight line which, stage left, comes quite close to the proscenium, while it extends obliquely stage right toward the back of the stage. The main part of these bleachers is to be imagined extending deep into the backstage. Stage left, near the proscenium, a small section of the headquarters building juts out . . . ; from its large balcony, used for public addresses, one has a view of the entire sports stadium. In front of the building, space is left as an acting area . . .*

*The sport stadium itself should appear to be lower than the stage. Behind the bleachers, an alpine landscape: mountains, forests, meadows, glaciers.*

*The vacant area of the stadium, facing the spectators, is to be imagined as the entrance to the field; space is needed here for the parade.*

SCHOENBERG, *The Biblical Way,* act 1, stage set 2

Schoenberg left behind several drafts of his stage set for the second part of act 1 of his 1927 play *The Biblical Way.* On graph paper he worked out the exact dimensions of the stadium and the bleachers and made pastel and watercolor pictures of the administrative building and the stadium. The bleachers surrounding the stadium are seen from the audience's perspective as a semicircle, on two pictures closing almost into a full circle. Nature behind the stadium appears either as bucolic green hills or as towering snow-covered peaks. In either case, nature is obviously separated from humans, who gather in the encircled area of the arena (fig. 5).

Utopias tend to be located in geometrically arranged, constraining spaces. Utopian spaces are transparent, providing no hiding place for humans. By their mere arrangement they confine human life. It is by no accident that most early utopias were imagined on islands. Being whole and complete requires definitive boundaries that isolate, protect, and control. Utopian space is a symbol of utopia itself, its main characteristic being its completion. There are no construction sites in utopias.

Schoenberg's most utopian works, *Die Jakobsleiter* ( Jacob's ladder), *Der*

Figure 5. Schoenberg's rendering of the administration building and stadium for *The Biblical Way*, stage setting for act 1, part 2, watercolor and colored pencil on cardboard (Catalogue raisonné 201). © 2006 Belmont Music Publishers/ Artists Rights Society (ARS), New York/VBK, Vienna.

*biblische Weg* (The biblical way), and *Moses und Aron,* were all left incomplete. Their incompletion signals contradictions inherent in Schoenberg's attempt to fuse his spiritual, musical, political, and specifically Jewish concerns into personally marked artworks. In the 1930s Schoenberg rationalized their incompletion by viewing them as preambles to his later political utopia. It is probably futile to ask which was Schoenberg's primary concern, the artistic manifestations of his utopian mindset or his political fantasies. Schoenberg himself seems to have answered this question differently at different times.

The interrelationship of the religious, the political, and the artistic/musical in Schoenberg's creative activities is highly complex in these incomplete works. *Die Jakobsleiter,* conceived as a representation of the striving for an abstract spiritual essence, remained religiously unspecific. The political utopia in *The Biblical Way,* although specifically Jewish, ultimately proved to be irreconcilable with the composer's spiritual beliefs. *Moses und Aron* reestablished the primacy of spiritual values, yet lost political significance. It was equally difficult for Schoenberg to reconcile his musical style with a Jewish utopia. The music of his three torsos—the complex musical language he imagined for *Die Jakobsleiter;* his experiment with the reintroduction of tonality and with rhythmic gestures of the march[1] on the few pages of musical drafts related to *The Biblical Way;* and the abstract twelve-tone music that conveyed Schoenberg's faith in the abstract nature of the Jewish God in *Moses und Aron*—were all markedly devoid of identifiable Jewish elements.

Schoenberg attempted to integrate Jewish elements in two other works: in an incomplete arrangement of a song from Palestine and in *Kol nidre,* his only completed Jewish work in the 1930s. *Kol nidre* is unique in Schoenberg's oeuvre, for in it the composer combined his political ideas with his religious convictions as well as Jewish idioms with his personal style. The fact that Schoenberg could not complete the arrangement of the song from Palestine and that *Kol nidre* remained at the periphery of both Jewish liturgical practice and the Schoenberg canon indicates the difficulty of such combinations.

### EPIPHANIES

Although Schoenberg's intense preoccupation with Jewish politics lasted for only a brief period in the 1930s, the composer and his apologists have repeatedly pointed out that his interest in Jewish questions dated from a much earlier time. Writing to Max Reinhardt in 1933, Schoenberg tried to justify his absorption in Jewish politics by insisting that his volte-face was the result of at least fourteen years of preparation, a number Ringer claimed was an "obvious allusion to Hitler's ubiquitous invocation of fourteen years of struggle."[2] Though Schoenberg was a true believer in fighting the foe with its own methods, nothing indicates that he intended to use the number as an allusion to Hitler. The date indicates the end of World War I, which, as Schoenberg claimed in 1933, first revealed to him the alienating power of anti-Semitism.[3] Life-determining anti-Semitic experiences are common in stories of reassumed Jewish identities. What is unusual about Schoenberg's case is that besides a vague reference to his experience during his military service, there are only two other incidents he associated with anti-Semitism: an episode in Mattsee, and his unsuccessful recruitment to the Bauhaus.

Unless Schoenberg is silent about other events, it seems that his experience in Mattsee was his only direct personal encounter with blatant anti-Semitism. In Mattsee, an Austrian resort town, where he planned to spend his vacation in June 1921, he received an anonymous card warning him that Jews were not welcome in the town.[4] His pupil Berg's reaction to the incident might reflect Schoenberg's own. "Do not tell or write anything to anybody; absolute discretion," Berg wrote to his wife. "Nobody must know about the 'anti-Jewish animosity.' Regarding Schoenberg's return: should it happen, it should not be construed that persecution of Jews caused it, but I believe you should say that Sch. did not like the climate. I hope nonetheless that things can be resolved there. After all, the wife of Schoenberg's brother is the daughter of Mattsee's mayor. . . . All the Austrian summer resorts are full of Jews and all the surrounding population is anti-semitic, but the latter would not think to even bend a single hair of the Jews."[5] Although it is possible to imagine that other similar incidents were hushed up in the Schoenberg circle, it seems that Mattsee was indeed unique in the composer's life. Schoenberg himself singled out this humiliating experience in an oft-quoted letter to Kandinsky in 1923: "Must not a Kandinsky have an inkling of what really happened when I had to break off my first working summer [in] five years, leave the place I had sought out for peace to work in, and afterwards couldn't regain peace of mind to work at all?"[6]

The letter was written on the occasion of Schoenberg's refusal to take a position in the Bauhaus project, on the basis of information he had received from Alma Mahler about the supposed anti-Semitic orientation of the group. The two letters he sent to Kandinsky are probably the most moving and sincere documents of Schoenberg's reaction to anti-Semitism. They differ from the composer's later writings on Jewish affairs, for he did not yet present himself as a leader and, at least in the first letter, declined to be distinguished from other Jews on the basis of his artistic merits. "Today I no longer wish to be an exception," he wrote in his initial anger. "I have no objection at all to being lumped together with all the rest."[7]

But the second letter to Kandinsky already reveals that he did not lump himself together with what he called the "tougher elements" of Jewry. Anti-Semitism will get rid of Einstein, Mahler, and himself, Schoenberg wrote, and will exclude him from his "natural sphere of action."[8] His natural sphere was, obviously, not Jewish, and, as the letter indicates (and his biography demonstrates), he would never be reconciled with his exclusion from German culture.

Neither the Mattsee episode nor the break with Kandinsky should be viewed, as they often have been, as direct inspiration for Schoenberg's most explicitly political work in the 1920s, *The Biblical Way*. Although the composer repeatedly stated that he started to work on the play in the early 1920s, the general outline dates from June 1926, five years after the Mattsee incident and three after the confrontation with Kandinsky.[9] The play seems to have been inspired by Schoenberg's 1924 contribution to a Zionist brochure, *Pro Zion!* Edited by Rudolf Seiden, the brochure contained statements by a number of prominent personalities about their stance toward Zionism, which they formulated on the basis of some Zionist writings Seiden had sent them.[10] Mäckelmann argues that Seiden, who, like Schoenberg, lived in Mödling at that time, approached the composer in full awareness of his interest in Jewish affairs.[11] Seiden's agenda, however, was quite different. *Pro Zion!* was a propagandistic project with which Seiden wanted to demonstrate how prominent non-Jewish personalities "particularly from political and ecclesiastical circles," in other words, people who might not necessarily be positively disposed to Zionism, reacted to the Zionist program. What is peculiar about Schoenberg's participation is precisely his inclusion among "non-Jewish intellectuals." Here is how Seiden justified the selection of contributors in his preface, in which, to his credit, he did not reveal the identity of his Jewish authors:

> I chose the subtitle "Mainly non-Jewish Voices about the Jewish Renaissance Movement" for the present brochure because I did not want to refuse two or three short contributions, the "pure race" of whose authors I cannot guarantee (I refer here to personalities who either left Judaism themselves or who are not of purely Jewish origin), and because I furthermore do not assume the right to list as Jews people who apparently did not regard themselves Jews on the basis of a (questionable) racial theory of Judaism; and finally because I don't want to get into pointless conflict with the ethnogeny of both sides.

Seiden thus did not want to exclude Schoenberg because of his ethnic background, and considered him nevertheless representative of "non-Jewish opinions."[12]

It is very probable that Schoenberg, who was frequently willing to formulate strong and definitive opinions on subjects known to him only by hearsay, read little more about Jewish politics than the three pamphlets Seiden sent him: *Judaism, Jewish Nation, Jewish Land* (a brochure edited by Seiden), reports on the first Zionist Congress in Basel (1897), and the Balfour

Declaration (1917).[13] Schoenberg's library contains hardly anything on Jewish politics (he did not even own Herzl's book),[14] a lacuna that explains his surprising unfamiliarity with contemporary Jewish politics. His short yet strongly opinionated reaction to these readings already contained the most important and most constant element of his future political views: the belief in aggressive military action. Here is the full text of Schoenberg's contribution to Seiden's *Pro Zion!*:

> Every contract implicitly presupposes a *power* that protects it. This [power] can also be the moral or the "spear point."[15] But experience teaches us that in general *solid* guarantees are needed where "the word of a man" won't be enough.
>
> In the life of people this higher power is either an *alliance* or the *weapon*, the war.
>
> Even law can adjudicate the fulfillment of a *contract* only *where* the power in the form of law exists between restricted borders: *inside the state*.
>
> One cannot believe that for a sufficient length of time it will be possible to find a power with the will, the interest, and the means to defend the Jews in Palestine against the enemies that surround them. And that one cannot talk about a lasting protection is best proved by the history of the Jews: *only as long as victorious wars protected their empire* [Reich][16] *were they able to safeguard their independence*. A significant time frame of overall protection would be required to protect the pioneers from all sides until they were duly equipped with defensive and attacking capabilities.
>
> *The re-establishment of a Jewish Empire* could happen only in the way similar events have always occurred in history: *not through words and morality, but through victorious weapons and a lucky confluence of interests*.[17]

Schoenberg's *Tendenzstück* (political play) *The Biblical Way* was based on the principles established in his statement in *Pro Zion!* It is not clear for what purpose Schoenberg wrote the play. He finished the typewritten final version of the text in 1927. Some musical sketches also survive, suggesting that the composer may have originally meant to incorporate at least incidental music.[18] In 1933, when the composer tried to convince Reinhardt to help produce *The Biblical Way*, he claimed it was written "for the inauguration of an open-air propaganda campaign"[19]—but no such plans were revealed at the time Schoenberg was working on the draft. More likely, he wanted to elaborate his ideas about an ideal Jewish state, already sketched in response to Seiden, and he considered the play, like the new compositional method he worked out in the previous years, part of the process of ascending "to higher and better order."[20]

Nobody seems to have shared Schoenberg's enthusiasm for *The Biblical Way*. Shortly after its completion in 1927, he read the first act to "H" (possibly Emil Herztka, director of Universal Edition), who, Schoenberg reported, "had the bad taste to give me his really hopelessly amateurish, conventional opinion." The criticism discouraged the composer, who recognized that "stupid as what he [H.] said, still it did show me that not everybody is going to like this thing either." They did not. Even Schoenberg admitted that "its rejection was so general, so absolute and unambiguous, that I finally said to myself: I know with certainty that it is not so bad as all the conventional experts think." Convinced that negative criticism was proof of artistic value, he declared that *The Biblical Way* was "stylistically the best" thing he had written, and claimed that "although its profundities offer the superior mind plenty of food for thought, [it] is vivid and theatrical enough to fascinate the simpler sort."[21] Still, both Reinhardt and later Franz Werfel ignored Schoenberg's urgent calls to help turn the play into a piece of political propaganda.[22] Even Ernst Schoen, who worked for Universal Edition in London and whom Schoenberg approached in the hope that he would help publish the play and persuade Reinhardt to produce it, seems to have been unable or unwilling to act on his behalf.[23] Neither the composer's political agenda nor his play's artistic quality was persuasive enough to win the cooperation of others.

A close look at the play makes it clear why Schoenberg had so much trouble selling it. The state the birth of which Schoenberg presented in *The Biblical Way* was a totalitarian one led by a dictator and supported by military power. Since in Schoenberg's state there is only one truth, no opposition is allowed. As Jonston, one of the characters who supports the leader Max Aruns, declares: "Whoever is convinced of doing the only right thing—and a true believer is [convinced]—tolerates no criticism, considers it nonsense."[24] A "leader has no use for resistance in his nearest circle," he continues, "he grasps far-reaching objectives."

In this industrialized and militarized state, the Jewish nation, stereotyped by Schoenberg as a "nation of scholars, artists, merchants and money-changers," is transformed into a "nation of combat-ready warriors," in other words, into "a healthy and strong nation." These warriors can endure anything since they know that they are "chosen to maintain the Messianistic Idea throughout the ages; the strict, unadulterated, relentless Idea: that there is only one, eternal, invisible and unimaginable God." As Aruns instructs the youth in his speech at the end of the festive parade of youth athletic clubs, "for the sake of your people, you sacrifice all your past striving toward those intellectual pursuits that have been useful in the Diaspora." In his 1933 political essays Schoenberg himself would again emphasize the importance of physical fitness (a common component of utopias) in the future Jewish state. Schoenberg's turn away from composition in 1933 can also be seen as an effort to enact Aruns's initiative to give up "intellectual pursuits" in favor of political activities.

Max Aruns, his opponent Fritz Sanda explains, is a true dictator, who although "called Master . . . in reality is the Commander-in-Chief, and he holds absolute power in his hands." He has to fight aggressively his opponents, whom Schoenberg identified, in expressionist fashion, as "the Capitalist," "the

Orthodox," "the Socialist," and "the Intellectual." Other enemies, like democracy, liberalism, pacifism, and enlightenment, joined Schoenberg's list of evils in his 1933 drafts. Like these personifications of evils, none of the characters, not even Schoenberg's double, Max Aruns, has any real human features.[25] As the composer explained to Werfel, they were only *"messengers for* [his] *ideas."* The role of individual characters is thus downplayed. So is emotion, or, as Schoenberg put it, "erotic experience." The two female characters, Aruns's wife and his devoted secretary, are unimportant *"as persons per se,"* the composer wrote to Werfel; their role consists only of *"incarnating their appropriated share of the idea."*[26] Only Sanda, the enemy, has feelings, for he is not focused on the "idea."

Max Aruns, on the contrary, has no right to be guided by personal emotions. When asked about his personal feelings by his wife, Christine, he declares them nonexistent.[27] The same requirement returns later in Schoenberg's political writings when he lists among the requirements for the leader "the elimination of all subjective tendencies, feelings, of any personal ambition."[28]

There are further similarities between *The Biblical Way* and Schoenberg's later political writings. The role of secrecy is emphasized in both the play and the drafts. In the play each functionary "has his own assigned duty, and does not learn more than is needed to execute it wisely."[29] Bad news is withheld, for it would make it difficult "to nourish and maintain . . . much needed optimism." The whole state is built on one idea, for, as characters declare repeatedly, "from a good idea, all things flow spontaneously." People's obligation is to grasp this idea ("all should focus on one idea—the national idea") and not to diverge from it ("each and every individual will have to think this way; not differently . . . !"). But beside its nationalist character, this unifying idea remains unexplained throughout the play. Explanation is not needed in a totalitarian setting, for "an idea, by virtue of its own correctness, is readily fulfilled."

Aruns's power does not lie solely in this abstract idea. The most disturbing image in the play is Schoenberg's description of the real basis of the new state's power: "As he did for the Hebrews at Jericho, God has given us into our hands a powerful weapon with which to overpower our enemies," Aruns declares. "We have our own trumpets of Jericho! An invention [that] enables us to aim rays at any point around the globe, and at any distance—rays which absorb the oxygen in the air and suffocate all living creatures." What Schoenberg imagined was a weapon of mass destruction, a disturbing premonition both of how the Jews would be exterminated and of recent developments in military technology. In their fear, frustration, or anger people frequently dream of such weapons. Particularly disquieting are the details of the description of Schoenberg's "Trumpets of Jericho," which imply a long rational process dedicated to its development. The central role of the weapon is most explicit in the first four-page draft of the scenario.[30] It is not Aruns's abstract idea but this secret weapon that forces the world to accept his proposal. As Schoenberg declared in *Pro Zion!*, not "words and morality" but only "victorious weapons" can ensure victory.

Aruns's belief that the secret of the weapon has been betrayed leads to his destruction. His wife abandons him, and his people stone him to death. Aruns realizes that despite his idealistic rhetoric he believed more in the material power of the weapon than in the spiritual persuasiveness of his idea. Before he dies he confesses: "Thus I have betrayed the Idea, relying upon a machine rather than upon the spirit."[31]

The scene of Aruns's death has strong associations with the Passion story. In the detailed outline Schoenberg presents the confrontation of the mob and the leader with direct references to the Gospels, unintentionally drawing a parallel between the rebellious Jewish immigrants as the killers of Aruns and the Jews as killers of Christ.[32] Aruns, like Christ, asks for forgiveness for the people who, losing trust, take his life:

> Lord, only now do I recognize it, and implore you: accept my blood as expiation.
> But do not let these poor innocent people atone for my sins.
> Lord, my God, save them! Give them a sign that you are castigating only me for my sins against the spirit, but that you will not let the Idea die with me.[33]

The particular circumstances of Max Aruns's death indicate that Schoenberg modeled his figure not only on Moses, who led his people out of slavery, but also on Christ, who was rejected by his own people.

The state does not fall with Aruns's death. His successor, Guido, still possesses the secret of the "Trumpets of Jericho" and under its protection leads his people to victory. In his final speech Guido announces that instead of using the "death-carrying rays of material power" against other nations he intends to send the "illuminating rays of [their] creed's concept" to enlighten mankind. "These material rays," he promises, will one day be only a "symbol" of what "flows spontaneously from the Idea." Yet his final command that his people should *"spiritualize"* themselves to set themselves "free of all that is material"[34] rings false under the protection of a weapon of mass destruction. Guido's triumph is an odd twist in the story, for it lessens the significance of Aruns's sincere doubt about the spiritual power of an idea that convinces with the help of a secret weapon.

## SPIRITUAL PREAMBLE: *DIE JAKOBSLEITER* AND *MOSES UND ARON*

Schoenberg's preoccupation with the striving for absolute freedom from material limitations dated from at least 1915, the time he began to work on *Die Jakobsleiter*. In 1922, still at work on the oratorio, he confessed to Kandinsky, who similarly strove to create representations of the abstract essence of art,[35] that the worst consequence of the war was "the overturning of everything one has believed in." In the last eight years, Schoenberg complained, he found himself

> constantly faced with new obstacles against which all thinking, all power of invention, all energy, all ideas, proved hopeless, for a man for whom ideas have been everything it means nothing less than the total collapse of things, unless he has come to find support, in ever increasing measure, in belief in something higher, beyond. You would, I think, see what I mean best from my libretto Jacob's Ladder (an oratorio): what I mean is—even though without any organizational fetters—religion. This was my one and only support during those years—here let this be said for the first time.[36]

Like Alexander Skryabin's *Mysterium* and Charles Ives's *Universe Symphony,* Schoenberg's monumental *Die Jakobsleiter* is an incomplete eschatological essay in music. Despite Schoenberg's repeated efforts in the 1920s and later in 1944 to finish the oratorio, *Die Jakobsleiter* had to wait to be reconstructed by Schoenberg's pupil Winfried Zillig (1905–63) after the composer's death. Although often discussed as related to Schoenberg's awakening Jewish identity, *Die Jakobsleiter* is not specifically Jewish in conception. The only possible reference to Judaism is the central role of "the Chosen One," but here, in the spirit of Romantic genius worship, the phrase describes an individual and not, in a Biblical spirit, a people.

The oratorio is best remembered for Schoenberg's quotation of the first lines of its text ("Whether to right or left, foreword or back, uphill or down, one must go on") in reference to the musical space created by twelve-tone music in "Composition with Twelve Tones." Schoenberg compared his system to Swedenborg's heaven as described in Balzac's *Séraphîta* (1835) (and reinvented in *Die Jakobsleiter*), where "there is no absolute down, no right or left, forward or backward."[37] This homogeneous space was, to be sure, not Swedenborg's, who populated his heaven with angels living and marrying just like humans, but Balzac's, who stripped Swedenborg's angels of all their human characteristics, especially of their gender.[38]

In Balzac's heaven "each world possessed a center to which converged all points of its circumference. These worlds were themselves the points which moved toward the centre of their system." There was, also, an absolute center: "each system had its centre in great celestial regions which communicated with the flaming and quenchless *Motor of all that is.*" What most fascinated Schoenberg was the unity, the oneness of this space, its organic composition: "from the greatest to the smallest of the worlds . . . all was individual, and all was, nevertheless, One and indivisible." Balzac's is a sophisticated utopian space, centralized, total, and organic, designed, however, not for humans but for angels who moved through the circles toward the center, more and more purified, becoming "lines of fire without shadow" and thus losing their physical body by entering the spheres of the absolute spiritual.[39] Séraphîta, who appears as a woman to the male and as a man to the female protagonist, also goes through the process of purification as he/she loses his/her human features in the transition into an angelic condition. Balzac's (and Schoenberg's) angels thus assumed a hermaphroditic existence, which, in effect, was the perfect embodiment of utopian beings devoid of difference and potential tension and thus representing wholeness and unity.[40]

The utopian project of eliminating tension through the removal of sexual difference and of creating a centralized space found their equivalent in Schoenberg's musical thought. Already in his 1911 *Harmonielehre* he had described the duality of major and minor modes as the duality of male and female. "The dualism presented by major and minor," Schoenberg wrote, "reminds us of male and female and delimits the spheres of expression according to attraction and repulsion." Hinting at the possibility of eradicating this duality, he remarked: "the angels, our higher nature, are asexual: and the spirit does not know repulsion."[41] Hermaphrodites, or as Schoenberg put it, "double gender," would give "rise to a higher race."[42] Going beyond human space was a common desire of utopian artists. In his nonrepresentational Suprematist phase Kazimir Malevich (1878–1935) designed floating geometric forms that, as art critic Roland Schaer observed, "had no real right side up and had left density behind in order to exist in a cosmic space free of gravitational references."[43]

Cleansing music of its material associations and raising it to the sphere of the spiritual was the focus of Schoenberg's *Moses und Aron*. The opera, another torso, was conceived, as Schoenberg explained in a letter to Gradenwitz, as "part of a nationalist trilogy," including, besides the opera, *The Biblical Way* and possibly *Die Jakobsleiter*.[44] *Moses und Aron* was related both to the longing for pure spirituality expressed in the Christian-Buddhist mysticism of the unfinished oratorio and to the nationalist strivings of *The Biblical Way*. Responding to the priest Asseino's criticism of Max Aruns of trying to be Moses and Aron in one person in the play, Schoenberg splits Aruns into two characters in his opera. Now it is Moses who "bears a certain intrinsic similarity" to Schoenberg, while Aron represents the corrupter of the pure idea of Moses. As the bearer of the "idea," Moses, like Max Aruns, is "not human at all."[45] Again, the characters do not interact like dramatis personae; as in *The Biblical Way*, they are only messengers of Schoenberg's ideas.

While in the play Schoenberg attempted to turn intellectuals into warriors, in *Moses* he dramatized the process Guido promised at the end of *The Biblical Way*: the spiritualization of a people. The idea Schoenberg presents in the opera is that of the "inconceivable God, of the Chosen People, and of the leader of the people,"[46] all three central to Schoenberg's political views in the 1930s. Focusing on its abstract nature, religion remains yet again denominationally neutral in the opera. While in *The Biblical Way* Max Aruns was willing to compromise with Jewish religious leaders, in *Moses* the protagonist fulfilled Aruns's hopes of interpreting the laws "according to their spirit and not their letter."[47]

Lacking political power (or a secret weapon), Moses fails to convert his people to his pure, unrepresentable, inconceivable idea. His failure is the opposite of Aruns's. Aruns dies because he corrupted the idea, Moses collapses because he could not turn the idea into political reality. Moses is not killed by his people like Aruns, but left lying on the ground while they march toward the promised land led by his opponent Aron. Schoenberg completed only the text for the third act. Its conclusion, the death of Aron caused by the recognition of the falsity of his misguided acts, is a forced solution that remains dramatically unconvincing after the powerful ending of the second act. Like the final triumph that follows Aruns's death in *The Biblical Way*, the victory of Moses over Aron oversimplifies the problem posed by the opera. Leaving it a torso was thus a powerful solution. The opera's incompleteness demonstrates, better than the completion of the third act could have done, the irreconcilable contradiction inherent in opposing the "idea" (here the spiritual essence of a religion) and its potentially corrupting representation (religious practice).

The fact that despite its incompletion *Moses und Aron* has become part of the music-historical canon is due not so much to its dramatic power (the opera still bears strong resemblance to an oratorio) as to its musical conception. *Moses und Aron* was the first large-scale work that Schoenberg built on a single twelve-tone row, thus demonstrating the large-scale organizational possibilities of his new compositional method. More significant for our purposes than the specific arrangements of the twelve-tone set in the opera, however, is the fact that *Moses und Aron*, like *Die Jakobsleiter*, offers special insight into the relationship between Schoenberg's musical and spiritual-religious convictions.

The unified musical space that Schoenberg strove to construct in *Die Jakobsleiter* found one of its clearest manifestations in his twelve-tone compositions. As Schoenberg explained in 1941, the first creative thought in a twelve-tone piece is the basic set.[48] To derive everything from this single set was the ideal that Schoenberg demanded from an organically constructed (and organically functioning) work of art, an ideal he formulated in *The Biblical Way* as a political maxim: "from a good idea all things flow spontaneously."[49] Schoenberg's multidimensional but completely unified musical space and his conception of a politically united Jewry are two sides of a creativity inspired by utopian ideals. But since the musical concept predates the political, it is tempting to hypothesize that Schoenberg constructed his utopian, homogeneous Jewish society on the model of an organic work of art.

The musical idea on which a whole composition is based has a broader meaning than a theme or twelve-tone row, although the latter, with its fundamental sameness in all permutations, probably comes the closest to the concept. The "idea" is also an "instantaneous creative vision," an inspiration or thought that, like Schoenberg's God in *Moses und Aron,* is indescribable in words: it is, as the composer put it in 1931, the "unnameable sense of sounding and moving space, of a form with characteristic relationships; of moving masses whose shape is unnameable and not amenable to comparison."[50]

Herein lies the problem, similar to the one Schoenberg struggled with in the religious context of *Moses und Aron.* To make this abstract, unnameable idea comprehensible to the listener, the composer must break the whole into parts. Schoenberg believed that the "inspiration, the vision, the whole, breaks down during its representation into details whose constructed realization reunites them into the whole."[51] But can the idea remain intact when, in its presentation, it loses its detachment from the physical, material domain? Rising into a Balzacian heaven means just the opposite: the achievement of a total dematerialization of the body, the substance of which is sublimated into a spiritual essence. Requiring from the listener the recognition of sameness in differently presented twelve-tone rows, thus denying the perceptual difference between horizontal and vertical musical dimensions, entails a similar striving toward spiritualization. Music is set free from its physical reality, its "body" is dissolved into an idea that inhabits a totally unified, homogeneous, nonphysical musical space.[52]

Although presented in a religious context, *Moses und Aron* is about the boundaries of this process of spiritualization. But instead of pointing to a solution, it magnifies the problem. The music, which Schoenberg proclaimed would bring the drama to life,[53] creates even more puzzles than the text alone suggests. In the text Schoenberg set up the basic conflict between idea and its representation, or, in terms of characters, between Moses and Aron. Aron can speak and communicate, which is represented by his singing in the tradition of the opera stage. Schoenberg represents the inability of Moses to communicate the idea of the "one, infinite, unperceived, inconceivable God"[54] by depriving him of a singing voice. Moses sings only once, when in his argument with Aron he uses his brother's tool of expressing his idea in music. His vocal line is the linear presentation of the basic set (in transposed inversion), his words a repetition of his main idea: "Purify your thinking. Free it from worthless things. Let it be righteous" (ex. 76). But can he persuade Aron of the necessity of keeping the idea pure when he himself has to resort to Aron's deceptive singing voice and hence to his brother's way of representing, translating, and thus corrupting the idea?

Schoenberg does not mark the presence of the inconceivable God with a straightforward presentation of the row, but with chords related to the basic set in a complicated way. The first pair of triads contains the first and last trichords in the row, while each of the following pair shares its boundary

Example 76. The twelve-tone row of *Moses und Aron*.

a. The primary row in *Moses und Aron*.

b. Moses sings, mm. 208–17 (vocal part only).

notes with the first two chords but adds one note from the second and third trichords of the row, respectively. The result is four triads, the last being the inversion of the first (both typically Schoenbergian atonal triads, consisting of a tritone and perfect fourth), and the second the inversion of the third (consisting of an augmented fifth and a minor third). All six chords have a major seventh as their boundary interval. The six-note motive that follows completes the row by adding the notes of the middle two trichords of the row (ex. 77).

Giving the row a vertical appearance, thus presenting its notes not in easily comprehensible succession but simultaneously, seems to correspond to Schoenberg's idea of the unimaginable and unrepresentable God whose voice he set by a twelve-part chorus, divided into singing and speaking parts, as if God possessed both the music of Aron and the prose of Moses. The end of the second act powerfully underlines the fall of Moses, for it leaves the downtrodden Moses alone with a single musical line that displays horizontally the prime, then the inverted, and finally the retrograde forms of the row (mm. 1108–36). The dramatic situation suggests that the idea, when revealed in an easily comprehensible way, loses its power.

Schoenberg never set to music the opera's last act. In fact, the inability

Example 77. Divine chords in *Moses und Aron.*

a. Divine chords in *Moses und Aron,* mm. 1–3.

b. The hexachord content of the divine chords.

of Moses to express the pure idea of God in music already suggested this coming silence. No matter how the twelve-tone row is displayed in connection with Schoenberg's inconceivable God, in Aron's part the music—and, metaphorically, music itself—marks corruption, the falsification of the pure idea.

Were Schoenberg's ideas of the "inconceivable God, the Chosen People and the leader of the people" truly "the essence of Israel's transcendent mission," as Ringer wished to see them? Was Schoenberg's "spiritual dilemma" essentially Jewish—as Ringer has proposed[55]—or did Schoenberg recast Judaism in his own image? The God of the Jews, as described by Jewish philosophers under the influence of Greek philosophy, does have abstract qualities similar to those of God in *Moses und Aron.* In Maimonides' view God's transcendence resists the human capacity for comprehension, so human efforts to characterize Him must be either allegorical or negative. This God is not anthropomorphic. But Schoenberg also presents Moses as "not human at all," thus attributing divine character to God's messenger.[56]

Then, too, the prohibition against representing God in graven images decisively set the ancient Jews apart from the surrounding peoples. But Schoenberg prohibits (as representation) not only images, among which he counts even the tablets of the law and the promised land, but also actions, and, by extension, the practice of the law itself. Moses judges Aron because he was "satisfied only by the act, the deed."[57] In the opera the contradiction between two passages of the Bible describing the same event differently, which puzzled Schoenberg, is turned into a basic difference between the attitudes of Moses and Aron toward idea and deed.[58] "You then struck the rock, instead of speaking to it, as you were commanded to do in order to make water flow from it," Moses accuses Aron in the third act. The Biblical command of "doing all the words of this Law," thus the redemptive power of right action, which is a basic concept of Talmudic tradition, is called into question by Schoenberg's idiosyncratic prohibitions. By reducing Judaism to its "spiritual essence," Schoenberg seems to have attempted to assimilate the Mosaic faith (which focused on the law rather than on contemplation) to Christian concepts of spirituality.

Schoenberg thus spoke truthfully when he confessed to Klatzkin in 1933 that he would prefer to establish his own religion.[59] And so he did in *Moses und Aron*. While strongly reminiscent of certain aspects of Judaism, the religious concept presented in the opera is nevertheless Schoenberg's own. It is completely cleansed of all elements that Schoenberg, true believer as he was in musical and religious purity, was unwilling to accept. Formulating his own abstract and purified concept of Judaism in the opera helped Schoenberg make the gesture of reconversion in Paris on 24 July 1933.[60] The gesture was at once sincere and political, for according to Jewish law apostates (converts to other religions) remained Jews, and hence no formal ceremony was needed for them to return to Judaism. This was the first step in turning his ideals, formulated inside the boundaries of his artistic world, into reality. The religion presented in *Moses und Aron* became Schoenberg's personal religion; the political ideals, first expressed in his contribution to *Pro Zion!* and in *The Biblical Way*, turned into frenzied, imagined activity expressed in his propagandistic writings of the 1930s.

### "AUTHENTIC JEWISH MUSIC": THE HANS NATHAN PROJECT

Although initially Schoenberg seems to have kept his interest in Jewish affairs in the sphere of political fantasy, in early 1937 he sketched a "Jewish Symphony," the program of which shows that the composer considered explicitly presenting his political ideas in music. In his outline for the program of the projected symphony Schoenberg demonstrated the same preoccupation with the antagonistic relationship between the "they" and the "we" as in his political writings:

| | |
|---|---|
| 1st Movement: | Predominance (superiority) provokes envy. |
| 2nd Movement: | a) What they think about us. |
| Scherzo | b) What we think about them. |
| | c) Conclusion. |
| 3rd Movement: | The sacred feasts and customs. |
| 4th Movement: | The day will come.[61] |

The group Schoenberg marked as "they" included not only the gentiles, but also the Jews, who, as Schoenberg had complained bitterly to Klatzkin in

1933, "have never shown any interest in my music. And now, into the bargain," Schoenberg wrote in anguish, "in Palestine they are out to develop, artificially, an authentically Jewish kind of music, which rejects what I have achieved."[62] His information about the development of "an authentically Jewish kind of music" came from Gradenwitz, a student of Joseph Rufer and a great admirer of Schoenberg, who settled in Tel Aviv in 1936. In that year Gradenwitz urged Schoenberg to write the theoretical book the composer had mentioned to him in 1934.[63] There was a pressing need for such a book in Palestine, Gradenwitz informed Schoenberg, where talented composers lacked theoretical knowledge. "Most composers are trying to create 'Jewish' music on a very crude level," Gradenwitz wrote to Schoenberg, "that is, whining Russian [music] and folkloristic concoctions, which your description in the foreword of the Choir Satires fits perfectly."[64]

Schoenberg soon came into contact with this Russian-sounding folk music. In 1937 Hans Nathan (1910–89), a graduate student in musicology at Harvard, approached Schoenberg for a contribution to a series of arrangements of Palestinian folk songs by famous composers.[65] The songs Nathan sent to his arrangers for selection originated in Middle Eastern and European traditions, the latter represented by songs of early Polish and Russian immigrants to Palestine. Most of these songs were published on postcards in the early 1930s by the Jewish National Fund, a Zionist organization founded in 1901 for purchasing land in Palestine. Nathan distributed the tunes "according to what [he] thought (or hoped) would meet the musical language of the composers."[66] Composers' reactions, as well as their arrangements, varied according to their temperaments and persuasions. Toch was deeply touched by the contact with current-day Palestine culture, Kurt Weill arranged one of the melodies in a "restrained march rhythm," while Milhaud expressed frustration with the poor musical quality of one of the songs that "constantly returns to the same tone" and "lacks character." He asked Nathan to send him "melodies that are more logical, more clearly defined. Perhaps Sephardic texts," suggested Milhaud, himself of Sephardic origin.[67]

Schoenberg's reaction was similar to Milhaud's. After receiving six melodies, he asked for at least ten or fifteen from which to select, for, as he wrote to Nathan, he wanted to arrange at least six, all for inclusion in Nathan's series. Furthermore, he wanted to know whether the arrangements would serve educational, political, or artistic purposes.[68] In his next (and last) communication he complained: "It is not at all easy to arrange these songs. . . . Above all, because they do not give me the impression of authenticity. I hear more Russian and Polish in them than Jewish. I might be mistaken, but it seems to me that they are art songs *[Kunstprodukte]*. In any case arrangers who write in the style of Stravinsky seem more suited to [arranging] them than I am."

Schoenberg's main problem with the arrangements lay, however, deeper than the songs' authenticity. He did not believe in producing national mu-

Example 78. Postcard with the song "Holem tza'adi."

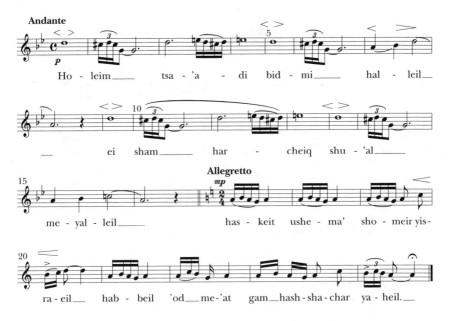

Ho - leim___ tsa - 'a - di bid - mi___ hal - leil___ ei sham___ har - cheiq shu - 'al___ me - yal - leil___ has - keit ushe - ma' sho - meir yis - ra - eil___ hab - beil 'od___me-'at gam___hash-sha-char ya - heil.___

(My step resounds in the dead of night. Somewhere in the distance a jackal is wailing. Hearken and hear, o sentinel of Israel! Behold, very soon the dawn will shine [Translation in Bohlman, *Israeli Folk Music*, xx]).

sic "synthetically." "I believe that Jewish national music exists where a Jewish genius works," he wrote to Nathan. "I cannot believe that more or less talented amateurs can come up with [anything] more than stylistic copies or mannerisms." He sent the melodies back to Nathan, adding that if he "had more time and had not been so tired, [he] would have done something that could be conceived as something beneficial for a Jewish national style in spite of [his] conviction."[69]

Although Schoenberg withdrew from the project, the one sketch that survives shows how he set out to arrange one of the melodies. Of the ten songs Nathan had sent him Schoenberg chose the one that sounded the least Russian and the most Oriental. Both parts of "Holem tza'adi" (My step resounds, also called Shirat ha-shomer [The sentinel's song]) are Arabic in character, which was closer to what Schoenberg imagined to be "Jewish" than the Russian tunes. The first part is similar to an Arabic melody for the call to prayer; the last eight measures contain a well-known Arabic motive (ex. 78).[70]

While the simple, repetitive, scalewise motion of the second part apparently left Schoenberg cold (after two attempts at harmonizing it he gave up

Example 79. Schoenberg's setting of the first part of "Holem tza'adi" (ASI U469), mm. 1–4.

the entire project), the unfamiliar sound of the first part seems to have appealed to his musical imagination. What inspired him was the intervallic content of the call-to-prayer melody, starting, like his row in *Moses und Aron,* with a minor second and a tritone. He identified these two intervals as the main idea, which he set out to "develop, modify, intensify, clarify," in the way he believed all musical ideas should be treated. Distilling a melody or an entire piece into one or two intervals and turning that intervalic content into the essential idea governing the whole was a typical analytic and compositional method for Schoenberg.[71]

The first measure of the setting already shows Schoenberg's preoccupation with the intervals of the minor second and tritone (ex. 79). The bass and the upper part of the piano part start with a downward or, since the bass part is an inversion of the upper part, an upward minor second, and then continue with a perfect fourth (right hand) or a tritone (left hand). The B–C minor second in the bass is also the transposed retrograde of the first two notes of the vocal melody. The upper part, although containing melodically a perfect fourth, vertically displays the tritone, while the lower part at the parallel location sounds a perfect fourth. From different pitches the second measure repeats the process of the first, only now it is the upper part that proceeds upwards and the lower downwards. In the fourth measure Schoen-

Example 80. Pitch content of the central motives of "Holem tza'adi."

berg brings the alteration of minor seconds and tritones/fourths to a stretto, displaying the intervals both vertically and horizontally. This is the only place in the setting where he uses all twelve tones of the chromatic scale in one measure.

While Schoenberg's draft of "Holem tza'adi" does not use his twelve-tone method, it demonstrates the composer's tendency to think in terms of circulating the pitches in the chromatic gamut. The first four trichords that he uses in the four motives of the first two measures (ex. 80) behave like the divine chords in *Moses und Aron.* The pitch content of the 3 + 3 notes of the two measures is both symmetrical and forms a hexachord on its own. But the second hexachord, like the third and fourth chords at the beginning of *Moses und Aron,* repeats notes from the first hexachord, more precisely from the second trichord. The second hexachord derives from the first and thus forms a logical continuation in terms of the tune's intervallic content. Throughout the first part of the setting the minor second–tritone/fourth motive dominates the entire musical spectrum both melodically and harmonically.

Schoenberg thus neutralized the audible musical characteristic of the tune by reducing it to its intervallic content and by forcing it into a vertically and horizontally unified space. Although this setting remained incomplete, the compositional technique Schoenberg used in his next Jewish piece, *Kol nidre,* shows a very similar approach.

JEWISH UNITY THROUGH RITUAL: *KOL NIDRE*

The idea for Schoenberg's *Kol nidre* came from Los Angeles Reform Rabbi Jakob Sonderling. A German émigré who came to the United States from Hamburg in 1923 and moved to Los Angeles in 1935, Sonderling encouraged innovations and changes in Conservative Reform Yom Kippur services.[72] This openness to innovation may have been one reason he was willing to collaborate with Schoenberg in the creation of a highly individual version of the Kol nidre service, about which Saminsky, then music director of New York's Temple Emanuel-El, predicted, "the Rabbis [would] raise Cain."[73]

Schoenberg, who was not a member of any Jewish congregation in Los Angeles, met Rabbi Sonderling through his friend Joseph Achron, who, after leaving Russia in 1922, emigrated to the United States in 1925 and settled in Los Angeles in 1934. Practical and religious considerations played an equal role in Schoenberg's acceptance of Sonderling's commission. Through the rabbi, the composer hoped to establish connections with wealthy Jews who would provide affidavits for his acquaintances trying to escape from Europe, which, after Hitler's occupation of Austria in March 1938, became even more urgent.[74] Schoenberg also believed that his collaboration with Sonderling could lead, after *Kol nidre*, to a series of liturgical pieces. Of these only a few measures of a setting of the Yom Kippur hymn "Yaaleh" (May it rise) survive.[75]

*Kol nidre* was the first liturgical composition Schoenberg attempted and the only one he completed. The adjustment to liturgical composition was not easy for him. His personal convictions about Judaism caused Schoenberg to rebel against both the text and the melody of the traditional Kol nidre. Many German Jews shared his squeamishness about the ritual. Originating as an incantation in the Babylonian period, Kol nidre is not a prayer but a legal formula. Although written in a confusion of tongues and tenses, and plagued by both legal and ethical inconsistencies, Kol nidre gained a central position in the ritual of the High Holy Days. The Ashkenazi version of the ritual reads as follows:

> All *nidrei, esarei, charamei, konamei, chinuyei, kinusei,* and *shevuei* (vows, prohibitive vows, oaths, vows of dedication, *konam*-vows, *konas*-vows, and equivalent terms) which we have vowed, sworn, declared, and imposed upon ourselves from this Day of Atonement until the next Day of Atonement may it come upon us for good. Regarding them all, we regret them. Let them all be released, forgiven, erased, null and void. They are not valid nor are they in force. Our vows *[nidreina]* are not vows. Our prohibitive vows *[esareina]* are not prohibitive vows. Our oaths *[shevu'atana]* are not oaths.[76]

The most puzzling aspect of the Ashkenazi text was the annulment of vows not only in retrospect but also for the year to come. Schoenberg, for one, was "horrified" and announced the text to be "truly immoral" and "false," as well as "diametrically opposed to the lofty morality of all the Jewish commandments."[77]

Schoenberg's judgment reflected the opinion of many anti-Semites, for whom the Kol nidre ritual was an easy target. In Russia, under anti-Semitic pressure an explanatory preface was added to the formula in 1860. In Germany after 1844 the entire text was dropped from the Reform ritual and replaced by Psalm 130.[78] The Kol nidre was reintroduced in the twentieth century partially because of the popularity of its melody, but also because in 1917 Joseph S. Bloch (1850–1923), a prominent Jewish publicist, proposed a dramatic theory about the origin of the text. Although Bloch's theory has never been proven, his idea that Kol nidre arose as a reaction to forced Jewish conversions to Christianity provided an emotional as well as rational basis for the revival of the prayer.[79]

This theory also helped Schoenberg reconcile himself to the Kol nidre. He read about the persecution of the Jews in Spain in Solomon Ibn Verga's *Shevet Yehudah* (c. 1520), a book Klatzkin lent him in 1933.[80] In his explanation of the Kol nidre ritual Schoenberg repeated the popular view that "whenever under pressure of persecution a Jew was forced to make oaths, vows or promises counter to his inherited belief in our religious principles, he was allowed to repent them and to declare them null and void. Thus," Schoenberg wrote in his notes on *Kol nidre*, "he was allowed to pray with the community as a Jew among Jews."[81]

Although all Reform prayer books use paraphrased, rationalized versions of the traditional text, Schoenberg's *Kol nidre* has the unmistakable mark of the composer's own Credo, emphasizing the idea of the "Chosen People," who are elected by the "One, Everlasting, Unseen, Unfathomable God" for a sacred task. Drafted by Sonderling, the final version of the text of Schoenberg's *Kol nidre* bears the mark of the composer's heavy revisions:

*Schoenberg's Text*

INTRODUCTION

*Sonderling's Text*

The Masterspirit gazed
upon void
Inert nothingness he
faced—silence—
emptiness, darkness.

1   The Kabalah tells a legend:
At the beginning God said: *"Let There Be Light."*     "Let There Be Light." The
Maker breathed the
Out of space a flame burst out.                        words and—out of
space—a light burst out.
Under the kisses of its rays
vast worlds began to
wheel, plants burgeoned,
wings fluttered, shapes
crawled and climbed,
life struggled into being.
Upon the light He gazed,
the Maker.
About to make the world,                              Then He took it, threw it
God crushed that light to atoms.                  down to earth, crushed
it to atoms.
The phosphorescent
fragments fell down
to ground,
and there they lay,
5   Myriads of sparks are hidden in our world.     half buried, hidden
in the furrows.

Not all of us behold them.
The self-glorious one, who walks arrogantly
   upright will never perceive one.

But the meek and modest—eyes downcast,
   he sees it.

"A light is sown for the pious."

The proud, self-glorious
   mortal, walking with
   eyes searching the
   heights will tread upon
   the sparks . . .
But the humble, the meek
   and modest one, going
   through life with
   downcast eyes, out of
   a sudden—discovers
   something shining
   on the ground
a spark—his spark; a
   light—his light,
   his message from the
   Maker.
   "A Light Is Sown For The
   Pious."
Tonight we come with eyes
   cast down. Where is our
   light?
Oh let us find our light.
Our Sorua lazadik.

10    Bishivo Shel Maalo Uvishivo Shel Mato
[in the sight of God and of the congregation]
In the Name of God!
We solemnly proclaim—that
Every Transgressor
Be it that he was Unfaithful to Our People Because of Fear
15    Or Misled by False Doctrines of Any Kind,
Out of Weakness or Greed
We Give him Leave
To be One with Us in Prayer Tonight.
A light is sown for the pious—
   a light is sown for the *repenting* sinner.
Kol nidre
20    All Vows and Oaths, and Promises and Plights of Any Kind
Wherewith we pledged ourselves
Counter to Our Inherited Faith in God
Who is One, Everlasting, Unseen, Unfathomable—
We declare These null and void.
25    We repent that these obligations have *estranged* us
From the sacred task we were *chosen* for.
We shall strive from this day of Atonement till the next
To avoid such and similar obligations,
So that the Yom Kippur to follow

30   May come to us for good.—
Whatever binds us to falsehood
May be absolved, released, annulled, made void and of no
    power.—
Hence all such Vows shall be no Vows.
All such Bonds shall be no Bonds.
35   All such Oaths shall be no Oaths.
[RECAP. OF THE PRAYER]
   We repent
   Null and void be our vows
   We repent them.
   A light is shown for the sinner.
[RECAP. OF INTRODUCTION]
   We give him leave to be ONE with us in prayer tonight.[82]

Schoenberg's text is a didactic explanation of how Kol nidre should be understood. Instead of the annulment of future vows, it contains the promise to abstain from such vows in the future. Even more Schoenbergian is his replacement of the word describing what is being absolved from "vows" to "whatever binds us to falsehood." He also included his definition of God in the text, thus transforming the legal formula into a prayer against "falsehood" that would break the unity of God's chosen people (see the Kol nidre proper in lines 20–35). In the second part of the introduction Schoenberg's underlining of "false doctrines" (line 15) reminds one of his lists of evils in his political statements and in *The Biblical Way*. Viewed in the context of the composer's political propaganda in the 1930s, Schoenberg's interpretation of the text suggests that he recognized the Kol nidre as the purifying ritual through which Jewish unity could be created on a religious basis.

POLITICAL IMPLICATIONS: "A FOUR-POINT PROGRAM FOR JEWRY"

The underlying political implications of Schoenberg's *Kol nidre* come into even sharper focus when we consider that he completed his propagandistic essay "A Four-Point Program for Jewry" in October 1938, just two months after the composition of *Kol nidre*. That the composer saw *Kol nidre* and his political propaganda essay as a unit is demonstrated by the fact that he combined his "Notes on Kol Nidrey" and the "Four-point Program" into a single document.[83] It is unclear why Schoenberg renewed his interest in Jewish affairs in 1938. It seems logical to see the escalation of events in Europe as triggering his involvement and the essay as a reaction to the violence of *Kristallnacht* (9 November 1938), the infamous Nazi attack on Jews throughout Germany and Austria. Yet the "Four-Point Program" predates *Kristallnacht* by a month.

The content of the "Four-Point Program" is very similar to the earlier writings. The four points in which Schoenberg summarized his central political views are as follows:

I. The fight against anti-Semitism must be stopped
II. A united Jewish party must be created
III. Unanimity in Jewry must be enforced with all means
IV. Ways must be prepared to obtain a place to erect an independent Jewish state.

Claiming that he had failed to find a magazine in the United States that would publish "A Four-Point Program for Jewry," Schoenberg sent the thirty-seven-page essay to Thomas Mann, asking him to help publish the article in Europe. Mann's recommendation, Schoenberg believed, could also help "overcome the superstition that a musician can write about nothing but music."[84] Although interested in the subject, Mann was shocked by Schoenberg's violent tone and the defamatory and personal rhetoric of the essay. Since Mann's is one of the most thoughtful and detailed contemporary reactions to Schoenberg's ideas about Jewish politics, it is worth quoting his letter at length:

> My natural reactions varied from the heartiest approval to a certain dismay over the frequently brutish tone, whether it be in the individual polemics or in the overall mental stance, which smacks indeed somewhat of fascism. Excuse the latter term, which is of course in no way applicable here. What I really mean is a certain predisposition toward terrorism, which to me signifies a tolerance for the fascist orientations. The reaction to such a brutal pounding and attack surely is humanly understandable, and yet I find that we should not give in to its temptation and that especially the unconditional power political orientation does not do justice to Judaism's particular spirituality, which you yourself so correctly describe as fundamentally religious in nature, is not a very appealing one.
>
> I need hardly mention that your article contains important and most persuasive points. It is above all the polemics against the anti-Semitism that seems most noteworthy to me. The appeal to reason and logic has indeed born so little fruit that it is hardly of any use any longer in the real world's battles.

To make publication possible, Mann encouraged Schoenberg to change his tone:

> There is for me no question about the desirability of getting your paper published. The practical implications have to be thought through most carefully; for one is dealing here with matters Judaic and the article therefore belongs in a Jewish publication. On the other hand, it is humanly only too understandable that Jewish periodicals cannot bring themselves to publish an article, in which the whole Jewish leadership is attacked with such radicalism and unbridled harshness of expression. In my opinion the defamatory and all too personal element in your article would have to be toned down before there

can be any thought of submitting it further. I am returning the manuscript to you with many thanks and with the suggestion that you go over it once more with the practical implications of publishing in mind.[85]

Surprisingly, Mann's criticism did not seem to have offended Schoenberg. Accustomed to outright rejections of his political views, he took the fact that Mann had not completely dismissed his essay as encouraging. In his answer to Mann he repeated his misgivings about democracy (in which "only those who say what people want to hear have the opportunity" to speak up), his belief that Jewish unity cannot be achieved without the use of strong methods, and his conviction that acts of violence are occasionally the only remedies. Schoenberg admitted to Mann that he was neither a "left-wing extremist" ("I would not grant the right to free expression of opinion to everyone, but only to those who can really say something that is worth saying"), nor a "right-wing extremist" ("I don't believe in the value of making everything equally dull"), but probably "a most progressive conservative who would like to bring forward and develop what's worth preserving." He could "appreciate the value of democracy," although he could not "ignore its weakest points: that those who exaggerate opportunity as its principle in an orthodox way are up to turn it upside down." He did not overlook "the ill of fascism, for those who through the power given to them don't do anything with it but hand it to the wrong hands." Though unusually uncertain of himself, he insisted that he was "not the one who writes: truth was writing."[86] He never revised the text. The "Four-Point Program," like his political writings from 1933 and 1934, remained unknown until Ringer published it in the appendix of *Arnold Schoenberg: The Composer as Jew* in 1990.[87]

Although unpublished, some of the political demands formulated in the essay found their way into the text of *Kol nidre*. Schoenberg reveals his political inspiration by the remark he added in the margin to Sonderling's words "Our people:" "not nationalistic enough."[88] In line seven Schoenberg added his pet word "arrogant" to Sonderling's text. A feature characteristic of the entire Jewish people in Schoenberg's "Four-Point Program" and thus justifying anti-Semitism,[89] now the adjective refers only to the "self-glorious" Jews who, because of their arrogance, cannot perceive the "myriads of sparks" in the world. The division between those who can and those who cannot see these hidden sparks signals that in *Kol nidre*, as in his political programs, Schoenberg envisioned a Jewish unity consisting of a chosen, leading elite and obedient masses.

### GIVING DIGNITY TO MUSIC IN *KOL NIDRE*

Schoenberg's revisions affected not only the words but the traditional melody as well, which had been responsible for keeping the Kol nidre ritual alive for centuries despite the controversies over the text. After examining seven variants of the traditional tune, Schoenberg, ever the compositional taskmaster, diagnosed serious flaws in the melody: "This melody in spite of its very striking beginning suffers from monotony which is principally caused through the minor key in which most of its parts are composed. . . . Furthermore there were some objections against the structural appearance of this melody. We are accustomed that melodies are 'built up' onto a certain climax. Nothing of this kind can be observed in this melody. It ends without any musical reason. It simply does not continue, but the ending is neither prepared, nor built up, nor emphasized. This is very unsatisfactory."[90] To provide the tune with "seriousness, and solemnity," and "to give this DECREE the dignity of a law, of an edict," Schoenberg decided that his main task consisted of "vitriolizing out the 'cello-sentimentality' of the Bruchs."[91] The result was, as Paul Dessau put it, a "highly heroic and dramatic interpretation of the prayer,"[92] which Schoenberg achieved by forcing the sentimental G-minor melody into a march-like rhythmic frame (see especially the chorus parts at mm. 94ff.).

Schoenberg used only the "striking" first part of the tune, creating his version after analyzing four of his models.[93] Although opposed to what he called "cheap embellishments and ornamentations," which he attributed to the singers of the melody, who, the composer remarked, have a "natural inclination towards sentimentality,"[94] Schoenberg kept most of the embellishments he found in his models. The most important change he made was his elimination of the expressive appoggiatura that is part and parcel of the second measure of all versions of the traditional tune. He shifted the meter so that in his rendition each of the first four measures contains only one pitch. Compared to his models, Schoenberg's first phrase is bare and angular, like Adolf Loos's puritan architectural designs (ex. 81).

Schoenberg uses the melody, with slight variants, twice in the piece: once in the G-minor orchestral accompaniment to the rabbi's recitation of the Kol nidre text, and a second time in A♭-minor sung unison by the chorus at the repetition of the same text. But even when the entire melody is absent, motivic variants of its opening permeate the score. As in "Holem tza'adi," Schoenberg distilled a three-note (two-interval) kernel of the tune, derived from the first three notes of the first line of the melody. This three-note motive lends unity to the piece, providing a link between sections with markedly different characters (ex. 82). The distinctly Oriental motive that dominates the orchestral prelude, for instance, contains both the prime and the inversion of the kernel (ex. 82b). By incorporating a major seventh into an inverted form of the original version, Schoenberg put his own stamp most clearly on the fourth and sixth versions of the motive ("d" and "f" in ex. 82). Even two notes, like in motive "e" (m. 27), can indicate the presence of the

Example 81. Comparison of the Kol nidre melody by Baruch Schorr, one of Schoenberg's models, and by Schoenberg.

Baruch Schorr (1906)

Schoenberg

Schorr

Schoenberg

Example 82. The six versions of Schoenberg's Kol nidre motive.

a. The Kol nidre motive at the beginning of Schoenberg's *Kol Nidre*, mm. 5–6.

b. Prime and inversion of the kernel of the motive, m. 9.

c. Inversion of the motive, mm. 15–16.

(*continued*)

Example 82 *(continued)*

d. Version with major seventh, mm. 15–16.

e. Two notes indicating the motive, m. 27.

f. Second version with major seventh, mm. 181–84.

unifying motive of the piece. This intricacy of motivic elaboration, exemplified by mm. 15–16 in which all parts play rhythmically and metrically different variants of the prime and the inversion of the motive, demonstrates Schoenberg's method of assimilating the traditional tune to his personal style so that it can serve as the material for abstract musical procedures (ex. 83).[95]

Despite this modernist approach, nineteenth-century associations abound in the piece. The orchestral prelude, for instance, is a typically nineteenth-century creation prologue. Schoenberg builds the text, which retroactively explains the music, around the line "A Light Is Sown For The Pious," a quotation from Psalm 97:11 that starts the evening service proper on Yom Kippur. He uses the command "Let there be light" to reveal his ideas about the nature of creation, not only God's but also his own artistic creation.[96]

More crucially, the central motive is hidden in a harmonic progression in which Mäckelmann accurately recognized Wagner's "Tarnhelm" motive from the *Ring*. Mäckelmann buried his discovery in footnotes, explaining that although Schoenberg must have been aware of the similarity between his and Wagner's harmonic progressions, "the different characteristics" of Schoenberg's harmonies in *Kol nidre* imply that he did not intend to quote Wagner here.[97] The progression (minor triads a major third apart, followed by a major triad a fifth higher), however, is an obvious reference to the "Tarnhelm" motive, quite in agreement with Schoenberg's interpretation of the

Example 83. Contrapuntal elaboration of the Kol nidre motive in mm. 15–16 in
Schoenberg's *Kol nidre*.

Kol nidre ritual (ex. 84). In the first act of *Götterdämmerung*, the Tarnhelm
is the magic object that helps Siegfried break his vow made to Brünnhilde
in order to satisfy the false oath that he makes with Gunther after he un-
knowingly drinks a potion. The harmonic progression at the beginning of
*Kol nidre*, combined with the idea of transformation-absolution implied by
the text, stands for a similar idea—for a false vow that needs to be absolved
by the Kol nidre ritual.

The reference to Wagner, however, is not the most uncomfortable aspect
of Schoenberg's *Kol nidre*. What Dessau meant by "dramatic" interpretation
was Schoenberg's hierarchical separation of rabbi (speaker) and congregation (chorus), one absolving, the other repenting sins. They even present
the melody in different keys (G minor and A♭ minor), the congregation reaching a *fortissimo* declaration of the main motive on G (m. 159) only after long
sections of forceful marches. The end of the work is marked by the return

Example 84. Comparison of Schoenberg's introductory harmonies in *Kol nidre* and Wagner's "Tarnhelm" chords.

of motive "f," providing a final gesture with which Schoenberg forces the original motive into what we might consider its most Schoenbergian or modernistic form (ex. 85). The authoritative presence of this motive at the end of *Kol nidre* suggests that it is not Schoenberg's penitent voice that we hear in the closing choral *fortissimo* "we repent."[98] The role Schoenberg assumes in *Kol nidre* is again that of the leader or of the rabbi who, acting like a priest, absolves the penitent Jews.

Although motivically complex, Schoenberg's setting of the Kol nidre reverts to what for Schoenberg was already an outmoded style. The tonal *Kol nidre* is indeed an odd fit in the company of the twelve-tone Violin Concerto, op. 36, and Fourth String Quartet, op. 37. Schoenberg was too squeamish to admit that his *Kol nidre* was indeed a "tonal piece" and described it to Saminsky somewhat defensively as a "modern (but not 'atonal')" work.[99] Despite the occasional twelve-tone aggregates—used in a pre-dodecaphonic, symbolic way, marking places where the text refers to the first light of creation (m. 33)—*Kol nidre* seems nevertheless to be a compromise, at least from Schoenberg's modernist point of view. It is the furthest point Schoenberg ever went in adapting his style to a Jewish idiom. *Kol nidre* thus arrived at a surprising synthesis of presenting Schoenberg's religious and political convictions in a musical idiom that bears the composer's personal mark yet remains explicitly related to Jewish tradition.

The magic wrought by the ritualistic annulment of earlier attachments—in Schoenberg's case the temporary abandonment of dodecaphony—was powerless in at least one respect. Schoenberg's gesture of working in a Jewish idiom did not bring the acknowledgment the composer expected. Three

Example 85. End of Schoenberg's *Kol nidre* (reduced score).

years after the first performance the disappointed Schoenberg wrote to Saminsky that he had "supposed that [the fact that he wrote a *Kol nidre*] would soon be known throughout the country." But, as he added bitterly, "it was not."[100] Adding insult to injury, Saminsky refused to perform the piece because, he wrote to Schoenberg, "it would be difficult to induce the Congregation, now extremely careful in expenditure, to allow even a small orchestra." Besides financial problems, however, Saminsky was also wary of Schoenberg's text, which, he explained, is "too far from the standard version of even the Reform Synagogue."[101] Saminsky's opposition offended Schoenberg. Aware of the differences between Jewish religious communities mainly in theory, Schoenberg did not take into consideration that Saminsky, the musical director of the most conservative Reform temple in New York, represented only one of many Jewish opinions. Nevertheless, Schoenberg saw in Saminsky's rejection a grim confirmation of his belief that the Jews were unwilling to accept his music.[102] This disappointment over the reception of *Kol nidre* may have contributed to Schoenberg's reluctance to write more liturgical music.

·    ·    ·

Schoenberg never realized that the main obstacle to achieving unity in his vision of Judaism was not "false doctrines" such as liberalism, intellectualism, democracy, or socialism (to list only a few of his favorite evils), but himself. As his works and writings demonstrate, he was in fact the most unassimilable element in a Jewish tradition, the diversity of which was incongruous with Schoenberg's belief in abstract, spiritual totality. That is why in addition to the "inconceivable God" and "the Chosen People," the principle of "the leader of the people" had to be presented as one of the central ideas in *Moses und Aron*, and, by extension, in all his work. In Schoenberg's view, only by following a strong-minded leader, accepting his interpretation of Jewish politics, Jewish religion, and Jewish music, could Jewish unity be achieved. His way of returning to Judaism was thus assimilating Judaism to his artistic convictions. These convictions preferred abstraction to practice, spirit to material, and idea to its representation. But preference did not mean that Schoenberg was willing to push his musical conceptions to the abstract extremes his followers have done or that he was inclined to actively engage in real political action. His political writings represent only excursions to utopia, experiments that applied musical conceptions to politics. The musical torsos demonstrate his inability to solve the self-imposed conflict between idea and its realization. The question of how "Jewish" these projects were could be answered only if one is willing to define what "Jewish" meant in such an idiosyncratic context.

# Chapter 8

# On the Ashes of the Holocaust

## Anxiety, Abstraction, and
## Schoenberg's Rhetoric of Fear

*The mind resists what it feels to be imaginatively valid but wants to disbelieve; and the task of the artist is to find a style and a form to present the atmosphere or landscape of atrocity, to make it compelling, to coax the reader into credulity—and ultimately, complicity. The fundamental task of the critic is not to ask whether it should or can be done, since it already has been, but to evaluate how it has been done, judge its effectiveness, and analyze its implications for literature and for society.*
LAWRENCE L. LANGER, *The Holocaust and the Literary Imagination* (1975)

In response to attempts by music critics Kurt List and René Leibowitz (1913–72) to focus attention on the twelve-tone construction of Arnold Schoenberg's shocking Holocaust memorial *A Survivor from Warsaw*, Henry Cowell described the piece by making a catalog of its surface gestures: "double-basses low, divided into three parts, tremolando; a muted trombone chord; repeated notes in a jerky rhythm in bassoons and oboes; burbling clarinets; muted strings in a figure of three notes occupying the space of two octaves and a major sixth." Cowell resisted the temptation to search for technically complex unifying relationships between the notes, and instead characterized the *Survivor* as "rhapsodic and impassioned," a work whose "categories of sound and rhythm . . . are precisely identical with those used in Opus 16 [*Five Orchestral Pieces*], a work written before the idea of the twelve-tone row was conceived."[1] Cowell made his comment in 1950, on the occasion of the *Survivor*'s New York premiere. Since then, Leibowitz's conviction that in the *Survivor* Schoenberg achieved "the highest synthesis of extra-musical and purely musical elements," in other words, that subject matter and artistic realization cohered into a work of exceptional aesthetic quality, has become the accepted view.[2] The "extra-musical," as the expression indicates, has been considered "extra," something beside the point. In this equation, then, aesthetics occupies a higher sphere, while subject matter, in this case the Holocaust, is considered only raw material put in the service of artistic expression and ultimately transcended by art. Accepted as this view may be in art criticism, the reduction of the Holocaust to disposable subject matter raises serious questions about the moral implications of art's autonomy.

Strangely, what has fallen outside of analytical interest seems to have included not only the subject matter, but, as Arnold Whittall pointed out in his entry on analysis in the *Oxford Companion to Music,* also "all the surface features" of music, "the stressed dissonances, unexpected shifts of texture, memorable melodic flights," in other words, everything that "listeners tend to find most immediately striking and memorable."[3] In an analytical climate that has expressly preferred depth to surface, hidden to obvious, it is no surprise that the expressive gestures of music have been generally banished from serious analyses of Schoenberg's work. To reestablish the relevance of surface elements and of their relation to subject matter to the analysis of Schoenberg's music, this chapter traces the expressionist gestures of fear and anxiety from Schoenberg's monodrama *Erwartung,* op. 17 (1909), "Premonitions" (the first of *Five Orchestral Pieces,* op. 16, 1909), and the twelve-tone *Begleitmusik zu einer Lichtspielscene,* op. 34 (1929–30), through *A Survivor from Warsaw,* op. 46 (1947). To explain Schoenberg's consistent reliance on these gestures I revisit art historian Wilhelm Worringer's theory about the interrelationship between anxiety and abstraction.

In *Erwartung* the musical gestures are intimately related to the text. Similar gestures appear also in instrumental pieces that, like "Premonitions," generate a similar sense of anxiety. But while the motivic construction of the monodrama is purposely loose, allowing a fast and extremely precise musical response to the text, "Premonitions" exhibits a more rationally organized thinking. This motivic organization can be seen as a reaction to what Worringer dubbed the "urge to abstraction," the result of which, Worringer argued, served to create an abstract order missing from the world characterized by disorder and growing anxiety. Viewing the changing focus of Schoenberg's musical language from expression to abstraction in Worringer's terms, the composer's discovery of twelve-tone technique, the ultimate abstraction in Schoenberg's style, can also be seen as a response to anxiety. In this context Schoenberg's attraction to abstraction can be understood less as a specifically Jewish tendency originating in the abstract potential of Judaism and in the Second Commandment against making graven images than as an attempted escape from expressionist anxiety. Yet gestures of anxiety, fear, and violence remained prevalent in Schoenberg's music even in twelve-tone compositions, as in *Begleitmusik* and the *Survivor.*

By combining his anxiety-producing musical idiom with horrifying subject matter, Schoenberg's abstract style finally achieved popular acclaim in the *Survivor.* This late work influenced not only the reception of Schoenberg's music but also interpretations of his Jewish identity. Since in the *Survivor* his strong, ethnically nonspecific, anxiety-ridden musical language was coupled with this tragic Jewish subject, Schoenberg's previous artistic utterances were turned into prophetic "premonitions" of Jewish fate.[4] Rather than retroactively turning Schoenberg's anxiety into a specifically Jewish experience, this chapter provides a background for the musical language of fear and violence in the *Survivor*. The effectiveness of this work was partially the result of Schoenberg's successful translation of gestures of abstract anxiety into specific gestures of violence, a procedure demonstrated also by Alban Berg's adaptation of expressionist gestures to realistic dramatic scenes in *Wozzeck*. The translation of abstract gestures to representation of concrete events, however successful, results in stylization, which, in the case of Holocaust art, raises ethical questions about the limits of artistic representation in general, and Schoenberg's approach in particular.

### CRIES OF DISTRESS

At the end of 1908 Richard Gerstl, a promising young painter and Schoenberg's private tutor in painting, eloped with the composer's wife, Mathilde. When Anton Webern persuaded Mathilde to return to her husband, "Gerstl positioned himself in front of his atelier mirror, tightened a noose around his neck, and plunged a butcher knife into his chest."[5] Not all suicides in the first decade of the twentieth century were as gruesome as Gerstl's. His staging, executing, and observing his own death, however, expressed the desire of a whole generation of artists to possess, in the spirit of Rainer Maria Rilke's *The Notebooks of Malte Laurids Brigge* (1907), their own death, and thus diminish the constant despair that made suicide a natural climax of life.

Schoenberg's credo that "art is the cry of distress uttered by those who experience at first hand the fate of mankind"[6] expressed the general mood of the time. In his *Harmonielehre* Schoenberg quoted his favorite authors, August Strindberg (who said that "life makes everything ugly") and Maurice Maeterlinck (who believed that "three-quarters of our brothers are condemned to misery"), to support his pessimistic worldview. Schoenberg and his fellow expressionists considered everything that was pleasant or comforting "superficial," and hence outside the realm of art. It was the world of no comfort that, in Schoenberg's belief, mattered most and needed to be expressed in art.[7]

Expressionist art did not promise relief. The artist's obligation was to observe, analyze, and express—not to ease—pain. Since pain was located inside the artist himself, self-portraits abound in paintings. An extreme case even among expressionists, Schoenberg painted at least eighty-five portraits of himself, none of which show the artist at ease, smiling, and happy (fig. 6). Adorno equated this expressionist "negation of illusion and play" with a tendency "toward the direction of knowledge."[8] He never specified what kind of knowledge was to be gained, but, as Adorno implied, it seems to have been restricted to the dark and threatening side of human nature.

Figure 6. Schoenberg, self-portrait, colored chalk on paper (Catalogue raisonné 262). © 2006 Belmont Music Publishers/Artists Rights Society (ARS), New York/ VBK, Vienna.

It is impossible to detect what precisely caused this expressionist malaise. To be sure, the decade culminating in World War I was an age of angst. Historical, economic, and political causes are easy to find, but it would be hard to argue that the early 1900s were psychologically more trying than post–World War I, pre–World War II, or post–World War II times. A primary difference, then, was that in the prewar period, which lacked the postwar ironic distance from emotion, anxiety, this age-old human feeling, produced a strong artistic response from a generation in search of itself.

Fear of the unknown sometimes manifested itself in fear of violence, which found its way into disturbing images in art, or, as Gerstl's manner of suicide exemplifies, into real-life enactment of violent artistic fantasies. Schoenberg became a central figure among expressionist artists because he was able to give musical voice to the fears that his fellow artists searched to express. For them his music was a fitting soundtrack to their anxious fantasies. In its abstraction, Schoenberg's music was also the perfect medium to express anxiety, the fear of the unknown and the unspeakable.

Unknown and unspeakable fear is the subject of Edvard Munch's famous picture *The Scream* (1893). "I was walking along the road with two friends," Munch recalls.

> The sun set. I felt a tinge of melancholy. Suddenly the sky became a bloody red.
> I stopped, leaned against the railing, dead tired, and I looked at the flaming clouds that hung like blood and a sword over the blue-black fjord and the city.
> My friends walked on. I stood there, trembling with fright. And I felt a loud, unending scream piercing nature.[9]

In the picture the sound is transformed into an image of a howling man who, while screaming, loses his personal features. In Thomas Harrison's description: "His eyes and mouth are holes, as though nature had made these organs of perception and articulation dysfunctional out of malice. The man cups the ears of his hairless head with his hands, trying to block out the piercing sounds of the swirling, circumambient universe. Wandering away from dark, retreating figures impervious to this clash of abstract forces, he is witness to a nightmare outside himself. Internal though it be, his anguish is caused by cosmic pressure."[10]

Cosmic pressure or emerging insanity, the cause of Munch's *Scream* remains unknown, and hence the picture is a paradigmatic image of anxiety (fig. 7). Anxiety is produced in the viewer partially by the contrast between the intense emotionality of the frontal figure and the staid calmness of two distinctly bourgeois men in the background. The latter's unawareness of abstract forces is depicted as deafness, for they do not seem to hear either the sounds of the universe or the scream of the figure facing us. These sounds, the intensity of which is indicated by the frontal figure's wide open mouth and blocked ears, remain imprisoned in the silent genre of the picture.

Figure 7. Edvard Munch, *The Scream,* lithograph. © 2006 The
Munch Museum/The Munch-Ellingsen Group/Artists Rights
Society (ARS), New York, used by permission.

The cosmic sound may be undecipherable, yet we suspect a word in the
howl. For anyone with an aural memory of shocking moments in twentieth-
century German opera, the missing word is *Hilfe* (help), the word Marie
screams at the moment of her murder in Berg's *Wozzeck,* or, to find an earlier and more abstract example, it is the word Schoenberg's female protagonist screams when frightened either by nature in darkness or by the phan-
toms of her overstressed imagination (ex. 86a–b). Schoenberg's scream must

Example 86. Three operatic screams.

a. Berg, *Wozzeck*, m. 103.

Hil - fe!

*seizes her and plunges the knife into her throat*

(Help!)

b. Schoenberg, *Erwartung*, mm. 188–93.

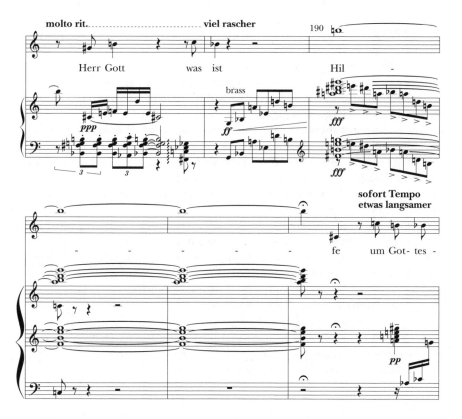

(Oh, God, what is it? Help!)

Example 86 *(continued)*

c. Wagner, *Parsifal,* act 2 (8 mm. after rehearsal number 154).

lach  -  te . . .

(I laughed.)

have been on Berg's mind, since he chose the same $b^2$ as his teacher to get a high note that could still be sung with the intensity of a *fortissimo*. Berg's second note, b, arrived at via a dramatic leap, is different from Schoenberg's $c\sharp^1$. Yet as the parentheses around the note indicate, it is the register and not the exact pitch that matters.

The scream in Schoenberg's *Erwartung* is an intensified version of the scream in Wagner's *Parsifal,* in which a wild, hysterical Kundry recalls her blasphemous laughter at the sight of the suffering Savior with the same immense leap ($b^2$ to $c\sharp^1$).[11] Kundry's scream, like the woman's in *Erwartung,* is unexpected and unprepared in the voice (ex. 86c). Both Wagner's and Schoenberg's climaxes are followed by a moment of silence. But while Kundry's high note is accompanied by a half-diminished seventh chord, Schoenberg increases the level of dissonance to an unprecedented degree by contrasting an A diminished triad with G♯ in the woodwinds and clashing the woodwind sonority with a brass chord comprising the notes of an E-minor pentachord, all underlined by the timpani's tremolo C♯. The result is a ninenote chord that would be hard to define in conventional harmonic terms. Its main characteristic is its intensity of dissonance created by major sevenths/diminished octaves that clash against all notes of the sonority.

### TROMBONES, OSTINATOS, AND OTHER MUSICAL SIGNS OF FEAR

Although the level of dissonance is certainly high in the woman's scream in *Erwartung,* it is not merely the pitch content that gives this moment its horrifying power. Because dissonance became part and parcel of Schoenberg's musical language, the composer had to rely on other means to create effects of terror. Sudden dynamic change (here, for instance, the *fortissimo* outburst is surrounded by *pianissimo* whispering), increased density of texture, extreme leaps, frightening, rushed melodic gestures, and constant melodic, harmonic, and textural discontinuity all contribute to the shocking effect. These are musical gestures that Adorno, describing *Erwartung*, aptly compared to "gestures of shock resembling bodily convulsions."[12]

Besides the presence of at least some of these gestures, what seems to be common in all of Schoenberg's depictions of terror is the composer's use of brass instruments, especially trombones. Because of their strong ecclesiastical associations (resulting from their frequent employment in early church music), trombones became signs of supernatural presence in eighteenth- and nineteenth-century operas. Richard Strauss still relied on this connotation when he underscored Jokanaan's pronunciations in *Salome* with a slow-moving choir of four trombones. Schoenberg followed suit when he doubled the vocal line in Shema Yisroel with trombones in the *Survivor*. Beginning with Mozart's Requiem (and Don Giovanni's fall into hell), trombones also recalled the Last Judgment and thus expressed human fear of cosmic violence. Berlioz thought that the instrument could portray almost everything, "from religious, calm and imposing accents to savage, orgiastic outbursts." Trombones "can chant like a choir of priests, threaten, utter gloomy sighs, a mournful lament or a bright hymn of glory," Berlioz wrote. "They can break forth into awe-inspiring cries and awaken the dead or doom the living with their fearful voices." In his expressionist works Schoenberg was relying on the last effect in Berlioz's list. As Berlioz observed, the character of timbre varied also by the degree of loudness.[13] As the passage leading to the woman's scream in *Erwartung* demonstrates, in *fortissimo* the sound is menacing and terrifying, especially since the brass are used in unison.

This menacing character is enhanced when the instruments are muted, a practice introduced at the beginning of the twentieth century and exploited by Strauss, who used muted trombones in *Salome* at moments of impending gloom and danger, indicating the presence of something uncanny, repugnant, and threatening.[14] Schoenberg's use of muted trombones bears a strong similarity to Strauss's, especially in its association with frightening, threatening moments. Even short, fanfare-like figures achieve this effect, like the one at the first melodic appearance of the trombones in *Erwartung*, coinciding, significantly, with the word "fear" in the text (ex. 87). The association of fear with muted trombone timbre remains constant throughout the monodrama.

Muted trombones can imply not only fear but also violence. At the moment when the woman cries out "Was? Lass los eingeklemmt!" (What's that? Is it caught?), the combination of the brass outbursts with percussive effects

Example 87. Schoenberg, *Erwartung*, mm. 11–12.

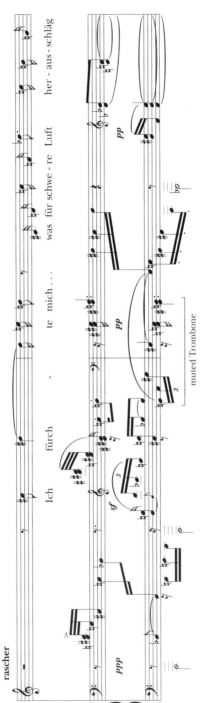

(I am afraid ... How heavy is the air that comes out of there ... )

Example 88. Schoenberg, *Erwartung,* mm. 40–41.

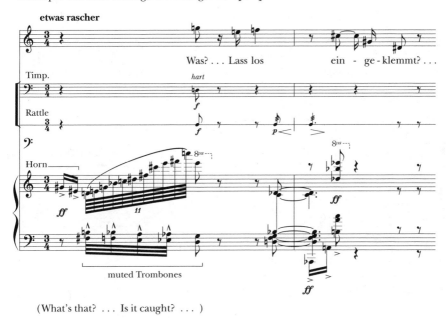

(What's that? . . . Is it caught? . . . )

has military connotations (ex. 88). Angst, at least in Schoenberg's version, thus has a strong component of fear of physical violence. Having any physical relationship with the outside world seems to trigger this kind of fear— hence the woman's horror when touching inanimate objects or living animals (ex. 89). The climax, again emphasized by the use of muted brass, is achieved here at the end of a steady buildup during which isolated, shockingly short musical motives in the woodwinds and the brass provide the intensifying power against the repeated static figures in the strings.

Since the opera is punctuated by similar moments of violence, the woman's increasingly frequent screams point beyond psychological torture. Her terrified recognition of her lover in the shadows makes her utter a scream that (especially because of its violent reverberation in the orchestra) recalls Herod's command to murder Salome in Strauss's opera. Herod's order is followed by a brutally naturalistic aural depiction of slaughter, mercifully hidden from the spectators' eyes by the falling curtain. Yet Strauss's high-pitched, shrieking woodwinds produce a brutal effect even without visual help. Strauss arrives at Herod's outburst by cutting short Salome's erotic ecstasy with a violent D-minor brass chord that aggressively cancels the previous C♯

Example 89. Schoenberg, *Erwartung*, mm. 109–11.

(How it glares . . . Not an animal, dear God, not an animal . . . )

tonality and pushes the ending a half tone below the tonality of the beginning of the opera (ex. 90a).

Schoenberg's orchestration is almost equivalent to Strauss's and creates
a similar effect (ex. 90b). Even the interval leading to the high B♭ in the voice
is the same in Schoenberg's and Strauss's scores. But while B♭ is nothing out
of the ordinary in Schoenberg's atonal melodic style, in the tonal context
of Strauss's music the note represents the ultimate dissonance. It clashes with
B♮, a note presented in the bass as the root of a French sixth chord in the
strings, which leads, by skipping the dominant, to the final C tonality. The
dominant is indicated only in the vocal figure leading to C.

Example 90. High B♭s in Strauss's *Salome* and Schoenberg's *Erwartung*.

a. Strauss, *Salome*, ending, mm. 358–75.

*(continued)*

Example 90 *(continued)*

Example 90 *(continued)*

b. Schoenberg, *Erwartung,* mm. 153–57.

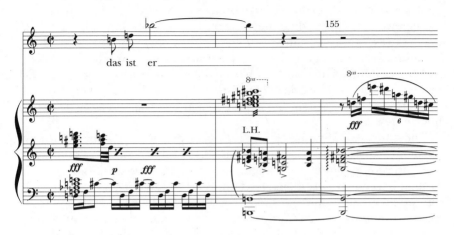

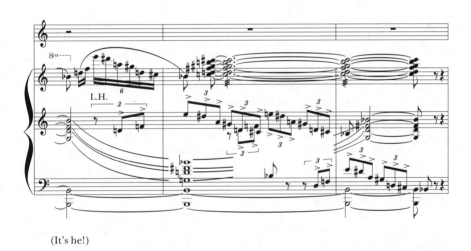

(It's he!)

Herod's outburst is followed by a *fortissimo* trumpet fanfare that unleashes chromatic runs and short repeated figures in the score. Besides A♭ and F♯, notes pointing to G, the dominant function is missing from these wild closing measures. Since it lacks tonal preparation and occurs via a chromatic sliding down, the C-minor ending is not a "natural" conclusion of the opera, just as Salome's death is not a natural closure of her life. The close affinity between these brutal moments in Schoenberg's and Strauss's operas indicates that the woman's frightened outcry in *Erwartung* "Das ist er" (It's he) is provoked by fear of her lover as a potential murderer. In the imagination of expressionist artists love and violence are closely related.

Stubborn ostinatos following or preceding moments of violence are common in Schoenberg's expressionist scores. Ostinato figures of various lengths are superimposed preceding the woman's false recognition of her lover in the dark (ex. 90b). The climax is followed by a figure that runs through all orchestral instrument groups in two rhythmic variations (woodwinds, strings, and brass, ending, significantly, with trombones). There is no concluding gesture. This most violent moment of the score is followed by a long silence, as if the world fell mute recognizing its powerlessness to respond to such intense human despair.

The difficulty of finding closure is a major problem in Schoenberg's expressionist works. Resolving tension has little role in Schoenberg's music, in which the constant use of dissonance neutralizes functional tension. In music in which climaxes are generated by musical gestures, it is logical that endings would also be achieved through gestures. Perhaps Schoenberg's most ingenious ending is that of *Erwartung*. The text itself calls for an unconventional ending. In this intensified *Liebestod,* ostensibly modeled on Isolde's in Wagner's *Tristan* and on Salome's, the woman is denied even the corpse of her lover. While Salome can reach perverse ecstasy and thus facilitate her own death, Schoenberg's protagonist is deprived of death. As the final words indicate, she is condemned to life in a loveless and spectatorless universe. The dissolution of the notes in the final bar of the opera is a mark of her cosmic loneliness. The last note, G♯, in the vocal part, which coincides with the first note of the entire opera (there sounded in the bassoon), indicates return rather than a closure. Before this last note dies away, saturation with augmented triads begins in the score. In the last measure the two most common atonal scales, the chromatic and the whole tone, collapse into one sonority. Three descending whole-tone scales in a low register run contrary to numerous ascending chromatic scales, some moving in parallel augmented triads. Schoenberg's musical space is completely saturated with chromatic notes and increasingly fast rhythmic motion. This is the total opposite of conventional closure. It opens up rather than closes, although what is beyond the opening we do not dare ask. The last measure, a barely audible sweep of simultaneous ascending and descending scales (*pppp* without crescendo), wraps the woman in menacing silence (ex. 91).

Schoenberg's ending does not indicate death. Again, Berg translates the moment into dramatic action when in *Wozzeck* he uses a similar technique of chromatic saturation to portray the rising water around the sinking figure of the bloodstained Wozzeck. Adjusting the gesture to the dramatic situation, instead of accelerating, he increasingly slows down the rhythmic motion. Here as elsewhere Berg's technique demonstrates how in realist drama

Example 91. Schoenberg, *Erwartung*, mm. 425–26.

(I searched.)

Schoenberg's gestures expressing abstract anxiety and loneliness can be transformed into musical representation of fatal action (act 3, mm. 284ff).

### URGE TO ABSTRACTION 1: "PREMONITIONS"

A similarly ambiguous ending closes Schoenberg's first movement of *Five Orchestral Pieces,* op. 16, which, in its extreme brevity, sounds like a radically condensed, abstract version of *Erwartung.* Its subtitle, "Premonitions," implies (like *Erwartung*) an unknown yet threatening future. Almost all gestures in the ending of "Premonitions"—the intensity of dissonance (D versus C♯ and A versus B♭ in the woodwinds), the hurried tempo *(sehr rasch),* and the increasing dynamics, which, although it decreases from *forte* to *piano* in the woodwinds and from *fortissisimo* to *forte* in the low strings, grows from *pianissimo* to *fortissimo* in the muted trombones during a quick period of four measures—serve to undermine the sense of closure (ex. 92). While the end of *Erwartung* falls into a fearfully empty space of eternal silence and loneliness, this movement exhibits a forced ending in which the music is brutally cut short at the moment of still increasing tension. What relates this ending to that of *Erwartung* is its chromatic and whole-tone saturation (reaching a climax in "Premonitions" in the six measures preceding measure 120), which in both scores serves as a perfect antidote against any sense of potential tonal orientation.

"Premonitions" shares many musical figures with *Erwartung.* Unexpectedly emerging brass fanfares, short, thematically unrelated, frightening gestures, sudden dynamic changes, use of ostinatos to build up tension, and the frequent employment of muted trombones are common in both scores. Tension is never resolved. The main climax is similar to the most violent moment in *Erwartung* (m. 155) in that both culminate in a highly dissonant chord sounded in all instruments of an immense orchestra. Both moments are discontinued at the dynamic and textural climax (ex. 93).

Although in terms of gestures and of horrifying effects the two works are similar, there is a striking difference between them. While according to Schoenberg opera allowed the suspension of tonality, in symphonic forms ("for which tonality is fundamental") tonality had to be replaced by other organizational principles.[15] And although Schoenberg described the entire opus 16 as "completely unsymphonic, devoid of architecture or construction, just an uninterrupted change of colors, rhythms and moods,"[16] "Premonitions" displays tight-knit motivic relatedness. Almost all the motives in the piece can be derived from the principal theme consisting of an arpeggiated augmented triad with half-step pickups preceding its root and third (ex. 94). The major thirds, as part of a whole-tone collection, and the half tones, as part of the chromatic collection, provide a motivic core that forms the foundation of the entire movement.

Example 92. Schoenberg, *Five Orchestral Pieces*, op. 16, "Premonitions," mm. 120–28 (reduced score).

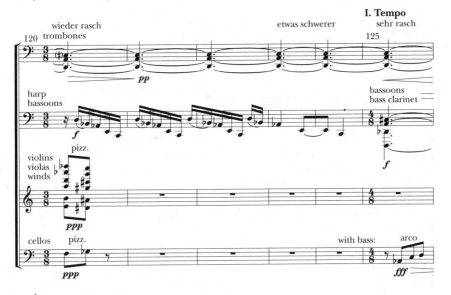

Example 93. "Premonitions," mm. 73–77 (reduced score).

*(continued)*

The secondary theme (presented, like the first, in the cello) is related to the first fanfare-like theme through its military character, manifested in the steady march rhythm of the paired eighth notes (ex. 95). The concluding repeated three notes turn into an ostinato that is soon incorporated into a three, then four-part contrapuntal string texture in which both the theme and its ostinato accompaniment are played in canon (mm. 49–63). Contrapuntal complexity increases as more instruments enter, resulting in a passage in which the secondary theme is presented in two-part canon in combination with two different versions of its rhythmic augmentation. An augmented version of the ostinato accompanies this contrapuntal elaboration (mm. 79–86). The passage culminates in a four-part stretto in measure 87.

A tendency to provide an abstract musical order in a work portraying anxiety, in other words, a chaotic state of the human psyche, is central in "Premonitions," much more than in *Erwartung,* in which the music, although not as motivically free as Webern claimed, preserves a flexibility in order to ex-

Example 93 *(continued)*

press the "thousands" of sensations Schoenberg claimed a person had simultaneously.[17] "Premonitions," an atonal piece that lacks the organizing
principles of a text, was more in need of structural organization than the
opera, and thus in it Schoenberg's natural attraction to abstract musical construction comes to its fore. Thus while *Erwartung*, at least partially, fulfilled
Schoenberg's desire to liberate music from cohesion and logic, "Premonitions" relied precisely on the "motivic working out" that the composer wanted
to abolish from music.[18] By favoring extremes of complexity over the aurally
cognizable aspects of music, Schoenberg enhanced the abstract potential of
music. Schoenberg and his disciples always presented this tendency toward
abstract organization as a "natural" or inevitable consequence of nineteenth-
century developments. More than a music-historical necessity, however, musical abstraction in Schoenberg's music seems to have been a response to
the need to create order in a chaotic universe.

Example 94. Primary theme of "Premonitions," mm. 1–3

Example 95. Secondary theme of "Premonitions," mm. 26–39.

### URGE TO ABSTRACTION 2: WORRINGER'S *ABSTRACTION AND EMPATHY*

It is precisely this psychological need for order that Wilhelm Worringer claimed to be the basic urge to abstraction. Using Worringer's principles one can argue that in Schoenberg's "Premonitions," while the gestures of music portray anxiety and fear of violence, the motivic structure presents a level of abstraction that corresponds to Worringer's category of artistic abstraction triggered by fear.

Art, Worringer argued in his 1907 doctoral thesis *Abstraction and Empathy,* is more than playful imitation. It fulfills deep psychological needs, and thus its history reflects concerns similar to that of religion. According to Worringer art originates either in the urge to empathy or in the urge to abstraction, the former accompanying the rare moments of "happy pantheistic relationship of confidence between man and the phenomena of the external world," the latter responding to "man's feeling of being lost in the universe." Abstraction, in Worringer's view, is a process of turning the frightening arbitrary world into something necessary and inviolable, into *"absolute* value."[19]

Worringer associated this anxiety with a primitive condition, and abstraction in art with primitive cultures and antirationalist Eastern civilizations. In primitive cultures, Worringer argued, abstraction is not the result of unskilled artists' attempt to imitate nature, but a necessity that helps expel fear from man's existence. Artists' most powerful urge in these cultures, Worringer wrote, was to take "the individual thing of the external world out of its arbitrariness and seeming fortuitousness," to eternalize it "by approximation to abstract forms and, in this manner," to find a "point of tranquility and a refuge from appearances." Getting rid of the last trace of life and the organic, abstract art creates law and necessity, Worringer observed, "while everywhere else the caprice of the organic prevails." To be sure, abstraction, despite its purity, does not have the purifying function of Aristotelian catharsis. But it creates "resting points, opportunities for repose, necessities in the contemplation of which the spirit exhausted by the caprice of perception could halt awhile."

Focusing his discussion on architecture and sculpture, Worringer identified the angst that abstraction tried to counteract as a "spiritual dread of space in relation to the extended, disconnected, bewildering world of phenomena." In his aesthetics the artistic preference that leads to abstraction approximates representation to a plane and suppresses the representation of space; in other words it excludes "all subjective adulteration." Representation or nonrepresentation of space was a crucial concept in Worringer's discussion of abstract art. It was space that surrounded organic and therefore ephemeral life in Worringer's view, thus its elimination elevated abstract art into a timeless sphere. "Just as the urge to empathy as a pre-assumption of aesthetic experience finds its gratification in the beauty of the organic," Worringer wrote, "so the urge to abstraction finds its beauty in the life-denying inorganic, in the crystalline or, in general terms, in all abstract law and necessity."

The denial of empathy, or, in Worringer's terms, of the human capacity to identify with life or with organic reality, leads art to what later Ortega y Gasset would call "the dehumanization of art" and what Worringer characterized as "the deepest and ultimate essence of all aesthetic experience . . . the need for self-alienation."[20] Philosopher Georg Lukács saw this tendency as a "flight from reality (from *in*human conditions into *trans*human solutions) and the grounding of an artistic practice which is determined by such flight and which necessarily manifest itself in *anti*human forms."[21]

By justifying abstraction as a psychological need and consequently as an acceptable artistic choice, and especially by focusing on spiritual, "inner experience" in contrast to outer phenomena,[22] Worringer came surprisingly close to the ideas propagated by abstract artists, most specifically the group around the Blaue Reiter. It was only after the publication of *Abstraction and Empathy* that Worringer became aware of the similarities between contemporaneous artistic strivings and the urge to abstraction he had described.[23] By 1912 the founders of the Blaue Reiter, Franz Marc and Kandinsky, recognized Worringer's significance.[24] The second volume of the almanac, which never appeared, was to have included an essay by Worringer.

Worringer's ideas about abstract art come very close to those of Schoenberg, who was also discovered by Kandinsky as a possible ally in the spiritualization of art. Spiritualization came through abstraction, and through the elimination of decorative, surface elements. The music that resulted was, in Lukács's terms, antihuman in that it implicitly excluded the audience by focusing on aurally nonsignificant inner relationships in the music. Yet as Schoenberg's expressionist works demonstrate, the all too human surface gestures of the music and the transhuman structural principles could exist side by side.

### URGE TO ABSTRACTION 3: *BEGLEITMUSIK* AND THE *SURVIVOR*

The need to find a new order that could replace the old led Schoenberg to the formulation of twelve-tone technique, the development of which was the end result of a utopian project of reaching a spiritual state of music. It was utopian in a sense that although it was rooted in a practical compositional problem (manifest already in the urge in "Premonitions" to create structure without the organizing principles of tonality), it reached a level of abstraction in which aurally imperceptible structural factors became the primary concern. The twelve-tone project that occupied several of Schoenberg's contemporaries had its roots in mystical spiritualist movements and, like those, offered a total solution to life's mysteries.[25] The unity of musical space, in which the comprehensibility of "a musical idea is independent of whether its components are made audible one after the other or more or less simultaneously,"[26] is in fact a denial of the physical reality of musical space, similar to what Worringer described in abstract art as the suppression of space.

Yet Schoenberg's twelve-tone technique could not (and was not intended to) control musical gestures of fear. Twelve-tone pieces preserve a gestural surface that links their sound to the expressionist works. Even at its most complex, Schoenberg's music reflects aspects of the human condition, just as Willem de Kooning's abstract art, as art critic Clement Greenberg argued, "harks back to the contour, particularly that of the human form."[27]

Schoenberg's twelve-tone *Begleitmusik zu einer Lichtspielscene,* op. 34, subtitled "Threatening danger, Fear, Catastrophe," bears a close resemblance to *Erwartung* and "Premonitions." The music of the "Catastrophe" is in fact quite similar to the violent moments in the earlier pieces. It occurs after an immense crescendo and an increase of tension produced by an ostinato, which culminates in a densely orchestrated, *fortissimo* twelve-tone aggregate sonority. The climactic measure is punctuated by accented blows in the brass and timpani (the presence of which suggests, as in Mahler's Sixth Symphony or in *Carmen,* the menacing closeness of death). Here, unlike in other Schoenberg scores, the violent climax does not mark the end of the passage; the blows are repeated with decreasing dynamics until they lose their brutal intensity and fade into the quiet reverberations of a shocking event (ex. 96).

Example 96. Schoenberg, *Begleitmusik zu einer Lichtspielscene,* op. 34, mm. 167–77 (reduced score).

(continued)

Example 96 *(continued)*

Other climaxes in the piece are even closer to those in "Premonitions" and *Erwartung.* Measure 43 reaches a double bar with a crescendo that is abruptly cut off. On the next page a new section starts that, in terms of its character, has no relation to the former event. The intensity of the previous measures is enhanced by short ostinatos in the low strings, by the frightening timbre of muted brass and percussion, and by sharp dissonances that create a sense of almost physically perceptible pain (ex. 97).

Military associations and gestures related to bodily reactions abound in the score. Around the first melodic presentation of the row in the oboe martellato and pizzicato strings convey a march quietly pushing forward. The strings' repetitive motion is punctuated by soft, threatening figures of the snare drums and timpani (ex. 98). The sudden *forte* outburst in measures 118–19 is followed by the return of mainly paired notes that sound like sighs. They are resting points, needed after the effort required by the violent outburst. As the *forte* gesture is related to a scream, the *pianissimo* gesture re-creates a sense of exhaustion (ex. 99).

In the reassuringly modernist framework of twelve-tone organization, Schoenberg felt free to make a less modernist move and end the piece with a passage that recapitulates the quiet beginning. Yet according to the program of *Begleitmusik,* provided by the subtitles, recapitulation means that every catastrophe is followed by anxious anticipation of the next cataclysm.

The work that most explicitly relied on the programmatic trajectory of

Example 97. Schoenberg, *Begleitmusik*, mm. 39–43 (reduced score).

*(continued)*

Example 97 *(continued)*

*Begleitmusik* is *A Survivor from Warsaw,* op. 46. A late twelve-tone piece, the *Survivor* harked back to the expressionist musical language of *Erwartung* even more than *Begleitmusik.* What was significantly different was that here Schoenberg's gestures of anxiety depicted a real historical event instead of unspecified psychological disturbances. His subject matter translated his abstract music into a naturalist representation of horror the way Berg's *Wozzeck* gave concrete dramatic meaning to certain fearful gestures of *Erwartung.* As Cowell remarked, the similarities between the *Survivor* and the earlier expressionist works were too explicit to be missed. The short, discontinuous, nervous phrases, the frightening, abrupt signals, the characteristically wide intervals, the unexpected accents, the sudden dynamic changes, and the

Example 98. Schoenberg, *Begleitmusik*, mm. 9–11 (reduced score).

Example 99. Schoenberg, *Begleitmusik*, mm. 118–20 (reduced score).

abundant use of augmented triads are all tied to expressions of anxiety, fear, and violence in Schoenberg's earlier style.

As in *Erwartung,* most of the characteristic musical gestures in the *Survivor* depict physical sensations with effective immediacy. Most produce sounds that are iconic, though stylized, versions of the sounds they represent. The orchestra, as in Schoenberg's early opera, reacts with minute sensitivity to every detail of the text. The whining minor seconds, which are the musical signs of the victims, mime the groaning and moaning described in the text (mm. 44–45). At the mention of the separation of families, the oboes and violins respond with a *molto espressivo* motive (m. 29). The irregularly alternating minor seconds in the viola in mm. 47–48 portray the irregular pulse of the narrator, beaten unconscious to the ground. The sudden fortissimo outbreak of the fanfares signifies the rising anger of the brutal Germans (m. 34), while the disquieting repetitions of short figures illustrate the nervous agitation of the terrified victims (mm. 36–37). The horror fanfares are the sounds of reveille, which opens the piece and which is later related specifically to the text ("the trumpets again," m. 32). The fanfares also appear in the strings, detached from their original brass sound, as if the victims had internalized the sound of the shocking reveille (m. 61). The military associations of brass instruments and the eerie atmosphere created by muted trombones are reinforced by the text and by the abundant use of percussion, among them military drum. But while in the expressionist works the military associations remained a vague reference to potential violence, in the *Survivor* they relate the hallucinatory scene to the sounds of brutal reality.

Schoenberg's translation of gestures of anxiety to the representation of atrocity resulted in significant changes of meaning. Screaming occurs here just as in *Erwartung,* but instead of a frightened woman, it is the tormentor who shouts. The counting of the prisoners is punctuated by these brutal, abrupt screams (*Abzählen,* m. 63, *Achtung,* m. 66, and *Rascher,* m. 68), all three breaking through a tense texture of *piano* dynamics. All three trigger sharp dissonances and fanfare figures in the orchestra (ex. 100).

The counting starts a process of increasingly denser ostinato figures, leading to a *fortissisimo* climax. The frightening climax, however, is not followed by silence as in the earlier pieces. As the Holocaust provided the subject for the gestures of anxiety, Schoenberg's belief in the possibility of transcending horror by spiritual-religious unity provides the *Survivor* with a cathartic closure (mm. 8off.). Powerful though this closure is, it is also a cliché of questionable appropriateness to Schoenberg's subject matter. Both the similarities and the differences between Schoenberg's earlier expressionist works and the *Survivor* raise questions about his artistic response to the Holocaust.

Example 100. Schoenberg, *A Survivor from Warsaw,* op. 46, mm. 61–70 (reduced score).

Example 100 *(continued)*

*(continued)*

Example 100 *(continued)*

## THE *SURVIVOR* PROJECT

Despite the widespread notion that the *Survivor* came into being as a spontaneous personal reaction to an account of a witness to the uprising in the Warsaw ghetto, it was in fact written to order. The original commission came not from Serge Koussevitzky, to whom the completed work eventually went, but from the Russian dancer Corinne Chochem, who planned to produce a gramophone album of new compositions by Jewish composers.[28] Schoenberg's piece was probably planned to commemorate the fifth anniversary of the Warsaw uprising (1943, April 19–May 16). The composer met Chochem in April 1947 through Ernst Toch, with whom he was again on friendly terms after their clash in Paris. It was Chochem who provided Schoenberg with the story of the Warsaw ghetto and with songs she suggested the composer use in the work.[29]

    The commission, however, was not realized as such. Apparently Chochem could not meet Schoenberg's financial demands. In Chochem's words, her "recognition and awareness as to what such a work would be to the Jewish cultural life and to the musical world in general [was] greater than [her] ability to pay adequately." Schoenberg was unwilling to lower his price. As he explained to Chochem, he had worked enough for idealistic purposes for which he had never been appropriately rewarded.[30] Ultimately Schoenberg offered the *Survivor* to the Koussevitzky Foundation in July 1947 as a fulfillment of a commission he had postponed three years earlier.[31]

Though Schoenberg had originally thought of a work for one or two speakers, a men's chorus, and small orchestra, in July he was apparently still willing to turn the piece into a symphonic poem, if Koussevitzky so desired. He did not change it, though, for he realized that without the text "it would not have been the same thing."[32] Because Koussevitzky neither acknowledged the receipt of the score nor sent the honorarium for the work for eight weeks, Schoenberg felt that the conductor did not appreciate the "great emotional quality of this composition," let alone its "artistic value."[33] But the work had such importance for the composer that he was willing to put aside his resentment and decided to send, in addition to his condensed score,[34] a fair copy to Koussevitzky, made by Schoenberg's ardent advocate René Leibowitz during his stay in Los Angeles in December 1947.

Even with the fair copy in hand, however, Koussevitzky did not plan to request rights for the first performance. Schoenberg originally promised the world première to Leibowitz, who had helped the composer complete the score and publicize the work. But Schoenberg forgot his promise[35] and gave the piece to Kurt Frederick, who premiered it in Albuquerque, at the University of New Mexico, on 4 November 1948. The program consisted of Bach-Stokowski's "Come Sweet Death," Schoenberg's new cantata played twice, and Jaromir Weinberger's Concerto for Timpani, concluding with Beethoven's Eighth Symphony. The success of the concert inspired Frederick to announce that Schoenberg was on the way to becoming a "popular composer."[36]

## AUTHENTICITY AND "PERSONAL PARABLE"

The subject matter of the *Survivor* appealed to Schoenberg both for its shocking content and for the story's dramatic musical potential; the moment at which the Jews, condemned to die, burst into singing suggests the heroic climax of a musical composition. *Sprechgesang* leading to a choral climax was a technique Schoenberg had already used at the end of *Gurrelieder*. For the climax of the *Survivor* an even more important prototype was Beethoven's Ninth Symphony. In place of the "Ode to Joy," Schoenberg used the Shema Yisroel, the supreme affirmation of the unity of God in Jewish thought. Like Kol nidre, the Shema is strongly associated with Jewish martyrdom, in Orthodox Judaism even with the heroism of those who sacrificed themselves for the sake of religion.[37] Traditionally recited at least twice a day, the first verse of the Shema is also the last prayer an observant Jew says before death. The text of the first part of the Shema comes from the Bible (Deut. 6):

4–7: Hear, O Israel: The Lord our God is one Lord; and you shall love the Lord with all your heart, and with all your soul, and with all your might. And these words which I command you this day shall be upon your heart; and you shall teach them diligently to your children, and shall talk of them when you sit in your house, and when you walk by the way, and when you lie down and when you rise.

8–9: And you shall bind them as a sign upon your hand, and they shall be as frontlets between your eyes. And you shall write them on the doorposts of your house and on your gates.

Reform Judaism uses only this first part of the three-part Shema.[38] Schoenberg goes even further by omitting the last two lines (8–9) of the first part. These lines refer to the signs that Jews should write upon the doorposts of their houses and may have sounded too particularistic for Schoenberg, a believer in an abstract, unfathomable God.[39]

Because of its central role in Judaism and because of its ritual connection to dying, memories of the recitation of the Shema frequently come up in accounts of Holocaust survivors. In 1946 American psychologist David P. Boder conducted interviews with 109 Holocaust survivors in camps for displaced persons in various European countries. Many reported regular shootings by the SS. "How were the people selected?" Boder asked a Polish survivor, E. Kalman. Randomly, was Kalman's answer. "Did those people say anything before they were shot?" asked Boder. "All that we heard was 'Shema Yisroel,' nothing else," answered Kalman.[40]

This account, like many others, could support the claim that Schoenberg's narrative was "authentic." Unstated though it was, the argument of authenticity seems to suggest that if what Schoenberg recounts in the *Survivor* is "true," nobody has the right to criticize his text. Schoenberg himself, cryptically as ever, insisted on the authenticity of his story, claiming in the preface of the published score that he had based his text "partly upon reports which [he had] received directly or indirectly." Leibowitz went so far as reproducing Schoenberg's expressionist text verbatim as if quoting the "survivor."[41] Schoenberg's statement, sent to Frederick, is no more revealing than the composer's published comment. "Schoenberg has reason to believe that such an event took place as described in the text," Schoenberg's assistant Leonard Stein responded, at Schoenberg's request, to the conductor's inquiry.[42] When faced with harsh criticism of his text by Kurt List, who compared it to Hollywood scripts, the offended composer responded: "I would say there is one decisive difference between me and Hollywood—this is the intention—the mind in which I do my things. Even if they would do quite the same, it would be different, because *Quod licet Jovis not licet bovis* [What is permitted to Jove is not permitted to cattle] and even if they would have done something of this kind before I would have done it, then they have stolen it from me."

In other words, Schoenberg felt that his status as a great composer granted him the right to do what might have been objectionable coming from Hollywood. But he misunderstood List's comparison. The critic was not initiating another *Prioritätstreit*—there was no copyright on the subject. In his response to List, the composer himself admitted that the events he described might be imaginary. "We should never forget this, even if such things have not been done in the manner in which I describe in the *Survivor*," he wrote to List. "This does not matter. The main thing is, that I saw it in my imagination."[43]

And, indeed, the text suggests an imaginary, almost hallucinatory scene. The narrator, in quite expressionist fashion, starts off his story by describing himself as a somewhat unconscious witness. References to this half-conscious state are maintained throughout the text: "I cannot remember everything;" "I have no recollection ; . . . ;" "I must have been unconscious." Right before the Shema the nightmarish, apocalyptic vision of wild horses underlines the horrifying scene of counting the prisoners. In this context the Shema itself might be part of a feverish dream.

Schoenberg, who in his expressionistic art often mixed his real-life experience with vivid, emotionally intense imagination, reacted with the same admixture to the experience of the Holocaust. Critics tried to prove or disprove Schoenberg's statements about the authenticity of his story, showing how the episodes confuse labor camp and ghetto experiences, or how actual survivors' narratives, like Kalman's quoted above, are in agreement with Schoenberg's imaginary account. Yet verifying the authenticity of the story cannot dispel the disquietude raised by Schoenberg's *Survivor*. Those who object to the text do not do so because they do not believe what Schoenberg said but because Schoenberg's representation of the Holocaust makes them uneasy.

Many have read the *Survivor*, like Schoenberg's *Kol nidre*, as a personal parable about the composer's return to Judaism. "Like the condemned Jews," Michael Strasser argues, "Schoenberg finally rebelled against the humiliations heaped upon him and forcefully reasserted his Jewish identity."[44] Although drawing a parallel between the victims of the Holocaust and Schoenberg runs the risk of reducing the Holocaust to Schoenberg's personal story and thus trivializing its tragedy, it is true that Schoenberg's treatment of the Holocaust in the *Survivor* was personal, although not necessarily the way Strasser suggested. Like Schoenberg's political views—which, however comparable they may be to other contemporaneous political currents, reflected the composer's fantasies rather than political reality—his representation of the Holocaust is best understood in the context of his own political and artistic vision. For the *Survivor* reiterates Schoenberg's main convictions about the necessary unity (spiritual as well as political) of the Jewish people and the inevitable triumph of the "idea."

As Schoenberg separated himself from the Jews in his political writings, in the *Survivor* the narrator is detached from the sufferers, and not only in the necessary narrative manner. Schoenberg's narrator talks about "them" and describes "their" fear. They sing the Shema now, Schoenberg seems to say, they who ignored it for many years. More disquietingly, the text's reference to the guilty and the innocent lends a judgmental dimension to the narration.[45] Despite its compassion, Schoenberg's rhetoric in the *Survivor* recalls the tone of his contentious political writings from the 1930s in which he accused the Jews of ideological disunity and faithlessness. One might suspect that Schoenberg chose the Warsaw ghetto as the subject of his cantata precisely because it was one of the rare occasions during the war when Jews organized armed resistance against their oppressors. As he stated in *Pro Zion!* in 1924, Schoenberg believed that Jewish survival could be secured only "through victorious weapons." In 1942 he put the emphasis on human sacrifice: "the possession of an independent country," he wrote to Pierre van Paasen, National Chairman of the Committee for a Jewish Army, "must be based upon the sacrifice of all the people who believe in their nationality."[46] Here Schoenberg talked about voluntary, heroic sacrifices, yet listening to the Beethovenian, triumphant ending of the *Survivor* it is hard not to think of the involuntary sacrifice of almost an entire people in the Holocaust, which, in grim accordance with the perpetrators' goals, finally united Jewry in destruction. In the *Survivor* the victims of insane and irrational brutality became martyrs whose sacrifice helped build a new nation.

### THE LIMITS OF ARTISTIC REPRESENTATION

On the occasion of the *Survivor*'s New York premiere in 1950 a skeptical Olin Downes remarked: "The subject [of the piece] is so moving, the imaginary scene so tragical, that in listening to Schoenberg's musical investiture one could easily believe it to be much more significant and inspired than it is."[47] The comment was intentionally malicious, probably triggered by the unexpected (and to Downes unwelcome) success of Schoenberg's new composition. Yet Downes pointed to a problem critics face even today. Because of the subject of Schoenberg's cantata, negative criticism was silenced almost immediately following the *Survivor*'s premiere and has remained largely *verboten*. Failing to profess sympathy for this work of Schoenberg's exposes one to the charge of being insensitive to one of the most horrifying events in human history. The unease some felt and still feel at listening to the work is either repressed or attributed to the gruesome subject.

    In concerts, the *Survivor* is commonly paired with Beethoven's Ninth; indeed, the composer of the *Survivor* has been elevated to an ethical pedestal established and formerly occupied solely by Beethoven. It is precisely this forceful ethical claim that needs to be put under a critical lens. For however therapeutic it may be in processing unbearable memories into programmatic archetypes, the *Survivor*, like other examples of Holocaust art, raises ethical questions about the limits of artistic representation.

Besides Downes, two other contemporary critics raised public objections to the *Survivor:* Kurt List and Theodor W. Adorno. Since both were ardent believers in Schoenberg's aesthetics, their objections are hidden in celebratory essays. Recalling their criticism is important, for they encourage a critical stance that challenges Schoenberg's claim to the moral status he attained by composing the piece. Greeting the *Survivor* in 1948 as a "work of classical perfection on a theme ostensibly unsuitable to such a treatment," List praised Schoenberg's new cantata because in it attention was successfully shifted from "the event itself to the art, from consequence and self-concern to aesthetic contemplation."[48] Yet despite his apparent approval, List raised serious concerns about the work's relationship to the event it represented. Adorno's reaction to the *Survivor* was even more contradictory than List's, for Adorno felt obliged to situate Schoenberg's new composition within his own post-Holocaust aesthetics. In fact, Adorno's criticism of the *Survivor* is central to understanding his over-quoted statement that "to write poetry after Auschwitz is barbaric."[49]

In Adorno's view postwar art was problematic in any event, whether it ignored the Holocaust or used it as subject matter. By ignoring the Holocaust art would become socially irresponsible and hence untruthful. Yet art that did take the Holocaust as its subject could run the risk of abusing real victims' experiences either through crude imitation, or through artistically powerful yet ethically false tropes of transcendence. Schoenberg's *Survivor* relies both on a realistic representation of horror and on the powerful trope of transcendence; the contrast between the two provides the work with its compelling Beethovenian narrative.

Comparing the representation of victims and perpetrators in Schoenberg's cantata and in anti-Nazi writer Friedrich Torberg's novel *Mein ist die Rache* (Vengeance is mine) helps pinpoint problems to which both List and Adorno reacted negatively. Torberg (1908–79), a fellow Viennese-Jewish émigré who came to Los Angeles and then settled in New York, may have known the composer through Alma Mahler-Werfel. In 1943 he presented Schoenberg with a copy of his little book, an imaginary account of a survivor of a Nazi labor camp.[50] Schoenberg enthusiastically responded to Torberg, congratulating him on his effective description of Nazi brutality. The book, Schoenberg confessed to Torberg, made him feel as if he himself experienced the cruelties the author described.[51]

Schoenberg's reaction suggests that he misunderstood Torberg's point in *Mein ist die Rache*. Although the novel contains schematic descriptions of Nazi brutality, the power of the narrative stems from Torberg's focus on the moral dilemma of the inmates, torn between their religious obligation to deny human vengeance and their desire for justice, between the instincts of self-preservation and the guilt that resulted from the recognition of such instincts. The conflict reaches its climax when the protagonist, who professes to believe in God's exclusive right to exact revenge, kills the sadistic commander of the camp, thereby taking revenge into his own hands. He escapes, reaches the United States, and for the rest of his life is tormented with horrible feelings of guilt, because he knows that his personal revenge must have cost the others their lives. Torberg seems to say that human revenge begets revenge, and that survivors may be guilty of others' deaths.

In the *Survivor* Schoenberg ignored the moral conflict of survival presented by Torberg, and instead reproduced the book's almost Spielbergian depiction of evil. In representing what Adorno thought to be aesthetically inaccessible,[52] Schoenberg (like Torberg) turned to clichés that come very close to what Hannah Arendt dubbed "satanic greatness," which she so vehemently rejected in connection with Nazi crimes. Arendt argued powerfully that the evil that infected the world during World War II had nothing to do with traditional human motivations. Reporting on Adolf Eichmann's trial Arendt came to the horrifying conclusion that this particular evil, however shocking the statement sounds, was the result of mere thoughtlessness. "This new type of criminal," Arendt maintained, "commits his crimes under circumstances that make it well-nigh impossible for him to know or to feel that he is doing wrong."[53] Because Arendt's definition was completely unrelated to traditional literary, theological, or philosophical concepts of evil, her views, especially the theory of the banality of evil, aroused outrage. Arendt refused to accept the psychological satisfaction of seeing evil as something with a motive and consequently as something that could be properly punished. Her new concept denied the sense of gratification elicited from judging human evil from a morally superior position.

In his representation of evil Schoenberg chose precisely the position that Arendt repudiated. List was embarrassed by this aspect of Schoenberg's text, in which, the critic wrote, "the immense tragedy begins to sound stale and melodramatic." As an example List quoted Schoenberg's treatment of the "German *Feldwebel* who gives the orders for the execution in a clipped Prussian accent out of Hollywood. . . . One is almost relieved," List writes, "and not only for obvious dramatic reasons—when the chorus finally breaks into the words of the Hebrew prayer." The reference to Hollywood signals that List recognized a discontinuity between the event represented and the artistic means Schoenberg utilized to represent it. In List's view Schoenberg had failed to grasp the tragedy of his subject matter. Schoenberg's text, List maintained, was "written out of sympathy, hardly out of true empathy, and certainly not out of personal experience."[54]

But is personal experience really indispensable to Holocaust art? In other words, do only victims have the right to produce artworks that address their experience? List does not seem to suggest this. On the contrary, List argued that Schoenberg's inability to cope with the gigantic problem of mass extermination forces him to escape into the realm of art and seek the gratification of a "higher truth" than the reality of life can provide.

Yet it seems that despite this twist of the argument List remained disturbed by the composer's use or abuse of real victims' memories for artistic purposes. More offensive than Schoenberg's clichéd representation of perpetrators, the discontinuity between the actual victims and their artistic counterparts forced List to raise ethical objections against the piece. For Schoenberg, he argued, "the tragedy of the Warsaw Ghetto is a stimulus [for] artistic creation. The prayer becomes a heroic climax and not, as it was in reality, the grotesque distortion of daily ritual. . . . The composer cannot comprehend the horror of extermination or the obsessional motives that force those who survived it to repeat endlessly and in unemotional tones the unspeakable terror of their experience. For Schoenberg, the real event becomes stuff for his program." Stunned by what he perceived as the work's artistic perfection, List finally allowed that Schoenberg's inability to grasp the events "does not matter." Yet even he had to admit that the Holocaust was "much too overwhelming to be used simply as a material" for art.

In his 1965 article "Engagement" Adorno put the moral dilemma in even stronger terms. When the Holocaust "is turned into an image . . . it is as though the embarrassment one feels before the victims were being violated." The victims, Adorno wrote, "are turned into works of art, tossed out to be gobbled up by the world that did them in." In the *Survivor*, Adorno warned, artistic stylization itself raised problems. "The aesthetic stylistic principle, and even the chorus' solemn prayer, make the unthinkable appear to have had some meaning; it becomes transfigured, something of its horror removed. By this alone an injustice is done [to] the victims."[55] Generic tropes of artistic representation tend to reduce the Holocaust's reality, immensity, and singularity to clichés, in some cases even to effects out of Hollywood. In its representation, the violent event loses its particularity; it becomes a source for artistic treatment, in List's words—"stuff."

One can argue that the Holocaust was also "stuff" for Schoenberg's artistic program in another sense. Although Schoenberg's style was well suited to express the horrors of the human soul long before World War II, the ideal subject for such a style was still missing. The experience of the Holocaust did not change the quality of expression; rather, it provided Schoenberg with a subject shockingly appropriate to his musical language. In the *Survivor* Schoenberg's iconic music representing atrocity provides the text with a physical immediacy that would be impossible to achieve through words alone. Adorno, as his observations about *Erwartung* demonstrate, knew about this sensual aspect of Schoenberg's expressionist style. In contrast to *Erwartung*, however, in the *Survivor* Schoenberg's music reacts more to physical than to psychological experience, and thus unconscious angst becomes palpable reality. This physical aspect of the music made Adorno uneasy. He cautioned that the "so-called artistic rendering of the naked physical pain of those who were beaten down with rifle-butts contains, however distantly, the possibility that pleasure can be squeezed from it."[56] Adorno talks about pleasure drawn from art, yet it is hard to dismiss the suggestion that latent sadistic impulses might contribute to our pleasure. For Holocaust art can and often does rely on what historian Saul Friedländer called a "union of kitsch and death."[57] In the *Survivor* Schoenberg's minute depiction of the rough physicality of human pain makes the music not only cinematic, to which List objected, but, as Adorno feared, an almost voyeuristic experience.

In his 1953 celebratory essay about Schoenberg's artistic development Adorno seems to have accepted Schoenberg's successful combination of style and subject matter with more ease. In this essay, instead of fearing potential exploitation of the Holocaust, Adorno approved the match, announcing that in the *Survivor* the sound of expressionist works such as *Erwartung* and *Begleitmusik* "finally meet what they had always prophesied. . . . Horror has never rung as true in music."[58] Here, Adorno argued, anxiety, which he called "Schoenberg's artistic core," ceased to express the "feebleness and impotence of the individual soul." Instead, anxiety identified itself "with the terror of men in agonies of death, under total domination." What Adorno praised, then, is what he saw as Schoenberg's effort to turn individual expression into social expression, the personal into communal.

But is this really what happens in the *Survivor?* One can just as easily read the piece—as Adorno did on another occasion—as one that exploits a communal tragedy for personal artistic purposes. For notwithstanding the effectiveness of the music, the immediate success of the *Survivor* was in great part due to the effect of its text. Combined with the raw persuasiveness of the dramatic narration, Schoenberg's notoriously difficult music finally became accessible and effective.

Adorno insisted that in the *Survivor* music regained its redeeming power by daring to articulate horror and to negate beauty. The audience, however, experiences a less abstract and more immediate moment of redemption, achieved not in the first but in the last part of the piece, which, instead of articulating horror, turns to conventional musical paradigms of transcendence. This last part of the *Survivor* has a decisively different effect than the first. The change of language from English to Hebrew is a signal for the change of style. The appearance of singing and, even more crucially, of the expressive excess of a more melodic style sharply differentiates the Hebrew prayer Shema Yisroel from the discontinuous, illustrative shock effects that accompany the narration in the first part. During the prayer the narration is suspended. The victims gain voice and with it an actual presence on stage (which, to Schoenberg's dismay, was overdramatized at the first New York performance at which, as Olin Downes reported, "the members of the chorus, as the narrator described the scene, rose to their feet, first one by one, the ranks filling more and more rapidly, until they stood, coats discarded, in the white shirts of the condemned").[59] The Shema is devoid of the descriptive aspects of the music that precedes it. The iconic motives disappear, and the orchestra ceases to perform an illustrative function. The trombones, until now instruments of fear and violence, regain their ecclesiastic function by doubling the melody of the prayer. The music, like the text of the Shema, is purged of physical associations and rises into the sphere of the spiritual. In this case, though, spirituality is achieved at a price. For it is hard to dismiss the feeling that the Shema stands for an illusory triumph—for the attempt to re-create the spirit of those whose bodies perished in the Holocaust. The artistic cliché of transcendence used here has little to do with the brutal reality.

As the ending suggests, the *Survivor* is more about the imaginary heroes than about the real victims, and hence it can be seen as an artistic expression of Schoenberg's political beliefs. It contributes to the myth of the triumph of the spirit in the face of disaster, in which Schoenberg, ever an advocate of the spiritual, deeply believed. Yet whose triumph was that? True, the Holocaust created a new Jewish nation—that of the survivors—united to an extent unheard of in modern Jewish history. But as many critics of Holocaust art argue, traditional artistic tropes of transcendence are not easily tenable in relation to the Holocaust.[60] Since there was nothing redeeming or spiritual in the Nazis' systematic murder of six million Jews, art that still works with traditional tropes of redemption might lose contact with the very event it commemorates. Can one soften the horror by calling the victims martyrs, although they had no choice? Is there an appropriate aesthetic solution to the memory of mass murder?

In its Beethovenian program, the *Survivor* appeals to a basic human need for redemption. It ascends from the depths of suffering to the heights of victory. As Adorno said, Schoenberg's musical setting of the prayer Shema Yisroel triumphs over barbarism not only by its dramaturgical force (attested by the daring utterance of the Hebrew prayer in the face of death), but also by its daring formalism. For, ironically, what stands for spiritual freedom in the face of physical extermination is a twelve-tone Shema, in fact, the row itself, presented in its entirety as a melody for the first time. The display of the twelve-tone row in such dramatic fashion makes the *Survivor* almost a didactic dodecaphonic composition, accessible, ironically, because of the tonal connotations of the row melody itself.[61] The twelve-tone row connects the two parts of the work, providing it with a spiritual unity and an essential continuity that is emphatically broken on the surface of the musical style. Dodecaphony thus became a means that united the dying victims and the triumphant survivors.

The compositional subtleties of Schoenberg's twelve-tone technique, however, serve another important function: they shield the *Survivor* against the charge of being merely descriptive. In fact, the Shema not only triumphed over barbarism, but also demonstrated the validity of twelve-tone music. As Leibowitz declared, dodecaphony provided the *Survivor* with a "purely musical plan."[62] In Leibowitz's belief the "purely aesthetic means" of the twelve-tone technique ensured the "autonomy" of the music. But as Schoenberg himself would have argued, the technique with which the composition was created had little or nothing to do with the music's expressive validity.[63] The strict technique was applied to purify and control the emotionally charged subject, just as in "Premonitions" intricate Brahmsian motivic complexity provided control over the expressive excess. This intellectual control, as the analyses of List and Leibowitz demonstrate, has a reassuring effect on critics, for it proves, falsely, as Adorno or Arendt would argue, that rationality still presides even amid the most inhuman terror.

To what extent should the relief brought by the Hebrew prayer, or the updated Romantic program of triumph through suffering, or the assurance of rational control erase the knowledge that the unity achieved in the *Survivor* was in reality not the unity of the heroes but that of the exterminated? However discomforting it may be, we must ask ourselves whether the catharsis the listener experiences upon listening to Schoenberg's cantata is not produced at least in part by satisfying voyeuristic impulses and, no less important, an irrepressible human desire to redeem even the irredeemable. Both instincts are human and help turn the *Survivor* into an effective artistic commemoration of the Holocaust. Yet although the work fulfils the crucial task of keeping the memory of the Holocaust before the public, respect for its subject should not silence thoughtful criticism and debate about the work itself and about the limits of artistic representation in general. Only by acknowledging the contradictions inherent in Schoenberg's project do we confront the moral quagmire and ethical confusion that artists face while searching for an appropriate artistic response to events that may ultimately lie beyond the grasp of human reason.

.    .    .

Artists' pre–World War I preoccupation with fear and horror went rapidly out of fashion after the experience of real wartime violence. Nine million casualties cured the obsession with death. Amnesia was the most common response to the horrors of that war. Even Schoenberg, who, in his extreme self-absorption, was usually slow to react to events of the outside world, abandoned his expressionist eccentricity. That many of his musical gestures remained closely related to fantasies of violence even after the change in his compositional style testifies that his belief in the artist's obligation to express the unexplored depths of the human soul was an unalterable component of his artistic personality.

His response to the Holocaust displayed the same artistic fantasies of violence that were always part of his musical language. As in his political utopias, reality had little influence on his strong artistic vision. The Holocaust merely provided justification for an art strongly rooted in expressions of fear and violence. "There is no longer beauty or consolation," Adorno wrote from a similarly justified position after World War II, "except in the gaze falling on horror, withstanding it, and in unalleviated consciousness of negativity holding fast to the possibility of what is better."[64] The glimpses of hope Schoenberg's *Survivor* offers are located either in the comfort provided by the rationality of his abstract compositional technique or in the redemptive power provided by his political utopia of Jewish unity. Yet knowledge of the irrational inspiration of his twelve-tone technique and the aggressive side of his political utopia can make one skeptical of what Schoenberg's glimpses of hope ultimately signify. The combination of gestures of fear and expression of violence with abstract musical concepts, as well as the mixture of the Romantic program of transcendence and a particular Jewish political utopia in the *Survivor*, result in a highly idiosyncratic work that can be celebrated as a powerful Holocaust memorial, or dismissed as triumphalist kitsch. Ringer, who presents the most essentialist argument of Schoenberg's Jewish persuasion, saw the *Survivor* as "a unique minidrama, a relentless crescendo from beginning to end of unmitigated horror defeated by unyielding faith," in other words, "a paean of Jewish suffering."[65] But lacking a religiously faithful belief in Schoenberg's artistic mission, one can just as easily hear the *Survivor* as Holocaust kitsch.[66]

Similarly, Schoenberg himself can be placed between two extremes, between a Jewish hero who, again in Ringer's words, "poured all his sorrow and the full measure of his Jewish pride"[67] into the *Survivor*, and a Holocaust idolater, a sinful transgressor of the Second Commandment of nonrepresentation, who insensitively represented the unrepresentable, or, to put it in even less sympathetic terms, exploited the Holocaust by assimilating it to his artistic idiom. These opposing options in the interpretation of the *Survivor* represent different attitudes toward Schoenberg and toward art in general. The *Survivor* is the only work in which Schoenberg, while remaining as tight-lipped and absorbed in anxiety as in his self-portraits, exposed himself to this eternal debate.

# Chapter 9

# A Taste for "the Things of Heaven"

## Cleansing Music of Politics

*"Wrestling Jacob" is an attempt to give a symbolical description of the religious struggles of the author, and as such it is a failure. Therefore it has only remained a fragment, and, like all religious crises, has ended in a chaos. The inference seems to be that all investigation of the secrets of Providence, like all attempts to take heaven by storm, are struck with confusion, and that every attempt to approach religion by the way of argument leads to absurdities.*

AUGUST STRINDBERG, *Notes to "Wrestling Jacob"* (1912)

Among Schoenberg's papers is an obituary of French painter, illustrator, and writer Adolphe Willette (1857–1926) from the *Berliner Tageblatt* with the composer's notes in the margin. "I am rising higher and higher," Willette was reported to have said on his deathbed with an expression of profound happiness. "Now I am ascending straight up, always up, continuously without stopping, quick as an arrow—straight to Paradise."[1] Willette had a peaceful exit from the world, strikingly dissimilar from the violent departure of Richard Gerstl, whose death remained an open wound for Schoenberg, his one-time friend and disciple.[2] Willette's death, in contrast, represented an ideal for the aging composer. He kept the article because, he wrote, Willette's death was "so exactly [like] the death in *Jakobsleiter.*"

Though he left it incomplete, Schoenberg never gave up *Jakobsleiter.* Its Balzacian/Swedenborgian rise to heaven, and its Strindbergian struggle for faith, stayed central to the composer's religious visions. Like Balzac's, Schoenberg's spiritual quest was more of a transcendental endeavor than a religious pursuit. Containing both Judaic and Christian elements, Schoenberg's conception of religion was nondenominational, tied to the abstract conceptions of his art. In fact, drawing a distinctive line between his religious and artistic projects is impossible. Like his involvement in Jewish politics, his ideas about religion had no practical implications. His rare attempts to put his art in the service of any religious ritual more specific than the worship of an abstract, unimaginable God resulted in awkward interactions between him and religious authorities.

Religion, though, did serve a real function in Schoenberg's last years. It fed into the cliché of the politically detached, spiritually engaged artist who, toward the end of his mission, turns his gaze upward and inward to sum up his life. The late works, however, are not unrelated to Schoenberg's earlier preoccupations. Despite the composer's repeated statements about his deeply apolitical attitude, works like the fragmentary *Israel Exists Again, Dreimal tausend Jahre,* and, most crucially, the texts he drafted for *Modern Psalms* reinforce Schoenberg's utopian political ideas. His uneasy relationship with Jewish organizations also remained constant. After *Kol nidre,* efforts to draw him into specifically Jewish projects resulted only in two small choral works: *Dreimal tausend Jahre* and *Psalm 130,* one a quiet, subdued celebration of the founding of the State of Israel, the other an esoteric setting of Psalm 130. Both works combine an increasing tendency to abstraction with a nostalgia for tonality.

Ringer has argued that these late works prove that by the end of his life Schoenberg fully identified himself as a Jew, embracing his Jewish heritage "with a fervour of one discovering an unsuspected treasure in his own backyard."[3] Instead of seeing these works as the final manifestations of a journey toward Jewish identity, one should recognize in them the same idiosyncratic combination of spiritual, political, and artistic concerns that characterized some of Schoenberg's earlier compositions. The best summary of Schoenberg's religious beliefs are the texts of *Modern Psalms,* which recycle many ideas from *The Biblical Way, Moses und Aron,* and his political writings. What the fragment of music Schoenberg composed for the first psalm reveals is that despite the composer's rhetoric of purity, his music preserved gestures of fear, frustration, and quest, thus keeping this last work close to the most human aspects of Schoenberg's art.

## REJECTION OF POLITICS

Schoenberg's intense political preoccupation in the 1930s had no public outlet and hence did not affect his reputation of being an apolitical artist. Schoenberg himself fostered this image. In 1950 he vehemently denied all his previous political interests, using his artistic achievements as proof of no time wasted on politics. "I was much too busy with my own development as a composer," Schoenberg wrote in 1950, "and, I am sure, I could never have acquired the technical and aesthetic power I developed had I spent any space of time to politics."[4] This statement shows the composer's late sensitivity to charges that could have dragged him out of the ivory tower of his aesthetics.

Schoenberg's attitude toward artists' political responsibility began to change toward the end of World War II. In 1945 he was still willing to send the texts of *The Biblical Way, Moses und Aron,* and his 1938 political essay "Four-Point Program for Jewry" to Kurt List, who wanted to publish an article about Schoenberg's relationship to Judaism in the journal *Commentary.* But when

List mentioned that *Commentary* might reprint parts of these texts and that Heinrich Jalowetz had also showed interest in them, Schoenberg immediately withdrew his manuscripts. He might have been alarmed by a cautionary remark List made about his disagreement with Schoenberg's conclusion in the "Four-Point Program," but, more likely, he recoiled as usual at the suggestion of public display of his political ideas.[5]

The same year, when asked to give a speech at the Western Jewish Institute in Los Angeles, Schoenberg refused to speak about anything besides music. With unusual modesty he admitted that he had little knowledge of the "other subjects" the organizers proposed and would speak rather on musical subjects.[6] On 9 October 1944 he drafted a short essay about collaboration with Nazi politics in Germany. A staunch noncompromiser all his life, Schoenberg now pleaded absolution for artists who were drawn into German politics for the mere reason that neither their race nor their art had forced them into exile. One can blame collaborators, he argued, only if one has "proved to be fearless in spite of the menace of the concentration camps and of torture." Those who emigrated, Schoenberg went on, did so only under pressure. And, he added, "even among real emigrees there are some who at first tried very hard to come to an agreement with the powers but had to give up finally." This expression of tolerance was a rarity for Schoenberg, to be explained, perhaps, by his low opinion of the moral standards of artists in general. "Treat them like immature children," he wrote. "Call them fools and let them escape."[7]

He made a similar plea when List attacked Shostakovich for having meddled in politics. "Even if it is a weakness in his character—he might be no hero, but a talented musician," Schoenberg wrote to List in defense of the Soviet composer. To make his separation of heroes and musicians even more definite, he added: "In fact there are heroes, and there are composers." And although "heroes can be composers," one "cannot require that."[8]

By 1948 Schoenberg's statements about the separation of art and politics became even more explicit. "It is absolutely pointless associating oneself with the political ideals of any existing parties," he preached to Josef Rufer, who complained about the frightening political situation in Berlin. "We who live in *music* have no place in politics and must regard them as something essentially alien to us. We are apolitical and the most we can do is endeavor to stay quietly in the background."[9] The major difference between the earlier statements and this one is that while previously Schoenberg had always left some room for his own special case, here he included himself in the group of politically nonconsequential artists. Thus he seems to have resumed the modest place he had assigned to himself when in 1928, writing about composers' role in wartime, he seemed to be satisfied with a secondary position. "Beethoven's 'Battle of Vittoria' was written only after Wellington's victory," he declared. "And in all political matters that seems to me the only form of

behaviour worth recommending to musicians as in keeping with the times—
*post festum.* Music then arrives just in time for the feast."[10]

This is precisely what he attempted after the founding of the State of Israel by composing *Israel Exists Again.* Its text, written by Schoenberg, recapitulates many ideas familiar from his political writings of the 1930s. Like
all of Schoenberg's works that directly address Jewish politics, *Israel Exists
Again* remained incomplete. The piece that in its subject relates the most to
the Israel fragment is a simple twenty-five-bar a cappella setting of "Gottes
Wiederkehr" (God's return), a poem by Dagobert David Runes. It is a crafts-
manlike, but surprisingly quiet and tame, work that stands in great contrast
to Schoenberg's grandiose plans of celebration.

### POST FESTUM: ISRAEL EXISTS AGAIN AND DREIMAL TAUSEND JAHRE

The text of *Israel Exists Again,* with which Schoenberg originally wished to
greet the new State of Israel, resulted from his collaboration with Friedrich
Torberg, whose book had been an inspiration for the *Survivor.* In October
1947 Torberg sent Schoenberg his poem "Kaddish" (1943), which he hoped
the composer would set. Schoenberg's first reaction was positive, and he
promised Torberg that he would set his poem after the completion of his
other projects. Although by 1949 Schoenberg seems to have forgotten Torberg's "Kaddish,"[11] he sought the writer's collaboration on a text that he intended to set as a *"post festum"* greeting of Israel. What Schoenberg had in
mind was a festive hymn that would express his joy over Israel's triumph and
would "celebrate the occasion of the possible festivities to which the peace
and the foundation of the new State of Israel gave rise." Though he was no
friend of Zionism and had "developed other plans" for the Jews, he now re-
joiced that Israel had fulfilled the principle he advocated: that "one has to
win a land with one's own blood."[12]

Schoenberg was spurred in his plans by an article suggesting that Israel,
now settled on its ancient land, would eventually turn to Christianity. This
suggestion, Schoenberg insisted, should be fought against and the opposite
should be expressed, though "in an indirect way," in his hymn. The text
should declare that "Jehovah triumphed over Hitler, Jehovah triumphed over
Bevin, and he will triumph over all our enemies." "This is consistent with my
religious conviction," Schoenberg added, and "it will not be difficult for me
to express it in music."[13]

Since Torberg repeatedly postponed his participation in the work, Schoenberg decided to set a poem by Dagobert David Runes, "Gottes Wiederkehr,"
which he found in the volume of the author's *Jordanlieder.*[14] Schoenberg knew
Runes from the Philosophical Library, then in the process of issuing a one-
volume compilation of Schoenberg's writings, *Style and Idea.* Most probably
Schoenberg picked Runes's nostalgic recollection of the sacred land because

it resonated with his ideas about his celebratory music for Israel. *Dreimal tausend Jahre* (Three times a thousand years) is about God's, and metaphorically His people's, return to Israel. At the same time it also suggests that the bond between the land and the people was never broken.

Schoenberg's slightly revised version of Runes's text reads as follows:

> Dreimal tausend Jahre seit ich dich gesehn,
> Tempel in Jerusalem, Tempel meiner Wehn!
> Und ihr Jordanwellen, silbern Wüsterband,
> Gärten und Gelände grünen, neue Uferland.
> Und man hört es klingen leise von den Bergen her,
> Deine allverschollnen Lieder künden Gottes Wiederkehr.

> [Three times a thousand years since I saw you,
> Temple in Jerusalem, temple of my pain!
> And you, wave of Jordan, silver stretch of desert,
> Gardens and lands are becoming green, new banks.
> And from the mountains come soft sounds,
> Your songs, long lost, are heralding God's return.][15]

Besides changing the title from "Gottes Wiederkehr" (God's return) to "Dreimal tausend Jahre," Schoenberg made other adjustments in the text. He turned Runes's three quatrains into a six-line strophe, added an exclamation point after "Wehn," made the fifth line impersonal yet aurally more perceptible by exchanging "Und mir ist als rauschen" (to me it sounds like murmuring) with "Und man hört es klingen leise" (literally: one hears it as softly sounding), neutralized the past tense by writing "allverschollnen" (long lost) instead of "alt-verschollnen" (old lost), and, most significantly, replaced "flüstend" (whispering) with the louder and more active "künden" (heralding).

While Schoenberg's changes to the text raise the volume of the poem, his music does not reflect this increased dynamics. The piece remains quiet throughout and does not end, as one would expect in a celebratory work, with a bang. Based on a combinatorial row (a row in which the second hexachord shares its pitch content with an inverted, transposed version of the first), this short piece is full of compositional intricacies (ex. 101). It starts by displaying the first hexachord of the row and its inversion transposed at a fifth in primary and retrograde forms, thus superimposing both vertical and horizontal mirroring possibilities (ex. 102). The musical illustration of the word *klingen* (*ppp* staccato notes in the upper parts) is combined with contrapuntal sophistication (the prime form of the row and its inversion at the fifth running below in canon; ex. 103).

Because of its soft dynamics, *Dreimal tausend Jahre* lacks the aggressive effect of the sharp dissonances that are so typical of Schoenberg's music. Probably reflecting the idea of return ("Wiederkehr") in the text, there is even

Example 101. Combinatorial row of Schoenberg's *Dreimal tausend Jahre.*

Example 102. Schoenberg, *Dreimal tausend Jahre,* mm. 1–4.

Example 103. Schoenberg, *Dreimal tausend Jahre*, m. 13.

a certain "upsurge of desire for tonality"[16] in this quiet work, especially for the purity of C major sound. Since the prime version of the row starts on G and the inversion a fifth below on C, G and C play a central role in the piece. The final harmony has C in the bass and G in the soprano (both shadowed by a major seventh, A♭ in the alto and B♮ in the tenor). This C ending is prepared by three incomplete dominant seventh chords, the first (in third inversion) coinciding with the quasi recapitulation (F–B–G in m. 17), the second (in first inversion) at the beginning of measure 19, and the last, blurred by the E♭ in the bass, in measure 20 (ex. 104).

Schoenberg sent *Dreimal tausend Jahre* as a contribution to a celebratory Schoenberg issue of the Swedish magazine *Prisma* in 1949.[17] Only after failing to complete *Israel Exists Again* and finishing his setting of Psalm 130 did Schoenberg think of including *Dreimal tausend Jahre* in his op. 50, a series of pieces he intended to offer to the State of Israel in place of the celebratory hymn he could not complete.[18]

Four days after the completion of *Dreimal tausend Jahre*, Schoenberg wrote down the first version of the text for *Israel Exists Again*. Instead of sending this version to Torberg, however, he drafted another text, in which he gave full vent to his frustration for being excluded from the culture to which he had belonged. "Ihr, die uns verachtet . . . " (You, who despise us) is again about superiority, addressed more to the gentiles than to the Jews. Although in the text Schoenberg renounces revenge and retaliation in the name of the Jews, his anger burns through the lines and leaves his world eternally split between an imagined community of "we" and that of a hostile "you":

Example 104. Schoenberg, *Dreimal tausend Jahre*, mm. 17–25.

*(continued)*

Example 104 (continued)

der - kehr, _____ Got - tes Wie - der - kehr. _____

Got - tes Wie - der - kehr. _____

Wie - der-kehr, _____ Got - tes Wie - der - kehr. _____

der - kehr, _____ Wie - der - kehr. _____

| | |
|---|---|
| Ihr, die uns verachtet, | You, who hate us, |
| Hab Acht: | Watch out: |
| Wir [erringen?] die Nacht, | We [win] the night |
| die uns Rache verschafft! | that brings us revenge! |
| Vergebung! | Forgiveness! |
| Wäre es so verwunderlich, | Would it be so surprising |
| wenn es uns nach Rache verlangte? | if we required revenge? |
| Zwei tausend Jahre haben wir | For two thousand years |
| mit euch gelebt | we lived with you |
| und haben euch kennen gelernt. | and have gotten to know you. |
| Wir kennen alle eure Schwächen. | We know all your weaknesses. |
| Wir wissen welches Unrecht | We know what injustice |
| euch Wert ist; | you value; |
| wir wissen wie wenig ihr | we know how little |
| wahren Wert erkennt. | you acknowledge real value. |
| Wir haben euch Kultur gebracht, | We brought you culture |
| wenn ihr wolltet, dass wir | when you wanted us |
| euren Handel organisieren. | to organize your trade. |
| Wir haben euch Sitte, Recht und | We gave you customs, |
| Gesetz gegeben, | justice and law, |
| durch unsere zehn Gebote, | through our ten |
| | commandments, |
| Wir haben euch gezeigt, dass wir | We showed you that |
| in alle euren Kirchen und | in all of your churches |
| Wissenschaft euch ebenbürtig sind. | and science we are equal to you. |
| Trotzdem habt ihr uns | Nevertheless you hated, |
| verachtet und habt uns ge- | avoided, and |
| mieden und ausgeschlossen, wo ihr | excluded us, where you could |

euch ohne behelfen konnten:
  Wäre es versonderlich, wenn wir
  Vergeltung wünschen?
Es ist unser Rang eines alten Volkes,
das uns bestimmt auf Rache
zu verzichten, ~~und~~ Vergeltung aber
zu übern, wie es diesem Rang geziemt:
  Indem wir fortfahren
  euch zu beschenken:
    Ihr die ihr Gott,
  Sitte, Recht und Gesetz
  durch Gottes zehn Geboten
von uns empfangen lassen werden
zu den Gnaden, die damals Gott

der Menschheit zugedacht hat.

do without our help:
  Would it be surprising if we
  wanted retribution?
It is our status as an old people
that determines us to renounce
revenge, ~~and~~ instead to retaliate
as is appropriate to this status:
  While we continue
  to be generous to you:
    You, who received
  your God, customs,
  justice and law from us
through God's ten commandments,
you will be received into the grace
that God
provided for humanity long ago.

Arnold Schoenberg, 27 April 1949[19]

Like most of Schoenberg's writings on Jewish politics, this was a private document, perhaps necessary for him to pen before he could write a text with less personal anger.

Tired of waiting for Torberg's reply, on 10 June Schoenberg sent the writer a slightly revised version of his first draft for *Israel Exists Again:*

Israel exists again!
It has always existed
though invisibly.
And since the beginning of time,
since the creation of the world
we have always seen the Lord,
and have never ceased to see Him.
Adam saw Him.
Noah saw Him.
Abraham saw Him.
Jacob saw Him.
But Moses
saw He was our God
and we His elected people:
elected to testify
that there is only one eternal God.
Israel has returned
and will see the Lord again.[20]

He was still dissatisfied with his text. The foundation of a new Israel, Schoenberg wrote to Torberg, should be expressed concomitantly with the recognition that it has always been in God's presence—and therefore existed spiritually even before it became a political reality.[21] Again, political reality and spiritual essence proved to be hard to reconcile in Schoenberg's creative imagination.

Shortly after receiving Schoenberg's letter, Torberg finally drafted his own version of the text, a somewhat lengthy, didactic elaboration of Schoenberg's ideas about the indestructible spiritual strength of God's chosen people and the everlasting mystical bond between the people of Israel and their God. What Torberg left out of his version was the reference to the specific role Schoenberg attributed to Moses, who, Schoenberg believed, was the founder of the belief in the inconceivable, invisible, eternal God and the one through whom God chose the people of Israel as his witness.

Schoenberg found Torberg's version too long, and he now disapproved of politicized lines about Haman, Pharaoh, Titus, and Hitler, who tried and failed to destroy the Jews, which Torberg had included at the composer's request.[22] By the time Schoenberg received Torberg's text, he had already composed the first three lines of the piece, which remained the only part he would set.[23] Schoenberg convinced himself that what had seemed illogical in his version of the text, namely, the connection between Israel's present existence as a "power" and its eternal existence as an "idea," needed no further explanation.[24] Ultimately Torberg approved Schoenberg's text, but he recommended some small changes, the most important of which was the inclusion of the name of Isaac between those of Abraham and Jacob, since, Torberg argued, God is always called "God of Abraham, of Isaac, and of Jacob."[25]

Schoenberg never adopted Torberg's suggestions. By July he seemed to have lost interest in the project. In its fragmentary form, *Israel Exists Again* occupies a metaphorical position among Schoenberg's late works. Many believe that the incompleteness of the work signifies Schoenberg's turning from openly political to personal, religious subjects.[26] Yet what the gestation of its text and the incompleteness of its music more likely demonstrate is that the composer, believer in the invisible and inconceivable, was incapable of writing *Gebrauchsmusik,* even to celebrate the State of Israel.

### ANOTHER KIND OF *GEBRAUCHSMUSIK:*
### THE PUTTERMAN PROJECT AND *PSALM 130*

In spite of unfinished projects such as Hans Nathan's commission and *Israel Exists Again,* Schoenberg's reputation as a Jewish composer was growing. Jewish organizations tried to gain prestige for their projects through the inclusion of the renowned modernist. David Putterman, cantor at New York's Park Avenue Synagogue, organized special musical services for which he commissioned contemporary composers. His negotiations with Schoenberg, lasting from 1943 through 1950, show the extent of his interest.

Putterman's first request was a composition for cantor, choir, and organ based on "some portion of the Sabbath Eve Liturgy." Schoenberg did not refuse the commission out of hand. "Maybe," he wrote to Putterman, "if the text produces at once a good idea, which I can carry out in a short time, I might do it."[27] Encouraged by such a response Putterman sent him English translations of five psalms (numbers 95. through 99) and "Mi Chomocho" (Who is like unto Thee), a Biblical text (Exodus 15:11) employed traditionally as a response after the Shema in the evening and morning services.[28]

Schoenberg refused to use the texts suggested by Putterman, partially because, as he said, they were too long, but more important, because he wanted to write something "which is closer to our present day's [sic] feelings."[29] The contemporary feeling Schoenberg referred to concerned a God who protected His people and punished their enemies. This time, however, Schoenberg did not compose his own text. He compiled lines from Exodus and two psalms:

Who is like unto thee, o Lord? [Exodus 15:11]

Nations rose up, and were angry. [Exodus 15:14]

Thou stretchest forth thy hand and the earth swallowed them [Exodus 15:12]

Lord, Almighty [Exodus 15:3]

thou hast become salvation to thy people, [Exodus 15:2]

thou wilt not make our enemies rejoice over us. [Psalm 29:2]

Deliver thy people, o Lord, from all his [sic] tribulations. [Psalm 24:22][30]

The fact that Schoenberg kept at least the first line of "Mi Chomocho" (Who is like unto Thee) impressed Putterman so much that he offered to substitute the composer's text for the traditional "Mi Chomocho" of the prayer book.[31] He did request, however, that Schoenberg open and close his piece with the original Hebrew lines of "Mi Chomocho." Schoenberg's second version of the text includes the Hebrew lines, but by the time he made this textual revision he had stopped composing. None of the fifteen versions of the opening melody he drafted include the Hebrew text. The few remaining musical sketches show Schoenberg wavering again between tonal nostalgia and twelve-tone obligation. The first sketches are drafted, significantly, with a key signature of C minor. But then the usual row charts appear, showing this plan to belong stylistically to the late works with combinatorial rows.[32]

For no apparent reason the project came to naught. Cable followed cable, and desperate letters urged Schoenberg to meet the deadline of the upcoming event. Even though the composer missed the first Sabbath Evening Service of Liturgical Music on 10 March 1944, Putterman did not lose hope and asked the composer to finish the composition for another musical service on 30 June.[33] Even after this date had passed, Putterman kept begging for the composition. "You simply *cannot* and *must* not disappoint us this time," he wrote to Schoenberg. "The Jewish people generally and our Synagogue's liturgical music specifically will be the poorer—unless we have this contribution from you to add to our cultural enrichment."[34]

And so it went, until Schoenberg offered his *Kol nidre* as a substitute for the new work in 1945. Disappointed, Putterman responded: "Words are much too inadequate for me to express our utter disappointment. We are completely heartsick. Almost two years . . . elapsed since we first had hopes of a liturgical piece from your creative genius—and now you suggest 'Kol Nidre'—which I know very well, because our mutual friend Dessau presented it most comprehensively at our meeting of the Jewish Music Forum in May 1942."[35]

This was not the end of the story, though. In October 1950 Schoenberg's secretary Richard Hoffmann wrote to Putterman requesting the return of the original text, which, Putterman assured Schoenberg, he had sent back years ago. "As I recall," Putterman wrote, "it was selected verses which you made from chapters in Psalms dealing with God's wrath upon people who did not conform to the teachings of righteousness, truth and love."[36]

The reason for Schoenberg's renewed interest in the text was another commission, now from the Jewish Agency for Palestine, which undertook the compilation of an anthology of Jewish music. As Benjamin Halpern, director of the Department of Education and Culture, informed Schoenberg, the volume would include "synagogal, Hasidic, Jewish folk music, oriental and modern Israeli music." They requested a composition for mixed chorus a cappella with Hebrew text. Schoenberg agreed but asked for a text and encouraged Halpern to contact Putterman to get back the one he had written for him six years earlier.[37]

Chemjo Vinaver (1895–1973), editor of the volume, recommended instead Psalm 130. He sent Schoenberg an old liturgical melody, "traditionally applied to this psalm for generations." "As you may know," Vinaver explained to the composer, "these sacred airs of our oral tradition are very rare. Nowadays they are not found even in our synagogues, where the authentic chant has been replaced by inferior innovations."[38] He also described the liturgical use of the text and its traditional manner of performance, based on the alteration of the leader of the prayer and the congregation.

After reassuring Vinaver that he had "profited from the liturgical motif" he received from him and that he had achieved an "approximately similar expression," Schoenberg declared: "Of course, you cannot expect music of this primitive style from me. I wrote a 12-tone piece."[39] Otherwise a traditionalist in Jewish liturgical music,[40] Vinaver approved: "Of course, I would not expect from you a composition not in the 12-tone system."[41]

The *Anthology of Jewish Music*, which appeared in 1953 with a jacket illustration by Marc Chagall, demonstrates perfectly Vinaver's conception of Jewish music. His publication consists of traditional Jewish tunes in his own transcriptions and of their polyphonic settings mainly by Eastern European synagogue composers from the first half of the century or earlier. In his volume Vinaver included Moses Milner's "Unsaneh tokef," first printed among the OYNM publications, creating a posthumous contact between Schoenberg and the Russian-Jewish composers. Besides Schoenberg's *Psalm 130,* Erich Itor Kahn's *Dance Song,* and Frederich Jacobi's *Teyfen l'hakshiv* (Let us listen), Vinaver's own compositions are the only contemporaneous ones among the twenty-seven polyphonic settings in the *Anthology.* No doubt Schoenberg's is the oddest fit in the collection. In fact, by sending the transcription of the psalm's Hasidic recitation to Schoenberg Vinaver might have hoped that he could win over the champion of modern music to his own traditionalist approach.

Despite Schoenberg's insistence on a twelve-tone setting, he did rely on the traditional melody Vinaver sent him. Although it would be hard to perceive aurally the relationship between a monophonic tune and Schoenberg's six-part setting, there are definitive correspondences between them. Unfamiliar with the Hebrew language, the composer closely followed the rhythm of the words in the traditional melody.[42] He digressed from his source only at two climactic settings of the word *Adonay* (Lord), where, instead of using two short and one long syllable, he prolonged the first short note and thus created a dotted figure. He also followed the melodic contour of his source, sometimes even matching the exact notes of the traditional tune. An avid enemy of ornaments in general, here he was willing to apply, although frugally, short melismas to correspond to some elaborate embellishments in the Hasidic tune (ex. 105).

*Psalm 130* is unique in Vinaver's *Anthology of Jewish Music* not only because of its extreme difficulty, but also because it contains *Sprechgesang,* an expressive declamation in between speaking and singing that Schoenberg associated with the divine in *Moses und Aron,* in which God, speaking from the burning bush, is represented by a combination of a singing and a speaking chorus. The speakers echo the singing in faster rhythm, thus blurring the comprehensibility of the singing. Since its first use in *Gurrelieder, Sprechgesang* had been an especially effective device for Schoenberg, who felt he could use it more freely than music with absolute pitches that, he wrote, create motives that produce obligations that need to be fulfilled.[43] *Sprechgesang,* Schoenberg believed, would generate no musical consequences. Metaphorically, then, *Sprechgesang* corresponds to Schoenberg's image of God, the "almighty one [who] is not obliged to do anything, is bound by nothing," as Moses declares at the end of the third act of the opera.

Schoenberg's use of *Sprechgesang* in combination with singing in *Psalm 130* has similarly divine connotations. Moreover, it also provides the piece, as Schoenberg put it, with its "dramatic character."[44] The six- and occasionally seven- or ten-part texture of the psalm is woven from the constantly varying proportions of speaking and singing voices. Contrast is achieved either by

Example 105. Comparison of the traditional melody Shir hamaalot with Schoenberg's *Hauptstimme* in *Psalm 130*.

(Out of the depths I cry to you, oh Lord, Lord, hear my voice. Let your ears be attentive to my cry for mercy.)

Example 106. Row of *Psalm 130*.

roughly superimposing the two kinds of expression, speaking voices closely following or preceding the singing parts (singing and speaking never join in homophony), or by displaying them in successive blocks (mm. 23–29). The culmination of the piece is achieved through the use of a dense vocal texture (mm. 38–40) that lacks the shadowing effect of speech. It is never clear, though, which one is the shadow, the musical or the speaking voice. In *Moses und Aron* the speaking voice carried the idea, while the singing voice represented corruption. In *Psalm 130* the symbolic roles of the two modes of performance are less sharply drawn, suggesting the combination of the human and the divine.

In contrast to the free flow of speaking voices, bound only by the rhythm of the text, the musical construction of the psalm is strictly organized. The entire piece is built on a combinatorial row (the inverted set transposed not a perfect fifth as in the other works in op. 50, but a major sixth below) (ex. 106). Blocks of the primary and inverted sets are contrasted, paired, and made to clash against one another, creating the imaginary musical space that would dissolve direction, as Schoenberg first described it in reference to *Die Jakobsleiter*. The notes of the vertical or horizontal blocks consist mainly of hexachordal subdivisions of the primary or the inverted sets and never mix with the notes from the other hexachords. Motivic development appears by treating the primary set as a thematic unit and breaking it down into shorter segments (mm. 17–20).

Naturally, in this twelve-tone composition there are no "free" notes.[45] The structure of the row, however, allows Schoenberg to highlight four major thirds, based on the respective notes of a diminished seventh chord (E–G♯, G–B, B♭–D, D♭–F). These four major thirds permeate the texture both melodically and harmonically. The beginning and end of the piece display these thirds as if they constituted its motivic substance. E–G♯ is the first interval sounded in measure 2, the tritone B♭–E at the beginning of measure 3 resolves to B♭–D, the mezzo soprano and alto parts sing G–B in measure 4, and the soprano and tenor pronounce the substitute name of God (Adonai) on a *ff* D♭–F interval in measures 4–5. The last two harmonies include all four major thirds, but incorporate also the notes of a diminished seventh chord to complete the aggregate (ex. 107).

Aligning these four major thirds in a row results in an octatonic scale. Like the C-major references in *Dreimal tausend Jahre* and *Israel Exists Again*, the occasional octatonic passages and consonant points of reference seem to imply nostalgia toward an earlier musical language. Schoenberg used the octatonic set first in the opening bars of *Die Jakobsleiter*, a work in search of an abstract musical language capable of reaching the realm of the spiritual. Because of their invariant character, octatonic structures are similarly effective for unifying musical space, just as is the method of rotating the twelve notes of a dodecaphonic set.[46]

Does this highly complex, abstract music relate in any way to the details of its text? Schoenberg might have insisted that it did not. In the foreword to the 1926 publication of four of his own texts he had asserted that "the musician is in the position of being relatively untouched by his text. He needs it mainly in order to arrange the vowels and consonants according to principles which would also be decisive without it."[47] And yet, while a far cry from the expressionistic word painting in the *Survivor*, the music of *Psalm 130* also reacts to the meaning of its text. An obvious example is measures 4–5, where

Example 107. *Psalm 130*.

a. Mm. 1–5.

Example 107 *(continued)*

(Out of the depths I cry to you, oh Lord)

Example 107 *(continued)*

b. Mm. 54–55.

(He will redeem Israel.)

the soprano and tenor parts complete the twelve-tone set at the word *Adonay* (ex. 107a). The climax of the piece is also related to the text. The *fortissimo,* ten-part chord in measure 38 coincides with the word *ha-chesed* (the mercy), which represents the side of God turned toward humans (ex. 108). Nor does it seem accidental that this climactic moment is not echoed by *Sprechgesang.* In these measures all the notes are meaningful in terms of their relation to the whole, namely, to the primary set of the piece.

Considering the first, emphatic proclamation of the substitute name for God in measure 4, it is strange that Vinaver requested that Schoenberg change *Adonay* to *ha-chesed* in four parts at the end of measure 37 because, he explained to the composer, the frequent use of the word *Adonai* was "not quite in keeping with the Jewish liturgical tradition, which prescribes that

Example 108. *Psalm 130*, mm. 37–39.

(The Lord has mercy in abundance.)

the name of God be used sparingly."[48] The word *Adonay* in the lower parts of measure 37 starts a repetition of the second part of line 7 and echoes the *Adonay* in the soprano part. Because of the homophonic setting of the four parts in measure 37, the name of God sounds only twice in a row. In measures 30–31 the word sounds five times consecutively (tenor, soprano, tenor, alto, mezzo soprano), but to that Vinaver did not object. It is hard to see why Vinaver suggested the change, unless he wanted to demonstrate the contrast between his and Schoenberg's knowledge of Jewish tradition. Schoenberg did not seem to mind the change and told his secretary to communicate his consent to Vinaver.[49] No edition, not even the complete edition of Schoenberg's works, contains the correction.

In this strictly constructed composition, the music fulfills Schoenberg's requirement for a work of art to be "so homogeneous in its composition that in every little detail it reveals its truest, inmost essence."[50] In Schoenberg's conception the music thus functions as a living organism, modeled on the human body (fashioned in God's image). Schoenberg imposes on this organism the pure "idea," expressed both by the tone row and by the unbounded speech, and thus creates a passage through the otherwise impenetrable divide that separates man from the purely spiritual. As in *Die Jakobsleiter,* in his last pieces Schoenberg searches for a mystical, transcendental function of music that does not simply represent what Louis Lambert in Balzac's novel called "the things of heaven,"[51] but actively strives to create the link between physical reality and what lies beyond.

### SAYING IT AGAIN: "MODERN MAN'S PRAYER"

In *Modern Psalms* Schoenberg tried once again to express the fundamentals of a new religion that would reflect his own ideals. Finding expression for a religion adequate for him, or, as he repeatedly said, "modern man," had preoccupied him at least since 1912 when he approached Richard Dehmel (1863–1920) for a text of a projected oratorio. The subject would be, he informed Dehmel,

> modern man, having passed through materialism, socialism, and anarchy and, despite having been an atheist, still having in him some residue of ancient faith (in the form of superstition), wrestles with God (see also Strindberg's "Jacob Wrestling") and finally succeeds in finding God and becoming religious. Learning to pray! It is *not* through any action, any blows of fate, least of all through any love of woman, that this change of heart is to come about. Or at least these should be no more than hints in the background, giving the initial impulse. And above all: the mode of speech, the mode of thought, the mode of expression, should be that of a modern man; the problems treated should be those that harass us. For those who wrestle with God in the Bible also ex-

press themselves as men of their own time, speaking of their own affairs, remaining within their own social and intellectual limits. That is why, though they
are artistically impressive, they do not offer a subject for a modern composer
who fulfills his obligations.

For the time being Schoenberg settled on the last chapter of Balzac's *Séraphîta,*
"The Ascent into Heaven," using it as the basis for *Die Jakobsleiter.* But, he added,
"I could never shake off the thought of 'Modern Man's Prayer.'"[52]

Elements that returned in his late texts were already present in this letter to Dehmel: the desire to express contemporary (that is, Schoenberg's
own) concerns, the longing for faith, the striving to create a connection between man and the transcendental, the approval of superstition as a fundamentally religious attitude, the concentration on an abstract and pure
"idea," and the shunning of action (in other words, traditional religious customs). As his religious inspiration gained more of a Judaic focus in the late
1920s and early 1930s, Schoenberg saw the new religion as a spiritualized,
abstracted form of the Mosaic faith. In *The Biblical Way* Max Aruns asks the
Orthodox Assenio, whom he wants to become the state's first high priest,[53]
to give the nation "a contemporary Law which would allow us to hold our
own amongst all the competing nations, and do not constrain us to live according to laws which were valid five thousand years ago." The practice of
religious traditions carried little value in Schoenberg's radical spiritualism.
What for Assenio sounded blasphemous was for Aruns the only possible way
to approach religion:

> In God's word only His spirit is eternal! The letter of the word is only its figu-
> rative appearance, adapted to a given time—namely, the circumstances of the
> wandering wilderness.
>
> But a nation in our own time cannot afford, every Friday, to shut down its
> blast furnaces and close its electrical plants. I demand . . . new laws . . . to al-
> low us to observe the living spirit of the law.[54]

By 1950 Schoenberg's ideas about politics and religion that he formulated
separately in *The Biblical Way* and in *Moses und Aron* were mixed into a peculiar amalgam. Strangely, it was the political overtones of his highly personal *Modern Psalms* that most marked his meditations as Jewish. Although
he planned to offer the new psalms, together with *Dreimal tausend Jahre* and
*Psalm 130,* to the State of Israel, he could not overcome his frustration with
feeling like an outsider among Jews. All his life Schoenberg had been convinced that it was the Jews in particular who did not appreciate him as an
artist.[55] He expressed this conviction in alarming terms in a letter to Albert
Einstein in 1924 ("In the hatred of [my music], the Jews and the Swastika
bearers are of one mind"), and more moderately in 1946 in a letter to the
editor of *The Jewish Yearbook:*

According to my experience, Jews look at me rather from a racial standpoint than from an artistic. They accordingly give me a lower rating than they give to their Aryan idols.

This is why I underlined four of my works which even by Jews are considered outstanding. It is one of my greatest triumphs that I could create something that forces even Jews to look with a slight admiration upon another Jew.[56]

Even when elected to be honorary president of the Music Academy in Jerusalem, he warned the director, Ödön Pártos (1907–77):

For years I had to observe with sorrow that, among the admirers of my art, of each ten, seven or eight were Christians and at the most two to three Jews. On the other hand most of the Jewish musicians were admirers of the Christian musicians, Stravinsky, Bartók, Hindemith. All these were also enemies of my music and theories and yet they found more support among Jews than I did.

Noblesse forbade me to take up a position against this. But now I must say: I will be very sad if this institute educates those who admire my enemies, instead of bringing up those who are ready to fight.

I cannot allow them not to take this remark as obligatory. I would have to resign, if I found an experience which was going against myself.[57]

Schoenberg did not live to witness the extent to which his suspicions became unjustified. After years of silence about his Jewish background, his name and work became connected to Judaism, and thus his whole life was read from the angle of his reconversion in 1933. The story, as we have seen, can be told in a different way. The texts of Schoenberg's late psalms, which describe not only his personal, nondenominational religion, but also his militant political convictions and personal frustration, provide material for a less essentialist interpretation of the composer's interest in Judaism.

There are ten numbered psalm texts, written between September 1950 and February 1951, seven complete but unnumbered texts, and one incomplete text, written after March 1951. What the several versions of titles for the first text and the whole series share is the designation of the texts as psalms ("A Psalm," "Modern Psalms," "Psalms, Prayers, and Other Conversations with God," and "Psalm 151").[58] As the number 151 indicates, Schoenberg considered his psalms continuations of the Biblical 150. Psalm 150 is a psalm of praise, concluding with the phrase: "Let everything that breathes praise the Lord." "All peoples praise you," Schoenberg continues. "But what can it mean to you whether I do it likewise or not?" This is a question a Biblical psalmist never asks. Thus despite their designation, Schoenberg's modern prayers diverge significantly from their Biblical models. They are neither poems of thanksgiving, nor hymns of praise, nor penitential offerings. They are not even prayers in a traditional sense, for Schoenberg never asks for anything—as he declares in his first psalm, "I must not and cannot make any claims." He interpreted the prayer as a mere metaphor for the bond that unites the praying man with a God who cannot be conceptualized or approached.

In his draft for the series of psalms Schoenberg numbered six groups of topics and then added other subjects that became more and more peculiar as the draft proceeded. Despite Schoenberg's fondness for organization, his grouping of texts does not show a desire for arranging his ideas systematically. Instead they seem like free associations, starting with the explanation of prayer but soon turning to topics connected to his personal frustrations and former political obsessions:

*First group: ideological*

No. 1 Yet I pray
    2 Hope becomes noticed
    3 Luck of the criminal
    4 Virtue and not credit
    5 Chosen-stubbornness
    6 Superstition
    7 Miracle of today
    8 Ten Commandments
    9 Jesus
  10 Love                        about 10–15
  11 Don't make a picture
  12 The number 13

*2nd group: Our Suffering*

3rd group: Our enemy—the cowardly Jew. The avaricious. Shylock

4th group: Expulsion of the criminal—The criminal is driven away from the Temple; the gambler; the cheater; gangster; the godless rabbi; Politician.

5th group: Israel's main task: national resettling on the basis of the true faith.

6th group: Israel's politics toward the East
*Freedom—restricted*
*It's good not to know about fate in advance*
*Sacrifice*
When you rebuild us, purify us and expel the criminal.

The cowardly lion and the stupid tiger

Faith and knowledge.[59]

In the third group Schoenberg already seems to have planned to speak up against the "enemy," whom, just as in his political propaganda from the 1930s, he identified with the "bad Jews," the cowards, the avaricious, and, as the reference in the fourth group tells us, the religious and political leaders ("the godless rabbi" and "Politician"). For the sake of a homogeneous community and pure faith, Schoenberg proposed to expel these elements from his ideal

community. With the fifth and sixth groups of psalms Schoenberg intended
to address the political situation of Israel, thus recycling his ideas about a
utopian Jewish state. The peculiarity of this part of the draft is that Schoenberg seems to have picked up the thread exactly where he had left it in the
1930s, as if Israel had not already come into existence. With a belief in the
future, the last topic, "sacrifice," expresses Schoenberg's wish for Israel to be
rebuilt and purified as a nation.

The subject of the enemy occupies a prominent role not only in the list
of topics but also in the completed texts. Psalm 3, although it belongs to the
"ideological psalms" according to Schoenberg's labeling, contains the only
plea expressed in his prayers: "Lord, I ask you not for the improvement of
my situation. But I ask you more ardently and earnestly that you punish the
criminal: Establish justice at least in this way."[60] In the same psalm Schoenberg identified the enemy as those who lived off what he considered his own
intellectual property: "I will never understand this: that these criminals, who
steal from me and rob me, are protected by luck, lead a good life, while I
have spent years of my life in poverty and worry." Psalm 4 attacks those who
serve evil forces. Schoenberg explains the injustice present in the world by
splitting humanity into two categories: the ones who serve the unfathomable
God cannot expect reward, while those bound to evil sell their souls for a
rich return. "Foreign peoples," Schoenberg declares in psalm 5, are the enemy of God's chosen people. They are "annoyed by the arrogance of our
calling ourselves 'the chosen people.' They fail to understand the martyrdom to which we are always exposed because of our persistence." "We must
remain like this," Schoenberg explains, "until all humanity understands God
as he should be understood."

According to Schoenberg, not only the idea of God but also man's relation to this abstract idea is unimaginable for humans. Since he believed that
no communication is possible between man and this incomprehensibly abstract God—for human conceptualization would turn God into an anthro-
pomorphous being—superstition represents one of the possibilities of faith
open to humans. Superstitious himself, Schoenberg was convinced that the
superstitious mind can recognize secret relationships hidden from common
eyes. "What truly moves us about superstition," Schoenberg writes in psalm
6, "is the faith of the superstitious, his faith in mysteries." The human mind
is weak to recognize mystical relationships. Otherwise, Schoenberg declares
in psalm 7, "many things would be revealed as the necessary and intentional
fulfillment of events predestined long ago."

Schoenberg's relation to traditional religions, especially to Judaism, about
which his knowledge did not seem to go beyond superficial assumptions, is
more complex. While in psalm 5 he presents Orthodoxy as a positive, stubborn force that kept God's idea alive among the Jews ("You endowed us with

steadiness, which sometimes degenerates into stubbornness and Orthodoxy, but enabled us to cling steadfastly to our task"), in the last two unnumbered texts Schoenberg again attacks Orthodoxy. Orthodoxy, he states, led the intelligentsia astray and into the hands of liberalism and materialism, for the intelligentsia could not but refuse to keep "all these detailed hygienic prescriptions." A stout noncompromiser himself, Schoenberg now renounces "the uncompromising severity of the Israelite religion, with which it limits even small, incidental details of the private lives of every individual—allowing no exceptions and no variations," and thus turns religion "into a spiritually useless instrument—a circumstance that in the end causes it to forfeit all success" (unnumbered psalms, "Man kann jedoch nicht behaupten . . . " [One cannot, however, assert . . . ] and "Wer dürfte den ersten Stein werfen" [Who may throw the first stone]).

His relationship to his earlier Christian inclinations is no less ambivalent. Curiously the longest psalm text, psalm 9, is about Jesus, "the purest, the most innocent, unselfish, and idealist being," who, Schoenberg writes, was unrecognized by Jewish historiography. Distressing for those who wish to emphasize the growing importance of Judaism in Schoenberg's thinking, the composer presented Jesus as "the king of the Jews and the son of God," a second Moses who wanted to lead his people "to the true faith in the One, Everlasting and Omnipotent" God.[61] But his people, the psalm goes on, who "knew how to further their own interests in the name of religion, had degraded the Nation." Schoenberg felt that it was a tragedy that Jesus' martyrdom was not represented truthfully. He believed that Jesus did not want to divide the Jewish nation. "On the contrary, he wanted to restore the religion in its purest form." The Bible failed to report his story, and thus the Jews, Schoenberg concludes, "were forced to consider [their] mosaic monotheism contrary to other forms of faith." The prominence of Jesus in this psalm suggests that Schoenberg's self-identification with Moses as a political leader may have been shifting toward Jesus, whose martyrdom was not recognized by his own people.

Strangest of all are the texts about love. There are only two kinds of love of which Schoenberg approved: spiritual friendship, similar to the love described in Balzac's *Séraphîta,* and procreative physical love. Disapproved by God, the sexual side of love "destroys the species and will finally wipe out humanity," Schoenberg preaches in psalm 10. It was Eve's sin, we learn, that led to the "unbalanced search for pleasure." Fear of damnation and "the mild deference of venereal disease" could not restrict man's boundless sexual desire (unnumbered psalm "Liebe ist der Verlangen der Kinder" [Love is the desire of children]). Culture is guilty of glorifying the excesses of love, Schoenberg claims five months before his death (unnumbered psalm "Wer dürfte den ersten Stein werfen?"). While in his political pamphlets he advocated every means to achieve Jewish unity, in these last texts he approves the power of church and state to fight physical love: "The power of the church must be at least equal to that of the state. Its organizations, however, must surpass politics in sensitivity—where every means is right as long as it secures power." Nothing can succeed, though, Schoenberg writes, for both the "shameless methods of politics" and "the uncompromising strength of militant laws" proved to be too weak to correct humanity in this respect. "Perhaps, however, we have been given the splitting of the atom in order to exterminate ourselves and our evils" (unnumbered psalm "Liebe ist das Verlangen der Kinder"). Instead of turning to the spirituality of religion, here, at least for a moment, Schoenberg imputes to religion the aggression of politics.

Schoenberg's discomforting invective against physical love is part of the composer's ultimate obsession with purity. In this obsessive view, religion, politics, and art all blur into a unified striving for absolute purity, politics being the forceful means to achieve the condition in which religion, instead of observing rituals, would become abstract, the same way human love would be transformed into spiritual friendship. This longing for the spiritual can be seen as typical in a composer approaching the end of his life. Yet Schoenberg's stubborn, self-righteous political rhetoric overshadows his quasi-religious images and thus creates an unpleasant association between his psalms and the ruthless political utopias of the twentieth century. Ironically, then, the spiritual cleansing of politics Schoenberg attempted in the last phase of his life failed. The texts of his psalms represent an amalgam of convictions in which religious, political, musical, and personal aspects of Schoenberg's thinking are so unified that separating them is no longer possible.

## ANOTHER FRAGMENT

The musical fragment that Schoenberg composed for the first psalm also defeats his striving for purity. Like the other pieces in op. 50, the first psalm is a twelve-tone composition, based on a combinatorial row Schoenberg called a "miracle" row because not only does its transposed inversion contain the same pitch classes as the primary form, but the second hexachord of the primary row is also a retrograde of its first hexachord. Despite its abstract complexity, the row also allows quasi-tonal motivic references. Starting from the first, third, or fourth notes of the hexachord, three consecutive notes form motives consisting of major/minor thirds (C–E♭[D♯]–E; A♭–C♭–C; B[C♭]–A♭[G♯]–G♮). The hexachords also include major and minor triads (based on A♭ in P 1–6, on G♭ in P 7–12, on B♭ in $I^5$ 1–6, and on C in $I^5$ 7–12) (ex. 109). Leaving out the second note from the first and the fifth note from the second hexachords produces augmented triads. The music

Example 109. Row of *Modern Psalm,* $P^0$ and $I^5$.

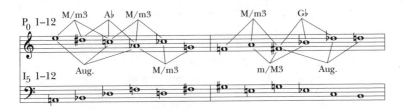

Example 110. Vocal parts of *Modern Psalm,* mm. 78–80.

([I ask for] miracle: fulfillments.)

of the psalm is permeated with these major/minor and augmented triads both melodically and harmonically. One finds even gestures of tonal resolution, as in the soprano and tenor parts in measures 78–80 (ex. 110).

But in one respect Schoenberg's setting of his first psalm text differs from his other late choral works. While *Sprechgesang* in *Psalm 130* recalled the God of Moses, in the first *Modern Psalm* the individual speaking voice harks back to Moses himself. At the beginning of *Moses und Aron* Moses says: "Einziger, ewiger, allgegenwärtiger, unsichtbarer und unvorstellbarer Gott!" (Only one, eternal, omnipresent, unperceived, and unimaginable God) (2 mm. after rehearsal number 6). The psalmist describes God with almost the same series of attributes ("Einziger, Ewiger, Allmächtiger, Allwissender, Unvorstellbarer" [The Only, Eternal, Almighty, Omniscient, Unimaginable]). But while the first words of Moses address God, in the psalm the self-searching question comes before the pronouncement of God's nature. "Wer bin ich, mich

Example 111. The psalmist's words in *Modern Psalm*, mm. 18–21 (reduced score).

(Who am I to think that my prayers are necessary?)

Example 112. *Modern Psalm,* mm. 14–16 (reduced score).

(What can it mean for you whether I do this or [not?])

der Macht der Blindheit entgegenzustellen?" (Who am I to combat the power and force of that blindness), asks Moses in the opera (3 mm. after rehearsal number 26). "Wer bin ich, dass ich glauben soll, mein Gebet sei eine Notwendigkeit?" (Who am I to believe that my prayer is necessary?), asks the modern psalmist. In the psalm this question thunders over everything else. Extracted from the second hexachords of the prime and its inversion, three-note motives, in close imitation and *fortissimo* dynamics in the chorus and orchestra, highlight this most important question (ex. 111). Moses was occupied with the definition of God. Schoenberg's psalmist, representing the composer's own voice, is in search of himself.

This personal voice evokes expressive gestures of fear, anger, and frustration that were missing from the other choral compositions of op. 50. Schoenberg signals the turn to personal questions in measure 14, where the muted horn, together with a bass-drum roll and strings playing close to the bridge, enters. The abrupt hitting of the notes is like a pang that suddenly changes the tone of the prayer (ex. 112). The same shivering string tremolos accompany the psalmist's questions about the necessity of prayer (m. 20).

Speaker and chorus share most of the text; the chorus, as a communal expression, neutralizes fear and pain by abolishing the expressive gestures that accompany the speaker. The prohibition of making images of God is ut-

Example 113. Prohibition to make images in *Modern Psalm,* mm. 26–28 (reduced score).

([I speak about the . . . ] Unfathomable, of whom I cannot or should not create a picture. On whom I cannot [and should not make a claim.])

tered, however, only by the speaker, accompanied, significantly, by two blocks of sonorities together completing the aggregate (ex. 113). These aggregate moments appeared in other Schoenberg compositions in association with a divine presence. Here, the *fpp* tremolos, played close to the bridge, produce a frightening effect, signaling fear of the consequences of trespassing the prohibition of the second commandment.

Instrumental interludes, like the one following the chorus's proclamation of the possibility of God's ignoring prayer, comment on the text. The vehement *forte* outburst of densely layered strings expresses anger, inexpressible in words without blasphemy. The interlude imbues the phrase that precedes *trotzdem* (in spite of this) with a strong emotional punch (ex. 114).

Example 114. First instrumental interlude in *Modern Psalm,* mm. 45–50 (reduced score).

*(continued)*

Example 114 *(continued)*

Example 114 *(continued)*

The second interlude, preceding the chorus's repetition of the word *trotz-dem*, similarly builds up a climax, now reminiscent of the frenzied ending of Salome's dance in Strauss's opera. In measures 68–69 the top notes of the first violin (F♯–G–C) provide a quasi-tonal progression, pointing to C as its goal. The dance gestures, evoked by the repeated rhythmic figures in the violins, indicate an additional layer of meaning to *trotzdem* by creating a link between the first psalm and those that attack sensuality as an irradicable human evil (ex. 115).

Yet the musical gestures again contradict Schoenberg's striving for purity. Like the texts, the music is also too personal and too expressive to reach the level of detachment the composer equated with spirituality. All in all, Schoenberg's personality was too weighty and too centered around the self to be able to rise unbound to heaven. This failure ultimately makes Schoenberg's music accessible to us, for the composer's weakness, and ultimately his inability to achieve his lofty goal, humanize his late works.

Example 115. Second instrumental interlude in *Modern Psalm,* mm. 68–71 (reduced score).

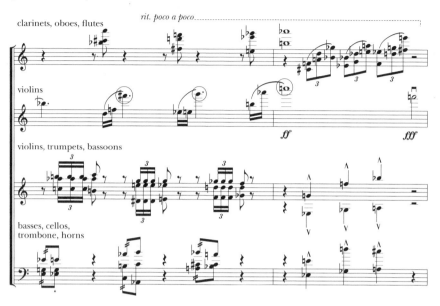

·   ·   ·

How does this utopian striving relate to Schoenberg's Jewishness? Do we do justice either to Schoenberg's artistic achievements or to Jewish spiritual movements if we try to label Schoenberg's (or anyone's) intellectual concerns as essentially Jewish or Christian, German or French, Western or Eastern, to mention only a few of the century's most hackneyed binarisms? Ignoring Schoenberg's Jewish background and especially its effect on his life would be a deliberate distortion of facts. Yet the reduction of the complexity of the composer's identity to a Jewish one, however defined, distorts our image of Schoenberg hardly the less, for it ignores a cultural milieu that played a far more important part in the formation of Schoenberg's personality than the Jewish religion he did not practice or the Jewish culture he only superficially absorbed. Until Hitler came to power and anti-Semitism became a gruesome political reality, this formative milieu included Jewish and Christian, as well as occasionally fashionable "Eastern" elements. Many, irrespective of their religious, racial, or national origin shared Schoenberg's strivings for purity and order in art and politics. "The division of Austrians, Germans, and other Europeans into Aryan and non-Aryan citizens—and this need hardly be proved any more—rests on a racialist attitude that was to find its final solution in the holocaust," art dealer Serge Sabarsky stated in a letter concerning a 1996 Festival of Austrian-Jewish culture. Sabarsky warned that to "make a distinction between Aryan and non-Aryan human beings belongs, *nolens volens*, to the theory of the Nürnberg laws, even if it is done ever so philosemitically."[62]

It was less an abstract spiritual essence that connected Schoenberg to Judaism than it was his fraught and confused relationship to his Jewish origin, which was distorted all the more by the murderous racist politics of World War II. Schoenberg's reaction to his expulsion from Germany was not unique, although the vehemence with which he saturated his new Jewish identity with aspects of the old German one does seem exceptional. This is the part of the story that most fascinates and disturbs. It tells us a great deal about the conflicts of identity faced by Jews in the first part of this century, and it warns that the results of coerced reconversions are rarely untainted by the sins of the coercers.

# POSTSCRIPT: "CASTLE OF PURITY"

*La nostalgie d'une pureté passée, la vocation d'une pureté à venir, la phobie de l'impureté présente, —voilà . . . ce que nous offre l'expérience.*

*[The nostalgia for a past purity, the call of a future purity, and the phobia about the present impurity—that is . . . what experience offers us.]*
VLADIMIR JANKÉLÉVITCH, *Le pur et l'impur* (1960)

Octavio Paz concludes his essay "The Castle of Purity" on Marcel Duchamp with these words:

> In his abandonment of painting there is no romantic self-pity, nor the pride of a titan; it is wisdom, *mad wisdom*. It is not a knowledge of this thing or that, it is neither affirmation nor negation; it is the void, the knowledge of indifference. Wisdom and freedom, void and indifference resolve themselves into a key word: purity. Something which cannot be sought after but which gushes forth spontaneously after one has traversed certain experiences. Purity is what remains after all the accounts have been made. Igitur finishes with these words: *Le Néant parti, reste le château de la pureté* [Nothingness having departed, there remains the castle of purity].[1]

The final quotation is from Stéphane Mallarmé's 1869 unfinished play-narration *Igitur ou la folie d'Elbehnon*.[2] Although it figures in the title, the word *purity* appears only on the last page of Paz's essay, as if putting into practice what Paz preaches—letting purity be what remains "after all the accounts have been made." Mallarmé's *Igitur* suggests that purity is more than a quality left behind after "Nothingness has departed." The play invokes purity as part of an Absolute, the last stage of a process of self-knowledge, a state of detachment and permanence, possibly death. Purity, as Mallarmé formulated it in less cryptic words in a letter to Henri Cazalis, is what "man has never reached and will never reach," an ideal that, because of the imperfection of the human mind, cannot be converted to reality.[3] With its stuffy and stifling furniture Igitur's castle symbolizes the protagonist's ancestors, his "pure" past that enables Igitur to complete his quest for his own purity (it is in this sense that Igitur talks about the purity of race). What purity is exactly we never learn: neither from Mallarmé, who weaves his cryptic narrative around the word (the key images in the text, the self, the night, and the mirror, are all striving to achieve absolute purity), nor from Paz, who exploits the word's magic power by keeping its meaning a secret.

Invoking purity is an appropriate closing gesture, and so this study on Jewish identities in music ends with an essay on purity. Consideration of the word's rich connotations is indispensable for understanding the immense rhetorical power purity possessed in twentieth-century art in general, and in the life and work of the Jewish protagonists of this book in particular. More than by any mysterious Jewish essence, the composers presented here are united by their preoccupation with purity, which connected them not only to each other but also to ancient religious and contemporaneous political and artistic concepts. Saminsky's polemic about "the music of the Bible" versus "the music of the ghetto" relied heavily on forceful Old Testament associations of purity. Bloch's inspiration was also Biblical. And although he seems to have been the most innocent of purity's political connotations, his strong belief in the determining factor of race in human character and in art associates him with contemporaneous theories of racial purity. In Schoenberg's work, religious, political, and artistic concepts of purity merge. Ultimately his uncompromising demand for purity silenced his work on Jewish subjects and resulted in torsos (similar to Mallarmé's or Duchamp's works that were also doomed to incompletion by their authors' pursuit of purity).

Saminsky's, Bloch's, and Schoenberg's quests for purity exemplify different aspects of the ideal as manifested in twentieth-century art. However different, though, their strivings were also related in greater or lesser degree to contemporaneous political currents, as they were to their emerging awareness as creative artists of their ethnic identity in an anti-Semitic climate. It would be tempting to argue that these artists' preoccupation with purity originated in their Jewish ethnicity and was thus connected to the central role purity played both in ancient Jewish religion and in modern Jewish nationalism. It is more probable, however, that it was not their Jewish background but rather their assimilated status that made the quest for purity so central in their artistic projects. Hard though it would be to prove, it could be that the urge for purification was stronger in artists of Jewish ethnicity than in their gentile contemporaries precisely because of their personal experience of being treated—covertly or openly—by the society in which they functioned as impurities.

Although Western European society in the first part of the twentieth century was predominantly secular, the obsession with purity that permeated cultural discourses retained religious, even magical, implications. When purity is evoked, religious connotations abound, which, though historically removed from twentieth-century art or politics, are crucial for comprehending the power the word came to posses. Understanding the philosophical concept of purity, as well as how purity evolved from its strictly cultic use to a more broadly understood religious concept, how it became associated with moral questions in general (and sexual taboos in particular), how it gained significance in secular thought, and how it was transformed into a powerful concept in politics and art, communicates something of the range of meanings that the word purity evokes.

In ancient religions purity and impurity were strongly associated with taboos. Western culture inherited the concept via Judaism, in which, as it survived in the book of Leviticus, a scrupulous system was built according to which things designated as pure and impure were strictly separated. In this chapter consideration of the different roles purity has played in society starts with its function in religious cults and ends with its reappearance in social utopias that used the rhetorical power of purity to facilitate the creation of artificially homogeneous societies. From the perspective of realized social utopias, purity can be seen as a tool of violence, hence the discomfort one feels in evoking the concept. Despite its central role in twentieth-century art, the significance of purity has been rarely if ever discussed, as if critics have wanted to "purify" history of the concept. The squeamishness is not surprising. The genocidal purification practiced during World War II and the numerous attempts at ethnic cleansings that still haunt the world have tainted the word with horrific associations. Yet however comforting it may be, silencing critical discussion of the concept leaves an important aspect of twentieth-century art unexplained. Studying different aspects of purity is revealing, for although its connotations had never been spelled out when the word reappeared in different historical and cultural contexts, the concept of purity has preserved the magical power of its primeval, cultic meaning.

## INEFFABLE PURITY

What, then, is purity? The question is crucial, but finally elusive. Since impurity is more commonly defined, the imagination must fill the vacuum created by the undefined character of purity. We can learn only about the impure, philosopher Vladimir Jankélévitch maintains, for "only the impure, with its roughness, disparity, and mixture, can offer a grip for our understanding."[4] Past, present, and future provide us with different experiences of purity, manifest, as Jankélévitch recognizes, in a nostalgia for the imagined purity of the past (paradise lost), in a longing for the purity of the future (utopia), and, above all, in the phobia created by the impurity of the present. Purity is a point of departure or arrival in the historical narrative, but never exists now. Translating his three categories of time into personal experience, Jankélévitch states: "pure is something I used to be and I will become—but, properly speaking, I am never pure."

What makes Jankélévitch's philosophical discussion of the concept appealing for the present study is that he sees purity as a deeply human concern. For him purity is a moral category that "serves us to measure and appreciate at least the degree of our impurity." It is, in other words, a "model, a system of reference, and a principle." It is only death, as Mallarmé's *Igitur* suggests and Jankélévitch confirms, that provides humans with the experience of purity. Death liberates humans from the passing of time and hence, like purity, "stops the advance of the future." The idyllic purity of the past and the messianic purity of the future exist only in the human imagination, for, Jankélévitch writes, "the original purity is not the most ancient time of history but belongs to a *completely different category* than history." In its existence outside of human time purity in fact resembles God, and human desire to achieve a state of purity is a longing to approach a divine state.

The elusiveness of purity only increases its significance. It remains, as Jankélévitch puts it, *"the invisible that allows us to see."* The process of purification, which is more important in human life than purity itself, is a restoration of our integrity, a process that, as described in *Igitur*, leads to self-knowledge. Purification strips the person (or the object) from foreign elements and restores his or her essence. Philosophical concepts of purity and essentialism are thus close, both relying on Plato's division of the world into essences and appearances.

There are plenty of examples to confirm Jankélévitch's philosophical observations. In every context purity preserves its elusive, ineffable, yet irresistible character. Purity laws in Judaism, for example, described only states of impurity and means of purification. Being pure meant being free from impurities. The path-breaking anthropological study *Purity and Danger* (1966) by Mary Douglas reveals already in its subtitle, *An Analysis of the Concepts of Pollution and Taboo*, that the focus of the book is pollution and not the ungraspable, unrepresentable concept of purity. It is precisely its indefinable character that has made the concept of purity such a dependable ideological weapon—hence one can read a second meaning into the title of Douglas's study: not simply "purity and danger" but "purity as danger."

And dangerous it was, for although philosophically ineffable, purity could become all too real in regulations that societies attempted to set up in order to put their strivings for purity into practice. In fact, we can add another experience of purity to Jankélévitch's categories of the imagined purity of the past, the impurity of the present, and the projected purity of the future: the experience of social violence as it has been exercised repeatedly in the name of institutionalized quests for purity. Though always present in human society, the dual concept of purity and impurity seems to have been especially effective where, as Mary Douglas observes, "the lines of structure, cosmic or social, are clearly defined."[5] Regulations to ensure purity assume a highly regulated society. Charles Hinnant associates the emergence of the concept with fear experienced in these strictly organized societies. "If it is preoccupied with threats to its security," Hinnant writes in his analysis of

*Gulliver's Travels,* "a society formulates rules about purity which mirror these fears."[6]

The significance as well as the practical and psychological implications of the concept differed considerably at different time periods. Yet something remained constant: a human need to divide the world and human action into pure and impure categories. The tendency is inevitably totalitarian, for the division creates a world in which everything occupies either a positive or a negative place in the totality of society. The more polarized the perception, the less room is left for anything that would fall in between. Preoccupation with purity thus signals totalitarian tendencies, be it in religion, which inclines virtually by definition to a utopian worldview, or in politics and the arts, which need not so incline.

## FROM CULT TO MORAL CONSTRAINT

As in Hinnant's model society, the religious division of the world into pure and impure is inspired in large part by fear. Judaism turned the same dual concept into elaborate regulations that, as Jacob Neusner points out, affected the law as a whole. Neusner's description of purity and impurity demonstrates Judaism's complex relationship to the concept. In Judaism, Neusner states, purity and impurity "refer to a status in respect to contact with a source of impurity and the completion of acts of purification from impurity."[7] It is worth stressing again that Jewish religious regulations describe the state of impurity and not the nature of purity. The lack of definition in this case is not simply a philosophical question. One can argue that in Judaism the indescribable nature of purity relates the concept to holiness and thus to the aniconic God of the Jews.

The Bible offers no rationale for the division, for—as the twelfth-century Jewish philosopher Maimonides, among others, maintained—the laws of purity and impurity "are decrees laid down by Scripture and not matters about which human understanding is capable of forming a judgment."[8] For Robertson Smith, an influential Bible scholar of the late nineteenth century, impurity still represented a status beyond rationalization. "Levitical legislation," he claimed, "reduces the fear of unknown or hostile powers to a matter of God's laws: uncleanness is hateful to God and must be avoided by all who have to do with the divinity." In contrast, Baruch A. Levine argued in the 1970s that impurity represented a "demonic conception of sin, offence, and transgression."[9] Demons disappeared from official Jewish religion, yet the focus on impurity in the Bible demonstrates that, as Jacob Milgrom observes in the commentary to the book of Leviticus, in "physical impurity . . . the demonic continued to reside. It was no longer an autonomous force but was inherent in the very nature of the impurity."[10]

Divine will or fear of demonic forces, however, does not explain the particulars of Jewish impurity laws. Various other explanations, among them sin, aesthetic considerations, holiness of the sanctuary, separation of Israel, health issues, the enhancing of priestly power, have been suggested by various authors. Milgrom proposes a more poetic exegesis. Finding that chief impurities (related to death, birth, menstruation, and scale disease or leprosy) can all be associated with death, he claims that purity laws were meant to separate "forces of life and death set loose by man himself through his obedience to or defiance of God's commandments." In other words, the laws produced a symbolic system that reminded Israel "of its imperative to cleave to life and reject death."[11]

At the time when purity laws mainly affected priests around Temple service and thus had primarily cultic significance, exegesis was not yet needed for the priestly writers. Purity laws both in and outside of the Temple mostly served to maintain the divine in the people's midst.[12] It was only after the destruction of the Temple that the interpretation of impurity laws became so central to religious debates that, Neusner states, the attitude toward impurity regulations emerged as one of the most decisive factors in differentiating emerging Jewish religious sects. More important than providing a distinguishing mark, however, the need for explanation also opened the way for secular interpretations of purity. With the explanations of Philo, Josephus, the Pharisees, and later early Christians, purity and impurity gained ethical significance.[13] Separated from its original cultic context purity became a sign of moral blamelessness, impurity a symptom of sin.

In the Talmudic period, Neusner explains, "rabbis' primary hermeneutical interest lay in the ethical or moral lessons to be derived from the purity-rules." Thus Pinhas B. Yair could make a long list of associations that lead from cleanliness via saintliness to the resurrection of the dead (which makes Milgrom's explanation of purity laws even more persuasive): "Heedfulness leads to [physical] cleanliness, cleanliness to purity, purity to separateness, separateness to holiness, holiness to humility, humility to the shunning of sin, the shunning of sin to saintliness, saintliness to the Holy Spirit, the Holy Spirit to the resurrection of the dead." Not a quintessentially rabbinic argument, Neusner warns, still, it demonstrates how far the metaphorical use of purity could be stretched. All in all, as Neusner demonstrates, the modern West inherited two important ideas about purity and impurity from ancient Israel: that they had a cultic significance, and that they can be interpreted as "metaphors for moral and religious behavior, primarily in regards to matters of sex, idolatry, and unethical action."

## PURITY AS METAPHOR

Christianity preferred this latter metaphorical use. Despite the fact that some purity regulations were still in force in early Christianity, purity rules were

regularly treated as "metaphorical or figurative of a higher reality."[14] Purity
thus became even more elusive, while impurity came to serve as the most powerful metaphor for sin.[15] Paul Ricoeur traces the development from the notion of defilement (an "archaic conception of fault") through sin ("a fundamental experience which includes *all* men and indicates the *real* situation of
man before God") and guilt ("a feeling of the unworthiness at the core of
one's personal being"),[16] in other words, from cultic regulations of impurity
through an internalized feeling of guilt. At the end of the process sin and impurity (or defilement) became one, an equation that, Ricoeur believes, ultimately erases the dividing line between physical and ethical categories:

> The anticipation of punishment, at the heart of the fear of the impure,
> strengthens this bond between evil and misfortune. Punishment falls on man
> in the guise of misfortune and transforms all possible sufferings, all diseases,
> all death, all failure into a sign of defilement. Thus the world of defilement
> embraces in its order of the impure the consequences of impure actions or
> events; step by step, there is nothing that cannot be pure or impure. Hence,
> the division between the pure and the impure ignores any distinction between
> the physical and the ethical and follows a distribution of the sacred and the
> profane which has become irrational for us.

In conjunction with impurity the concept of sin is a rather narrow one. Although Ricoeur states that "an indissoluble complicity between sexuality and
defilement seems to have been formed since time immemorial," it was Christianity that limited discussions about impurity to sexual impurity. In this context, Ricoeur observes, purity becomes identified with virginity. And this is
precisely how narrowly the word was still understood at the end of the nineteenth century. Mainly because of Church propaganda, purity was used almost exclusively to refer to one aspect of morality: the abstinence from sexual relations. This meaning was so firmly established that in his *Little Essays
of Love and Virtue* (1922) Havelock Ellis, the most popular sexologist of his
time, took for granted that purity's exclusive meaning was chastity. However
limiting in an ethical sense, the sexual connotation of purity and impurity
is nevertheless powerful. In fact, one suspects that the squeamishness about
bringing the concept of purity into critical focus is at least partially due to
the symbiosis between impurity and sexuality.

### DARK OVERTONES: RACIAL PURITY

Separating purity from its original cultic context had its threatening aspects.
Alongside the narrowing of its moral significance, its metaphorical use allowed a broader spectrum of associations outside of the religious sphere.
Sometimes even in religion, adherence to purity could evoke violence. In
ancient Judaism, for instance, Temple purity was so severely guarded that in

the Sanhedrin impurity was listed among the sins that were punished by death. "If a priest served [at the altar] in a state of impurity, his fellow priests did not bring him to the *bet din*," the Sanhedrin states, "but the young priests took him outside of the Temple court and split open his brain with clubs."[17]

Similar descriptions inspired Barrington Moore to search for manifestations of violence exercised in quest of purity from Biblical times through the twentieth century. The French Revolution, he claims, turned purity into a secular concept, in which, Moore states, ethical exclusiveness became even more amplified, and violence as an enforcing measure more likely to be used than in religious practice. Focusing on the violent potential of purity, he concludes that "the secular aspect [of purity] may have reached its apex under Fascism and Stalinism."[18]

Indeed, the secularization that followed the Enlightenment did not diminish, but rather enhanced, the yearning for purity. The concept was transformed, but its power has not diminished in secular societies. Purity's function, Marcel Poorthuis and Joshua Schwartz write in *Purity and Holiness*, shifted "from the social to the psychological realm and from the religious even to the racist."[19] This particularly dangerous discourse of purity, of which anti-Semitism was a notorious manifestation, became an obsession in the nineteenth century. Yet while Moore seeks to establish a connection between forceful application of Biblical impurity laws and political violence exercised in order to achieve racial purity, Poorthuis and Schwartz carefully draw a distinction between religious and political concepts: "Racist purity was a pernicious transformation of ultimately Biblical ideas. The difference should be duly noted: whereas in the Bible pure and impure denote two possible states of the individual, modern racism created an insurmountable dualism transferring these concepts to an opposition between a so called 'chosen race' and all other races, which were considered more or less inferior." Unlike religion, racism does not offer purification. There is no connecting passage between racist categories of pure and impure.

The position of Jews in race theories was ambiguous. In Europe where racism was practiced with considerable anti-Semitic bias, Jews were among the most frequent targets. For Chamberlain Jews' racial purity was a myth, a falsification of the past, which Jews were forced to overtake when they became "conscious of their racial sin." "In order to wipe out the irretrievable past, in order to fuse that past with the present, in which wisdom and the power of will should set a limit to sin and make a place for purity," Chamberlain wrote, "the whole Jewish history from the beginning had to be falsified, and the Jews [had to be] represented as a people chosen above all other peoples by God and of stainlessly pure race, protected by Draconian laws against every crossing."[20] Summarizing the results of his pseudo-scientific knowledge Chamberlain stated: "A chief result of this anatomical survey is that the Jewish race is in truth a permanent but at the same time a mongrel race which always retains this mongrel character." Although he admitted that "all historically great races and nations have been produced by mixing," Chamberlain defined mongrel as the mixing of incompatible races, between which the difference "is too great to be bridged over."

Since impurity became irretrievably linked to sin and guilt, Chamberlain could maintain that "race and nationality . . . possess a significance which is not only physical and intellectual but also moral." Seemingly only an anthropological curiosity, racial purity became a moral yardstick for the different races. "In men," Chamberlain stated, "any want of organic racial consistency, or fitness in the parent stock, means above all things a lack of moral and intellectual coherence." This conviction made moral judgment astonishingly easy. If the Jewish race is impure, the Jews as a people and as individuals are morally tainted.

In contrast to Europe, in the United States, where the discussion of race focused on questions of slavery and immigration, some considered Jews as a model race that maintained its "racial purity." In *Race or Mongrel*, Alfred Schultz, a chief advocate of racial purity in the United Stated, spoke up against "the intermarriage of people of one color with people of another," which, he argued, "always leads to deterioration."[21] Comparing Chamberlain's and Schultz's notions of Jewish racial purity shows how flexibly racial ideology could be adjusted to ideological agendas. The mongrel, according to Schultz, was "the result of a fertile cross between two varieties of the same species." Schultz's example of "pure race" is the Jews, because, Schultz wrote, Jews "had in a very early time a knowledge of that law of nature which demands purity of blood." Schultz's historically erroneous claim that "the wonderful instincts of the Israelites led them to evolve a religion which had race purity as its central idea" shows how widespread the notion was that the Jewish religion was based on racial segregation. Concluding his chapter on the Jews, Schultz stated: "The Jews have overcome well-nigh insurmountable obstacles; they are succeeding everywhere, because they have been and do remain true to themselves, that is, true to their race instincts. They demonstrate to the world that the blood that courses in the veins of the individual is more sacred than gold, silver, territory, flag, and country. . . . Race purity is the secret of the success of the Jews."

A myth of pure Jewish blood was cherished even by the Jews, so much so that in the 1905 *Jewish Encyclopedia* "Purity of Race" occupies a separate entry. In it Joseph Jacobs, much in the spirit of Schultz, spoke up against intermarriage, arguing that it lessens fertility. The entry is cautiously formulated and avoids giving a definitive answer to the question of whether Jews are racially pure, yet it suggests that Jacobs is in favor of racial purity, which he backs up with anthropological and historical reasoning.[22] Not surprisingly, the new 1976 *Encyclopedia Judaica* omits the entry completely.

Purity of race is a long stretch from the original, cultic meaning of purity.

Yet it is one connotation that cannot be ignored when purity is recalled in twentieth-century politics and arts. While in a religious context purity continued to refer to sanctity and holiness, in a secular environment its invocation urged separation, in the form of either political xenophobia or artistic elitism.

## PURITY OF ART

Already in the nineteenth century, critics' celebration of the aesthetic autonomy of absolute music signaled an emerging preoccupation with purity in music. Yet the two currents—program music that attributed poetic meaning to instrumental compositions, and absolute music that tried to set music free from the "extramusical"—could still coexist in contemporary aesthetics.

Twentieth-century aesthetics was less tolerant. Partially because artists felt even more insecure about their role in society than their predecessors, their thirst for certitude, provided by purity, increased. Absolute music (consciously stripped of social contexts) became valued as a musical manifestation of purity, while program music (or any music that acknowledged the social function of art) was viewed as impure. The association of program music with impurity was justified by reference to the exploitation of such music by repressive totalitarian regimes, while the purity of absolute music was demonstrated by its cultivation in free societies. Guarded almost to the extent of paranoia from meaning or associations outside of the strictly technical, absolute music achieved a self-reflective purity (promoted by Clement Greenberg) that was one of the most common paradigms of modernism.[23] Abstract art (in other words, art without referential subject matter), the counterpart of absolute music, was a maximalization of this tendency toward purification.

But abstract art was even more. It was, as Worringer noticed, a symptom of an anxiety that manifested itself in the fear of contracting impurities. The intensity of this fear signaled a deepening sense of personal, social, and political instabilities, and thus reconnected the striving for purity to its primordial religious roots. Abstract art took its inspiration from spiritual movements such as Theosophy (especially the Christian version advocated by Rudolf Steiner), Swendenborgian spiritualism,[24] or, as in Schoenberg's case, from self-created, abstracted versions of traditional religions. Artists aspired to divine heights and considered artistic creativity comparable to divine creation, and art as a way to rise toward God.[25]

Abstract art was also motivated by essentialist philosophy, especially by Platonism and German Idealism. Mark Cheetham relates the passionate pursuit of purity in twentieth-century art to a revival of Neoplatonism. Paul Gauguin and Piet Mondrian, the founders of abstraction in art, Cheetham claims, "quite unambiguously answered Plato with their new art." Abstract art, in this view, is a quest for essentials, and, according to Cheetham, purity is "the image of and vehicle to absolute, universal truth."[26] Appearances in art were then left behind in favor of some invisible essence, which could not be communicated or presented in any conventional way.

Abstract artists believed that they, like the soul in Plotinus's Neoplatonist philosophy, must withdraw to their innermost self to have, in Plotinus's words, a "vision, not of some light . . . but of the light within itself, unmingled, pure, suddenly gleaming before [him]."[27] For Plotinus, purification was indispensable to escape the shadows of reality. For falling into matter, according to the philosopher, hinders the soul. In abstract art, especially in painting where "matter" could not be completely ignored (unless one silences one's art like Duchamp), matter was to provide only "the initial step in the process of purification."[28]

Besides their heavy reliance on philosophical concepts of purity, abstract artists also built on purity's political connotations. As an aesthetic ideology, pure abstract art, Cheetham claims, has "the potential for authoritarian rigidity." "The new spirit is characterized by certainty; it does not question, it offers a solution," wrote the artists in the journal *De Stijl*.[29] Abstract artists' conviction that only abstract art can be valid inspired an aggressive, militant rhetoric, similar to that used in totalitarian politics of the time. And although abstract artists tried to detach their art from contemporary politics, they were far from being politically indifferent. In fact, they deeply believed that through their art they could construct an ideal state that would be modeled on their artistic vision. This new state was a utopian site, purified, whole, and exclusive.

The defining presence of purity in twentieth-century art signaled a strange combination of anxiety and hubris: anxiety about being unrelated to the social realities of the present (and hence claiming such a relation artistically irrelevant), and hubris of wanting to influence the future to a degree unheard of in the history of the arts since Plato's dictum about art's obligation to shape society. This hubris is perhaps the most disquieting aspect of the philosophy of modern art. Although abstract artists like Mondrian and Kandinsky had no sympathy for Nazi politics and aesthetics (which designated most abstract art as degenerate), their ideals have nevertheless been compared to Nazi ideology. As Cheetham observes, "the shock value of a comparison between these quests for absolute answers through mechanisms of purification can alert us to the ideological implications of purity in abstract painting."[30]

### RECAPITULATION

Although both in painting and music Schoenberg remained an expressionist, his relation to abstract artists and hence to the artistic quest for purity was the strongest among the protagonists of this book. The similarities between his and Kandinsky's ideas are indeed so striking that it would be difficult to distinguish between those that demonstrate mutual influence and those that were merely coincidental. Admiring the abstract potential of music, Kandinsky consciously modeled his art on musical principles. Schoenberg's ideas on music, first published in his 1911 *Harmonielehre*, provided inspiration for many artists of his time. Thanks to *Harmonielehre*, many parts of which were accessible even to artists not versed in music, Schoenberg's name became the emblem of the new tendencies that Kandinsky dubbed "the spiritualization of art." Kandinsky could have substituted the word *pure* for spiritual, for the meaning of the two easily collapsed into a single concept. Spiritual and material, pure and impure were on the opposite extremes of the same scale of measuring artistic value. The lower, materialistic segment of Kandinsky's spiritual triangle was populated by artists who, in Kandinsky's words, "flatter base needs; in an ostensibly artistic form [they] present what is impure." Satisfying "base needs" meant material success, which artists at the top of the spiritual triangle despised. Instead of profiting from their work, Kandinsky argued, spiritually minded artists are "scorned and disliked," yet they drag "the heavy weight of resisting humanity forward and upward."[31]

Echoing Schopenhauer, Kandinsky and Schoenberg agreed that art's object was "an Idea in Plato's sense."[32] Both believed in the divine mission of the artist, which was to capture in art the timeless essence of this "idea." Both distinguished the idea from style (or appearances), which, Schoenberg claimed, was "inconsequential."[33] Art, Schoenberg declared, should have something in common with the eternal and the infinite, which he sought to achieve "through a fluctuating . . . unending harmony . . . that does not always carry with it certificate of domicile and passport carefully indicating country of origin and destination," in other words, through abandoning tonality. The words *idea, truth, essence, eternity,* and *infinity* were used almost interchangeably to express an abstract, higher reality that both Schoenberg and Kandinsky imagined as something absolutely pure and detached from material reality.

The means to approach this "truth" was intuition for Kandinsky and instinct for Schoenberg, both words designating an unconscious aspect of the creative act. This unconscious realm was activated by inner necessity, which forced the artist to create. Schoenberg admitted, at least in 1911, that this final truth was impossible to reach, for knowing it would prove to be unbearable. The impossibility of the task, however, did not stop the search. Discussing the possible use of the chromatic scale Schoenberg suggested in 1911 that a future theory "would . . . reach the only correct solution." "There is only one content, which all great men wish to express," he wrote in an article about Mahler in 1912, "the longing for its future form, for an immortal soul, for dissolution into the universe—the longing of this soul for its God."[34] After his discovery of the twelve-tone system, his cautious approach to the final truth gave way to more confidence in the correctness of the path he had taken.[35]

Schoenberg's obsession with purity reached beyond his artistic activity. His Jewish religion was not any preexisting faith but rather the result of the composer's effort to purify Judaism of all worldly associations. Schoenberg's God "in all its purity and depth"[36] bears a striking resemblance to philosophical concepts of purity: possessing an indescribable spiritual quality, Schoenberg's God ultimately remains beyond human comprehension. Jankélévitch makes a similar parallel between "sovereign purity" and God, whom, he writes, "one does not discuss except by using negative terms,"[37] in other words, by describing what God is not.

Like any utopia, Schoenberg's political utopia was another manifestation of a quest for purity. The total repression of political opposition, or even the slightest criticism, is a requirement for a homogenized society. As in real political situations in which the rhetoric of purity becomes dominant, violence is a constant threat in Schoenberg's utopian state. Yet since he was a true believer in spiritual essences, he was never tempted by theories of racial purity.[38] His utopian state was based on a spiritual, and not on a biological, unity.

While for Schoenberg race remained an ambiguous and unattractive concept, for Bloch it served as a guiding principle in his artistic self-definition. He used it not as a scientific term describing specific ethnic groups but as a vague category explaining the psychological constitution of individuals. Though a believer in the determining power of race, Bloch remained blind to the dangerous potential of the race concept. He seems to have never given any serious thought to purity in connection with race. Yet the racialized aesthetics that his statements about his music helped create could never be completely detached from assumptions about racial hierarchies and racial purity.

As *Jézabel* and the *Sacred Service* demonstrate, in his art Bloch was ever in search of purity. Probably the most intriguing aspect of Bloch's quest was his willingness to reduce impurity, in the spirit of Havelock Ellis, to sexual instinct. In *Jézabel* Bloch contrasted the pure, moral spirit of the Jews with Jezebel's boundless sexual desire that knew no moral restraint. In Bloch's black-and-white scenario, morality, in quest of purity, leads to the repression of the sexual drive. In the opera purification equals chastity, achieved by Jehu's painful renunciation of his desire. This is a conclusion that contradicts Bloch's confessed belief in the necessity of satisfying one's biological needs.[39] A later convert to Ellis's theories on the determining role of sexuality in human psychology, Bloch advocated a kind of purity in *Jézabel* that was inconsistent with his personal conviction.

The rhetoric of purity is the most pungent in Saminsky's writings. An abstraction for Schoenberg and an artistic dream for Bloch, purity was strongly tied to political reality for Saminsky. His obsession with it in music is no less passionate than the racial political propaganda of his time. In arguing for "racially pure" music Saminsky comes closest to bald racist rhetoric. "Music rooted in the race is perhaps the only one that has successfully resisted the great historical and social-industrial cataclysm of these decades,"[40] Saminsky stated in 1932. The three races "least affected by their European environment" and hence the providers of the musical revolution of the twentieth century were, in his opinion: the Russians (the "true Russians," of course, not the Europeanized ones like Chaikovsky), the Hungarians, and the Jews. In all three, at the end of a struggle against "bequeathed cultural habits," "the power of . . . inner racial impulse determines" that race triumphs over civilization. The difference between individual composers belonging to these three races, Saminsky argues, is that "the revolution of Stravinsky and Bartók is race conscious," while Skryabin and Schoenberg are involuntarily driven "by the inner force of race against their inheritance."

Considering Saminsky's passion for racial determinism, it is surprising that he also speaks up against cultural separatism, acknowledging "the blessing of racial interchange and cross-fertilization." The context of this statement was the United States, Saminsky's new home since 1920, the music of which had, according to him, neither "stringent nor homogeneous" racial background. In the United States racial art, which Saminsky saw manifested in "the daring spatial logic of the Grand Central Terminal in New York" and in "the torrential sweep of Walt Whitman's verse," originated not in the "soil" but rather in "the spiritual flux above it."

He was, however, less willing to allow "racial cross-fertilization" when it came to Jewish music. Simultaneously anti-Semitic and philo-Hebraic in persuasion, Saminsky passionately fought against "contamination" of Jewish music. In *Music of the Ghetto and the Bible* he attacks "Judaic" music, the "froth and dregs" of which, "picked up in the bazaar of the Orient and the street-gutter of the Occident, have darkened and disfigured the noble countenance of Hebrew musical art."[41]

For Saminsky, music of the Bible was the "pure old font" of Hebrew music, while that of the ghetto was the impure music, "contaminated, partly europeanized, partly orientalized in the Exile." East and West were then equally guilty of contaminating Jewish music. Western and Eastern musical idioms were both alien to Hebrew music, which was rooted in the "pure" idiom of the music of the Bible. A revitalized Jewish music was possible, in Saminsky's view, only through purification. The actual result of the process was never clear. While he repeatedly stated that Oriental "poison" should be eliminated from Jewish music, Saminsky never clarified whether he also meant to rid Jewish music of Western idioms, which, he believed, "discolored and distorted the very essence of Jewish habit and behavior."

Saminsky's argument mimics the racist propaganda of his day by inversion: "Aryan" is replaced by "Jewish" on the positive end and "Jewish" by "Aryan" on the negative. "We have to realize," Saminsky wrote, "that the Jewish people *did not* judaize the 'Aryan-pure' music of the West. Just the opposite, Jewish music has been itself 'aryanized.'" Reversing the positive and negative poles does not lessen the dubious import of Saminsky's rhetoric. The reason such an argument remained relatively harmless in practice was not a lack of venom but a lack of political power behind it. Old Biblical associations, racist prejudice, and elitist modernist intolerance all met in Saminsky's passionate argument. That he was willing to rely on all these associations in 1934, when the political consequences of propagating race purity were already visible, proves the lasting power of the ideology of purity.

Sharply dividing Jewish music into "music of the Bible" and "music of the ghetto," Saminsky set up an opposition that parallels the exclusive categories of pure and impure. Saminsky's belief in the purity of the ancient music of the Bible corresponds in fact to what Jankélévitch designates as humans' nostalgia for the purity of a lost paradise. The present, for Saminsky, as for all obsessed with purity, was impure, as Jankélévitch writes, "a land of ruins." Saminsky's efforts were close to Jankélévitch's theologian of history who "regards these debris as an archeologist who tries to reconstruct the splendors that cannot be known."[42]

.    .    .

Is there a direct connection between concepts of purity such as one finds in areas as wildly diverse as Old Testament law, racial prejudice in political propaganda, and the pursuits of modern art? Assuredly not. Although the word "purity" creates a rhetorical association between them, there is no practical link. Yet discussing these manifestations of purity together is nevertheless crucial, not only for understanding the concept, but also—and particularly—for uncovering the source of its rhetorical power.

Although Schoenberg's, Bloch's, and Saminsky's preoccupations with purity did not originate solely in their Jewish background, their assimilated status in societies that were never completely free from anti-Semitic paranoia increased their personal, social, and political insecurities. It was thus not their renounced or newly asserted Jewish identity, nor a hidden Jewish essence, that triggered their intense quest for purity, but rather the precarious social status of religious, ethnic, and national difference.

Jewish identity is not an essence. Its significance in a person's life depends on contexts: personal, national, cultural, religious, political, and historical, to name only a few from the eternal list that keeps Jewish identities in a constant flux. In the new theoretical framework of postethnic or multiracial theory David Biale argues against identity politics that "sees categories like race and ethnicity as static and essential." Biale prefers a theory that considers race not "a natural category but rather one that is socially constructed and imposed on groups. Instead of basing identity on these categories," Biale asserts, "a new construct would posit that identity can be individually chosen.

Identity in such a theory is fluid and often multiple." This approach, Biale admits, is somewhat utopian, for, as present-day ethnic tensions demonstrate, "even if race is a figment of our imagination, it is a figment that has real consequences."[43] It would also be hard to apply a postethnic approach to the first half of the twentieth century, a time period that, especially for Jews, was probably the furthest from the postmodern ideal of self-chosen identity.

Still, acknowledging that the nature of Jewish identity is multifaceted is a necessary requirement for understanding the protagonists of this book. For not only do countries host multiple cultures, but so do individuals. The contradictions between the Jewish backgrounds and the anti-Semitic tendencies of the composers in this book can variously be marked as a psychologically abnormal condition (stigmatized as "Jewish self-hatred") or acknowledged as a logical consequence of their multiple and sometimes conflicting identities. What moves us to compassion is precisely the fact that none of these composers was pure. They were, like the rest of us, torn between the claims of different personal, familial, ethnic, religious, social, and cultural impulses. Denying the significance of their Jewish background would make their personal stories incomprehensible. Yet limiting their individuality to a pure, shared Jewish essence smacks of racism's crude reduction. Nowhere was this danger more apparent than in the life of Jews in twentieth-century Europe.

# NOTES

## INTRODUCTION

1. Ringer, 201.

2. Jehoash Hirshberg, "Jewish Music," V, 2(i), Grove Music Online, ed. L. Macy (accessed 20 February 2007), *www.grovemusic.com.* Curt Sachs's definition of Jewish music at the First World Congress of Jewish Music in Paris, 1957, quoted by Edwin Seroussi in ibid., I, 1.

3. Matthew Baigell and Milly Heyd, eds., *Complex Identities: Jewish Consciousness and Modern Art* (New Brunswick, NJ: Rutgers University Press, 2001), xiv. "By Jewish art, the coeditors mean an art created by Jewish artists in which one can find some aspect of the Jewish experience, whether religious, cultural, social, or personal" (ibid.).

4. David Biale, Michael Galchinsky, and Susan Heschel, eds., *Insider/Outsider: American Jews and Multiculturalism* (Berkeley: University of California Press, 1998), 9.

5. Liah Greenfeld, "God's Firstborn: England," in *Nationalism: Five Roads to Modernity* (Cambridge, MA: Harvard University Press, 1992), 52.

6. John Hatchinson and Anthony D. Smith, *Nationalism* (Oxford: Oxford University Press, 1994), 51.

7. Lion Feuchtwanger, "Nationalisme et judaisme," *Revue juive de Genève* 3 (December 1934): 102.

8. Sigmund Freud's letter of thanks to B'nai B'rith, May 1926, in *Sigmund Freud, Briefe 1873–1939,* ed. Ernst and Lucie Freud (Frankfurt am Main: Fischer, 1980), 381. Freud's definition is similar to Otto Weininger's description of Jewishness as "neither a race nor a people nor a recognized creed" but "a tendency of mind . . . a psychological constitution." Otto Weininger, *Sex and Character* (London: William Heinemann, 1906), 303.

9. Gdal Saleski, *Famous Musicians of Jewish Origin* (New York: Bloch, 1949), xiii.

10. Joseph Yasser, "On Jewishness in Music," in *Commission a Jewish Musical Work! A Handbook of Procedures to Guide Organizations, Local Community Councils and Composers*

*Who Will Participate in the National Jewish Music Council's Nation-wide Project to Encourage the Creation of New Jewish Musical Works*, prepared by the National Jewish Music Council (New York, 1963), 19.

11. David Ewen, *Hebrew Music: A Study and an Interpretation* (New York: Bloch, 1931), 44–45.

12. "General Guides," in *Commission A Jewish Musical Work!*, 16.

13. Isadore Freed, "The Qualities of Jewish Music," ibid., 17.

14. Ringer, 196.

15. Heinrich Berl, *Das Judentum in der Musik* (Stuttgart: Deutsche Verlags-Anstalt, 1926), 11.

16. Ringer, 195–96.

17. Ibid., 195.

18. Berl, *Das Judentum in der Musik*, 131, 125–26. Berl bases his discussion about Schreiber on Max Brod's *Adolf Schreiber: ein Musikschicksal* (Berlin: Im Welt, 1921).

19. Max Brod, "Jewish Musicians in the Diaspora," in *Israel's Music* (Tel Aviv: Sefer Press, 1951), 31–32.

20. *Lexikon der Juden in der Musik: Mit einem Titelverzeichnis jüdischer Werke*, ed. Theo Stengel and Herbert Gerigk (Berlin: Bernhard Hahnefeld, 1940), 41.

21. Brod, "Jewish Musicians in the Diaspora," 26–27.

22. In a recent book (*Bloch, Schoenberg, Bernstein: Assimilating Jewish Music* [Oxford: Oxford University Press, 2003]) David M. Schiller discusses Schoenberg and Bloch from the perspective of assimilation. But even his approach, as his subtitle suggests, is tied to assumptions about the existence of an abstract concept of "Jewish music" that these composers supposedly assimilated to Western idioms.

23. Peter Gradenwitz, *Of Music of Modern Israel* (New York: National Jewish Music Council, 1940), 11.

24. Peter Gradenwitz, *The Music of Israel: Its Rise and Growth through 5000 Years* (New York: W. W. Norton, 1949), 238.

25. Bloch's letter to Schoenberg (5 November 1933, original in ASI), in which Bloch, already an American citizen, cordially greets his great European contemporary on the occasion of Schoenberg's arrival to the United States, apparently remained unanswered.

26. Bloch's letter to Albert Elkus, 26 January 1947 (UCB Bloch Col.), Bloch's emphasis.

27. Abraham Zvi Idelsohn, "My Life (A Sketch)," *Jewish Music Journal* 2, no. 2 (May/June 1935): 10. Reprinted in *Yuval* 5 (*The Abraham Zvi Idelsohn Memorial Volume*, ed. I. Adler, B. Bayer, and E. Schleifer) (1986): 18–23.

CHAPTER 1

1. Leonid Sabaneev, "The Jewish National School in Music," *Musical Quarterly* 15, no. 3 (July 1929): 448. Subsequent quotations come from pp. 468 and 448–49. The article was based on Sabaneyev's *Yevreyskaya natsional'naya shkola v muzike* (The Jewish national school of music) (Moscow, 1924).

2. About the origin of the term see Richard Taruskin, "What Is a *Kuchka?*" in *Musorgsky: Eight Essays and an Epilogue* (Princeton: Princeton University Press, 1993), xxxiii–xxxiv.

3. Albert Weisser, *The Modern Renaissance of Jewish Music. Events and Figures: East-ern Europe and America* (New York: Bloch, 1954), 11–12.

4. Mikhail Beizer, *The Jews of St. Petersburg: Excursions through a Noble Past*, ed. Martin Gilbert, trans. Michael Sherbourne (Philadelphia: Edward E. Elson, 1989), 292.

5. John D. Klier, "The Russian Jewish Intelligentsia and the Search for National Identity," in John Morison, ed., *Ethnic and National Issues in Russia and East European History: Selected Papers from the Fifth World Congress of Central and East European Studies, Warsaw, 1995* (New York: St. Martin's Press, 2000), 131–45.

6. Ahad Ha'am, "The Jewish State and the Jewish Problem" (1897), in *Nationalism and the Jewish Ethic: Basic Writings of Ahad Ha'am*, ed. Hans Kohn (New York: Herzl, 1962), 79–80.

7. Ahad Ha'am, "Summa summarum" (1912), ibid., 149.

8. Simon Dubnow, "The Jewish Nationality Now and in the Future," in Dubnow, *Nationalism and History: Essays on Old and New Judaism*, ed. Koppel S. Pinson (Philadelphia: Jewish Publication Society of America, 1958), 172.

9. The only Russian-language Jewish periodical at the time, *Voskhod* fought for Jewish rights but rejected political Zionism.

10. Ernest Renan, "Qu'est-ce qu'une nation?" (lecture given at the Sorbonne in 1882), in French in Dubnow, *Nationalism and History*, 79.

11. Dubnow, "Letters on Old and New Judaism (1897–1907)," ibid., 95–96.

12. See Dubnow, "The Affirmation of the Diaspora: A Reply to Ahad Ha'am's 'Negation of the Diaspora,'" ibid., 182–91.

13. *Bund* here stands for the Algemeyne yidisher arbeterbund in Lite, Poylen un Rusland (General Federation of Jewish Workers in Lithuania, Poland, and Russia), a Jewish socialist party, founded in 1897. In 1906 it merged with the Russian Social Democratic Labor Party. Because of its determination to fight for cultural autonomy, the *Bund* left the Russian party in 1909. See Salo W. Baron, *The Russian Jew under Tsars and Soviets* (New York: Macmillan, 1976), 143, and Jonathan Frankel, *Prophecy and Politics: Socialism, Nationalism, and the Russian Jews 1862–1917* (Cambridge: Cambridge University Press, 1981), 171–258.

14. "K voprosu o Sione i territorii" (Toward the question of Zion and the territories), in Frankel, *Prophecy and Politics*, 342.

15. Issued on 3 May 1882, the so-called May Laws forbade Jews to settle anew outside towns and to carry on any business on Sundays and Christian holidays. See Baron, *The Russian Jew under Tsars and Soviets*, 44–47.

16. About anti-Jewish tsarist legislation see Heinz-Dietrich Löwe, *The Tsars and the Jews: Reform, Reaction and Anti-Semitism in Imperial Russia, 1772–1917* (Chur, Switzerland: Harwood, 1993).

17. *Regesti i nadpisi* (Digests and inscriptions), published by the ORP in 1899. See Christoph Gassenschmidt, *Jewish Liberal Politics in Tsarist Russia, 1900–1914: The Modernization of Russian Jewry* (New York: New York University Press, 1995), 7; Beizer, *The Jews of St. Petersburg*, 219. The title *Yevreyskaya starina* emulated the long-established *Russkaya starina*. About *Yevreyskaya starina* see Gassenschmidt, *Jewish Liberal Politics in Tsarist Russia*, 74.

18. See Abraham G. Duker, "'Evreiskaia Starina': A Bibliography of the Russian-Jewish Historical Periodical," *Hebrew Union College Annual* 8–9 (Cincinnati, 1931–32): 525–603.

19. For a new edition of Marek and Ginzburg's collection see *Yevreyskiye narod-nïye pesni v Rossii* (Yiddish folksongs in Russia), ed. Dov Noy (Ramat Gan: Bar-Ilan University Press, 1991). For more about the Ginzburg and Marek collection see Weisser, *The Modern Renaissance of Jewish Music,* 32–39. About Yiddish folklore, see Itzik Nakhmen Gottesman, *Defining the Yiddish Nation: The Jewish Folklorists of Poland* (Detroit: Wayne State University Press, 2003).

20. Earlier the tsarist government did not allow Jewish historical societies. See Binyamin Lukin, "Archive of the Jewish Historical and Ethnographic Society: History and Present Condition," *Jews in Eastern Europe* (summer 1993): 45.

21. Semyon An-sky, "Yevreysokye narodnoye tvorchestvo" (Jewish folk art), *Perezhitoye* (The past) (St. Petersburg, n.d.), vol. 1, 277–78, in Semyon An-sky, *The Jewish Artistic Heritage: An Album,* ed. Alexander Kantsedikas (Moscow: "RA," 1994), 27.

22. About details of the expeditions' musical findings see Lydmila Sholochova, "The Phonoarchive of Jewish Folklore at the Vernadsky National Library of Ukraine," trans. Illia Labunka (Kiev: Vernadsky National Library of Ukraine, 2001), at www .archives.gov.ua/Eng/NB/Phonoarchive.php, and *Stanovleniye i razvitiye yevreyskoy muzïkal'noy folkloristiki v rossiyskoy imperii v nachale XX st.* (Formation and development of the study of Jewish musical folklore in the Russian empire at the beginning of the twentieth century) (Kiev: Natsional'naya Muzïkal'naya Akademiya Ukraini im. P. I. Chaikovskovo, 2000). See also Jacob Shatsky, "S. Ansky, the Folklorist," in H. A. Abramson, ed., *Vitebsk Amol* (New York, 1956), in Avram Kampf, *Jewish Experience in the Art of the Twentieth Century* (South Hadley, MA: Bergin & Garvey, 1984), 204n9.

23. About Kiselgof see Beizer, *The Jews of St. Petersburg,* 265, and Sholochova, *Stanovleniye i razvitiye yevreyskoy muzïkal'noy folkloristiki,* chs. 2–4.

24. *Jüdische Volkslieder,* vol. 1, ed. G. Kopït and M. Shalit, and vol. 2, ed. S. Kiselgof (Petrograd: Rotaprint-Druck, 1915). To date four CDs from the Vernadsky Phonoarchive (Institute for Information Recording and Vernadsky National Library) have been released: *Treasure of the Jewish Culture in Ukraine* (1997); *The Historic Collection of Jewish Music 1912–1947:* vol. 1, Materials of J. Engel Ethnographic Expedition 1912 (2001); vol. 2, Materials from the Zinoviy Kiselgof Collection: Religious Songs; vol. 3, Materials from the Zinoviy Kiselgof Collection: Jewish Folk Music and Theater (2004).

25. About the various Jewish cultural organizations see Beizer, *The Jews of St. Petersburg,* 289–93, and Gassenschmidt, *Jewish Liberal Politics in Tsarist Russia,* 76. Whether the increased number of new societies reflected the spread of Jewish culture, or only the expansion of government control, is hard to tell. By legalizing Jewish organizations authorities tried to distinguish between revolutionary and nonrevolutionary elements among the Russian Jews (see Löwe, *The Tsars and the Jews,* 195).

26. Gassenschmidt, *Jewish Liberal Politics in Tsarist Russia,* 76. According to published copies of the charter, the OYNM was officially approved on 4 March 1908. The first meeting took place on 30 November. About the protocols and dates of the OYNM see Rita Flomenboim, "The National School of Jewish Art Music: Joel Engel (1868–1927) and Michail Gnessin (1883–1957)," Ph.D. diss. (Bar-Ilan University, 1996); James Loeffler, "Society for Jewish Folk Music," in *YIVO Encyclopedia of East European Jewish History and Culture,* ed. Gershon D. Hundert (New Haven: Yale University Press, forthcoming); and Galina Kopytowa, "Die Aktivitäten und Veranstaltungen der 'Gesellschaft für Jüdische Volksmusik' in St. Petersburg/Petrograd," in Jascha Nemtsov and

Ernst Kuhn, eds., *Jüdische Musik in Sowjetrußland: die "Jüdische Nationale Schule" der zwanziger Jahre* (Berlin: Ernst Kuhn, 2002), 103.

27. According to Rosovsky, the St. Petersburg district commissioner who headed the committee that gave permission to the establishment of new societies.

28. Here Rosovsky refers to Musorgsky's chorus *Iisus Navin* (also known as "Joshua"), in which the composer used a Jewish melody. For more about Musorgsky's chorus see ch. 2.

29. Israel Rabinovitch, *Of Jewish Music, Ancient and Modern*, trans. A. M. Klein (Montreal: Book Center, 1952), 155. Rabinovitch's source is Solomon Rosovsky, "The Society for Jewish Folk Music: Personal Reminiscences," *Jewish Music Forum Bulletin* 9 (December 1948): 9–10. See also Kopytowa, "Die 'Gesellschaft für Jüdische Volksmusik' in St. Petersburg/Petrograd," 67.

30. L. Zeitlin is sometimes confused with Lev Moiseievich Tseitlin (or Zeitlin) (1881–1952). About Lev Mordukhov Tseitlin see Paula Eisenstein Baker, "Leo Zeitlin's Eli Zion: An Attribution Chiseled in Stone," *Strings* 6, no. 1 ( July/August 1991): 18–24; "Who Was 'L. Zeitlin' of the Society for Jewish Folk Music?" *Yivo Annual* 23 (1996): 233–57; and most recently, "Jewish Motives in an Early-20th-Century Work: Leo Zeitlin's *Eli Zion*," *International Journal of Musicology* 6 (1997): 231–79.

31. The names of board members are listed in "Fun der vervaltung fun der geselshaft fan yidishe folks-musik in Petersburg" (From the Board of the Society for Jewish Folk Music in Petersburg), YIVO Institute for Jewish Research (New York), Records of Jewish Music Societies, Society for Jewish Folk Music, St. Petersburg, 6/324–31.

32. The Moscow branch of the OYNM was chartered on 9 May 1913. Its name was changed to Obshchestvo Yevreyskoy muzïki in 1918. According to Kopytowa, the Moscow branch was established at the end of 1912 (see Kopytowa, "Die 'Gesellschaft für Jüdische Volksmusik' in St. Petersburg/Petrograd," 112). Information on the other branches has been taken from Paula Eisenstein Baker, "Sheet Music as Artifact: The Publications of the St. Petersburg Society for Jewish Folk Music and the Moscow Society for Jewish Music," unpublished paper.

33. The chair of the music division of MEK, Professor Anutchin, was the chief editor of *Russkiye Vedomosti*, the musical column of which was edited by Engel. See Weisser, *The Modern Renaissance of Jewish Music*, 31.

34. By 1908 Alexander Glazunov, who took over the direction of the Conservatory in 1905, had achieved the complete abolition of quotas. See *Alexander Glazunow: Sein Leben in Bildern und Dokumenten*, ed. Detlef Gojowy and Herbert Günther (Munich: List, 1986), 102, quoted in Detlef Gojowy, *Arthur Lourié und der russische Futurismus* (Laaber: Laaber-Verlag, 1993), 16. See also Kopytowa, "Die 'Gesellschaft für Jüdische Volksmusik' in St. Petersburg/Petrograd," 62–63.

35. Flomenboim, "The National School of Jewish Art Music," 65.

36. The program of the concert that took place on 21 January 1909 featured the following pieces: Cantata in honor of Sholom-Aleichem, in celebration of his twenty-five years of literary activity (text by M. S. Rivesman, music by E. I. Shklyar); Variations on the folk melody "Freylekhs" (by H. Kopït); "Song of Songs" (by Rimsky-Korsakov); "Der furman un di eysenban" (The conductor and the railways, folk song); "Der parom" (The ferry, folk song, arranged by Shklyar); "Faryomert, farklogt" (Depressed, dejected, text and melody by Goldfaden, arranged by Shklyar); "B'shadmith

Beth-Lechem" (In the field of Bethlehem, text by Shapiro, music by Shklyar); Jewish Rhapsody for piano two hands (by V. Zolotarev); "Yevreyskaya pesnya" (by Musorgsky); "Di gilderne pave" (The golden peacock, folk song, arranged by Shklyar); "Alte kashe" (Eternal question, folk song, arranged by Shklyar). See YIVO, Records of Jewish Music Societies, Society for Jewish Folk Music, St. Petersburg, 2/115–17.

37. The topics of the lectures are listed in M. I. Vainshtein, "Obshchestvo Yevreyskoy narodnoy muzïki kak faktor kul'turnoy zhizni Peterburga nachala XX v." (The Society for Jewish Folk Music as a factor in the cultural life of St. Petersburg in the early twentieth century), in N. V. Yukhnyova, ed., *Etnografiya Peterburga-Leningrada: materialï yezhegodnïkh nauchnïkh chteniy* (Leningrad: Nauka, 1988), 34; and Kopytowa, "Die Aktivitäten und Veranstaltungen der 'GfjV' in St. Petersburg/Petrograd," in *Jüdische Musik in Sowjetrußland*, 103–22.

38. See Vainshtein, "Obshchestvo Yevreyskoy narodnoy muzïki," 35.

39. The first (1913) and second (1914) editions were published in Berlin by Leo Winz, the third (1923) by Yuval.

40. According to Idelsohn the word *skarbove* comes from the Latin word *sacra*. The Polish word *skarb* means treasure, while the word *skarbove* in Yiddish means "common" or "trite" (in this context probably traditional). (To add to the confusion, the Russian word *skorb* means "grief.") *Niggun* (plural *niggunim*) is a type of vocal tune associated with the Hasidic movement.

41. This mode also exists as one of the prayer modes or *shteygers* called *ahavah rabbah* (great love) because of the initial words of the prayer preceding the Shema in the Ashkenazi morning service. According to Idelsohn, the *ahavah rabbah* mode is the only one that has no connections with the Biblical modes. Idelsohn attributed its existence to Tartar influence. See Abraham Z. Idelsohn, *Jewish Music: Its Historical Development* (New York: Dover, 1992), 84–89.

42. Beizer, *The Jews of St. Petersburg*, 188–90.

43. In Judaism the deer is a symbol of swiftness (according to the Mishna the swiftness of a deer implies the oneness of purpose and quickness of reflex), or, as in Psalm 42:2, of the soul. In depictions of hunting scenes in medieval manuscripts, the "loving doe," pursued by evil hunters, represented the persecuted people of Israel. See Marc Michael Epstein, *Dream of Subversion in Medieval Jewish Art and Literature* (University Park: Pennsylvania State University Press, 1997), 22, 128n21.

44. The name originates in a reference to the birth of Naphtali, who was the son of Rachel's maid, Bilhah, because by giving her maid to Jacob to help her to conceive, Rachel "wrestled" with her sister Leah.

45. Abraham Goldfaden (1840–1906) was a founder of Yiddish theater. Mark Varshavsky (1848–1907) wrote Yiddish poems and popular songs.

46. Examples are Saminsky's "Gebet fun reb Levi Yitskhok" (no. 67) and "Patsh, patsh kikhelakh" (no. 69).

47. The folk song appeared later in Idelsohn's collection of Eastern European folk songs: *Hebräisch-orientalischer Melodienschatz*, vol. 9, *Der Volksgesang der osteuropäischen Juden* (Leipzig: Friedrich Hofmeister, 1932), no. 39, p. 14.

48. Richard Taruskin, "Entoiling the Falconet," in *Defining Russia Musically: Historical and Hermeneutical Essays* (Princeton: Princeton University Press, 1997), 152–85.

49. M. Rudinov, "Der Yiddishe Kompozitor M. Milner," *Yiddishe Kultur* 2 (1953): 40, quoted by Rita Flomenboim, "The Fate of Two Jewish Operas in the Soviet Union

during the 1920s and 1930s," in Joachim Braun, Heidi Tamar Hoffmann, and Vladimir Karbusicky, eds., *Verfemte Musik: Komponisten in den Diktaturen unseres Jahrhunderts* (Frankfurt am Main: Peter Lang, 1997), 135–36.

50. Rosovsky's account, in Weisser, *The Modern Renaissance of Jewish Music*, 44.

51. Shklyar's song is one of four songs in the OYNM series that has Russian as its first text. In all four, Yiddish translation is provided under the Russian text. In Shklyar's song the Yiddish text appears only in Hebrew characters, which might indicate that the song was mainly performed in Russian.

52. Albert Weisser, "Lazare Saminsky's Year in Russia and Palestine: Excerpts from an Unpublished Autobiography," *Musica Judaica* 2, no. 2 (1977–78): 12.

53. M. F. Gnesin, "N. A. Rimsky-Korsakov v obshchenii s uchenikami" (N. A. Rimsky-Korsakov in conversation with his pupils), in Vainshtein, "Obshchestvo Yevreyskoy narodnoy muzïki," 31.

54. Vainshtein quotes Saminsky's "Yubiley Peterburgskoy konservatorii i yevrei" (ibid., 31), while Weisser's account comes from a personal conversation with Rosovsky that took place in 1950 (Weisser, *The Modern Renaissance of Jewish Music*, 44). Shklyar studied with Rimsky-Korsakov between 1895 and 1899. Saminsky attended the Conservatory between 1906 and 1910, and Rosovsky graduated in 1909 (see Kopytowa, "Die 'Gesellschaft für Jüdische Volksmusik' in St. Petersburg/Petrograd," 70, 74).

55. Domenico de Paoli et al., *Lazare Saminsky: Composer and Civic Worker*, Eminent Composers of Hebrew Music (New York: Bloch, 1930), 57. Saminsky's influence might have been limited while he lived in Tiflis between 1911 and 1918.

56. Weisser, "Lazare Saminsky's Years in Russia and Palestine," 11–12.

57. "Fun der vervaltung fun der geselshaft fan yidishe folks-musik in Petersburg" (YIVO 6/324–31). On the top of the first page there is the same illustration of the harp of David as on the cover page of the OYNM series of sheet music. The text seems to be based on a 1910 Russian document ("Ustav obshchestvo yevreyskoy narodnoy muzïki," in German translation in Kopytowa, "Die 'Gesellschaft für Jüdische Volksmusik' in St. Petersburg/Petrograd," 68).

58. Weisser, *The Modern Renaissance of Jewish Music*, 45–46. The source of Weisser's information is M. Braunzaft, *Ha-'askolah ha-muzikalit ha-yehudit* (The school of Jewish music) (Jerusalem, 1940). For Rosovsky's account see Avraham Soltes, "The Hebrew Folk Song Society of Petersburg: The Historical Development," in Irene Heskes and Arthur Wolfson, eds., *The Historic Contribution of Russian Jewry to Jewish Music* (New York: National Jewish Music Council, 1967), 22.

59. I have found no data about the exact date of the dissolution of the St. Petersburg OYNM. YIVO preserves a concert program of 28 March 1919 (in Paula Eisenstein Baker, "Who Was 'L. Zeitlin' of the Society for Jewish Folk Music?," 252n7). The final concert took place on 14 October 1922. Joachim Braun, quoting Joseph Yasser, attributes the dissolution of the OYNM to its being "incompatible with the spirit of the time." See Joachim Braun, *Jews and Jewish Elements in Soviet Russia: A Study of a Socio-National Problem in Music* (Tel Aviv: Israeli Music Publications, 1978), 47. A letter from Achron to Rosovsky (4 May 1922) suggests that the OYNM ceased to exist because of administrative failure: "Our society has recently ceased to exist legally due to quite an absurd reason: we had to reorganize the society to ensure its continued existence." For Achron's letter see Phillip Moddel, *Joseph Achron* (Tel Aviv: Israeli Music Publications, 1966), 56.

60. "Obshchestvo Yevreyskoy Muzïki" (Society for Jewish Music) (1926), brochure distributed by the Society for Jewish Music, Moscow, YIVO, RG 37 [C] 2/3–9.

61. Symphonic music: Alexander Krein, Symphony; M. Gnesin, Songs of the Ancient Homeland and Variations on Jewish Themes for String Orchestra; I. Aysberg, Jewish Rhapsody for Piano and Orchestra. Chamber music: Achron, Symphonic Variations for Piano and songs; Ernest Bloch, *Baal Shem* for Violin and Piano; A. Veprik, Suite for Violin and Piano, "Severe Melody" for Clarinet and Piano, and Sonata for Piano; H. Hamburg, "From the Song of Songs," for Alto and Piano; M. Gnesin, "Fantasy" for String Quartet, Clarinet, and Percussion, songs, and other pieces; A. Krein, Suite for String Quartet, Clarinet, and Percussion and songs; G. Krein, Prelude for String Quartet, Flute, and Piano and songs; D. Milhaud, songs; M. Milner, Sonata for Piano, songs, and other works; M. Ravel, songs; L. Saminsky, piano works; L. Zeitlin, "Jewish Melody" for Alto and Piano; Y. Engel, Suite "Dybbuk" for String Orchestra, Clarinet, and Bass, songs, and other works (ibid.).

62. Joachim Braun, "The Jewish Art School in Russia," in Judith Cohen, ed., *Proceedings of the World Congress on Jewish Music,* Jerusalem, 1978 (Tel-Aviv: Institute for the Translation of Hebrew Literature, 1982), 199. About Saminsky's campaign for the use of synagogue music see ch. 2.

63. Joseph Yasser, "The Hebrew Folk Society of St. Petersburg: Ideology and Technique," in Heskes and Wolfson, *The Historic Contribution of Russian Jewry to Jewish Music,* 31–32.

## CHAPTER 2

1. Efros describes the same period also as "Vasnetsovism," "Ropetovism," and "Stasovism," referring to the work of landscape painter Viktor Vasnetsov (known for his ornamental murals in the Kiev St. Vladimir Cathedral and his sets for Ostrovsky's *Snow Maiden,* inspired by peasant handicrafts and woodcuts), architect Petrov Ropet (known for his "cockerel edifices," designed for the Russian section of the World Fair in 1878), and critic Vladimir Stasov (whose name Efros associated with "balalaika analogies").

2. Abram Efros, "Lampa Aladina (K vïkhodu v svet kapitalnogo izdaniya S. A. Anskogo Yevreyskaya narodnaya khudozhestvennaya starina)" (Aladdin's Lamp [On the occasion of the publication of S. A. An-sky's fundamental edition 'Jewish Folk Art Antiquities']), in A. Sobol and E. Loiter, eds., *Yevreyskiy mir* (Moscow, 1918), book I, pp. 299–300. Translated in An-sky, *The Jewish Artistic Heritage,* 10, 13–15.

3. See Olin Downes's interview with Diaghilev (*New York Times,* 19 January 1916), in Richard Taruskin, *Stravinsky and the Russian Traditions: A Biography of the Works through Mavra* (Berkeley: University of California Press, 1996), vol. 1, 502–18.

4. The admiration for Biblical Hebrews could easily exist alongside everyday anti-Semitism. About Musorgsky's anti-Semitism, for instance, see Taruskin, *Musorgsky,* 379–83.

5. Richard Taruskin, *Opera and Drama in Russia as Preached and Practiced in the 1860s* (Rochester, NY: University of Rochester Press, 1981), 65.

6. Jay Leyda and Sergei Bertensson, eds. and trans., *The Musorgsky Reader: A Life of Modest Petrovich Musorgky in Letters and Documents* (New York: W. W. Norton, 1947),

53. Ts. A. Cui, "Musical Chronicle: Mr Serov's *Judith*," in Stuart Campbell, ed. and trans., *Russians on Russian Music, 1830–1880: An Anthology* (Cambridge: Cambridge University Press, 1994), 147–48.

7. "Osnovan na narodnïkh izrailskikh pesnyakh" (See autograph in Rossiyskaya natsional'naya biblioteka imeni M. E. Saltikova-Shchedrina, St. Petersburg), in Márta Papp and János Bojti, eds. and trans., *Modeszt Muszorgszkij. Levelek, dokumentumok, emlékezések* (Modest Musorgsky: letters, documents, reminiscences) (Budapest: Kávé Kiadó, 1997), 598.

8. See N. Rimsky-Korsakov, *Polnoye sobraniye sochineniy: literaturnïye proizvedeniye i perepiska* (Collected works: literary works and correspondence) (Moscow: Gos. Muzïkal'-noye izd-vo, 1981), vol. 5, 31; and Vladimir Stasov, *Izbrannïye sochineniya* (Selected works), vol. 2, *Modest P. Musorgsky* (Moscow: Iskusstvo, 1952), 210. See also Boris Schwarz, "Musorgsky's Interest in Judaica," in Malcolm Hamrick Brown, ed., *Musorgsky: In Memoriam 1881–1981* (Ann Arbor, MI: UMI Research Press, 1982), 89–92.

9. In a 1934 Russian dictionary entry (D. N. Ushakov, *Tolkovïy slovar' russkogo yazïka*, vol. 1 [Moscow, 1934], p. 868) all definitions of *zhid* indicate a derogatory meaning. See John Doyle Klier, "Zhid: The Biography of a Russian Pejorative," *Slavonic and East European Review* 60, no. 1 (1982): 15.

10. Taruskin, *Musorgsky*, 382–83.

11. Taruskin locates the source for a new, neonationalist attitude toward folk music in Stasov's essay "Russian Folk Ornament." See Taruskin, *Stravinsky and the Russian Traditions*, vol. 1, 502–3.

12. About Engel's professional activities see Soltes, "The Hebrew Folk Song Society of Petersburg," 16.

13. Menashe Ravina, *Yoel Engel, v'hamisukah ha-yehudith* (Yoel Engel and Jewish music) (Tel Aviv, 1949), translated by Rabinovitch in *Of Jewish Music, Ancient and Modern*, 148. Jehoash Hirshberg, *Music in the Jewish Community of Palestine 1880–1948: A Social History* (Oxford: Clarendon Press, 1995), 79.

14. Stasov, "Posle vsemirnoy vïstavki" (After the world exhibition), *Yevreyskaya biblioteka* 7 (1879): 257–81, in Ilya Gintsburg, "Jüdische Nationalkunst (Gedenken eines gelehrten Russischen Kritikers)," *Ost und West* 5, no. 10 (1905), in Mirjam Rajner, "The Awakening of Jewish National Art in Russia," *Jewish Art* 16–17, no. 1 (1990): 107.

15. Vlad. Karenin (pseudonym of Stasov's niece, Varvara Komarova), *Vladimir Stasov: Ocherk ego zhizni i deyatel'nosti* (Vladimir Stasov: a sketch of his life and work), 2 vols. (Leningrad, 1927), vol. 1, 103. In Yuri Olkhovsky, *Vladimir Stasov and Russian National Culture*, Russian Music Studies 6, ed. Malcolm Hamrick Brown (Ann Arbor, MI: UMI Research Press, 1983), 40.

16. Rajner, "The Awakening of Jewish National Art in Russia," 110.

17. "Stasov" in *Yevreyskaya entsiklopediya*, vol. 14, pp. 560–61.

18. Vladimir Stasof and David Günzburg, *L'ornament hébrue* (Berlin: S. Calvary, 1905), 7, quoted in Seth L. Wolitz, "The Jewish National Art Renaissance in Russia," in Ruth Apter-Gabriel, ed., *Tradition and Revolution: The Jewish Renaissance in Russian Avant-Garde Art 1912–1928* (Jerusalem: Israel Museum, 1987), 24.

19. Mark Antokolsky, "O V. V. Stasove" (About Stasov), in E. D. Stasova, ed., *Vladimir Vasilievich Stasov. 1824–1906. K 125-letiyu so dnya rozhdeniya. Sbornik statei i vospominanii* (Vladimir Vasil'evich Stasov. 1824–1906. In honor of the 125th an-

niversary of his birth. A collection of articles and reminiscences) (Moscow: Iskusstvo, 1949), 38, in Olkhovsky, *Vladimir Stasov and Russian National Culture*, ix.

20. Stasov, "Posle vsemirnoy vïstavki," pp. 280–81, in Rajner, "The Awakening of Jewish National Art in Russia," 108.

21. The incident is described by Jacob Weinberg in *The Day* (New York, 7 August 1938), quoted in Rabinovitch, *Of Jewish Music, Ancient and Modern*, 147.

22. Zalman Shazar, "Our Teachers at the Institute of Baron Ginzburg," *Heavar* 6 (Tel Aviv, 1958), in Kampf, *Jewish Experience in the Art of the Twentieth Century*, 204n11.

23. Yuliy Engel, "Pamyati V. V. Stasova" (To the memory of V. V. Stasov), *Russkaya muzïkal'naya gazeta* 41 (14 October 1907): 893.

24. Stasov to Engel, 11 February 1904, in J. D. Engel, *Glazami sovremennika: izbrannïye stat'i o russkoy muzïke 1898–1918* (Through the eyes of a contemporary: selected articles on Russian music), ed. I. Kunin (Moscow: Sovetskiy Kompozitor, 1971), 476. Also in Joachim Braun, *Jews and Jewish Elements in Soviet Music: A Study of a Soviet-National Problem in Music* (Tel Aviv: Israeli Music Publications, 1978), 34.

25. Engel to Stasov, 23 February 1904, in Engel, *Glazami Sovremennika*, 476.

26. Weisser, *The Modern Renaissance of Jewish Music*, 49. The stereotypes reflect views on Rimsky-Korsakov (St. Petersburg) and on Chaikovsky (Moscow). There were also practical reasons behind Saminsky's decision. He argued that through Jurgenson Moscow composers had easier access to publication than did their St. Petersburg colleagues. In the unpublished paper "Sheet Music as Artifact: The Publications of the St. Petersburg Society for Jewish Folk Music and the Moscow Society for Jewish Music," Paula Eisenstein Baker suggests that the OYM might have initially served as a publishing venue for Engel.

27. About the post-Revolution, communist reinterpretation of the Saminsky-Engel debate see Beregovski, "Jewish Folk Music" (1934), in Mark Slobin, *Old Jewish Folk Music: The Collections and Writings of Moshe Beregovski* (Philadelphia: University of Pennsylvania Press, 1982), 21; and Kopytowa, "Die 'Gesellschaft für Jüdische Volksmusik' in St. Petersburg/Petrograd," 87–88.

28. Saminsky, "The Value of Jewish Domestic Songs: A Reply to Julius Engel," reprinted in *The Music of the Ghetto and the Bible* (New York: Bloch, 1934), 232. For the Russian original see *Iz istorii yevreyskoy muzïki* (From the history of Jewish music in Russia: proceedings of the international scientific conference "90 Years of the Jewish Folk Music Society in Petersburg-Petrograd [1908–1919]"), St. Petersburg, 27 October 1998 (St. Petersburg: Jewish Community Center of St. Petersburg Center for Jewish music, 2001), 125–64.

29. Flomenboim, *The National School of Jewish Art Music*, 58–60.

30. In *The Music of the Ghetto and the Bible* there is only one short reference to political Zionism as the impetus for the Jewish musician's return "to his age-old song" (48).

31. Ibid., 65.

32. Excerpts from Engel's answer to Saminsky (orig. in *Razsvet* 7 [1915]) are published by Rabinovitch, *Of Jewish Music, Ancient and Modern*, 173.

33. Saminsky, *The Music of the Ghetto and the Bible*, 251–52, 247.

34. In Marvin Zuckerman and Marion Herbst, *The Three Great Classic Writers of Modern Yiddish Literature*, vol. 3, *Selected Works of I. L. Peretz* (Malibu, CA: Joseph Simon Pangloss, 1996), 386. For more about the fights for Yiddish culture, see Gottesman, *Defining the Yiddish Nation*.

35. An-sky's article, *Voskhod* 10 (9 March 1906), in Frankel, *Prophecy and Politics*, 160.

36. In a letter sent to the committee of emigration on 24 July 1924, Engel stated: "I am no Zionist, but I regard the national element in general and in human creation in particular as of supreme importance, and this brings me closer to Zionism." In Hirshberg, *Music in the Jewish Community of Palestine 1880–1948*, 87.

37. Stasov, "Po povodu postroyki sinagogi v. S.-Petersburg" (Concerning the construction of the synagogue in St. Petersburg), *Yevreyskaya biblioteka* 2 (1872): 453–73, in Rajner, "The Awakening of Jewish National Art in Russia," 106–7.

38. Saminsky, *The Music of the Ghetto and the Bible*, 40. Subsequent quotations come from pp. 249, 251, and 73.

39. Klier, "Zhid: The Biography of a Russian Pejorative," 11.

40. Hirshberg, *Music in the Jewish Community of Palestine 1880–1948*, 11–22.

41. Saminsky, *The Music of the Ghetto and the Bible*, 241–42, 60.

42. Idelsohn, *Jewish Music: Its Historical Development*, 24.

43. Saminsky, *Music of the Ghetto and the Bible*, 235.

44. Rabinovitch, *Of Jewish Music, Ancient and Modern*, 173–74.

45. See "Georgia" in *Encyclopedia Judaica* 7 (Jerusalem: Macmillan, 1971), 425.

46. Saminsky, *The Music of the Ghetto and the Bible*, 153, Saminsky's emphasis. Subsequent quotations come from pp. 243 and 32–33.

47. The term "Jewish self-hatred" originates in Theodor Lessing's *Der jüdische Selbsthaß* (Berlin: Jüdischer Verlag, 1930). See also Sander L. Gilman, *Jewish Self-hatred: Anti-Semitism and the Hidden Language of the Jews* (Baltimore: Johns Hopkins University Press, 1986).

48. Although Saminsky does not identify Kiselgof as his source, in the score of Joseph Achron's arrangement for violin and piano ("Hebreyish viglid," no. 37) Kiselgof is acknowledged as the collector and transcriber of the original song.

49. According to A. Z. Idelsohn's statistics, only 11 percent of Jewish folk songs are in a major key, while eighty-nine are in minor (or minor-related) modes. See his "Musical Characteristics of East-European Jewish Folk-Song," *Musical Quarterly* 17, no. 4 (October 1932): 636–37; and *Hebräisch-orientalischer Melodienschatz*, vol. 9, *Der Volksgesang der osteuropäischen Juden*, xiv–xv.

50. In the Yemenite volume of his *Thesaurus* Idelsohn lists the song "Ani hadal" among the *neshid* songs of the Yemenite Jews. About the *neshid* songs see Idelsohn, *Gesänge der jemenischen Juden*, zum ersten Male gesammelt, erläutert und herausgegeben (Leipzig: Breitkopf & Härtel, 1914), 12–14; and Amnon Shiloah, *Jewish Musical Traditions*, Jewish Folklore and Anthropology Series, ed. Rachael Patai (Detroit: Wayne State University Press, 1992), 187–88.

51. In *The Music of the Ghetto and the Bible* (236) Saminsky refers to the rabbi as "Shneur Zalman of Liadi, Lithuania (1747–1813)."

52. Ibid., 236 and 238.

53. Idelsohn, *Hebräisch-orientalischer Melodienschatz*, vol. 9, xiii.

54. Moshe Beregovski, "The Altered Dorian Scale in Jewish Folk Music (On the Question of the Semantic Characteristics of Scales)" (1946), in Slobin, *Old Jewish Folk Music*, 562–63.

55. Saminsky, *The Music of the Ghetto and the Bible*, 230–31.

56. See Eisenstein, "Leo Zeitlin's Eli Zion" and "Jewish Motives in an Early-20th-Century Work."

57. Saminsky, *The Music of the Ghetto and the Bible*, 128; Sabaneev, "The Jewish National School in Music," 462.

58. Jonathan Anthony Powell, "After Scriabin: Six Composers and the Development of Russian Music," Ph.D. diss. (King's College, Cambridge, 1999), 157.

59. Leonid Sabaneev, *Modern Russian Composers*, trans. Judah A. Joffe (New York: International Publishers, 1927), 182.

60. The song also appeared as the third of Krein's *Tri pesni getto* (Three songs of the ghetto, 1929) in Russian and German translations.

61. Taruskin, "Chernomor to Kashchey: Harmonic Sorcery," in *Stravinsky and the Russian Traditions*, 267.

62. For an explanation of Skryabin's harmonic language see Taruskin, "Scriabin and the Superhuman: A Millennial Essay," in *Defining Russia Musically*, 308–59.

63. A. W. Binder, *Biblical Chant* (New York: Philosophical Library, 1959), 107.

64. Sabaneev, "The Jewish National School in Music," 462.

65. Efros, "Aladdin's Lamp," 9–10.

66. Ibid., 12.

67. Wolitz, "The Jewish National Art Renaissance in Russia," in Apter-Gabriel, *Tradition and Revolution*, 38.

68. "Di vegen fun der Yidisher malerei" (The paths of Jewish painting), in *Oifgang* (Kiev: Kulturlige, 1919), in Kampf, *Jewish Experience in the Art of the Twentieth Century*, 32.

69. For the potential relation between the Second Commandment and abstract art see Kampf, *Jewish Experience in the Art of the Twentieth Century*, especially the chapter "Reaching for the Absolute." See also Elisheva Revel-Neher, "'With Wisdom and Knowledge of Workmanship': Jewish Art without a Question Mark," and Margaret Olin, "Graven Images on Video? The Second Commandment and Jewish Identity," in Baigell and Heyd, *Complex Identities*, 12–33; 34–50. In her essay "To Figure, or Not to Figure: The Iconoclastic Proscription and Its Theoretical Legacy" (in Catherine M. Soussloff, *Jewish Identity in Modern Art History* [Berkeley: University of California Press, 1999], 67–84), Lisa Saltzman relates the Biblical prohibition to Adorno's post-Auschwitz aesthetics.

70. "Di vegen fun der Yidisher malerei," 34.

CHAPTER 3

1. Ashley Montagu, *Man's Most Dangerous Myth: The Fallacy of Race*, 2nd ed. (New York: Columbia University Press, 1945), 1.

2. Jacques Barzun, *Race: A Study in Modern Superstition* (London: Methuen, 1938), 5. Subsequent quotations come from pp. 283, 269, 9, and 299. For a more contemporary argument against race-thinking see Paul Gilroy, *Against Race: Imagining Political Culture beyond the Color Line* (Cambridge, MA: Belknap Press of Harvard University Press, 2000).

3. Throughout the text I use the term "racism" according to its primary definition to describe "the assumption that psychocultural traits and capacities are determined by biological race and that races differ decisively from one another." Although the dictionary associates racism also "with a belief in the inherent superiority of a particular race and its right to domination over others" (*Webster's Third New Interna-*

*tional Dictionary of the English Language,* ed. Philip Babcock Gove [Springfield, MA: Merriam-Webster, 1993], 1870), I use "racialism" to refer to theories in which racial prejudice, discrimination, or racial hatred are predominant. About "culturalist" racism see Etienne Balibar, "Is There a 'Neo-Racism'?" in Balibar and Immanuel Wallerstein, *Race, Nation, Class: Ambiguous Identities,* trans. Chris Turner (London: Verso, 1991), 23–24; also in Gilroy, *Against Race,* 32–39.

4. Barzun, *Race,* 132–33.

5. Montagu, "Are the Jews a 'Race'?" in *Man's Most Dangerous Myth,* 218–35.

6. John M. Efron, *Defenders of the Race: Jewish Doctors and Race Science in Fin-de-siècle Europe* (New Haven: Yale University Press, 1994), 4, 7.

7. Benjamin Disraeli, *Coningsby or the New Generation,* The World's Classics (London: Oxford University Press, 1931), 245–46, 248–49.

8. Richard Wagner, *Judaism in Music,* in *Richard Wagner's Prose Works,* vol. 3, trans. William Ashton Ellis (New York: Broude Brothers, 1894), 84, 86.

9. Disraeli, *Coningsby,* 249.

10. Wagner, *Judaism in Music,* 82.

11. Bloch's letter to Fleg, 8 February 1903, in Lew. 1, 186. All letters quoted are in French; unless noted otherwise, all translations are mine.

12. Bloch to Fleg, 9 April 1902, LC Bloch Col., part of the letter is in Lew. 1, 175.

13. Otto Lessmann's review (*Allgemeine Musik-Zeitung* [Berlin, 26 June 1903]), in Lew. 1, 201.

14. Camille Mauclair, "Le livret d'Opéra et le poème de drame lyrique," *La revue (Ancienne "Revue des revues")* 89 (1 January–15 March 1911): 471–72, in Lew. 1, 489. In English in David L. Sills, "Ruminations on *Macbeth,*" in *EBS Bulletin* 18–19 (1986–87): 12.

15. In Bloch's *Macbeth* there are clear references to both *Salome* and *Boris Godunov.* Lady Macbeth's listening to her husband's crime above a low tremolo recalls Salome's listening to Jokanaan's execution (act 1, scene 2). Some of Macbeth's monologues resemble Boris's, the appearance of Banco's spirit recalls Boris's hallucination, while the porter's song evokes the tavern scene in *Boris.*

16. Bloch remained unaware of Debussy's dislike of him. Jealous of Robert Godet's attention, Debussy made hostile remarks about Bloch, especially after Godet and Bloch broke up. In a letter on 4 September 1916 he asked Godet: "How could Robert Godet support this man who is like a commercial traveler and a dangerous fool?" In Lew. 1, 307. For Bloch's criticism of Debussy's lack of grandeur see his letter to Fleg, 8 February 1903, LC Bloch Col.

17. *Le rire* (10 December 1910).

18. For Prunières's quotation of Rolland's letter see Prunières, "Les concerts—Israël d'Ernest Bloch," *La revue musicale* 8, no. 2 (1 December 1926), in Lew. 1, 491.

19. Suzanne Bloch, "Lucienne Bréval," *EBS Bulletin* 18–19 (1986–87): 6.

20. Bloch to his sister Loulette, 26 February 1901, in Lew. 1, 143.

21. Bloch to Fleg, 11 March 1911, LC Bloch Col., part of the letter in Lew. 1, 536; Bloch to Fleg, 17 April 1911, in Lew. 1, 537.

22. Bloch to Fleg, 11 March 1911, in Lew. 1, 536.

23. "I also understand Wagner in his 'Judenthum in Music' (where he says) 'mit uns leiden und leben, in einem Worte, mit uns *Menschen* zu werden' [to suffer and live with us, in a word to become men with us]. Yes! If only this were possible! But

we are mistaken by our easy adaptation. . . . French with the French and German with the Germans." Ibid.

24. Wagner, *Judaism in Music*, 100; Bloch to Pizzetti, 13 October 1911, in Lew. 1, 549.

25. Bloch to Fleg, 11 March 1911, LC Bloch Col., parts of the letter in Lew. 1, 536.

26. Fleg's memoir appeared in 1928 as part of André Billy's series "Leurs raisons" (Their reasons), monographs in which the various authors explained their affiliations (Catholic, feminist, socialist, democratic, syndicalist, etc.). See Edmond Fleg, *Why I Am a Jew*, trans. Louise Waterman Wise (New York: Bloch, 1945), 1–17.

27. Fleg to Bloch, 20 July 1908, in Lew. 1, 411; Fleg, *Why I Am a Jew*, 35.

28. In 1906 Lucien Moreau became a recipient of a tenured chair at the Institute d'Action Française. See Lew. 1, 411.

29. Fleg, *Why I Am a Jew*, 36.

30. Bloch to Fleg, 24 January 1912, in Lew. 1, 561.

31. Bloch to his parents, end of May 1900, in Lew. 1, 136; and 24 March 1902, in Lew. 1, 173.

32. Ernest Bloch, "Man and Music," translated from the original French by Waldo Frank, *Seven Arts* 1, no. 5 (March 1917), reprinted in *Musical Quarterly* 19, no. 4 (October 1933): 377.

33. About Bloch's admiration of Catholicism and its rites, see Bloch's letter to his sister, 26 February 1901, in Lew. 1, 143, 145.

34. Bloch to Fleg, 24 January 1912, LC Bloch Col., part of the letter in Lew. 1, 561–62. Bloch's sister and her husband converted publicly to Protestantism, which made Bloch's mother break all relationships with her daughter until Bloch's vigorous intervention. See Suzanne Bloch, "Bloch's Reaction to Religion at Age 19," *EBS Bulletin* 13 (1981): 1; and the letter of Bloch's mother to Loulette, 14 March 1902, in Lew. 1, 173.

35. Fleg to Bloch [1912?], in *Correspondance d'Edmond Fleg pendant l'affaire Dreyfus*, ed. Andre E. Elbaz (Paris: Librairie A.-G. Nizet, 1976), 156–57. (The editor of the volume, Andre E. Elbaz, dates the letter to 1911, but from the content it is clear that Fleg responds directly to Bloch's letter of 24 January 1912.)

36. Bloch to Fleg, 4 February 1912, LC Bloch Col.

37. Bloch to Fleg, 18 May 1912, LC Bloch Col., part of the letter in Lew. 1, 565.

38. The "Jewish cycle" consists of three orchestral pieces and three psalms: the *Israel Symphony* (1912–15); the *Trois poèmes juives* (Three Jewish Poems) (1912–13); Fleg's French paraphrases of psalms 114, 22, and 137 (Two Psalms and a Prelude, 1912; Psalm 22, 1914); and *Schelomo* (1916). Some consider the First String Quartet (or at least its first movement) part of the cycle. The source of the designation is unclear, but it might originate in the publicity surrounding Bloch's first years in the United States.

39. Typescript of Lawson's biography with Bloch's marginal notes (14 May 1941), Judah Magnes Museum, Berkeley, California (Bloch's emphasis). Lawson's biography was part of the Works Projects Administration; see Ruth Raphael, "Ernest Bloch at the San Francisco Conservatory of Music," *Western States Jewish Historical Quarterly* 9, no. 3 (April 1977): 199.

40. Bloch to Downes, 9 July 1954 (orig. in English), in Schiller, *Bloch, Schoenberg, and Bernstein*, 55–56.

41. This part of the letter is quoted only in French in Lew. 1, 291.

42. For Godet's review see *Le Petit Temps* (June 19, 1903), in José-Flore Tappy, ed., *Ernest Bloch, Romain Rolland, Lettres (1911–1933)*, Collection "Les Musiciens" (Lausanne: Editions Payot Lausanne, 1984), 31. Information on Bloch's taking Godet as a student from Suzanne Bloch's oral communication.

43. Godet to Bloch, 28 October 1904, LC Bloch Col.

44. Bloch to Fleg, 21 February 1906, LC Bloch Col., parts of the letter in Lew. 1, 344–45.

45. See the preface to Hippolyte Taine, *Histoire de la littérature anglaise* (Paris: Librairie Hachette, 1864).

46. Godet to Bloch, 31 July 1904, LC Bloch Col.

47. Bloch to Fleg, 30 November 1906, in Lew. 1, 369. Lucienne Bloch lists *Les prophètes d'Israël* (1892) among her father's books, but she does not specify the author. Lucienne Bloch Dimitroff, "Impressions of Ernest Bloch," in *The Spiritual and Artistic Odyssey of Ernest Bloch: A Centenary Retrospective* (Charleston, SC: Piccolo Spoleto, 1980), 34. Godet also recommended Karl Budde, *Geschichte der althebräischen Literatur* (Leipzig: C. F. Amelangs Verlag, 1906), and Emil Schürer, *Geschichte des jüdischen Volkes im Zeitalter Jesu Christi* (Leipzig: J. C. Hinrichs, 1886–90). Godet to Bloch, 12 December 1906, in Lew. 1, 370.

48. Bloch to Fleg, 30 November 1906, in Lew. 1, 369.

49. Mary Tibaldi Chiesa, "Ernest Bloch," *La revue musicale* 15, no. 143 (February 1934): 129.

50. To justify his admiration for the prophets of the Old Testament, Chamberlain tried to prove that they, like all his heroes including Jesus, did not belong to the Jewish race. Among the "debased" Jews, Chamberlain argued, God kept the prophets uncorrupted to provide future humanity with a pure seed from which a new faith could grow. Houston Stewart Chamberlain, *The Foundations of the Nineteenth Century*, trans. John Lees (London: John Lane, Bodley Head, 1911), vol. 1, 466–72. As his footnotes show, Chamberlain relied heavily on William Robertson Smith's *The Prophets of Israel and Their Place in History to the Close of the Eighth Century B.C.* (New York: D. Appleton, 1897).

51. Geoffry G. Field, *The Evangelist of Race: The Germanic Vision of Houston Stewart Chamberlain* (New York: Columbia University Press, 1981), 171.

52. Ibid., 220.

53. Robert Godet, "Préface de la version française," in H. C. Chamberlain's *La genése du XIXᵉ siècle* (Paris: Librairie Payot, 1913), xlii.

54. Godet to Bloch, 24 February 1911, part of the letter in Lew. 1, 535.

55. See Chamberlain, *Foundations of the Nineteenth Century*, vol. 1, 117–20.

56. Bloch to Fleg, 4 February 1912, parts of the letter in Lew. 1, 562–63.

57. Bloch to Fleg, 2 January 1912, part of the letter in Lew. 1, 559. Bloch used a different translation from Godet's, which indicates that he looked up the passage in his own Bible. About Chamberlain's views see Field, *The Evangelist of Race*, 194.

58. Godet to Bloch, 8 and 12 February 1912, LC Bloch Col.

59. See Chamberlain, *The Foundations of the Nineteenth Century*, vol. 1, 337. Chamberlain significantly distorts Graetz's statements. Referring to the persecution brought upon the Jews as a consequence of Christian accusation of their being the killers of Jesus, Graetz writes: "The Messianic vision which had indistinctly floated in

the minds of the people, but which had now taken a tangible form, was certainly something new; and this novel apparition, *with its mask of death*, was to inflict new and painful wounds upon the nation" (my emphasis). In the other quoted passage Graetz describes Jesus' decision not to address the whole nation but only "a particular class of the Judaeans." "The middle classes," Graetz writes, referring to the historical and not to the present-day Jewish middle classes, "were not wanting in godliness, piety and morality, and consequently a call to them to repent and forsake their sins would have been meaningless." It is similarly untrue that Graetz was unwilling to admit Jesus' exceptional character. Jesus' "high-minded earnestness and spotless moral purity were his undeniable attributes," he writes. He even compares Jesus' "gentle disposition" and "humility" to Hillel's. See Heinrich Graetz, *History of the Jews*, vol. 2 (Philadelphia: Jewish Publication Society of America, 1893), 170–71, 149, and 151.

60. Bloch to Fleg, 2 July 1912, in Lew. 1, 566.

61. Godet to Bloch, 25 October 1913, in Lew. 1, 611.

62. Godet to Bloch, ibid., LC Bloch Col. (This part of the letter is not in Lewinski.)

63. Moeller van den Bruck, *Zeitgenossen* (Minden, 1906): 120ff. *Oesterreichische Rundschau* (November 1905–January 1906) no. 5, 455, quoted in Field, *Evangelist of Race*, 230.

64. Godet to Bloch, 25 October 1913, in Lew. 1, 611.

65. Morhardt asked Bloch to deliver a letter to Godet about the schemes of P. Roches (editor of the Parisian revue *Art décoratif*), which Godet attributed to Morhardt. Godet became furious that Bloch had meddled in his affairs. (According to Lewinski's personal communication, the dispute concerned Roches's search for a Camille Claudel sculpture for a projected exhibition.) See Lew. 1, 609.

66. Godet to Bloch, 25 October 1913, in Lew. 1, 611.

67. Godet to Bloch, 9 November 1913, in Lew. 1, 613.

68. Bloch named Godet as one of three people with whom he had the most intense spiritual kinship. The other two were his lovers Béatrix Rodès and Winifred Howe (Bloch to Howe, 9 April 1934, UCB Bloch Col.).

69. Bloch to Godet, 13 November 1920, in Lew. 2, 274–76.

70. Godet faulted Bloch's First String Quartet for its formal chaos and arbitrary, inorganic juxtapositions of fragments that resulted in lack of unity. See Godet, "Suisse—La musique en Suisse romande," *La revue musicale* 2, no. 5 (March 1921): 275.

71. Godet, "Suisse—La musique en Suisse romande," *La revue musicale* 2, no. 6 (April 1921): 83–84.

72. Bloch to Fleg, 22 April 1921, in Lew. 2, 320.

73. Bloch to Godet, 21 July 1925, in Lew. 2, 623.

74. Bloch to Howe, 18 March 1934, UCB Bloch Col. Most letters in the UCB collection are in English, unless noted otherwise.

75. Bloch to Lillian Hodgehead and Ada Clement, 6 July 1934, UCB Bloch Col.

76. Bloch to Howe, 27 October 1935, UCB Bloch Col.

77. Bloch to Hodgehead, 6 April 1934, UCB Bloch Col. Bloch's reference to Italy pertains to a review that appeared in Italy in 1934. "The only nasty dissonance in Italy, at the premiere of the Sacred Service (Jan. 1934), the *insulting* article published—again by *Jews!*—in the review 'Israel!'" Bloch to Clement and Hodgehead, 23 December 1950, UCB Bloch Col. For more about the Italian review of Bloch's *Sacred Service*, see ch. 5.

78. Bloch wrote to his niece Evelyn Hirsch about the first performance of his *Three Jewish Poems:* "I've always had the Jews against me: in Geneva, when in 1914 I conducted my *Three Jewish Poems,* the Jews were hostile: 'This is not Jewish!' The 'Great Rabbi,' a title that he granted to himself—Guinsburg, I think, went from one person to the next, criticizing the piece, 'there are bells in this work, the Jews don't have bells.'" 18 January 1954, in Lew. 1, 624.

79. Godet to Bloch, 6 March 1914, in Lew. 1, 625.

80. Ibid. (The above part is not in Lew. 1.)

81. See Wagner, "A Communication to My Friends," in *Richard Wagner's Prose Works,* vol. 1, *The Art-Work of the Future,* trans. William Ashton Ellis (New York: Broude Brothers, 1966), 358.

82. Maria Tibaldi Chiesa's program note for the work's performance in Rome at the Accademia di Santa Cecilia (22 January 1933), approved by Bloch.

83. Bloch to Fleg, 30 January 1913, in Lew. 1, 591.

84. Bloch to Rolland, 25 November 1912, in *Ernest Bloch, Romain Rolland, Lettres,* 22.

85. Hannah Arendt, *The Origins of Totalitarianism* (San Diego: Harcourt Brace, 1973), 74.

CHAPTER 4

1. On the fluid quality of Jewish identity see the preface to David Theo Goldberg and Michael Krausz, eds., *Jewish Identity* (Philadelphia: Temple University Press, 1993).

2. Bloch to Fleg, 13 August 1909, LC Bloch Col.

3. The creative power of artists had been viewed since the nineteenth century as determined by its unconscious nature. See Ruth Solie, "The Living Work: Organicism and Musical Analysis," *Nineteenth-Century Music* 4, no. 2 (fall 1980): 155.

4. Bloch to Fleg, 16 July 1911, in Lew. 1, 543.

5. Bloch to Fleg, 9 April 1902, 19 April, 1 May, and 15 May 1904, LC Bloch Col.

6. See Bram Dijkstra, *Idols of Perversity: Fantasies of Feminine Evil in Fin-de-siècle Culture* (New York: Oxford University Press, 1986).

7. Bloch to Fleg, 15 May 1904, LC Bloch Col.

8. Bloch might not have known Wilde's *Salome* before he saw Strauss's opera in Leipzig, in March 1907. He admired Strauss's music, although he found the "color" false. See Bloch to his wife, Marguerite Bloch, 7 March 1907, in Lew. 1, 381.

9. Probably because of the scandal surrounding Wilde's name in England, the anonymous author of a short English review that calls attention to Trowbridge's new play does not mention Wilde as a possible model either. (The review, without any bibliographical citation, was glued to the last page of a copy of the 1903 edition signed by Trowbridge to his aunt, now in the Sterling Memorial Library at Yale University.)

10. Dijkstra, *Idols of Perversity,* 381.

11. See Dijkstra's analysis of *Salome,* ibid., 396–98.

12. W. R. H. Trowbridge, *Jézabel: drame en un acte, en prose* (Paris: Edition de la Plume, 1903), 90.

13. Bloch to Fleg, 1 and 15 May 1904, LC Bloch Col.; Bloch to his wife, 16 May 1904, in Lew. 1, 277.

14. Bloch to Fleg, 15 May 1904, LC Bloch Col.

15. Bloch to Fleg, 2 December 1908, LC Bloch Col.

16. Bloch to Fleg, undated letters (from 1909), LC Bloch Col.

17. Bloch to Fleg, no date [1909?], LC Bloch Col.

18. Three versions of Fleg's libretto have survived. The earliest *(Lib1)* is a hand-written libretto, bound in four booklets, with pages of music paper containing Bloch's drafts of themes inserted between the pages of the text. The page preceding the text of act 4 is dated by Bloch as 1911. *Lib1* differs considerably from the other two libretti. Two copies of Fleg's 1917 revised typewritten libretto *(Lib2)* exist (one containing Bloch's notes). (Both *Lib1* and the two copies of *Lib2* had been in Suzanne Bloch's private collection.) The published libretto *(Lib3)* agrees with this 1917 revised version. The small differences might be attributed to editorial work that preceded publication. Fleg's own date (1910) at the end of the published version might refer to the first completion of the libretto. Dedicated to Ernest Bloch, *Lib3* was published in 1927 in the May/June volume of *La revue littéraire juive* (365–97) and in the same year as Edmond Fleg, *Iezabel: Midrash ou histoire inspirée des écriture* (Paris: Lipschutz Editeur, 1927).

19. Fleg might have relied on Trowbridge, who also leaves out Ahab from his *Jézabel.*

20. Bloch to Fleg, no date [1909?], LC Bloch Col.

21. *Lib3*, 45.

22. Bloch's handwritten prose scenario (forty-three pages in four small booklets, divided by acts, LC Bloch Col., box 6, folder 8) seems to be a free paraphrase of *Lib1.* David Z. Kushner, in *Ernest Bloch: A Guide to Research* (New York: Garland, 1988, p. 265), misidentified Bloch's prose scenario as Fleg's libretto, as did David L. Sills in "Bloch's Manuscripts at the Library of Congress," *MLA Notes* 42, no. 4 (June 1986): 738n24.

23. Bloch to Fleg, 21 August 1911, LC Bloch Col.

24. *Lib3*, 96.

25. The sketches surviving in the LC Bloch Col. include two versions of the continuity drafts for act 1, one from before Bloch's emigration in 1916, the other from 1918 (the draft of act 1 in box 6, folder 1 corresponds with *Lib2*, while the one in folder 2 is based on *Lib1*); a fairly complete draft for the first part of act 2 (folder 3), corresponding with *Lib2* and thus written in New York; various sketches, some from 1919, some, judging from the appearance of the character Abdias, who disappeared from the revised version, from 1911; some sketches for act 4 (folder 5), the date of which cannot be determined; two sets of thematic indices, one from 1911, completed in New York (folder 6), the other from around 1918 ("Esquisses & Notes," folder 7, twenty-five pages within bound sketchbook); and Bloch's handwritten scenario (folder 8). Early thematic sketches survived in *Lib1.*

26. Bloch to Fleg, 21 August 1911, LC Bloch Col.

27. Undated letter of Bloch to Fleg, part of projected preface (1910–11), in Lew. 1, 317, 319.

28. Bloch to Fleg, 21 August 1922, LC Bloch Col.

29. Ralph P. Locke, "Constructing the Oriental 'Other': Saint-Saëns's *Samson et Dalila,*" *Cambridge Opera Journal* 3, no. 3 (November 1991): 261–302.

30. Bloch to Fleg, 21 August 1911, LC Bloch Col.

31. Bloch to Fleg, 5 August 1911, LC Bloch Col.

32. In an interview with Olin Downes Bloch stated: "The themes [in my compositions] are all my own and are not even in the manner of the traditional Jewish melodies, which themselves are of doubtful antiquity. Superficially my works are not Jewish at all. The learned Jews will no doubt reject them altogether." Olin Downes, "Ernest Bloch at Sixty," *New York Times,* 27 October 1940.

33. In his afterword, "La poète au musicien," to his 1917 revised libretto Fleg recommended that Bloch look up melodies in the *Jewish Encyclopedia,* not as "sources for imitation but for inspiration" *(Lib2).* Bloch copied out all of the melodies he found in the 1905 *Jewish Encyclopedia* and put together an eighty-five-page booklet of the themes thus collected. See Alexander Knapp, "The Life and Music of Ernest Bloch," *Jewish Quarterly* 28, nos. 2–3 (summer–fall 1980): 27. About Bloch's visit to the New York Public Library see his letters to his wife (December 1916, ibid.); to Alfred Pochon, 3 January 1917, in Lew. 2, 63; and to Fleg, 11 August 1918, in Lew. 2, 155.

34. Bloch to Fleg, 11 August 1918, LC Bloch Col. Bloch used the motive again in his *Suite hébraïque* (1951).

35. In today's practice the name *Ne'ilah* (closing) refers to the closing of the heavenly gates as judgment is sealed.

36. Bloch to Fleg, 5 August 1911, LC Bloch Col.

37. In the original version Bloch planned to mark this moment with the "profession of faith" motive.

38. David Z. Kushner, "The 'Jewish' Works of Ernest Bloch," *Journal of Synagogue Music* (June 1985): 31; Alexander Knapp, "The Jewishness of Bloch: Subconscious or Conscious?" *Proceedings of the Royal Musical Association* 97 (1970–71): 107.

39. Bloch to Fleg, 21 August 1911, LC Bloch Col.

40. See Móricz, "Sealed Documents and Open Lives: Ernest Bloch's Private Correspondence," *Notes* 62, no. 1 (September 2005): 74–86.

41. The postponement of the opera's completion, Bloch wrote to Fleg, was necessary, for it allowed his style to mature (Bloch to Fleg, 26 October 1919, in Lew. 2, 223).

42. Bloch to Madelaine Fleg, 26 January 1916, in Lew. 1, 695.

43. Bloch's program notes for the concert held at the Accademia di Santa Cecilia, Rome, 22 January 1933, pp. 7–8 (original in Italian). My translation differs slightly from Suzanne Bloch's. "Hebrew Oratory" is Bloch's reference to his *Sacred Service.*

44. The relationship between the oversensitive Bloch and his father, who was frequently violent, especially with the composer's mother, was difficult. See Jacques Tchamkerten, *Ernest Bloch ou Un prophète en son temps* (Geneva: Editions Papillon, 2001), 7–8. In a letter to Fleg (16 July 1911, in Lew. 1, 542) Bloch confessed that he was anxious that he might have inherited his father's character.

45. The name of the mode is derived from the prayer *magen avot,* which is a summary of the seven benedictions of the Amida (see Idelsohn, *Jewish Music,* 78–84).

46. Lazar Saminsky, "'Hebrew Song Lives in Modern Music': Racial Expression Intensified in Last Decade through Research Work—Jewish Composers Classified in Eastern and Western Groups—Influence of Bible Seen in Important Productions—Schönberg and Bloch Considered," *American Music* 41, no. 1 (15 November 1924): 9; and his article in the *La revue musicale* (October 1921): 268.

47. Olin Downes, "Three Boston Premieres for Bloch," in *Olin Downes on Music:*

*A Selection from His Writings during the Half-Century 1906 to 1955*, ed. Irene Downes (New York: Simon and Schuster, 1957), 57.

48. Erich H. Müller, "Das Judentum in der Musik," in Theodor Fritsch, ed., *Handbuch der Judenfrage: Die wichtigsten Tatsachen zur Beurteilung des jüdischen Volkes* (Leipzig: Hammer-Verlag, 1932), 323–33. There is a quarter tone in the violoncello part of *Schelomo*, one measure before rehearsal number 36.

49. Guido M. Gatti, "Ernest Bloch," *Musical Quarterly* 7 (January 1921): 28.

50. Hannah Arendt, *Rahel Varnhagen: The Life of a Jewish Woman*, rev. ed., trans. Richard and Clara Winston (New York: Harcourt, Brace, Jovanovich, 1974), 224.

CHAPTER 5

1. Italo Calvino, "The Count of Monte Cristo," in *t zero*, trans. William Weaver (New York: Harcourt, Brace, Jovanovich, 1976), 145, 151–52.

2. *Seven Arts* 1, no. 5 (March 1917): 504, 506.

3. Waldo Frank, "The Chosen People," in *Our America* (New York: Boni & Liveright, 1919), 78. For more about the *Seven Arts* see Carol J. Oja, *Making Music Modern: New York in the 1920s* (Oxford: Oxford University Press, 2000), 303–4.

4. Ernest Bloch, "Man and Music," *Seven Arts* 1, no. 5 (March 1917): 493–503, reprinted in *Musical Quarterly* 19, no. 4 (October 1933): 375–79.

5. For more about Rosenfeld's role in shaping the modernist scene in America, see Oja, *Making Music Modern*, 302–10.

6. Paul Rosenfeld, "The Music of Ernest Bloch," *Seven Arts* 1, no. 4 (February 1917): 413, 415.

7. In a letter to his mother (14 February 1918) Bloch reported on the numerous reviews of his music in Jewish papers, regretting that he could not read Hebrew (or Yiddish) (in Lew. 2, 140).

8. Rosenfeld, "The Music of Ernest Bloch," 413. Subsequent quotations come from pp. 416–18.

9. About contemporaneous criticism of Rosenfeld's style see Oja, *Making Music Modern*, 308.

10. Sylvia Glass, "Semitic Silhouettes xvi—Psalmist in Israel," *Opinion: A Journal of Jewish Life and Letters* 3 (October 1933): 16.

11. Bloch to his mother, 5 February 1918, in Lew. 2, 140.

12. Siegmund Spaeth, "Jews Interpreters More than Composers. Ernest Bloch Says It Is because in Music, as in Everything, They Assimilate and Imitate—More Sincere Jewish Art to Come," *Evening Mail*, 26 April 1917.

13. Olin Downes, "Ernest Bloch, the Swiss Composer, on the Influence of Race in Composition," *Musical Observer* 14, no. 3 (March 1917): 11.

14. Wagner, *Judaism in Music*, 90–91.

15. Bloch to Downes, 24 January 1917, in Schiller, *Bloch, Schoenberg, and Bernstein*, 26–27.

16. Downes, "Ernest Bloch, the Swiss Composer, on the Influence of Race in Composition," 11.

17. H. E. Krehbiel, "Ernest Bloch's Experiment In the Music of Jewry: A Jewish Composer and the Music Which He Feels To Be Racial—Spirit versus Traditional

Idiom—M. Bloch's Views on Form and the Radicalism of Novices—Themes from His Work," *New York Tribune*, 29 April 1917.

18. Bernard Rogers, "Swiss Composer's Aim: To Sing Himself," *Musical America* (12 August 1916): 3.

19. In Gatti, "Ernest Bloch," 27. Gatti does not specify his source.

20. Bloch's story was written down by Boaz Piller (1887–1964), a member of the Boston Symphony Orchestra, who had maintained friendly relations with Bloch since the composer's debut in Boston (typescript in UCB, Bloch Col.). In French in Lew. 2, 53.

21. Bloch to his wife, 27 January 1917, in Lew. 2, 70.

22. In Hugo Leichtentritt, *Serge Koussevitzy, the Boston Symphony Orchestra, and the New American Music* (Cambridge, MA: Harvard University Press, 1947), 82.

23. Olin Downes, "Composer Conducts Symphony. Bloch's 'Jewish Poems' Create Profound Impression," *Boston Post*, 24 March 1917.

24. Bloch to his mother, 7 May 1917, in Lew. 2, 96.

25. "Ernest Bloch's 'Jewish Cycle' Given at Final Concert of Friends" (unsigned), *New York Tribune*, 4 May 1917; H. F. P., "Unique Music by Ernest Bloch Receives Notable Exposition," *Musical America* (12 May 1917): 9.

26. Suzanne Bloch, "Ernest Bloch," *Keynote* ( July 1980): 21.

27. Bloch to Fleg, 3 September 1916, LC Bloch Col., part of the letter in Lew. 2, 31–32.

28. Bloch wrote to his sister that his mother "could not find herself there at all! The types were so different, spoke so differently that she felt like a stranger." Bloch to his sister (Mme Samuel Hirsch), January 1922, in Lew. 2, 351.

29. See Bloch's letter to his sister, 6 May 1939, in *EBC Bulletin* 12 (1979–80): 1.

30. Bloch to Fleg, 6 April 1918, LC Bloch Col., in Lew. 2, 147–48.

31. Ibid., 148. (Some sentences are missing from Lew. 2.)

32. Bloch's letter to his mother, describing the same experience, 5 April 1918, in Lew. 2, 147.

33. "[Schindler] believes," Bloch wrote to his wife, "that he will be able to make some rich Jews interested here who will be happy to learn that there exists a man who lives, suffers and dreams about an art music that is inspired by Judaism!" 9 December 1916, in Lew. 2, 51.

34. Bloch to Fleg, 11 August 1918, in Lew. 2, 155.

35. Bloch to Fleg, 4 January 1920, LC Bloch Col.

36. In his *Famous Musicians of Jewish Origin* (p. 655) Saleski lists clarinetist Simon Bellison, violinists G. Miestechkin and G. Besrodny, violist N. Moldavan, cellist J. Cherniavski, and pianist L. Berdichevski as members of "Zimro." Kopytowa lists M. Rosener as second violinists and B. Nachutin as pianist ("Die 'Gesellschaft für Jüdische Volksmusik' in St. Petersburg/Petrograd," 95). In 1919 Prokofiev wrote his *Overture on Hebrew Themes* for the group.

37. Joseph Yasser suggested that Bloch heard former OYNM member Leo Nisvitzky in Switzerland and that he was influenced by his style (see Soltes, "The Hebrew Folk Song Society of Petersburg," 25). Izaly Zemtsovsky repeated the claim ("Jiddischismus in der Musik: Bewegung und Phänomen," in Nemtsov and Kuhn, *Jüdische Musik in Sowjetrußland*, 5). Saminsky wrote that Bloch told him that "his father was a

Russian Hebrew and that in his boyhood he was nursed on traditional Eastern tunes sung in the family" (Saminsky, "Hebrew Song Lives in Modern Music," *Musical America* 41, no. 4 [15 November 1924]: 9).

38. Bloch to Fleg, 4 November 1919, LC Bloch Col.

39. Bloch to Rolland, 22 March 1917, in *Ernest Bloch, Romain Rolland: Lettres,* 79.

40. Bloch to his wife, 11 February 1917, in Lew. 2, 77.

41. Bloch to his sister, 18 January 1954, in Lew. 2, 88–89.

42. Bloch to Fleg, 29 May 1919, in Lew. 2, 195.

43. Bloch to his mother, 11 November 1920, in Lew. 2, 273.

44. H. E. Krehbiel, "Song Recital Vies for Honors with Concert," *New York Tribune,* 6 November 1920.

45. A critic for the *New York Evening Post,* for instance, wrote: "Mr. Bloch's ideal of the Jewish music of the future is apparently the grotesque, hideous, cackling dispute of the Seven Jews in Richard Strauss's *Salome.* . . . Nearly all of Bloch's music is hot in the mouth with curry, ginger and cayenne. . . . Mr. Bloch got plenty of applause from a large audience, largely of the Oriental persuasion." In Nicolas Slonimsky, *Lexicon of Musical Invective: Critical Assaults on Composers since Beethoven's Time* (New York: Coleman-Ross, 1953), 66–67, partially in "Opinions of Mr. Bloch's Music Expressed by Daily Newspaper Critics," *Musical America* (12 May 1917): 10.

46. *America* was performed on 20 December 1928 in San Francisco (Alfred Hertz), Ann Arbor ( Joseph E. Maddy, with University School of Music Orchestra), Providence (Walter H. Butterfield, with Brown University Orchestra), New York (Walter Damrosch), Cincinnati (Fritz Reiner), and Los Angeles (George Schnéevoigt). Performances followed on the 21st and 22nd in Boston (Serge Koussevitzky), Philadelphia (Ossip Gabrilowitsch), and Chicago (Frederick Stock). In Cleveland *America* was premiered on 27 December (Nicolai Sokoloff). See Lew. 2, 783.

47. Oscar Thompson's criticism *(The Evening Post),* in *Musical America* (29 December 1928): 7; Richard Stokes's review *(The Evening World),* ibid., 8.

48. Olin Downes, "Ernest Bloch in the Academy: Recognition for a Great Composer Who Has Made Home Here—His Music Deserves More Attention from Performing Artists," *New York Times,* 3 May 1947; Paul Rosenfeld, "Bloch and His 'Sacred Service,'" in *Discoveries of a Music Critic* (New York: Harcourt, Brace, 1936), 165; Irving Weil's review *(The Journal),* in *Musical America* (29 December 1928): 8.

49. Dika Newlin, "The Later Works of Ernest Bloch," *Musical Quarterly* 23, no. 4 (October 1947): 454. Her article incited Bloch's anger: "After 25 years of complete silence about me, the 'Quarterly' published a study (?) which pretends to be *technical* (!) and shows the *total* ignorance and stupidity of the *so called* musicologists! Even the musical examples are *appalling!* I was itching to answer, to correct these imbecilities, but what is the use!" Bloch to Clement and Hodgehead, 14 November 1947, UCB Bloch Col.

50. Daniel Gregory Mason, *Tune In America: A Study of Our Coming Musical Independence* (New York: Alfred A. Knopf, 1931), 161–62. On 21 May 1933 the following statement by Mason appeared in the *New York Times:*

> I am distressed to find that certain statements in my book, *Tune In America,* are being misinterpreted as anti-Jewish propaganda, and even as friendly to jingoism and Hitlerian nationalism.

We should never have had an American music at all, whether childish or mature, without the assistance of our Jewish friends and co-workers. It is therefore quite as important to our honesty as to their welfare that we should extend to them the hand of brotherhood and grateful fellowship in their present troubles. This is a time when the whole art-loving world must unite against the intolerance, the brutal egotism, that wherever they appear threatens the very life of art.

In David Z. Kushner, "Ernest Bloch, Daniel Gregory Mason and The Jewish Question," *American Music Teacher* 38, no. 6 ( June/July 1989): 18.

51. Daniel Gregory Mason, "Is American Music Growing Up? Our Emancipation from Alien Influences," *Arts and Decorations* (November 1920), in Mason, *Tune In America,* 160 and 106. Before his arrival in the United States, Bloch's name reached Mason through his friend Alfred Pochon (1878–1959). Mason contacted Romain Rolland, who enthusiastically supplied Mason with further information about the composer. After reporting on Bloch's career so far, Rolland characterized Bloch as "being profoundly Hebrew in the poetic and religious sense of the word." In his Jewish works, Rolland wrote, Bloch "tries to revive the spirit of his race. But he is free in spirit and lacks any kind of fanaticism." Rolland to Mason, in *Ernest Bloch, Romain Rolland: Lettres,* 53.

52. John Tasker Howard, *Our American Music: Three Hundred Years of It* (New York: Thomas Y. Crowell, 1946), 411, 414.

53. In Saminsky, *The Music of the Ghetto and the Bible,* 9.

54. In Saleski, *Famous Musicians of Jewish Origin,* 22. Saleski does not specify his source.

55. David Ewen was such a Bloch enthusiast that he dedicated his book *Hebrew Music* to Bloch.

56. "Ernest Bloch," in Isaac Landman, ed., *The Universal Jewish Encyclopedia: An Authoritative and Popular Presentation of Jews and Judaism since the Earliest Times,* vol. 2 (New York: Universal Jewish Encyclopedia Co., 1940), 398–99.

57. Nicolas Slonimsky, "This *America* Deep in His Fervent Soul," *Boston Evening Transcript,* 15 December 1928. In a letter to Slonimsky on 31 December 1928 Bloch thanked Slonimsky for his "excellent" article (in French in Lew. 2, 793).

58. Bloch to Hodgehead and Clement, 23 April 1925, UCB Bloch Col.

59. Bloch to Fleg, 24 December 1918, LC Bloch Col.

60. Bloch to Fleg, 4 January 1920, LC Bloch Col.

61. Bloch to his mother, 22 May 1917, in Lew. 2, 98.

62. Bloch to Hodgehead and Clement, 23 April 1925, in Suzanne Bloch, "The Mass Bloch Never Wrote," *EBS Bulletin* 4 (1972): 1.

63. Bloch to Fleg, 30 May 1923, in Lew. 2, 439.

64. Bloch to Hodgehead and Clement, 14 January 1925, UCB Bloch Col., in Lew. 2, 573. (This part of the original letter is French.)

65. Bloch incorporated the Credo and Gloria from a Gregorian Mass into his second Sonata for Violin and Piano ("Poème mystique," 1924). See also Bloch's letter to Frederick Jacobi, 6 October 1931, UCB Bloch Col., in French in Lew. 2, 549.

66. Bloch had already met Cantor Rinder during his Cleveland years (1920–25). See Rosa Perlmutter Rinder, *Music, Prayer, and Religious Leadership, Temple Emanu-El, 1913–1969* (oral history transcript, tape-recorded interview conducted by Malca Chall in 1968–69), 47.

67. Rafael, "Ernest Bloch at the San Francisco Conservatory of Music," 207; "Sets New Music to Jewish Service. Ernest Bloch, in Switzerland, Is Composing Liturgic Harmony for Use in Synagogues," *New York Times,* 19 October 1930. About Warburg's offer of $10,000 see Lew. 2, 861. In March 1930 Bloch also became the recipient of the Jacob and Rosa Stern Fund, which provided him with $5,000 a year for a ten-year period (see Lew. 2, 855).

68. Bloch to Rinder, 8 September 1930, UCB Bloch Col.; Bloch to Rinder, 5 March 1931, UCB Bloch Col.

69. Bloch to Rinder, 8 September 1930, UCB Bloch Col.; Bloch to Howe, 7 September 1930, UCB Bloch Col. About Bloch's relationship to Howe see Móricz, "Sealed Documents and Open Lives."

70. Bloch's program note for the New York performance of the *Sacred Service* (Schola Cantorum, 25th season, 1933–34, 11 April 1934), 6. Copies of the program are in UCB Bloch Col.

71. The traditional Sabbath Morning Service consists of three main parts, the Shema Yisroel (Hear O Israel), the Tefillah (also known as the Amidah), which consists of nineteen blessings, and the Torah service. These three parts are framed by preliminary mediations, including the Mah Tovu, and concluding prayers, including the mourners' Kaddish. Instead of setting the texts in this liturgical order, Bloch selected excerpts, primarily choral responses, of the Hebrew text of the service and arranged them in five parts according to dramatic and musical considerations. In Bloch's rearrangement the first part starts with Mah Tovu, a prayer from the preliminary meditations, and continues with sections from the liturgical first part, containing the Shema and its blessings. Bloch's second part, the Kedusha, consists of excerpts taken from the liturgical Amida. Part three in Bloch's *Sacred Service* starts with the conclusion of the Amida and ends with excerpts from the Torah service. Part four consists of the conclusion of the Torah service. The last part of Bloch's service contains sections from the Alenu, the "Jewish Pledge of Allegiance" from the last part of the service, the English proem to the Kaddish, and the return of the Tzur Yisroel from part one. For the end of this part Bloch replaced the hymn En Kelohenu with the concluding hymn of the evening service, the medieval Adon Olom.

72. Alfred Frankenstein, "Bloch's 'Sacred Service' Heard First Time in S. F.," *San Francisco Chronicle,* 29 March 1938.

73. Olin Downes, "Bloch's Profession of Faith: His Setting of a Jewish Sacred Service Presents Composer's Conception of the Unity of Man and Nature," *New York Times,* 6 August 1933.

74. Olin Downes, "Schola Cantorum in Bloch's Premiere," *New York Times,* 12 April 1934.

75. Paul Rosenfeld, "The Bloch Sacred Service," *New Republic* 78 (25 April 1934): 310.

76. Paul Rosenfeld, "Bloch and His *Sacred Service*," in *Discoveries of a Music Critic,* 167. Bloch reported his disappointment about Rosenfeld's changed views of his work in a letter to Albert Elkus: "I know what *kind* of music (?) he loves now! I can only pity the poor man—He is unsettled himself, neurotic, undeveloped, without compass . . . and he had probably the morbid faculty of wanting to *destroy* what he has loved. . . . I have known a few people like that, in my long, long experience—the saddest experiences, in our lives." Bloch to Elkus, 20 March 1935, UCB Bloch Col.

77. Ernest Newman, "Bloch's Sacred Service," *Sunday Times* (London), 3 April 1938, reprinted in *EBS Bulletin* 4 (1972).

78. Bloch repeatedly expressed his concern about the Jewish reception of the *Service*. On 17 November 1933 he wrote to Clement and Hodgehead: "but *this* has been no life, no existence, only an *inferno* of complications, conflicting interests, hidden reasons,—*fears*, yes, from the Jews, themselves!" His wife reported a couple of days earlier: "How will the Jews receive his last message! He told me that the wealthy ones have been brilliant by their indifference . . . it does not astonish me. . . . I am afraid that his opponents will be mostly among his brethren of race." Marguerite Bloch to Clement and Hodgehead, 4 November 1933, UCB Bloch Col.

79. Bloch to Samuel Laderman, 30 December 1950, in Schiller, *Bloch, Schoenberg, and Bernstein*, 68.

80. Mary Tibaldi Chiesa et al., "Il 'Servizio Sacro' di Ernest Bloch esequito a Torino e trasmesso per radio," *Israel* 19, no. 17 (25 January 1934): 3–6. Subsequent translations are mine.

81. Bloch to Clement and Hodgehead, 6 September 1934, UCB Bloch Col. The Berlin performance was conducted by A. Weinbaum on 15 January 1934. See also Bloch to Clement and Hodgehead, 6 July 1934. The Jüdische Kulturbund, formed in 1933 by Joseph Goebbels's Ministry of Public Enlightenment and Propaganda, was a Jewish cultural organization that employed Jewish musicians and actors. It functioned until 1941. In view of the history of the organization, Bloch's claim that Nazis participated in the performance of his Jewish Service seems misguided.

82. [Olin Downes], "Bloch, Composer Here to Conduct," *New York Times*, 27 March 1934.

83. Bloch to Clement and Hodgehead, 6 April 1934, UCB Bloch Col.

84. Tibaldi Chiesa et al., "Il 'Servizio Sacro' di Ernest Bloch."

85. Bloch to Rinder, 26 November 1930, UCB Bloch Col.; Rinder's typescript of Bloch's letter (26 November 1930), UCB Bloch Col.

86. Bloch to Howe, 16 November 1930, UCB Bloch Col.; Bloch to Hodgehead, 12 September 1930, UCB Bloch Col.

87. Bloch to Clement and Hodgehead, 7 January 1933, UCB Bloch Col.

88. Bloch's correspondence in the 1930s shows that apart from his first enthusiasm he kept a sober distance from the politics of Soviet Russia.

89. The Mixolydian theme appears in a notebook of basso ostinatos with the inscription "For possible Jewish Service." Suzanne Bloch, "Ernest Bloch—Student of Choral Music: Some Personal Recollections," *American Choral Review* 10, no. 2 (winter 1968): 53–54.

90. Bloch to Rinder, 26 November 1930, UCB Bloch Col.

91. See Glass, "Semitic Silhouettes," 17. Saminsky also related the Gregorian melody of the Magnificat to its "well-known source, the ancient Temple chant of the people of Israel." Saminsky, *The Music of the Ghetto and the Bible*, 177.

92. Bloch heard rehearsals of *Parsifal* in Bologna during his Italian sojourn in the fall of 1931. See Bloch's letter to Clement and Hodgehead, 25 October 1931, UCB Bloch Col.

93. Saminsky, *The Music of the Ghetto and the Bible*, 176, 178.

94. Bloch to Rinder, 5 March 1931, UCB Bloch Col.

95. Schiller, *Bloch, Schoenberg, and Bernstein*, 32.

96. Rosa Perlmutter Rinder, *Music, Prayer, and Religious Leadership, Temple Emanu-El, 1913–1969*, 51.

97. See Eliyahu Schleifer's entry "Jewish Music," in *The New Grove Dictionary of Music and Musicians,* ed. Stanley Sadie and John Tyrrell (New York: Grove, 2001), vol. 13, 57. See also Idelsohn, *Jewish Music,* 84–89.

98. Bloch included only the proem to the Kaddish in his service, leaving the actual prayer as an ad libitum addition to the synagogue version of the piece during the Tzur Yisroel section in part five.

99. Bloch to Rinder, 5 March 1931, UCB Bloch Col.

100. Kurt List, "Ernest Bloch's 'Sacred Service': Musically Untraditional, but Authentically Jewish," *Commentary* 8 (December 1950): 588.

101. "I still receive warm echoes from Chicago—It compensates me for the *horrible* article by *Kurt List,* in 'Commentary' (Dec. 1950) which they had the nerve and cruelty to send me, even asking for a . . . commentary! . . . They are 'Schoenbergians' and, thus, hate me—I am 'in the way,' apparently." Bloch to Clement and Hodgehead, 23 December 1950, UCB Bloch Col. Bloch expressed even more bitter sentiments about List's review in a letter to Samuel Laderman:

> About *"Commentary,"* yes I had received the magazine, with a typewritten note—not even signed!—"Mr Kurt List suggested that you might be interested in this issue of 'Commentary'—We would appreciate your comment on his article or on the magazine in general." I was appalled and trembling! Mme. Bloch, after the first paragraph, did not even want to go further!—Alas, there must *always* be such *dirt* to *mar* the beautiful impressions which gave me the courage to live. . . . Well, my first impulse was to write to [the editor] E. Cohen that the only *commentary* I could make was in quoting *Schopenhauer:* either: "There is a difficulty in properly judging works which become all the harder, the higher their character; often there are no persons competent to understand the work, and often no unbiased or honest critics." . . . Or to say: "My commentary? I wonder who is the most despicable, K. List, for writing such an article, or *you,* to send it to me. . . ." And also to deplore that "the best Jews were burned and tortured by Hitler, when some of the worst escaped and now *poisoned* America!" But Mme. Bloch said that I ought simply write to E. Cohen "No *Commentary*"!

Bloch to Samuel Laderman, 30 October 1930, in Schiller, *Bloch, Schoenberg, and Bernstein,* 67, 69.

102. Bloch to Rinder, 5 March 1931, UCB Bloch Col.

103. Bloch to his parents, 8 May 1900, in Suzanne Bloch, "Bloch's Reaction to Religion at Age 19."

104. Romain Rolland, *Jean-Christophe,* vol. 2, "The House" (New York: Carroll & Graf, 1996), 374–76; "The Market Place," 140; "The House," 376; "The Market Place," 171–72.

105. List, "Ernest Bloch's 'Sacred Service,'" 589.

106. See Schiller, *Bloch, Schoenberg, and Bernstein,* 46–53; Tibaldi Chiesa et al., "Il 'Servizio Sacro' di Ernest Bloch," 4.

107. Bloch's program note for the New York performance of the *Sacred Service,* 9–10.

108. Bloch to Clement, 1 March 1932, UCB Bloch Col.

109. Bloch to Rinder, 26 November 1930, UCB Bloch Col.

110. Bloch to Clement, 3 May 1931, UCB Bloch Col.

111. Bloch to Rinder, 5 March 1931, UCB Bloch Col.

112. According to Bloch the ending should be "such a *moving* music that people must fall in each others' arms—and leave the Temple *better men*, more *human*, with more *compassion, love, generosity*, indulgence for each other." Ibid.

113. "Then in the enormous silence, outside of space, comes an impersonal voice, with the Law of Eternity, that everything was and will be, that He Is, He Shall Be, without beginning, without end. Then the Christianity comes in, God becoming more in the shape of man—'He is my God, my Living Liberator.' Then the motif of the third part when the man is purified of heart." Bloch's description of the fourth strophe of *Adon Olom* in a lecture given at the San Francisco Conservatory, 16 September 1933 (a copy of Bloch's draft is in the Judas Magnes Museum, Berkeley, CA).

114. Bloch to Rinder, 5 March 1931, UCB Bloch Col.

115. Bloch to Downes, 9 July 1954, in [Downes], "Bloch, Composer Here to Conduct."

116. "Despite all prejudice against the *blacks* here—and the obstacles are *insurmountable*—I met some admirable blacks. The *Indians* are of a wonderful race and spiritually they are infinitely superior to those who subjugated and deprecated them. I read a book by an *Indian* whose daughter I knew, and who is an admirable artist who died of the influenza. No 'American' wrote anything so uplifting and profound." Bloch to his sister, January 1922, in Lew. 2, 351. He probably refers to a book by Charles Eastman (1858–1939), whose daughter Irène Eastman he knew.

117. Bloch to Fleg, 23 January 1918, in Lew. 2, 153. Godet was in Bloch's mind, since in a previous paragraph he mentions that Godet will receive the Legion of Honor: "Is it probably the translation of the pan-Germanist Chamberlain that earned him that little red ribbon?"

118. Bloch to his sister, January 1922, in Lew. 2, 351, 353.

119. Bloch to Downes, 9 July 1954, in Schiller, *Bloch, Schoenberg, and Bernstein*, 56.

### CHAPTER 6

1. Frank E. Manuel and Fritzie P. Manuel, *Utopian Thought in the Western World* (Cambridge, MA: Belknap Press of Harvard University Press, 1979), 1.

2. Claude Lefort, *L'invention démocratique: les limites de la domination totalitaire* (Paris: Fayard, 1981), 98, quoted by Frédéric Rouvillois, "Utopia and Totalitarianism," in Roland Schaer, Gregory Claeys, and Lyman Tower Sargent, eds., *Utopia: The Search for the Ideal Society in the Western World* (New York: New York Public Library/Oxford University Press, 2000), 322.

3. See Karl Mannheim, *Ideology and Utopia: An Introduction to the Sociology of Knowledge*, trans. Louis Wirth and Edward Shils (San Diego: Harcourt Brace Jovanovich, 1936); Ernst Bloch, *The Principle of Hope*, 3 vols., trans. Neville Paice, Stephen Paice, and Paul Knight (Oxford: Basil Blackwell, 1986), and *The Utopian Function of Art and Literature: Selected Essays*, trans. Jack Zipes and Frank Mecklenburg (Cambridge, MA: MIT Press, 1988).

4. Wilde quoted in Bloch, *The Utopian Function of Art and Literature*, 17; Nicholas

Berdyaev, "Democracy, Socialism and Theocracy," in *The End of Our Time*, trans. Donald Attwater (London: Sheet, 1933), 188, quoted in the preface to Aldous Huxley, *Brave New World* (New York: Harper & Row, 1946), ii.

5. Edward Rothstein, "Utopia and Its Discontents," in Edward Rothstein, Herbert Muschamp, and Martin E. Marty, eds., *Visions of Utopia* (Oxford: Oxford University Press, 2003), 25–26.

6. About Adolf Loos's utopian concept of architecture see Herbert Muschamp, "Service Not Included," ibid., 29–35. Schoenberg's admiration of Loos is demonstrated in his letter to Albert Einstein, 1 November 1930, in E. Randol Schoenberg, "Arnold Schoenberg and Albert Einstein: Their Relationship and Views on Zionism," *JASI* 10, no. 2 (November 1987): 157–58. About the parallel between Karl Kraus's, Ludwig Wittgenstein's, Loos's, and Schoenberg's ideals of cleaning language, grammar, and expression see Lydia Goehr, "Adorno, Schoenberg, and the *Totentanz der Prinzipien*—in Thirteen Steps," *Journal of the American Musicological Society* 56, no. 3 (fall 2003): 609; Allan Janik and Stephen Toulman, *Wittgenstein's Vienna* (New York: Touchstone, 1973); and Carl Schorske, *Fin-de-siècle Vienna: Politics and Culture* (New York: Vintage Books, 1981).

7. Arnold Schoenberg, *Theory of Harmony*, trans. Roy E. Carter (Berkeley: University of California Press, 1978), 369–70.

8. Schoenberg, "Is It Fair?" (undated, Rufer C 116), in Richard Drake Saunders, *Music and Dance in California and the West* (Hollywood, CA: Bureau of Musical Research, 1948), 11.

9. See Schoenberg's "Prospectus of the Society for Private Musical Performances" (1918), in *S/Reader*, 152; Schoenberg, "New Music, Outmoded Music, Style and Idea" (1946), in *Style/Idea*, 123. See, e.g., Ringer, "Creation, Unity, and Law," in Ringer, 67–82. Schoenberg's striving to achieve maximum unity is emphasized by Anton Webern in his "The Path to New Music," in *The Path to the New Music*, ed. Willi Reich, trans. Leo Black (Bryn Mawr, PA: Theodore Presser, 1963), 9–41.

10. Although from the mid-1910s Schoenberg acknowledged the role of the intellect in composition, he never gave up the Romantic conception of intuitive creation. See Joseph Auner, "'Heart and Brain in Music': The Genesis of Schoenberg's *Die glückliche Hand*," in Juliane Brand and Christopher Hailey, eds., *Constructive Dissonance: Arnold Schoenberg and the Transformation of Twentieth-Century Culture* (Berkeley: University of California Press, 1997), 112–30.

11. Communism, Schoenberg wrote in 1932, "looks out from the totality of the present-day situation to a utopian but fantastic future. . . . All such efforts, be they now pacifism, Christianity, communism, the Salvation Army, loving thy neighbor; all these that are based on the assumption that man is good enough must fail because man is, at least in this sense, not good enough." "About Power, Majority, Democracy, Fascism, Etc., Especially also Mussolini" (August 1932), in *S/Reader*, 235.

12. Cherusci: Lat. A Germanic tribe in northwestern Germany that defeated the Romans and hence became a national symbol in nineteenth-century Germany.

13. Carl Engel, "Schoenberg and 'Sentiment,'" in Merle Armitage, ed., *Schoenberg: Articles by Arnold Schoenberg, Erwin Stein [et al.] 1929–1937* (New York: Freeport, 1937), 157.

14. See Schoenberg's letter to Albert Einstein, 1 January 1924 ("I am considered,

at least abroad, to be the leading German composer . . ."), in Randol Schoenberg, "Arnold Schoenberg and Albert Einstein," 155.

15. Gershom Scholem, "Jews and Germans," *Commentary* 42 (November 1966): 33. See also Sidney M. Bolkosky, *The Distorted Image: German Jewish Perceptions of Germans and Germany, 1918–1935* (New York: Elsevier, 1975), 67.

16. Schoenberg to Alma Mahler, 28 August 1914, in *S/Reader,* 126.

17. "Music" (from "Guide-Lines for a Ministry of Art," ed. Adolf Loos, 1919), in *Style/Idea,* 369.

18. Summer 1921 (or 1922), in Joseph Rufer, "Hommage à Schoenberg," in Egbert M. Ennulat, ed., *Arnold Schoenberg Correspondence: A Collection of Translated and Annotated Letters Exchanged with Guido Adler, Pablo Casals, Emanuel Feuermann and Olin Downes* (Metuchen, NJ: Scarecrow Press, 1991), 2.

19. "Nicht mehr ein Deutscher," ASI doc., Bio 417.

20. "National Music (2)" (1931), in *Style/Idea,* 173.

21. Schoenberg's letter to Peter Gradenwitz, 20 July 1934, in Lazar, 110.

22. Radio interview with Schoenberg in 22 August 1949, in *S/Reader,* 340–41. Schoenberg's claim about the Nazi regime's alleged support of Klenau is true. Klenau's *Rembrandt von Rijn* (1937) and *Die Königin* (1940) were performed in Berlin's State Opera House. Klenau defended the use of twelve-tone technique in many journal articles. See Erik Levi, "Towards an Aesthetic of Fascist Opera," in *Fascism and Theatre: Comparative Studies on the Aesthetics and Politics of Performance in Europe, 1925– 1945,* ed. Günter Berghaus (Providence: Berghahn, 1996), 260–76; and Thomas Phleps, "Zwölftöniges Theater—'Wiener Schüler' und Anverwandte in NS-Deutschland" (Twelve-tone theater—"Viennese students" and related figures in National Socialist Germany), in *"Entartete Musik" 1938—Weimar und die Ambivalenz: Ein Projekt der Hochschule für Musik Franz Liszt Weimar zum Kulturstadtjahr 1999,* ed. Hanns-Werner Heister (Saarbrücken: Pfau-Verlag, 2001), 179–215.

23. "Im Jahre 1883 ist Wagner gestorben," ASI doc., Jew 8Fa. (My translation here and in other writings from ASI follows Maja Reid's.)

24. The Jewish musical organization Mailamm (Hebrew acronym for the English America-Palestine Association of Musical Sciences) was founded in 1931 in New York at the initiative of Miriam Zunser. See Artur Holde, *Jews in Music: From the Age of Enlightenment to the Present* (New York: Philosophical Library, 1959), 284.

25. Wagnerian German nationalists, Schoenberg wrote in defense of Hans Pfitzner in 1947, all had "a small anti-Semitic tarnish." "A Solemn Declaration about Pfitzner" (10 September 1947), in *S/Reader,* 317.

26. "When We Young Jewish Artists," in *Style/Idea,* 503–4.

27. "Judenfrage," ASI doc., Jew 7.

28. Schoenberg to Anton Webern, 4 August 1933, in Lazar, 106.

29. Berg to Webern, 26 August 1933, in H. H. Stuckenschmidt, *Schoenberg: His Life, World and Work,* trans. Humphrey Searle (London: John Calder, 1977), 370.

30. "Jewry's Offer of Peace to Germany" (1939), ASI doc., Jew 8A (continuation of "A Four-Point Program"), orig. in English.

31. "Jeder junge Jude" (part of "PUJ Program"), ASI doc., in German in Lazar, 455.

32. Schoenberg to Klatzkin, 13 June 1933, in Lazar, 105. Schoenberg probably

came into contact with Klatzkin when the *Encyclopedia Judaica* published an article on the composer. See Schoenberg to Klatzkin, 16 December 1931, ASI corr. All letters are in German and my translation, unless noted otherwise.

33. Schoenberg to Albert Einstein, 1 January 1924, in Randol Schoenberg, "Arnold Schoenberg and Albert Einstein," 155.

34. "To create a national Jewish music is a holy task, and especially interesting for Jews—who in great numbers in former times, as well as in our days, have helped Aryan music to become as perfect as it is today—for we can prove our superiority in spiritual matters in creating this new Jewish music." "The Jewish Situation," 29 April 1934, in *S/Reader*, 252.

35. Schoenberg to [?], 28 June 1933, ASI doc., Jew 8G5; Schoenberg to Elsa Bienenfeld, 16 September 1933, ASI corr.

36. Schoenberg to Wise, 12 May 1934, in Randol Schoenberg, "Arnold Schoenberg and Albert Einstein," 166.

37. Schoenberg was such a devoted nationalist that at the end of World War I he worked out a detailed political proposal for avoiding a communist coup in postwar Austria. He proposed the establishment of battalions consisting of the "stable and sensible elements of the bourgeoisie," which would take over "all heavy armored airplanes, mine throwers, artillery, machine guns" and halt "any revolutionary movement." The proposal was not approved by the Ministry of War. The offended composer remarked: "courage was lacking." "Politik" (10 November 1932), ASI doc., Deut 397, in Ena Steiner, "Mödling Revisited," *JASI* 1, no. 2 (February 1977): 78–79.

38. Stein, 86–87.

39. "Judenfrage," ASI doc., Jew 7. Here Schoenberg refers to his musical achievements, especially to the organization of "Musikalische Privataufführungen," which in the article "The Truth about Schoenberg" Cesar Saerchinger called "an artistic tyranny such as I have never witnessed before or since" (see Armitage, *Schoenberg*, 91).

40. "Notizen zur jüdischen Politik" (2 September 1933), ASI doc., Jew 5. (The reference is to the same musical organization.) Schoenberg to Stephen Wise, 12 May 1934, in "Arnold Schoenberg and Albert Einstein," 165–66.

41. "Judenfrage," ASI doc.

42. "I've never said that I am Zionist, only that I wanted to found a Jewish Unity Party." Schoenberg to Hans Nachod, 7 October 1933, in John A. Kimmey, Jr., ed., *The Arnold Schoenberg—Hans Nachod Collection*, Detroit Studies in Music Bibliography 41 (Detroit: Information Coordinators, 1979), 36. Schoenberg, "On Jewish Affairs" (c. 1937), ASI doc., C62, part of it published in Lazar, 109.

43. Schoenberg to Toch, undated letter (June 1933?), part of "Programm zur Hilfe u. Aufbau der Partei," ASI doc., Jew 8 G2, in German in Lazar, 449.

44. "Ich beabsichtige in den Ver. Staaten . . . ," typewritten draft, part of "Programm zur Hilfe u. Aufbau der Partei," ASI doc., Jew 8 G3 (undated, probably from summer 1933), translated in Ringer, 136–37.

45. "This is the very tragicomedy of the Jewish democracy: everybody has the right to utter his opinion. . . . Should, for instance, another people be divided into 7 parties, the Jewish-Zionist-Party must consequently be divided into 7 times 77 parties!" "The Jewish Situation," in *S/Reader*, 255. "Judenfrage," ASI doc.

46. "PUJ Program" (1 February 1934), ASI doc., Jew 3a.

47. "Judenfrage," ASI doc.

48. "PUJ Program," ASI doc.; "Notizen zur jüdischen Politik," ASI doc.

49. "PUJ Program," ASI doc.; "On Jewish Affairs," ASI doc.

50. "PUJ Program," ASI doc.

51. "Forward to a New Jewish Unitary Party" (1 December 1933), ASI doc.

52. Schoenberg to Klatzkin, 13 June 1933, in Lazar, 105.

53. "Forward to a New Jewish Unitary Party," ASI doc. Original typescript in English.

54. "PUJ Program," ASI doc.

55. Ringer, 137–38. The quotation comes from Schoenberg's comments on racial politics ("Der auf die Spitze," Verm 357b, 25 September 1933), ASI doc., also in *S/Reader,* 242.

56. "My own fight taught me that my enemies are inferior. For a long time I was stupid enough to respect certain windbags, although they ignored me. At that time I still took them for peers and equals. They stood firm against my criticism: today I know that whoever does not hold me in the highest regard is inferior." Schoenberg to Heinrich Jalowetz, 19 August 1933, ASI corr.

57. "PUJ Program," ASI doc.

58. "Judenfrage," ASI doc.

59. "PUJ Program," ASI doc.

60. "I do not wish to hide the fact that I am ignorant about this area of history; on the contrary, I consider this an advantage for me. For it is not my wish to do something original; but rather, the right thing; but especially: the necessary and successful thing." "Judenfrage," ASI doc.

61. "Eine neue Realpolitik," ASI doc., Jew 6d.

62. Ringer, 60.

63. See Schoenberg, "Faschismus ist kein Exportartikel" (1935), in *Arnold Schönberg, Stil und Gedanke: Aufsätze zur Musik,* ed. Ivan Vojtěch, Arnold Schönberg Gesammelte Schriften 1 (Frankfurt am Main: Fischer, 1976), 316, also in English in *S/Reader,* 271.

64. Michael Mäckelmann, *Arnold Schönberg und das Judentum: der Komponist und sein religiöses, nationales und politisches Selbstverständnis nach 1921,* ed. Constantin Floros, Hamburgischer Beiträge zur Musikwissenschaft 28\(Hamburg: Karl Dieter Wagner, 1984), 193–94.

65. Ringer, 131, 137.

66. Schoenberg's comment on Erich Krämer's article "Traum und Wirklichkeit," *Vossische Zeitung,* 20 August 1932, "Über Macht, Mehrheit, Demokratie, Faschismus etc. insbesondere auch Mussolini" (29 August 1932), in English in *S/Reader,* 235. "PUJ Program," ASI doc.

67. Lilly Toch, *The Orchestration of a Composer's Life,* oral history transcript (interviewed by Bernard Galm, 1971 and 1972), Oral History Program, University of California, Los Angeles, 1978, vol. 1, 319, 322. Toch's attitude toward Nazi Germany and toward his own Jewish origin was different from Schoenberg's. "We have no choice," he said, "but wait until those people become human again." As far as his Judaism was concerned, he did not let Nazi propaganda influence his attitude: "I cannot accept Hitler's decision that I am not I; that he says I am another being doesn't make me another being. . . . Why should the Nazis have to tell me that I am a Jew and must be a Jew? What is their right: I am who I am." Ibid., 320–21.

68. "Judenfrage," ASI doc.; "PUJ Program," ASI doc.

69. "If the German government demonstrates even a reasonable interest in this idea, I will take the liberty, in the near future, of submitting a plan which is currently being worked out by specialists in accordance with my ideas. This should result in an agreement about the pace of the emigration (four- or five-year plan) and about the participation of German industry (in other words, about helping the German unemployed) in the requirements for the resettlement; in return, we hope that our request for a milder treatment of the Jews still living in Germany will be met with understanding." "Amerikanische reiche Juden . . . ," handwritten document (no date), ASI doc., Jew 8 G3.

70. Furtwängler to Schoenberg, 7 August 1933, ASI corr.; "Vorschlag an Furtwängler," no date, ASI doc.

71. "Jewry's Offer of Peace to Germany," ASI doc., orig. in English.

72. In a striking document written after Schoenberg's wife left him in 1908, the composer wrote: "Facts prove nothing. He who sticks with facts will never get beyond them to the essence of things. I deny facts. All of them, without exception. They have no value for me for I elude them before they can pull me down." "Testament-Entwurf," c. 1908, in *S/Reader*, 54.

73. Schoenberg's response to Hans Behr's invitation, dated 18 July 1933, is part of the "Programm zur Hilfe u. Aufbau der Partei," ASI doc., Jew 8D. Schoenberg's date book has the address of Behr on the suggested date (Notiz-Kalendar 1933, 21 July, ASI).

74. Schoenberg, as indicated in the draft, intended to publish his statement. "Einsteins falsche Politik," ASI doc., Jew 4, in Randol Schoenberg, "Arnold Schoenberg and Albert Einstein," 180.

75. "Die Gesetzte zum Schutze des geistigen Eigentums," May 1933, ASI doc., Jew 8E.

76. Schoenberg to Nachod, 18 September 1933, in *The Schoenberg—Hans Nachod Collection*, 35.

77. Schoenberg to the Exekutiv-Komitee des Jüdischen Weltkongresses, 14 August 1933; Schoenberg to Verdine Schlionsky, 19 August 1933; Schoenberg to Rosovsky, 23 December 1933, ASI corr.

78. Schoenberg to Rabbi Joseph S. Shubow, 23 December 1933, ASI corr.

79. "Forward to a New Jewish Unitary Party," ASI doc. A somewhat different version of the text is published in *S/Reader*, 251–56.

80. See Irene Heskes, "Arnold Schoenberg: Shaper of Twentieth-Century Music Creativity," in *Passport to Jewish Music: Its History, Traditions, and Culture* (Westport, CT: Greenwood Press, 1994), 279, and "Shapers of American Jewish Music: *Mailamm* and the Jewish Music Forum, 1931–62," *American Music* 15, no. 3 (fall 1997): 318.

81. "2 Speeches on the Jewish Situations, 1934, 1935," in *Style/Idea*, 501–5.

82. "The Jewish Government in Exile" (draft for a broadcast, 1946?), ASI doc., orig. in English. Published in part in Lazar, 108, and Ringer, 147–48.

83. Klatzkin to Schoenberg, 3 May 1946, ASI corr.

84. "My Attitude toward Politics," 16 February 1950, in *Style/Idea*, 505.

85. This and subsequent quotations about Schoenberg's plan of the future Jewish state are taken from his "Notizen zur jüdischen Politik" and "PUJ Program," ASI doc., unless noted otherwise.

86. "Amerikanische reiche Juden . . . ," ASI doc.

87. In German in Lazar, 444.

### CHAPTER 7

1. Some of the sketches have key signatures; see Lazar, 67–71; see figure 8, ibid., 69.

2. Schoenberg to Reinhardt, 24 May 1933, in Lazar, 95; Ringer, 133.

3. Schoenberg to Gradenwitz, 20 July 1933, in Lazar, 110.

4. For more details see ibid., 49–51.

5. Berg to his wife, 28 June 1921, ibid., 50–51.

6. Schoenberg to Kandinsky, 4 May 1923, in *S/Reader,* 169.

7. Schoenberg to Kandinsky, 20 April 1923, ibid., 168.

8. Ibid., 170, 172.

9. See Schoenberg's letter to Berg (16 October 1933, in Stein, 184) and to Reinhardt (24 May 1933, in Lazar, 444–45). Cf. Lazar, 56.

10. The contributors to the volume included (according to Seiden's specification) a medical doctor, an army general, a journalist, two dramaturges, an Arab writer, an art historian and architect, two writers, the Polish ambassador in Vienna, two professors, an author of books on the Orient, a historian, a Hungarian democrat, the mayor of Kassel, Arnold Schönberg (the "most modern living composer"), a poet, and a story-teller. Rudolf Seiden, ed., *Pro Zion! Vornehmlich nichtjüdische Stimmen über die jüdische Renaissancebewegung* (Vienna: Samuel Insel, 1924), 7–9.

11. Mäckelmann, *Arnold Schönberg und das Judentum,* 56–57.

12. *Pro Zion!,* 7. It is interesting to note that neither Lazar nor Mäckelmann mentions that Seiden emphasized that his contributors were "non-Jewish." Lazar tacitly leaves out the "non-Jewish" from his specification of contributors; see Lazar, 53.

13. See Lazar, 53, and Mäckelmann, *Arnold Schönberg und das Judentum,* 56. See also Lazar's comment on Schoenberg's knowledge of Jewish politics in Lazar, 135n129.

14. Only eleven books on Jewish subjects are found in Schoenberg's library, among them only four that Schoenberg could have owned at the time of his contribution to *Pro Zion!:* Matti Aikio, *Der Sohn des Hebräers,* ed. Niels Hoyer (Munich: Georg Müller, 1914); Heinrich Hirsch Graetz, *Volkstümliche Geschichte der Juden,* 10th ed., 3 vols. (Vienna: R. Löwit, [191?]) and the same published in 192?; Joseph ha-Kohen, *Emek habacha,* trans. and ed. Dr. M. Wiener (Leipzig: O. Leiner, 1858); and Josephus Flavius, *Geschichte des Jüdenischen Krieges,* trans. and ed. Heinrich Clementz (Berlin: Benjamin Harz, 1923).

15. The expression "Speeres Spitze" in the text is a reference to Wotan's words toward the end of *Die Walküre:* "Only the man who braves my spear-point can pass through this sea of flame!"

16. Among the contributors Schoenberg is the only one who uses the word *Reich* (empire) to refer to the new Jewish state.

17. Schoenberg's contribution to *Pro Zion!,* 33. Second part translated also in Lazar, 54. Schoenberg's emphasis.

18. See Lazar, 56. A further mystery surrounding Schoenberg's possible intentions for the play is that a short musical draft has text underlay in English. The ad-

dition of the English text could be explained had Schoenberg written it in 1933 when he planned to turn the play into an essential part of his worldwide propaganda campaign. But Schoenberg dated the accompanied version of the melody as "1926 or 1927" (see ibid., 68). The English text ("freedom for all! Throughout the world liberty and independence mankind embrace, freedom of thought, worship of God, tolerance, equality for every race") does not appear in the final version. Nor does its wording correspond to the general spirit of the play, which was far from an appeal for liberty for all.

19. Schoenberg to Reinhardt, 24 May 1933, ibid., 95. In a letter to Ernst Schoen Schoenberg claimed that he "conceived" the play in 1923 or even earlier. See Schoenberg to Schoen, 25 September 1933, ASI corr.

20. Schoenberg to Nikolas Slonimsky, 3 June 1937, in Slonimsky, *Music since 1900* (New York: Charles Scribner's Sons, 1971), 1316.

21. Schoenberg to Erwin Stein, 5 August 1927, in Stein, 127; Schoenberg to Werfel, no date (1933?), in Lazar, 112; Schoenberg to Klatzkin, 26 May 1933, ibid., 96.

22. Instead of Schoenberg's play, Reinhardt staged Werfel's *The Eternal Road,* for which Kurt Weill wrote the music. See *Speak Low (When You Speak Love): The Letters of Kurt Weill and Lotte Lenya,* ed. Lys Symonette and Kim H. Kowalke (Berkeley: University of California Press, 1996), 138–45.

23. Schoenberg to Ernst Schoen, 25 September, 3 October, and 14 October 1933, ASI corr.

24. For an explanation of names in *The Biblical Way* see Lazar, 73–86; *The Biblical Way, JASI* 17 (1994): 191. Subsequent quotations come from pp. 193, 233, 221, 231, 235, and 251.

25. How closely Schoenberg modeled Aruns on himself is demonstrated by details such as Aruns being considered a monarchist (251), his theories arousing opposition in everyone (179), and, on a more personal level, his wife's abandoning him for another man.

26. Schoenberg to Werfel, no date (1933?), in Lazar, 112.

27. The name Christine indicates that Max Aruns's wife was not Jewish. She tells her husband: "I am not completely of your kind" (see Lazar, 75); *The Biblical Way,* 245.

28. "PUJ Program," ASI doc.

29. *The Biblical Way,* 193. Subsequent quotations come from pp. 201, 199, 173, 185, and 239.

30. See Lazar, 57.

31. *The Biblical Way,* 319.

32. Lazar, 89.

33. *The Biblical Way,* 319.

34. Ibid., 327, 329.

35. See Peg Weiss, "Evolving Perceptions of Kandinsky and Schoenberg: Toward the Ethnic Roots of the 'Outsider,'" in *Constructive Dissonance,* 35–57.

36. Schoenberg to Kandinsky, 20 July 1922, in Stein, 70–71.

37. "Composition with Twelve Tones (1)" (1941), in *Style/Idea,* 223. For the relationship between Schoenberg's compositional ideas in *Die Jakobsleiter* and Balzac's *Séraphîta* see Richard Taruskin, "Scriabin and the Superhuman," in *Defining Russia Musically,* 349–59.

38. See Jacques Borel, *"Séraphîta" et le mysticisme balzacien* (Paris: Librairie José

Corti, 1967), 233–34. Schoenberg owned Swedenborg's *Theologische Schriften,* trans. Lothar Brieger-Wasservogel ( Jena: Diedrichs, 1904).

39. Honoré de Balzac, *Seraphita,* trans. Katharine Prescott Wormeley (Boston: Roberts Brothers, 1889), 191.

40. In Gabriel de Foigny's late-seventeenth-century utopia *Les avantures de Jaques Sadeur* hermaphrodites populate his utopian island.

41. Schoenberg, *Theory of Harmony,* 96. About the ideal of androgyny in *Jakobsleiter* see Jennifer Shaw, "Androgyny and the Eternal Feminine in Schoenberg's Oratorio *Die Jakobsleiter,*" in Charlotte Cross and Russell A. Berman, eds., *Political and Religious Ideas in the Works of Arnold Schoenberg* (New York: Garland, 2000), 61–83.

42. Webern quoting Schoenberg in *The Path to the New Music,* 37.

43. Roland Schaer, "Utopia and Twentieth-Century Avant-Gardes," in Schaer et al., *Utopia: The Search for the Ideal Society in the Western World,* 284.

44. Schoenberg to Gradenwitz, 20 July 1934, in Lazar, 110. Schoenberg did not name the third piece.

45. Defending himself from Berg's supposed suspicion that he used Strindberg's *Moses* as a model, Schoenberg writes: "but one thing you must grant me (I insist on that): everything I have ever written bears a certain intrinsic similarity with myself." Schoenberg to Berg, 9 August 1930, in Juliane Brand, Christopher Hailey, and Donald Harris, eds., *The Berg-Schoenberg Correspondence: Selected Letters* (New York: W. W. Norton, 1987), 407. Schoenberg to Walter Eidlitz (who in 1933 sent his own book on Moses to Schoenberg), 15 March 1933, in Stein, 172.

46. Ibid.

47. See the general outline of the play in Lazar, 63.

48. "The basic set functions in the manner of a motive. This explains why such a basic set has to be invented anew for every piece. It has to be the first creative thought." "Composition with Twelve Tones (I)," 219.

49. *The Biblical Way,* 239.

50. Schoenberg's answer to German psychologist Julius Bahl's question about the most important phases in composing a song, in Reich, *Schoenberg: A Critical Biography,* 238.

51. Schoenberg, "Constructed Music" (c. 1931), in *Style/Idea,* 107.

52. "In formulating the notion concerning the *unity of the musical space* I relied on an assertion that . . . chords are the vertical product of the overtones, but the scale is the horizontal product. I carried this thought to its conclusion and consequently arrived at the concept whereby the vertical and the horizontal, harmonic and melodic, the simultaneous and the successive were all in reality comprised within one unified space." "Vortag/12 T K/Princeton," ed. Claudio Spies, *Perspectives of New Music* 13 (1974), in Patricia Carpenter and Severine Neff, *Arnold Schoenberg, The Musical Idea and the Logic, Technique, and Art of Its Presentation* (New York: Columbia University Press, 1995), 389.

53. "[Music] itself . . . creates the figures for whom only schematic outlines were furnished." Schoenberg to Werfel, in Lazar, 112.

54. Moses's first words in the opera.

55. Ringer, 53, 63.

56. Schoenberg to Eidlitz, 15 March 1933, in Stein, 172.

57. Act 3.

58. In his letter to Eidlitz Schoenberg called "the divergence between: 'and thou shalt smite the rock' and 'speak ye unto the rock'!" "almost incomprehensible." 15 March 1933, in Stein, 172. The discussed Biblical passages are Exodus 17:6 and Numbers 20:8. The same contradiction is discussed also in *The Biblical Way* (307) in the argument between Aruns and Assenio.

59. Schoenberg to Klatzkin, 13 June 1933, in Lazar, 105.

60. The document of reconversion is reproduced in facsimile in Ringer, 135.

61. The sketches, including the basic set, are dated 7 January, 9 February, and 10 February 1937 (see U311, U312, U461, U559 in ASI). See Stuckenschmidt, *Schoenberg*, 421.

62. Schoenberg to Klatzkin, 19 July 1938, in Stein, 205.

63. Schoenberg to Gradenwitz, 20 July 1934, ASI corr. Manuscripts related to this project were published in Carpenter and Neff, *Arnold Schoenberg, The Musical Idea and the Logic, Technique, and Art of Its Presentation.*

64. Gradenwitz to Schoenberg, 3 December 1936, ASI corr. Gradenwitz refers to Schoenberg's statements about the incongruity of primitive musical material and sophisticated compositional technique in the preface to his *Three Satires,* op. 28 (1925).

65. Nathan's final collection contains arrangements by Kurt Weill, Darius Milhaud, Arthur Honegger, Stephan Wolpe, Aaron Copland, Paul Dessau, Ernst Toch, and Erich Walter Sternberg. Nathan published the arrangements in two series (each containing six folders), as *Folk Songs of the New Palestine (Composed by the true builders, the pioneers; and arranged by a group of eminent Jewish composers, including several of the leading musical personalities of our time),* ed. Dr. Hans Nathan, trans. Harry H. Fein (New York: Nigun, 1938). Republished in Philip V. Bohlman, *Israeli Folk Music: Songs of the Early Pioneers,* ed. Hans Nathan (Madison: A-R Editions, 1994).

66. Nathan's preface, in Bohlman, *Israeli Folk Music,* xi.

67. Toch's letter (26 May 1937), Weill's letter (30 May 1938), and Milhaud's letter (11 August 1938) to Nathan, ibid., xii.

68. Schoenberg to Nathan, 22 September 1937, ASI corr.

69. Schoenberg to Nathan, 11 February 1938, ASI corr. In 1950 Schoenberg expressed similar concerns about creating Jewish national music: "If only elements of the *biblical cantillation* should be used, why not also exclude all modern musical instruments and use only those of Bible-times. . . . If in spite of that, a national flavor is desired and possible—let it have it. But why keep people away from *progress in music,* when they are allowed to profit from products of all technical, scientific, legal, social, medical, and philosophical progress?" "Four Statements," 28 January 1950, in *S/Reader,* 339.

70. "Holem tza'adi" appears in Nathan's series in Milhaud's arrangement. The fast part is published in Baron Rodolphe d'Erlanger, ed., *La musique arabe,* vol. 6 (Paris: Librairie orientaliste Paul Guenthner, 1959). See Nathan's preface in Bohlman, *Israeli Folk Music,* xi.

71. See "Brahms the Progressive" (1947), in *Style/Idea,* 407.

72. Max Vorspan and Lloyd P. Gartner, *History of the Jews of Los Angeles,* Regional History Series of the American Jewish History Center of the Jewish Theological Seminary of America (San Marino, CA: Huntington Library 1970), 211.

73. Saminsky to Schoenberg, 20 April 1941, ASI corr.

74. Walter Rubsamen, "Schoenberg in America," *Musical Quarterly* 37, no. 4 (October 1951): 476. The correspondence between Schoenberg and Sonderling concerns mainly the obtaining of affidavits (see Schoenberg to Sonderling, 1 December 1938, and Sonderling to Schoenberg, 3 January 1939, ASI corr.).

75. Schoenberg starts his description of *Kol nidre* (document 2) suggesting that he considered it to be the first in a series: "I decided to compose at first the Kol Nidrey." (*S. Werke* B/19, xi, also in *S/Reader*, 282.) Schoenberg's sketch is entitled "Jahlech" (see ibid., 35).

76. Stuart Weinberg Gershon, *Kol nidrei: Its Origin, Development, and Significance* (Northvale, NJ: Jason Aronson, 1994), 35.

77. Schoenberg to Paul Dessau, 22 November 1941, in Stein, 212. In his notes to *Kol nidre* (document 2) Schoenberg wrote: "Nobody could understand why Jews should be allowed to make oaths and vows and promises, which they could consider as null and void. No sincere no honest man could understand such an attitude." Orig. in English, in *S. Werke* B/19, xii, also in *S/Reader*, 282.

78. Herman Kieval, "The Curious Case of Kol nidre," *Commentary* 46, no. 4 (October 1968): 56.

79. About Joseph Bloch's theory see *Encyclopaedia Judaica*, vol. 10 (Jerusalem: Macmillan, 1971–72), 1167.

80. Schoenberg asked for the book in 1933 and returned it in 1938 (see Klatzkin to Schoenberg, 7 July 1938, and Schoenberg to Klatzkin, 19 July 1938, ASI corr.).

81. Schoenberg's notes on *Kol nidre* (document 2).

82. The emphasis is Schoenberg's. Orig. in English. See *S. Werke* B/19, 36–39.

83. "Notes on Kol Nidrey and a 4 point program," ASI C60.

84. Schoenberg to Thomas Mann, 28 December 1938, ASI corr. (trans. ASI). No letters from 1938 survive from Schoenberg to any magazines or agencies or from magazines or agencies to Schoenberg that would indicate that he indeed sent out his essay for publication.

85. Mann to Schoenberg, 9 January 1939, ASI corr. (trans. based on ASI).

86. Schoenberg to Mann, 15 January 1939, ASI corr. (trans. ASI). Partially in *S/Reader*, 232.

87. See Appendix C in Ringer, 230–44.

88. *S. Werke* B/19, 39.

89. "Nevertheless, the arrogance of Jews is the very cause of anti-semitism. Only this term does not refer to the behavior or attitude of the single person, but to the whole of us, to the entire Jewry. Every non-Jew believes, consciously or subconsciously, that in every Jew is alive the feeling that he is different from all other peoples by his belonging to God's elected people. This is what they antagonizingly call great presumption, and to that they react with contempt and hatred." "A Four-Point Program for Jewry," in Ringer, 232–33.

90. *S. Werke* B/19, xi, also in *S/Reader*, 281–82. The *Complete Edition* identifies five of Schoenberg's sources: Leon Kornitzer (1928), Baruch Schorr (1906), Reuben B. Rinder (1931), Joseph Heller (1914), and H. Weintraub (1859).

91. Schoenberg's letter to Dessay, 22 November 1941, in Stein, 213. Schoenberg referred to Max Bruch (1838–1920), whose *Kol nidre* for cello and orchestra achieved such popularity that Bruch became an honorary Jewish composer, appearing in Saleski's *Famous Musicians of a Wandering Race* (9) as a composer with "Hebraic mu-

sical inheritance." Bruch, a composer with clerical Protestant background, composed *Kol nidre* for the Jewish community in Liverpool.

92. See Paul Dessau, "Arnold Schoenbergs 'Kol nidre,'" originally published in *Jewish Music Forum* (1941), reprinted in Fritz Hennenberg, ed., *Notizen zu Noten* (Leipzig: Reclam, 1974), 105.

93. Schoenberg copied the melodies of Kornitzer, Schorr, Rinder, and Heller under each other. See *S. Werke* B/19, 15–19.

94. Schoenberg's notes on *Kol nidre* (document 1), ibid., xi.

95. Dessau calls attention to these measures; see his "Arnold Schoenbergs 'Kol nidre,'" 106. About a different approach to the combination of foreign material and his style, see Joseph Auner, "Schoenberg's Handel Concerto and the Ruins of Tradition," *Journal of the American Musicological Society* 49, no. 2 (summer 1996): 264–313.

96. In 1941 he started his lecture "Composition with Twelve Tones" with these curious remarks: "To understand the very nature of creation one must acknowledge that there was no light before the Lord said: 'Let there be Light.' And since there was not yet light, the Lord's omniscience embraced a vision of it which only His omnipotence could call forth. . . . In fact, the concept of creator and creation should be formed in harmony with the Divine Model; inspiration and perfection, wish and fulfillment, will and accomplishment coincide spontaneously and simultaneously. In Divine Creation there were no details to be carried out later. 'There was Light' at once and in its ultimate perfection." *Style/Idea*, 214–15.

97. Michael Mäckelmann, "Ein Gebet für Israel, als die Synagogen brannten. Über Schönbergs 'Kol nidre'—zum Gedenken an den Pogrom der Kristallnacht 1938," *Neue Zeitschrift für Musik* 11 (November 1988): 8.

98. Many saw in Schoenberg's setting of Kol nidre an autobiographical gesture, as Eric Werner put it, a "personal sacrifice of atonement, an offer of expiation." See Werner's review in "Current Chronicle" in *Musical Quarterly* 44, no. 2 (April 1958): 243. The same argument is repeated by Dika Newlin, in "Self-revelation and the Law: Arnold Schoenberg in His Religious Works," *Yuval* 1 (1968): 218.

99. Schoenberg to Saminsky, 6 February 1941, ASI corr.

100. The first performance of *Kol nidre* took place in the Ambassador Hotel in Los Angeles during a Yom Kippur service. Rabbi Sonderling was the reciter, Schoenberg conducted the orchestra. See Rubsamen, "Schoenberg in America," 476. Schoenberg to Saminsky, 6 February 1941, ASI corr.

101. Saminsky to Schoenberg, 20 April 1941, ASI corr.

102. The audience of "The Jewish Music Forum," where Dessau introduced Schoenberg's *Kol nidre,* was more receptive than Saminsky. See Dessau to Schoenberg, 24 December 1941, ASI corr. "It is such a pity that people like Saminski *[sic]* decline to adopt the piece for use in the synagogue, on ritual and musical grounds. I believe it must be tremendously effective both in the synagogue and in the concerthall." Schoenberg to Paul Dessau, 22 November 1941, in Stein, 213.

CHAPTER 8

1. "Current Chronicle," *Musical Quarterly* 36, no. 3 (July 1950): 450–51.

2. Leibowitz's 1949 article is quoted in Reich, *Schoenberg: A Critical Biography*, 222.

3. *Oxford Companion to Music,* ed. Alison Latham (Oxford: Oxford University Press,

2002), 62. Whittall made this comment in his description of Heinrich Schenker's method of analysis.

4. Adorno, for one, maintained that *Erwartung* and *Begleitmusik* prophesied the horror of the Holocaust. See Theodor W. Adorno, "Arnold Schoenberg 1874–1951," trans. Samuel and Shierry Weber, in *Prisms* (London: Neville Spearman, 1967), 172. First published in 1953 as "Arnold Schönberg (1874–1951)," in *Die Neue Rundschau.*

5. Thomas Harrison, *1910: The Emancipation of Dissonance* (Berkeley: University of California Press, 1996), 168.

6. Schoenberg, "Aphorismen," *Die Musik* 9 (July–September 1909–10): 159, trans. in Reich, *Schoenberg: A Critical Biography,* 56.

7. Schoenberg, *Theory of Harmony,* 2.

8. Theodor W. Adorno, *Philosophy of Modern Music,* trans. Anne G. Mitchell and Wesley V. Blomster (New York: Continuum, 1985), 41.

9. Munch's diary entry from 22 January 1892, in Reinhold Heller, *Edvard Munch: The Scream,* Art in Context (New York: Viking Press, 1973), 65.

10. Harrison, *1910: The Emancipation of Dissonance,* 164.

11. About the Wagnerian scream see Philip Friedheim, "Wagner and the Aesthetic of the Scream," *Nineteenth-Century Music* 7, no. 1 (summer 1983): 63–70.

12. Adorno, *Philosophy of Modern Music,* 42.

13. Hector Berlioz and Richard Strauss, *Treatise on Instrumentation,* trans. Theodore Front (New York: Edwin F. Kalmus, 1948), 302, 305.

14. See 2 before rehearsal number 99 through 101, rehearsal number 161, 2 before rehearsal number 256, and 4 after rehearsal number 267 in Strauss's *Salome.*

15. Schoenberg, *Theory of Harmony,* 370. See also Susan McClary, *Feminine Endings: Music, Gender, and Sexuality* (Minnesota: University of Minnesota Press, 1991), 107.

16. Schoenberg to Strauss, 14 July 1909, in Slonimsky, *Music since 1900,* 207, and in Auner, "'Heart and Brain in Music,'" 126.

17. Webern, "The Path to Twelve-Note Composition," in *The Path to the New Music,* 53–54. "It is *impossible* for a person to have only *one* sensation at a time. One has *thousands* simultaneously." Schoenberg to Busoni, c. 18 August 1909, in *S/Reader,* 70–71.

18. "I strive for: complete liberation from all forms, from all symbols of cohesion and of logic. Thus: away with 'motivic working out.' Away with harmony as cement or bricks of a building." Ibid., 70. About the relation between this almost futuristic vision and Schoenberg's later adherence to order see Auner, "'Heart and Brain in Music.'"

19. Wilhelm Worringer, *Abstraction and Empathy: A Contribution to the Psychology of Style,* trans. Michael Bullock (London: Routledge and Kegan Paul, 1953), 15–17. Subsequent quotations come from pp. 16, 20, 35, 37, and 4.

20. José Ortega y Gasset, *The Dehumanization of Art and Other Essays in Art, Culture, and Literature,* trans. Helene Weyl (Princeton: Princeton University Press, 1948). (The Spanish original was published in 1925.) Worringer, *Abstraction and Empathy,* 23.

21. Georg Lukács, *Die Zerstörung der Vernunft, Werke,* ix, 708, quoted in Geoffrey C. W. Waite, "Worringer's *Abstraction and Empathy:* Remarks on Its Reception and on the Rhetoric of Criticism," in *The Turn of the Century: German Literature and Art, 1890–1915,* ed. Gerald Chapple and Hans H. Schulte, Modern German Studies 5, ed. Peter Heller (Bonn: Bonvier Verlag, Herbert Grundmann, 1981), 207.

22. Worringer, *Abstraction and Empathy*, 30.

23. See Worringer's preface to the third edition of the book, ibid., xiv–xv.

24. See Klaus Lankheit, "A History of the Almanac," in Wassily Kandinsky and Franz Marc, eds., *The* Blaue Reiter *Almanac*, New Documentary Edition by Klaus Lankheit, Documents of 20th-Century Art, ed. Robert Motherwell (New York: Viking, 1974), 30.

25. See Taruskin, "Scriabin and the Superhuman."

26. Schoenberg, "Twelve-Tone Composition," 9 May 1923, in *Style/Idea*, 208.

27. Clement Greenberg, "Foreword to an Exhibition of Willem de Kooning," in *Clement Greenberg: The Collected Essays and Criticism*, vol. 1, Perceptions and Judgments 1939–1944, ed. John O'Brian (Chicago: University of Chicago Press, 1986), 121.

28. Michael Strasser, "A Survivor from Warsaw as Personal Parable," *Music and Letters* 76, no. 1 (February 1995): 52–53.

29. After suggesting the song "I believe the Messiah will come," the English translation of which was not readily available to her, Chochem sent Schoenberg two versions of a partisan song, "Never say that there is only death for you," sung in the Vilna ghetto, along with the English translation of its text. See Chorine Chochem to Schoenberg, 2 April 1947, ASI corr.

30. Chochem to Schoenberg, no date, in Strasser, "A Survivor from Warsaw as Personal Parable," 53. Schoenberg to Chochem, 23 April 1947, in German in Nuria Schoenberg, ed., *Arnold Schoenberg (1874–1951): Lebensgeschichte in Begegnungen* (Klagenfurt: Ritter Klagenfurt, 1992), 410.

31. Initially Schoenberg offered his Variations for Windband or the section "Soul arrives in heaven" from *Jakobsleiter* to Koussevitzky (see Schoenberg's cable to Koussevitzky, 7 April 1944, ASI corr.). On 7 July 1947 he informed the conductor that now he could send a new composition. In Strasser, "A Survivor from Warsaw as Personal Parable," 54.

32. Strasser, "A Survivor from Warsaw as Personal Parable," 54; Schoenberg to Koussevitzky, 24 August 1947, ibid.

33. Schoenberg to Koussevitzky, 1 January 1948, ASI corr.

34. Because of Schoenberg's eye condition at that time, he used special large music paper.

35. After the premiere of the *Survivor* Schoenberg wrote to Leibowitz: "If I have promised you the world premiere of the Survivor, I am very sorry, I have entirely forgotten it, and I also did not know that Mr Frederick will come before you. It was a surprise to me and I did not know whether you had not already performed it in Darmstadt. But what is the advantage of a world premiere? I am sure you will make a premiere which will compare better than the very best world premiere which would be possible." 12 November 1948, in Stein, 257.

36. "Destiny and Digestion," *Time* (Albuquerque, 15 November 1948): 56.

37. See Schiller, *Bloch, Schoenberg, and Bernstein*, 97. The use of the Shema may have been suggested to Schoenberg by Rabbi Sonderling, who also provided the composer with a phonetic transcription of the text (ASI L25S29).

38. Reform Judaism rejects the notion of "reward and punishment" indicated by the second part (Deut. 11:12–21) and the particularistic view recalled by the third (Num. 15:37–41).

39. Unfamiliar with the Hebrew text, initially Schoenberg also left out the ex-

pression "oov<sup>e</sup>ḥol m<sup>e</sup>ōdeḥo" (with all thy might) from mm. 89–90, and "b<sup>e</sup>shivt<sup>e</sup>ḥo b<sup>e</sup>veteḥo" (when you sit in thy house) from m. 94 of the score he sent to Koussevitzky.

40. Donald L. Niewyk, ed., *Fresh Wounds: Early Narratives of Holocaust Survival* (Chapel Hill: University of North Carolina Press, 1998), 90. Schiller quotes a similar episode from Jewish combatant Jakob Smakowski's diary (in Reuben Ainsztein, *The Warsaw Ghetto Revolt* [New York: Holocaust Library, 1979], 164) in *Bloch, Schoenberg, and Bernstein,* 97–98.

41. Leibowitz's article (originally published in a German newspaper on 15 November 1949) is translated in Reich, *Schoenberg: A Critical Biography,* 222.

42. Leonard Stein to Kurt Frederick, 7 October 1948, in Schiller, *Bloch, Schoenberg, and Bernstein,* 96.

43. Schoenberg to List, 1 November 1948, in Nuria Schoenberg Nono, ed., *Arnold Schoenberg Self-portrait: A Collection of Articles, Program Notes and Letters by the Composer about His Own Works* (Pacific Palisades, CA: Belmont Music Publishers, 1988), 105.

44. Strasser, "A Survivor from Warsaw as Personal Parable," 60.

45. "The sergeant and his subordinates hit everybody; young or old, strong or sick, guilty or innocent."

46. Schoenberg to Paasen, 13 September 1942, in Lazar, 114.

47. Olin Downes, "Schoenberg Work Is Presented Here: Mitropoulos and Philharmonic Offer Cantata, 'Survivor From Warsaw,' at Carnegie Hall," *New York Times,* 14 April 1950.

48. Kurt List, "Schoenberg's New Cantata," *Commentary* 6, no. 5 (November 1948): 470, 472.

49. Theodor W. Adorno, "Cultural Criticism and Society," in Adorno, *Prisms,* 34.

50. Friedrich Torberg, *Mein ist die Rache* (Los Angeles: Privatdruck der Pazifischen Press, 1943).

51. "I read the book at once and it impressed me tremendously. True or not, this story characterizes the Nazis and their so-called philosophy in an extremely correct manner, all what they speak and do. . . . For several days I lived under the depressing feeling as if I would have been present at all these cruelties. I wished every anti-Nazi could read your book—then we need not be afraid that Germans might escape their punishment." Schoenberg to Torberg, 21 September 1943, ASI corr., orig. in English.

52. Adorno, "Arnold Schoenberg 1874–1951," 172.

53. Hannah Arendt, *Eichmann in Jerusalem: A Report on the Banality of Evil* (Middlesex: Penguin, 1965), 276.

54. List, "Schoenberg's New Cantata," 469–70. Subsequent quotations come from pp. 471–72.

55. Theodor W. Adorno, "Commitment," in *Notes to Literature,* vol. 2, ed. Rolf Tiedemann, trans. Shierry Weber Nicholsen (New York: Columbia University Press, 1991), 87–88.

56. Ibid.

57. Cf. Saul Friedländer, *Reflection of Nazism: An Essay on Kitsch and Death* (New York: Harper and Row, 1984).

58. Adorno, "Arnold Schoenberg 1874–1951," 172.

59. Olin Downes, "Schoenberg Work Is Presented Here." Reacting to Downes's review, Schoenberg wrote angrily to Mitropoulos: "I would like to learn whether Mr.

Olin Downes was right when he wrote about action—I say action in the cantata—according to which the singers took off their coats. It seems to me that you should have seen that I did not compose such an action, not only because of higher taste, but also because the concert stage is not a theatre." Schoenberg to Mitropoulos, 26 April 1950, in *S/Reader,* 346.

60. See Susan Gubar, *Poetry after Auschwitz: Remembering What One Never Knew* (Bloomington: Indiana University Press, 2003).

61. See Richard Taruskin, "A Sturdy Musical Bridge to the 21st Century," *New York Times,* 24 August 1997.

62. René Leibowitz, "Le 'Survivant de Varsovie' d'Arnold Schoenberg," in *L'artiste et sa conscience* (Paris: L'Arche, 1950), 101.

63. See Schoenberg to Rudolf Kolisch, 27 July 1932 ("my works are twelve-note *compositions,* not *twelve-note* compositions"), in Stein, 164–65.

64. Theodor W. Adorno, *Minima Moralia: Reflections from Damaged Life,* trans. E. F. N. Jephcott (London: NLB, 1974), 25.

65. Ringer, 203.

66. See Taruskin, "A Sturdy Musical Bridge to the 21st Century."

67. Ringer, 203.

## CHAPTER 9

1. "The Last Vision of Adolph Willette" (1926), *Berliner Tageblatt* (5 February 1926), Bio. 289, ASI doc., in Ringer, 178.

2. When in 1944 Otto Kallir recounted to the composer how he had found Gerstl's paintings, Schoenberg bitterly remarked in the margin of Kallir's letter: "Talent is fate. Very talented—to remind me of this right now." Kallir's letter to Schoenberg, 9 September 1944, in Jane Kallir, *Arnold Schoenberg's Vienna* (New York: Galerie St. Etienne and Rizzoli, 1984), 90n27.

3. Ringer, 191.

4. Schoenberg, "My Attitude toward Politics" (1950), in *Style/Idea,* 505.

5. List to Schoenberg, 11 December 1945, ASI corr., and Schoenberg to List, 24 January 1946, in Stein, 237–38.

6. Schoenberg to Dr. S. M. Neches, Dean, Western Jewish Institute, 7 July 1945, ASI corr., orig. in English.

7. "A Dangerous Game" (9 October 1944), ASI doc., orig. in English.

8. Schoenberg to List, 17 October 1944, in Stein, 219.

9. Schoenberg to Rufer, 25 May 1948, orig. in German, ibid., 255.

10. "Does the World Lack a Peace-Hymn?" (1928), in *Style/Idea,* 501.

11. Torberg to Schoenberg, 5 October 1943; Schoenberg to Torberg, 10 October 1947; Torberg to Schoenberg, 21 January 1949; and Schoenberg to Torberg, 31 January 1949, ASI corr.

12. Schoenberg to Torberg, 4 March 1949, ASI corr.

13. Schoenberg to Torberg, 29 March 1949, ASI corr. The reference is to Ernest Bevin (1881–1951), foreign secretary of the British Labour government, who opposed Zionist claims for a Jewish State.

14. In Schoenberg's library there is a copy of Dagobert David Runes's *Jordanlieder,*

dedicated to the composer on his birthday, 13 September 1949. Schoenberg thanked Runes for the present on 21 October 1949 (see ASI corr.)

15. Translation by Martin Thurn-Mithoff, in Arnold Schönberg, *Das Chorwerk*, cond. Pierre Boulez, Sony S2K 44571.

16. Schoenberg to Rufer, 25 May 1948, in Stein, 255.

17. Schoenberg's letter to Jane Lundblad (11 June 1949, ASI corr.) makes it clear that the composer did not write *Dreimal tausend Jahre* on commission from *Prisma*.

18. Originally bearing the opus number 49B, *Dreimal tausend Jahre* for four-part mixed chorus is related to Schoenberg's 1929 settings of three German folk songs (*Three Folksongs*), the revised first number of which he included in his *Three Folksongs*, op. 49 (1948). The only reference to Schoenberg's intention to offer the series of op. 50 to Israel is his letter to Chemjo Vinaver on 29 May 1951. See Chemjo Vinaver, ed., *Anthology of Jewish Music: Sacred Chant and Religious Folk Song of the Eastern European Jews* (New York: Edward B. Marks Music Corporation, 1953), 203.

19. Handwritten copy in ASI, 418c U450, orig. in German, my translation.

20. The second version of Schoenberg's text, sent to Torberg, 10 June 1949, ASI corr. In *S. Werke* B/19, 138, orig. in English.

21. Schoenberg to Torberg, 10 June 1949, ASI corr.

22. "Whosoever ventured to silence this eternal discourse of ours, / Whosoever tried to destroy us, / Haman of Persia, / or the Pharaoh of Egypt, / Titus of Rome, or the Führer of Germany, / Has only succeeded in destroying himself. / It cannot be otherwise. / Nobody can destroy God. / Nobody can destroy Israel, His witness." Torberg's text in Torberg to Schoenberg, 16 June 1949, ASI corr.; Schoenberg's initial request to Torberg, 29 March and 20 June 1949, ASI corr.

23. As in *Moses und Aron*, Schoenberg planned to set the text for mixed chorus (singing and speaking) and orchestra, based on a combinatorial row. The incomplete fair copy is dated 18 May 1949. (For the sketches see *S. Werke* B/19, 139–43.)

24. Schoenberg to Torberg, 20 June 1949, ASI corr.

25. Torberg to Schoenberg, 30 July 1949, ASI corr.

26. Mäckelmann, *Arnold Schönberg und das Judentum*, 350.

27. Putterman to Schoenberg, no date (1943), ASI corr.; Schoenberg to Putterman, 12 November 1943, ASI corr., orig. in English.

28. "Who is like unto Thee, O Lord, among the mighty / Who is like unto Thee, glorious in holiness, / Fearful in praises, doing wonders? / Thy children beheld Thy sovereign power, / As Thou didst cleave the sea before Moses; they exclaimed, / 'This is my God! The Lord shall reign forever and ever.'" (Text sent by Putterman on 23 November 1943 to Schoenberg. ASI corr.)

29. Schoenberg to Putterman, 15 December 1943, ASI corr.

30. *S. Werke* B/19, 145.

31. Putterman to Schoenberg, 22 December 1943, ASI corr.

32. See *S. Werke* B/19, 146–49.

33. Putterman to Schoenberg, 1 March and 19 May 1944, ASI corr.; Putterman to Schoenberg, 19 May 1944, ASI corr.

34. Putterman to Schoenberg, 14 November 1944, ASI corr.

35. "But I want to use the opportunity of this letter to tell you that I have composed a 'Kol Nidre,' which you could acquire from G. Schirmer. . . . This piece is, as regards to its text very different from the usual Kol Nidre. It is my own idea of what

the persecuted Jews of Spain might have prayed, and I can not deny that in ortho-dox circles it might arouse some opposition." Schoenberg to Putterman, 13 Febru-ary 1945, ASI corr., partially in Lazar, 133n116. Reply by Putterman to Schoenberg, 27 December 1945, ASI corr.

36. Putterman to Schoenberg, 11 October 1950, ASI corr.

37. Halpern to Schoenberg, 2 May 1950; Schoenberg to Halpern, 13 May 1950, ASI corr.

38. Vinaver to Schoenberg, 29 May 1950, ASI corr.

39. Schoenberg to Vinaver, 24 June 1950, ASI corr.

40. In a review Kurt List blamed Vinaver for having more of a musicological than a musical interest: "by using the reformed tune of the 19th century, or even more archeological tradition . . . [Vinaver] banishes music to the realm of musicology." Kurt List, "A Year of Jewish Music: Creative Effort in Concert Hall and Synagogue," *Commentary* 7 (February 1949): 183.

41. Vinaver to Schoenberg, 29 June 1950, ASI corr.

42. Vinaver's transcription of the text, with markings for short and long syllables, also helped him. *S. Werke* B/19, 102–3.

43. Schoenberg to Leibowitz about the performance of *Sprechgesang* in the *Survivor*, 19 November 1948, in Stein, 257.

44. Schoenberg to Vinaver, 29 May 1951, ASI corr.

45. The apparent exceptions are almost certainly mistakes. A misreading of notes in C clef in the second soprano part in m. 32 in which the two missing notes of the presented hexachord should be F and G♭ explains the otherwise out-of-place D and E♭ in the soprano clef. The only other instance of notes free of hexachordal consid-erations is not so easily explainable. In the four lower parts in m. 51 the second and third chords consist of notes seven through twelve of the inverted set, except two notes, one of which (G♯) is a repetition of note twelve (this would be the only case of note repetition in a given hexachordal constellation in the entire piece), and note C, which does not belong to the presented hexachord.

46. See Taruskin, "Scriabin and the Superhuman," especially 349–59.

47. In Jelena Hahl-Koch, ed., *Arnold Schoenberg, Wassily Kandinsky: Letters, Pictures and Documents,* trans. John C. Crawford (London: Faber and Faber, 1984), 89.

48. Vinaver to Schoenberg, 14 September 1950, in *S. Werke* B/19, 103. Used as the pronunciation of the sacred tetragammaton YHVH, Adonay also acquired sanc-tity, and thus in writing it is usually substituted by two letters.

49. Schoenberg's secretary to Vinaver, 3 November 1950, ibid.

50. "The Relationship to the Text," in *Style/Idea,* 144.

51. Honoré de Balzac, *Louis Lambert,* trans. Katharine Prescott Wormeley (Boston: Robert Brothers, 1889), 8.

52. Schoenberg to Dehmel, 13 December 1912, in Stein, 35–36.

53. *The Biblical Way,* 241.

54. Ibid., 305.

55. "III. a) Anti-Semites personify me as a Jew, my direction as Jewish.

b) a) but almost no Jews have followed my direction

b) in contrast, perhaps the only ones who have continued further in my direction are Aryans: Anton von Webern, Alban Berg, Winfried Zillig, Norbert von Hannenheim, Nikos Skalkottas

c) and the composers (except for my pupils) who stand closest to me are Aryans: Bartok, Hauer, and Hindemith."

"My Enemies," 6 October 1933, in *S/Reader,* 242. In 1950 Schoenberg wrote: "It is curious that Jews are always the last ones to accept my achievements, whether in Israel or in the rest of the world. They perform everything: Debussy, Ravel, Hindemith, Stravinsky, Shostakovich, Bartok etc.—but not me! In spite of my contributions, they are my greatest enemies." "Four Statements," 28 January 1950, ibid., 340.

56. Schoenberg to Albert Einstein, 1 January 1924, in Randol Schoenberg, "Arnold Schoenberg and Albert Einstein," 155; Schoenberg to the editor of *The Jewish Year Book,* 28 March 1946, in Stein, 238. The attachment of Schoenberg's list of compositions did not survive.

57. Schoenberg to Ödön Pártos, 15 June 1951, in Stuckenschmidt, *Schoenberg,* 519.

58. See *S. Werke* B/19, 119.

59. ASI man. 134, orig. in German.

60. Arnold Schoenberg, *Moderne Psalmen,* ed. Rudolf Kolisch (Mainz: Schott, 1956), my translations.

61. André Neher in his chapter on Schoenberg (in *They Made Their Souls Anew,* trans. David Maisel, SUNY Series in Modern Jewish Literature and Culture, ed. Sarah Blacher Cohen [New York: State University of New York Press, 1990], 150) impugns the significance of this text because of its uniqueness.

62. Ernst Gombrich, *The Visual Arts in Vienna Circa 1900: Reflections on the Jewish Catastrophe* (On the Occasion of the Seminar Fin de Siècle Vienna and Its Jewish Cultural Influences, 17 November 1996) (Spider Web, 1997), 9.

## POSTSCRIPT

1. Octavio Paz, "The Castle of Purity," in Octavio Paz, *Marcel Duchamp: Appearance Stripped Bare,* trans. Rachel Phillips and Donald Gardner (New York: Viking, 1978), 89–90.

2. Stéphane Mallarmé, *Igitur ou la folie d'Elbehnon* (Paris: Librairie Gallimard, 1925), 63.

3. Mallarmé to Henri Cazalis, 14 May 1867, trans. Bradford Cook, in Stéphane Mallarmé, *Selected Poetry and Prose,* ed. Mary Ann Caws (New York: New Directions, 1982), 87–88.

4. Vladimir Jankélévitch, *Le pur et l'impur* (Paris: Flammarion, 1960), 9. Subsequent quotations come from pp. 8, 25–26, 15, 24, and 16.

5. Mary Douglas, *Purity and Danger: An Analysis of the Concepts of Pollution and Taboo* (London: Routledge, 1966), 114.

6. Charles H. Hinnant, *Purity and Defilement in* Gulliver's Travels (New York: St. Martin's Press, 1987), ix.

7. Jacob Neusner, *The Idea of Purity in Ancient Judaism,* The Haskell Lectures, 1972–1973, Studies in Judaism in Late Antiquity from the First to the Seventh Century 1, ed. Jacob Neusner (Leiden: E. J. Brill, 1973), 1.

8. Maimonides, *Mishnah Torah: The Book of Cleanness,* viii, *Immersion Pools* 11:12, trans. Herbert Danby (New Haven: Yale University Press, 1954), 535; Neusner, *The Idea of Purity in Ancient Judaism,* 7.

9. W. Robertson Smith, *The Religion of the Semites* (1899), ibid., 9; Baruch A. Levine, *In the Presence of the Lord: Aspects of Ritual in Ancient Israel* (1974), ibid.

10. *The Anchor Bible. Leviticus 1–16.* A New Translation with Introduction and Commentary by Jacob Milgrom (New York: Doubleday, 1991), 766–67. Subsequent quotations come from pp. 1002–1003.

11. Ibid. About dietary laws in Leviticus see Douglas, *Purity and Danger,* especially 42–58.

12. Michael Newton, *The Concept of Purity at Quamram and in the Letters of Paul* (Cambridge: Cambridge University Press, 1985), 7.

13. Neusner, *The Idea of Purity in Ancient Judaism,* 11. Subsequent quotations come from pp. 72, 78, and 108.

14. Ibid., 63.

15. St. Paul was especially influential in shifting focus from ritual impurity to moral impurity as sin. See Jonathan Klawans, *Impurity and Sin in Ancient Judaism* (Oxford: Oxford University Press, 2000), especially 150–57.

16. Paul Ricoeur, *The Symbolism of Evil,* trans. Emerson Buchanan (Boston: Beacon Press, 1967), 7–8. Subsequent quotations come from pp. 27–29.

17. See "Purity" in *Encyclopedia Judaica,* vol. 13, 1411. The Sanhedrin contains descriptions of courts of justice and judicial procedures. It is disputed whether its content reflects historical facts or an ideal.

18. Barrington Moore, *Moral Purity and Persecution in History* (Princeton: Princeton University Press, 2000), xi.

19. M. J. H. M. Poorthuis and Joshua Schwartz, eds., *Purity and Holiness: The Heritage of Leviticus* (Leiden: Brill, 2000), 21. Subsequent quotations come from pp. 22–23.

20. Chamberlain, *The Foundations of the Nineteenth Century,* vol. 1, 392. Subsequent quotations come from pp. 389, 317, and 319.

21. Alfred Schultz, *Race or Mongrel* (Boston: L. C. Page, 1908), 7. Inspired by the racial theories of A. de Gobineau, H. S. Chamberlain, A. Wirts, and L. Woltman, Schultz intended his book as anti-immigration propaganda. Subsequent quotations come from pp. 34–35 and 44.

22. "It has, besides, been shown that the fertility of intermarriages is much below that of pure Jewish marriage, and consequently the proportion of persons of mixed descent would decrease in geometrical proportions." "All history points to the purity of the race; some anthropological facts are against it." *The Jewish Encyclopedia,* vol. 10 (New York: Funk and Wagnall's, 1905), 284.

23. Clement Greenberg, "Abstract Art," *The Nation* (15 April 1944), in *Greenberg: The Collected Essays and Criticism,* 203–4.

24. Mark A. Cheetham, *The Rhetoric of Purity: Essentialist Theory and the Advent of Abstract Painting* (Cambridge: Cambridge University Press, 1991), 14.

25. Schoenberg repeatedly made the comparison between divine and artistic creation: "I have often not known immediately if something I have written is beautiful, only that it was necessary. 'And God saw that it was good,' but only after he had finished creating." "Aphorisms from *Die Musik,*" 1909, in *S/Reader,* 65.

26. Cheetham, *The Rhetoric of Purity,* xii.

27. Plotinus, *Enneads,* trans. Stephen Mackenna (London: Faber and Faber, 1956), V, 5, 7; quoted ibid., 5.

28. Ibid., 22.

29. Ibid., 105.

30. Ibid., 135.

31. Wassily Kandinsky, *Concerning the Spiritual in Art and Painting in Particular* (1912), Documents of Modern Art 5 (New York: George Wittenborn, 1947), 28, 26.

32. Quoted in Cheetham, *The Rhetoric of Purity,* 17.

33. Schoenberg, *Theory of Harmony,* 413. Subsequent quotations come from pp. 128–29, 326, and 387.

34. Schoenberg, "Gustav Mahler," in *Style and Idea,* 464.

35. In his notes to his planned book on the musical idea he admitted that presently it was impossible for him to define the "total goal" in musical terms. But then he added: "But if one sets out to reach Utopia, then at most the route can be correct." Schoenberg, *The Musical Idea,* 149.

36. *The Biblical Way,* 201.

37. Jankélévitch, *Le pur et l'impur,* 8.

38. In his notes about the musical idea Schoenberg wrote: "The joining of like kinds is unfruitful (racial purity). We shall see how far the Germans get with this" (*Musical Idea,* 149). In his last psalm (unnumbered psalm "Inzucht, Blutschande . . ." [Inbreeding, incest]) he stated: "In breeding, incest is forbidden, because they destroy the race. National inbreeding, national incest is as dangerous to the race as to the family and the people." In Stuckenschmidt, *Arnold Schoenberg,* 520.

39. "Sex is a function, like breathing, sleeping, eating, but it is more formidable than the rest. If it is not satisfied, everything collapses, brain, nerves, etc. One cannot cheat nature. It takes revenge. Unfortunately we know nothing about this force and our education taught us nothing about this most important thing." Bloch to his wife, 20 November 1924, Lew. 2, 546.

40. Lazar Saminsky, *Music of Our Day: Essentials and Prophesies* (New York: Thomas Y. Crowell, 1932), 117. Subsequent quotations come from pp. 118–119, 121, 117, and 124.

41. Saminsky, *Music of the Ghetto and the Bible,* 73. Subsequent quotations come from pp. 3, 76, and 7.

42. Jankélévitch, *Le pur et l'impur,* 15.

43. David Biale, "The Melting Pot and Beyond: Jews and the Politics of American Identity," in Biale et al., *Insider/Outsider,* 29–30.

# BIBLIOGRAPHY

Adorno, Theodor W. "Arnold Schoenberg 1874–1951." In *Prisms*. Translated by Samuel and Shierry Weber, 147–72. London: Neville Spearman, 1967.

———. "Commitment." In *Notes to Literature*. Vol. 2. Edited by Rolf Tiedemann. Translated by Shierry Weber Nicholsen, 76–94. New York: Columbia University Press, 1991.

———. "Cultural Criticism and Society." In *Prisms*. Translated by Samuel and Shierry Weber, 17–34. London: Neville Spearman, 1967.

———. *Minima Moralia: Reflections from Damaged Life*. Translated by E. F. N. Jephcott. London: NLB, 1974.

———. *Philosophy of Modern Music*. Translated by Anne G. Mitchell and Wesley V. Blomster. New York: Continuum, 1985.

Ahad, Ha'am. *Nationalism and the Jewish Ethic: Basic Writings of Ahad Ha'am*. Edited by Hans Kohn. New York: Herzl, 1962.

*The Anchor Bible. Leviticus 1–16*. A New Translation with Introduction and Commentary by Jacob Milgrom. New York: Doubleday, 1991.

An-sky, Semyon. *The Jewish Artistic Heritage: An Album*. Edited by Alexander Kantsedikas. Moscow: "RA," 1994.

Apter-Gabriel, Ruth, ed. *Tradition and Revolution: The Jewish Renaissance in Russian Avant-Garde Art 1912–1928*. Jerusalem: Israel Museum, 1987.

Arendt, Hannah. *Eichmann in Jerusalem: A Report on the Banality of Evil*. Middlesex: Penguin, 1965.

———. *The Origins of Totalitarianism*. New York: Harcourt Brace, 1973.

———. *Rahel Varnhagen: The Life of a Jewish Woman*. Revised edition. Translated by Richard and Clara Winston. New York: Harcourt, Brace, Jovanovich, 1974.

Armitage, Merle, ed. *Schoenberg: Articles by Arnold Schoenberg, Erwin Stein [et al.] 1929–1937*. New York: Freeport, 1937.

Auner, Joseph. "'Heart and Brain in Music': The Genesis of Schoenberg's *Die glück-

*liche Hand.*" In *Constructive Dissonance: Arnold Schoenberg and the Transformation of Twentieth-Century Culture.* Edited by Juliane Brand and Christopher Hailey, 112–30. Berkeley: University of California Press, 1997.

———. *A Schoenberg Reader: Documents of a Life.* New Haven: Yale University Press, 2003.

———. "Schoenberg's Handel Concerto and the Ruins of Tradition." *Journal of the American Musicological Society* 49, no. 2 (summer 1996): 264–313.

Baigell, Matthew, and Milly Heyd, eds. *Complex Identities: Jewish Consciousness and Modern Art.* New Brunswick, NJ: Rutgers University Press, 2001.

Balibar, Etienne, and Immanuel Wallerstein. *Race, Nation, Class: Ambiguous Identities.* Translated by Chris Turner. London: Verso, 1991.

Balzac, Honoré de. *Louis Lambert.* Translated by Katharine Prescott Wormeley. Boston: Roberts Brothers, 1889.

———. *Seraphita.* Translated by Katharine Prescott Wormeley. Boston: Roberts Brothers, 1889.

Baron, Salo W. *The Russian Jew under Tsars and Soviets.* New York: Macmillan, 1976.

Barzun, Jacques. *Race: A Study in Modern Superstition.* London: Methuen, 1938.

Beizer, Mikhail. *The Jews of St. Petersburg: Excursions through a Noble Past.* Edited by Martin Gilbert. Translated by Michael Sherbourne. Philadelphia: Edward E. Elson, 1989.

Bellman, Jonathan. *The Exotic in Western Music.* Boston: Northeastern University Press, 1998.

Berl, Heinrich. *Das Judentum in der Musik.* Stuttgart: Deutsche Verlags-Anstalt, 1926.

Berlioz, Hector, and Richard Strauss. *Treatise on Instrumentation.* Translated by Theodore Front. New York: Edwin F. Kalmus, 1948.

Biale, David, Michael Galchinsky, and Susan Heschel, eds. *Insider/Outsider: American Jews and Multiculturalism.* Berkeley: University of California Press, 1998.

Binder, A. W. *Biblical Chant.* New York: Philosophical Library, 1959.

Bloch, Ernest. "Man and Music." Translated from the original French by Waldo Frank. *Seven Arts* 1, no. 5 (March 1917): 493–502. Reprinted in *Musical Quarterly* 19, no. 4 (October 1933): 375–79.

Bloch, Ernst. *The Principle of Hope.* 3 vols. Translated by Neville Paice, Stephen Paice, and Paul Knight. Oxford: Basil Blackwell, 1986.

———. *The Utopian Function of Art and Literature: Selected Essays.* Translated by Jack Zipes and Frank Mecklenburg. Cambridge, MA: MIT Press, 1988.

Bloch, Ernst, et al. *Aesthetics and Politics.* London: NLB, 1977.

Bloch, Suzanne. "Bloch's Reaction to Religion at Age 19." *Ernest Bloch Society Bulletin* 13 (1981): 1.

———. "Ernest Bloch." *Keynote* (July 1980): 19–23.

———. "Ernest Bloch and Roger Sessions at the Cleveland Institute." *Ernest Bloch Society Bulletin* 17 (1985): 4–7.

———. "Ernest Bloch—Student of Choral Music: Some Personal Recollections." *American Choral Review* 10, no. 2 (winter 1968): 51–54.

———. "Lucienne Bréval." *Ernest Bloch Society Bulletin* 18–19 (1986–87): 4–7.

———. "The Mass Bloch Never Wrote." *Ernest Bloch Society Bulletin* 4 (1972): 1.

Bloch Dimitroff, Lucienne. "Impressions of Ernest Bloch." In *The Spiritual and Artistic Odyssey of Ernest Bloch: A Centenary Retrospective,* 33–34. Charleston, SC: Piccolo Spoleto, 1980.

Bohlman, Philip V. *Israeli Folk Music: Songs of the Early Pioneers.* Edited by Hans Nathan. Recent Researches in the Oral Traditions of Music 4. Madison: A-R Editions, 1994.

Bolkosky, Sidney M. *The Distorted Image: German Jewish Perceptions of Germans and Germany, 1918–1935.* New York: Elsevier, 1975.

Borel, Jacques. *"Séraphîta" et le mysticisme balzacien.* Paris: Librairie José Corti, 1967.

Brand, Juliane, and Christopher Hailey, eds. *Constructive Dissonance: Arnold Schoenberg and the Transformation of Twentieth-Century Culture.* Berkeley: University of California Press, 1997.

Brand, Juliane, Christopher Hailey, and Donald Harris, eds. *The Berg-Schoenberg Correspondence: Selected Letters.* New York: W. W. Norton, 1987.

Braun, Joachim. "The Jewish Art School in Russia." In *Proceedings of the World Congress on Jewish Music,* Jerusalem, 1978. Edited by Judith Cohen, 198–203. Tel-Aviv: Institute for the Translation of Hebrew Literature, 1982.

———. *Jews and Jewish Elements in Soviet Music: A Study of a Socio-National Problem in Music.* Tel Aviv: Israeli Music, 1978.

Brod, Max. *Adolf Schreiber: ein Musikschicksal.* Berlin: Im Welt, 1921.

———. *Israel's Music.* Tel Aviv: Sefer Press, 1951.

Calvino, Italo. "The Count of Monte Cristo." In *t zero.* Translated by William Weaver, 137–52. New York: Harcourt, Brace, Jovanovich, 1976.

Campbell, Stuart, ed. and trans. *Russians on Russian Music, 1830–1880: An Anthology.* Cambridge: Cambridge University Press, 1994.

Carpenter, Patricia, and Severine Neff. *Arnold Schoenberg, The Musical Idea and the Logic, Technique, and Art of Its Presentation.* New York: Columbia University Press, 1995.

Chamberlain, Houston Stewart. *The Foundations of the Nineteenth Century.* 2 vols. Translated by John Lees. London: John Lane, Bodley Head, 1911.

———. *La genèse du XIX^me siècle.* Translated by Robert Godet. Paris: Librairie Payot, 1913.

Cheetham, Mark A. *The Rhetoric of Purity: Essentialist Theory and the Advent of Abstract Painting.* Cambridge: Cambridge University Press, 1991.

Cohen, Richard I. *Jewish Icons: Art and Society in Modern Europe.* Berkeley: University of California Press, 1998.

Cross, Charlotte M., and Russell A. Berman. *Political and Religious Ideas in the Works of Arnold Schoenberg.* New York: Garland, 2000.

Dawidowicz, Lucy S. *The Jewish Presence: Essays on Identity and History.* New York: Holt, Rinehart and Winston, 1960.

Dessau, Paul. "Arnold Schoenbergs 'Kol nidre.'" Originally published in *Jewish Music Forum* (1941). Reprinted in *Notizen zu Noten.* Edited by Fritz Hennenberg, 105–9. Leipzig: Reclam, 1974.

Dijkstra, Bram. *Idols of Perversity: Fantasies of Feminine Evil in Fin-de-siècle Culture.* New York, Oxford: Oxford University Press, 1986.

Disraeli, Benjamin. *Coningsby or the New Generation.* The World's Classics. London: Oxford University Press, 1931.

Douglas, Mary. *Purity and Danger: An Analysis of the Concepts of Pollution and Taboo.* London: Routledge, 1966.

Downes, Olin. "Bloch, Composer Here to Conduct." *New York Times,* 27 March 1934.

———. "Bloch's Profession of Faith: His Setting of a Jewish Sacred Service Presents Composer's Conception of the Unity of Man and Nature." *New York Times*, 6 August 1933.

———. "Composer Conducts Symphony. Bloch's 'Jewish Poems' Create Profound Impression." *Boston Post*, 24 March 1917.

———. "Ernest Bloch at Sixty." *New York Times*, 27 October 1940.

———. "Ernest Bloch in the Academy: Recognition for a Great Composer Who Has Made Home Here—His Music Deserves More Attention from Performing Artists." *New York Times*, 3 May 1947.

———. "Ernest Bloch, the Swiss Composer, on the Influence of Race in Composition." *Musical Observer* 14, no. 3 (March 1917): 11.

———. *Olin Downes on Music: A Selection from His Writings during the Half-Century 1906 to 1955*. Edited by Irene Downes. New York: Simon and Schuster, 1957.

———. "Schoenberg Work Is Presented Here: Mitropoulos and Philharmonic Offer Cantata, 'Survivor from Warsaw,' at Carnegie Hall." *New York Times*, 14 April 1950.

———. "Schola Cantorum in Bloch's Premiere." *New York Times*, 12 April 1934.

Dubnow, Simon. *Nationalism and History: Essays on Old and New Judaism*. Edited by Koppel S. Pinson. Philadelphia: Jewish Publication Society of America, 1958.

Duker, Abraham G. "'Evreiskaia Starina': A Bibliography of the Russian-Jewish Historical Periodical." *Hebrew Union College Annual* 8–9 (Cincinnati, 1931–32): 525–603.

Efron, John M. *Defenders of the Race: Jewish Doctors and Race Science in Fin-de-siècle Europe*. New Haven: Yale University Press, 1994.

Einstein, Albert. *About Zionism: Speeches and Letters*. Translated and edited by Leon Simon. New York: Macmillan, 1931.

Eisenstein, Paula Baker. "Jewish Motives in an Early-20th-Century Work: Leo Zeitlin's *Eli Zion*." *International Journal of Musicology* 6 (1997): 231–79.

———. "Leo Zeitlin's Eli Zion: An Attribution Chiseled in Stone." *Strings* 6, no. 1 (July/August 1991): 18–24.

———. "Who Was 'L. Zeitlin' of the Society for Jewish Folk Music?" *Yivo Annual* 23 (1996): 233–57.

Elbaz, Andre E., ed. *Correspondance d'Edmond Fleg pendant l'affaire Dreyfus*. Paris: Librairie A.-G. Nizet, 1976.

Engel, Yuliy. *Glazami sovremennika: izbrannïye stat'i o russkoy muzïke 1898–1918* (Through the eyes of a contemporary: selected articles on Russian music). Edited by I. Kunin. Moscow: Sovetskiy Kompozitor, 1971.

———. "Pamyati V. V. Stasova" (To the memory of V. V. Stasov). *Russkaya muzïkal'naya gazeta* 41 (14 October 1907): 893.

Ennulat, Egbert M., ed. *Arnold Schoenberg Correspondence: A Collection of Translated and Annotated Letters Exchanged with Guido Adler, Pablo Casals, Emanuel Feuermann and Olin Downes*. Metuchen, NJ: Scarecrow Press, 1991.

Epstein, Marc Michael. *Dream of Subversion in Medieval Jewish Art and Literature*. University Park: Pennsylvania State University Press, 1997.

Ewen, David. *Hebrew Music: A Study and an Interpretation*. New York: Bloch, 1931.

Feuchtwanger, Lion. "Nationalisme et judaisme." *Revue juive de Genève* 3 (December 1934): 102–4.

Field, Geoffry G. *The Evangelist of Race: The Germanic Vision of Houston Stewart Chamberlain*. New York: Columbia University Press, 1981.

Fleg, Edmond. *Iezabel: Midrash ou histoire inspirée des écriture.* Paris: Lipschutz Editeur, 1927.

———. "Iezabel: Midrash ou histoire inspirée des écriture." *Revue littéraire juive* (May/ June 1927): 365–97.

———. *Why I Am a Jew.* Translated by Louise Waterman Wise. Edited by André Billy. New York: Bloch, 1945.

Flomenboim, Rita. "The Fate of Two Jewish Operas in the Soviet Union during the 1920s and 1930s." In *Verfemte Musik: Komponisten in den Diktaturen unseres Jahrhunderts.* Edited by Joachim Braun, Heidi Tamar Hoffmann, and Vladimír Karbusicky, 135–47. Frankfurt am Main: Peter Lang, 1997.

———. "The National School of Jewish Art Music: Joel Engel (1868–1927) and Michail Gnessin (1883–1957)." Ph.D. dissertation. Bar-Ilan University, 1996.

Frank, Waldo. *Our America.* New York: Boni & Liveright, 1919.

Frankel, Jonathan. *Prophecy and Politics: Socialism, Nationalism, and the Russian Jews 1862–1917.* Cambridge: Cambridge University Press, 1981.

Frankenstein, Alfred. "Bloch's 'Sacred Service' Heard First Time in S.F." *San Francisco Chronicle,* 29 March 1938.

Freud, Ernst, and Lucie Freud, eds. *Sigmund Freud, Briefe 1873–1939.* Frankfurt am Main: Fischer, 1980.

Friedheim, Philip. "Wagner and the Aesthetic of the Scream." *Nineteenth-Century Music* 7, no. 1 (summer 1983): 63–70.

Friedländer, Saul. *Reflection of Nazism: An Essay on Kitsch and Death.* New York: Harper and Row, 1984.

Gassenschmidt, Christoph. *Jewish Liberal Politics in Tsarist Russia, 1900–1914: The Modernization of Russian Jewry.* New York: New York University Press, 1995.

Gatti, Guido M. "Ernest Bloch." *Musical Quarterly* 7 (January 1921): 20–38.

Gershon, Stuart Weinberg. *Kol nidrei: Its Origin, Development, and Significance.* Northvale, NJ: Jason Aronson, 1994.

Gilman, Sander L. *Jewish Self-hatred: Anti-Semitism and the Hidden Language of the Jews.* Baltimore: Johns Hopkins University Press, 1986.

Gilroy, Paul. *Against Race: Imagining Political Culture beyond the Color Line.* Cambridge, MA: Belknap Press of Harvard University Press, 2000.

Glass, Sylvia. "Semitic Silhouettes xvi—Psalmist in Israel." *Opinion: A Journal of Jewish Life and Letters* 3 (October 1933): 14–17.

Goberman, David. *Graved Memories: Heritage in Stone from the Russian Jewish Pale.* New York: Rizzoli, 2000.

Godet, Robert. "Suisse—La musique en Suisse romande." *La revue musicale* 2, no. 5 (March 1921): 275.

———. "Suisse—La musique en Suisse romande." *La revue musicale* 2, no. 6 (April 1921): 83–84.

Goehr, Lydia. "Adorno, Schoenberg, and the *Totentanz der Prinzipien*—in Thirteen Steps." *Journal of the American Musicological Society* 56, no. 3 (fall 2003): 595–636.

Gojowy, Detlef. *Arthur Lourié und der russische Futurismus.* Laaber: Laaber-Verlag, 1993.

Goldberg, David Theo, and Michael Krausz, eds. *Jewish Identity.* Philadelphia: Temple University Press, 1993.

Gombrich, Ernst. *The Visual Arts in Vienna Circa 1900: Reflections on the Jewish Cata-*

*strophe*. On the Occasion of the Seminar Fin de Siècle Vienna and Its Jewish Cultural Influences, 17 November 1996. Spider Web, 1997.

Gottesman, Itzik Nakhmen. *Defining the Yiddish Nation: The Jewish Folklorists of Poland*. Raphael Patai Series in Jewish Folklore and Anthropology. Detroit: Wayne State University Press, 2003.

Gradenwitz, Peter. *The Music of Israel: Its Rise and Growth through 5000 Years*. New York: W. W. Norton, 1949.

————. *Of Music of Modern Israel*. New York: National Jewish Music Council, 1940.

Graetz, Heinrich. *History of the Jews*. 6 vols. Philadelphia: Jewish Publication Society of America, 1893.

Greenberg, Clement. *Clement Greenberg: The Collected Essays and Criticism*. Vol. 1, *Perceptions and Judgments 1939–1944*. Edited by John O'Brian. Chicago: University of Chicago Press, 1986.

Greenfeld, Liah. *Nationalism: Five Roads to Modernity*. Cambridge, MA: Harvard University Press, 1992.

Gubar, Susan. *Poetry after Auschwitz: Remembering What One Never Knew*. Bloomington: Indiana University Press, 2003.

Hahl-Koch, Jelena, ed. *Arnold Schoenberg, Wassily Kandinsky: Letters, Pictures and Documents*. Translated by John C. Crawford. London: Faber and Faber, 1984.

Harrison, Thomas. *1910: The Emancipation of Dissonance*. Berkeley: University of California Press, 1996.

Hatchinson, John, and Anthony D. Smith. *Nationalism*. Oxford: Oxford University Press, 1994.

Heller, Reinhold. *Edvard Munch: The Scream*. Art in Context. New York: Viking, 1973.

Heskes, Irene. *Passport to Jewish Music: Its History, Traditions, and Culture*. Westport, CT: Greenwood Press, 1994.

————. "Shapers of American Jewish Music: *Mailamm* and the Jewish Music Forum, 1931–62." *American Music* 15, no. 3 (fall 1997): 305–20

Heskes, Irene, and Arthur Wolfson, eds. *The Historic Contribution of Russian Jewry to Jewish Music*. New York: National Jewish Music Council, 1967.

Hinnant, Charles H. *Purity and Defilement in* Gulliver's Travels. New York: St. Martin's Press, 1987.

Hirshberg, Jehoash. *Music in the Jewish Community of Palestine 1880–1948: A Social History*. Oxford: Clarendon Press, 1995.

Holde, Artur. *Jews in Music: From the Age of Enlightenment to the Present*. New York: Philosophical Library, 1959.

Huxley, Aldous. *Brave New World*. New York: Harper & Row, 1946.

Idelsohn, Abraham Zvi. *Gesänge der jemenischen Juden*. Zum ersten Male gesammelt, erläutert und herausgegeben. Leipzig: Breitkopf & Härtel, 1914.

————. *Hebräisch-orientalischer Melodienschatz*. Vol. 9, *Der Volksgesang der osteuropäischen Juden*. Leipzig: Friedrich Hofmeister, 1932.

————. *Jewish Music: Its Historical Development*. New York: Dover, 1992.

————. "The Kol Nidrei Tune." *Hebrew Union College Annual* 8–9 (1931–32): 493–509. Reprinted in *Contributions to a Historical Study of Jewish Music*. Edited by Eric Werner. New York: Ktav, 1976.

————. "Musical Characteristics of East-European Jewish Folk-Song." *Musical Quarterly* 17, no. 4 (October 1932): 634–45.

————. "My Life (A Sketch)." *Jewish Music Journal* 2, no. 2 (May–June 1935). Reprinted in *Yuval* 5 (*The Abraham Zvi Idelsohn Memorial Volume*). Edited by I. Adler, B. Bayer, and E. Schleifer (1986): 18–23.

*Iz istorii yevreyskoy muziki* (From the history of Jewish music in Russia: proceedings of the international scientific conference "90 Years of the Jewish Folk Music Society in Petersburg-Petrograd [1908–1919]"). St. Petersburg, 27 October 1998. St. Petersburg: Jewish Community Center of St. Petersburg Center for Jewish Music, 2001.

Janik, Allan, and Stephen Toulman. *Wittgenstein's Vienna.* New York: Touchstone, 1973.

Jankélévitch, Vladimir. *Le pur et l'impur.* Paris: Flammarion, 1960.

Kallir, Jane. *Arnold Schoenberg's Vienna.* New York: Galerie St. Etienne and Rizzoli, 1984.

Kampf, Avram. *Jewish Experience in the Art of the Twentieth Century.* South Hadley, MA: Bergin & Garvey, 1984.

Kandinsky, Wassily. *Concerning the Spiritual in Art and Painting in Particular* (1912). Documents of Modern Art 5. New York: George Wittenborn, 1947.

Kandinsky, Wassily, and Franz Marc, eds. *The* Blaue Reiter *Almanac.* New Documentary Edition by Klaus Lankheit. Documents of 20th-Century Art. Edited by Robert Motherwell. New York: Viking, 1974.

Karl, Frederick R. *Modern and Modernism: The Sovereignty of the Artist 1885–1925.* New York: Atheneum, 1985.

Kieval, Herman. "The Curious Case of Kol nidre." *Commentary* 46, no. 4 (October 1968): 53–58.

Kimmey, John A., Jr., ed. *The Arnold Schoenberg—Hans Nachod Collection.* Detroit Studies in Music Bibliography 41. Detroit: Information Coordinators, 1979.

Klawans, Jonathan. *Impurity and Sin in Ancient Judaism.* Oxford: Oxford University Press, 2000.

Klier, John Doyle. "The Russian Jewish Intelligentsia and the Search for National Identity." In *Ethnic and National Issues in Russia and East European History: Selected Papers from the Fifth World Congress of Central and East European Studies, Warsaw, 1995.* Edited by John Morison, 131–45. New York: St. Martin's Press, 2000.

————. "Zhid: The Biography of a Russian Pejorative." *Slavonic and East European Review* 60, no. 1 (1982): 1–15.

Knapp, Alexander. "The Jewishness of Bloch: Subconscious or Conscious?" *Proceedings of the Royal Musical Association* 97 (1970–71): 99–112.

————. "The Life and Music of Ernest Bloch." *Jewish Quarterly* 28, nos. 2–3 (summer–fall 1980): 26–30.

Krehbiel, H[enry]. E[dward]. "Ernest Bloch's Experiment In the Music of Jewry: A Jewish Composer and the Music Which He Feels To Be Racial—Spirit Versus Traditional Idiom—M. Bloch's Views on Form and the Radicalism of Novices—Themes from His Work." *New York Tribune,* 29 April 1917.

————. "Song Recital Vies for Honors with Concert." *New York Tribune,* 6 November 1920.

Kuhn, Ernst, Jascha Nemtsov, and Andreas Wehrmeyer, eds. *"Samuel" Goldenberg und "Schmuyle": Jüdisches und Antisemitisches in der russischen Musikkultur. Ein internationales Symposium.* Studia Slavica musicologica 27. Berlin: Ernst Kuhn, 2003.

Kushner, David Z. "A Commentary on Ernest Bloch's Symphonic Works." *Redford Review* 21, no. 3 (September 1967): 99–137.

————. *Ernest Bloch: A Guide to Research.* Garland Composer Resource Manuals. Edited by Guy A. Marco. New York: Garland, 1988.

————. *Ernest Bloch and His Music.* Glasgow: William MacLellan, 1973.

————. "Ernest Bloch, Daniel Gregory Mason and the Jewish Question." *American Music Teacher* 38, no. 6 (June–July 1989): 16–20.

————. "The 'Jewish' Works of Ernest Bloch." *Journal of Synagogue Music* (June 1985): 28–41.

Langer, Lawrence L. *Admitting the Holocaust: Collected Essays.* New York: Oxford University Press, 1995.

————. *The Holocaust and the Literary Imagination.* New Haven: Yale University Press, 1975.

Lazar, Moshe. "Arnold Schoenberg and His Doubles: A Psychodramatic Journey to His Roots." *Journal of the Arnold Schoenberg Institute* 17, nos. 1–2 (June and November 1994): 8–150.

Lefort, Claude. *L'invention démocratique: les limites de la domination totalitaire.* Paris: Fayard, 1981.

Leibowitz, René. *L'artiste et sa conscience.* Paris: L'Arche, 1950.

Leichtentritt, Hugo. *Serge Koussevitzy, the Boston Symphony Orchestra, and the New American Music.* Cambridge, MA: Harvard University Press, 1947.

Lessing, Theodor. *Der jüdische Selbsthaß.* Berlin: Jüdischer Verlag, 1930.

Levi, Erik. "Towards an Aesthetic of Fascist Opera." In *Fascism and Theatre: Comparative Studies on the Aesthetics and Politics of Performance in Europe, 1925–1945.* Edited by Günter Berghaus, 260–76. Providence: Berghahn, 1996.

Lewinski, Joseph and Emmanuelle Dijon. *Ernest Bloch: sa vie et sa pensée.* Vol. 1, *Les années de galères (1880–1916).* Geneva: Editions Slatkine, 1998.

————. *Ernest Bloch: sa vie et sa pensée.* Vol. 2, *La consécration américaine (1916–1930).* Geneva: Editions Slatkine, 2001.

————. *Ernest Bloch: sa vie et sa pensée.* Vol. 3, *Le retour en Europe (1930–1938).* Geneva: Editions Slatkine, 2005.

————. *Ernest Bloch: Sa vie et sa pensée.* Vol. 4, *Le havre de paix en Oregon (1939–1959).* Geneva: Editions Slatkine, 2004.

*Lexikon der Juden in der Musik: mit einem Titelverzeichnis jüdischer Werke.* Edited by Theo Stengel and Herbert Gerigk. Berlin: Bernhard Hahnefeld, 1940.

Leyda, Jay, and Sergei Bertensson, eds. and trans. *The Musorgsky Reader: A Life of Modest Petrovich Musorgky in Letters and Documents.* New York: W. W. Norton, 1947.

List, Kurt. "Ernest Bloch's 'Sacred Service': Musically Untraditional, but Authentically Jewish." *Commentary* 8 (December 1950): 586–89.

————. "Schoenberg's New Cantata." *Commentary* 6 (November 1948): 468–73.

————. "A Year of Jewish Music: Creative Effort in Concert Hall and Synagogue." *Commentary* 7 (February 1949): 174–84.

Locke, Ralph P. "Constructing the Oriental 'Other': Saint-Saëns's *Samson et Dalila.*" *Cambridge Opera Journal* 3, no. 3 (November 1991): 261–302.

Loeffler, James. "Concert Music." In *The YIVO Encyclopedia of East European Jewish History and Culture.* Edited by Gershon D. Hundert. New Haven: Yale University Press, 2008.

————. "'The Most Musical Nation': Jews, Culture, and Nationalism in the Late Russian Empire." Ph.D. dissertation. Columbia University, 2006.

———. "Society for Jewish Folk Music." In *The YIVO Encyclopedia of East European Jewish History and Culture*. Edited by Gershon D. Hundert. New Haven: Yale University Press, 2008.

———. "Yuliy Engel' i razvitiye yevreyskogo muzïkal'nogo natsional'nizma" ( Joel Engel and the development of Jewish musical nationalism). In *Iz istorii yevreyskoy muzïki v rossii* (On the history of Jewish music in Russia). Vol. 2, *Materialï mezhdunarodnoy nauchnoy konferentsii yevreyskaya professional'naya muzïka v rossii*. (Materials of the international scientific conference on the professional Jewish music in Russia). Edited by G. V. Kopytova and A. S. Frenkel, 251–64. St. Petersburg: Jewish Community Center of St. Petersburg Center for Jewish Music, Russian Institute for the History of the Arts, 2006.

Löwe, Heinz-Dietrich. *The Tsars and the Jews: Reform, Reaction and Anti-Semitism in Imperial Russia, 1772–1917*. Chur, Switzerland: Harwood, 1993.

Lukin, Binyamin. "Archive of the Jewish Historical and Ethnographic Society: History and Present Condition." *Jews in Eastern Europe* (summer 1993): 45–61.

Mäckelmann, Michael. *Arnold Schönberg und das Judentum: Der Komponist und sein religiöses, nationales und politisches Selbstverständnis nach 1921*. Hamburgischer Beiträge zur Musikwissenschaft 28. Edited by Constantin Floros. Hamburg: Karl Dieter Wagner, 1984.

———. "Ein Gebet für Israel, als die Synagogen brannten. Über Schönbergs 'Kol nidre'—zum Gedenken an den Pogrom der Kristallnacht 1938." *Neue Zeitschrift für Musik* 11 (November 1988): 3–8.

Mallarmé, Stéphane. *Igitur ou la folie d'Elbehnon*. Paris: Librairie Gallimard, 1925.

———. *Selected Poetry and Prose*. Edited by Mary Ann Caws. New York: New Directions, 1982.

Mannheim, Karl. *Ideology and Utopia: An Introduction to the Sociology of Knowledge*. Translated by Louis Wirth and Edward Shils. San Diego: Harcourt Brace Jovanovich, 1936.

Manuel, Frank E., and Fritzie P. Manuel. *Utopian Thought in the Western World*. Cambridge, MA: Belknap Press of Harvard University Press, 1979.

Marek, P. S. and Saul M. Ginzburg, eds. *Yevreyskiye narodnïye pesni v Rossii* (Yiddish folksongs in Russia). Reprint edited by Dov Noy. Ramat Gan: Bar-Ilan University Press, 1991.

Mason, Daniel Gregory. *Tune In America: A Study of Our Coming Musical Independence*. New York: Alfred A. Knopf, 1931.

Mauclair, Camille. "Le livret d'Opéra et le poème de drame lyrique." *La revue (Ancienne "Revue des revues")* 89 (1 January–15 March 1911): 471–72.

McClary, Susan. *Feminine Endings: Music, Gender, and Sexuality*. Minneapolis: University of Minnesota Press, 1991.

Moddel, Phillip. *Joseph Achron*. Tel Aviv: Israeli Music Publications, 1966.

Montagu, Ashley. *Man's Most Dangerous Myth: The Fallacy of Race*. 2nd ed. New York: Columbia University Press, 1945.

Moore, Barrington. *Moral Purity and Persecution in History*. Princeton: Princeton University Press, 2000.

Moore, MacDonald Smith. *Yankee Blues: Musical Culture and American Identity*. Bloomington: Indiana University Press, 1985.

Móricz, Klára. "Ancestral Voices: Anti-Semitism and Ernest Bloch's Racial Conception of Art." In *Western Music and Race.* Edited by Julie Brown, 102–14. Cambridge: Cambridge University Press, 2007.

———. "Anxiety, Abstraction, and Schoenberg's Gestures of Fear." In *Essays in Honor of László Somfai on His 70th Birthday: Studies in the Sources and the Interpretation of Music.* Edited by László Vikárius and Vera Lampert, 303–24. Lanham, MD: Scarecrow Press, 2005.

———. "The Confines of Judaism and the Illusiveness of Universality in Ernest Bloch's *Avodath Hakodesh* (Sacred Service)." *repercussions* 5, nos. 1–2 (spring–fall 1996): 184–241.

———. "Sealed Documents and Open Lives: Ernest Bloch's Private Correspondence." *Notes* 62, no. 1 (September 2005): 74–86.

———. "Sensuous Pagans and Righteous Jews: Changing Concepts of Jewish Identity in Ernest Bloch's *Jézabel* and *Schelomo*." *Journal of the American Musicological Society* 54, no. 3 (2001): 440–94.

Müller, Erich H. "Das Judentum in der Musik." In *Handbuch der Judenfrage: Die wichtigsten Tatsachen zur Beurteilung des jüdischen Volkes.* Edited by Theodor Fritsch, 324–34. Leipzig: Hammer, 1932.

National Jewish Music Council. *Commission A Jewish Musical Work! A Handbook of Procedures to Guide Organizations, Local Community Councils and Composers Who Will Participate in the National Jewish Music Council's Nation-wide Project to Encourage the Creation of New Jewish Musical Works.* New York: National Jewish Music Council, 1963.

Neher, André. *They Made Their Souls Anew.* Translated by David Maisel. SUNY Series in Modern Jewish Literature and Culture. Edited by Sarah Blacher Cohen. New York: State University of New York Press, 1990.

Nemtsov, Jascha, and Ernst Kuhn, eds. *Jüdische Musik in Sowjetrußland: die "Jüdische Nationale Schule" der zwanziger Jahre.* Berlin: Ernst Kuhn, 2002.

Neusner, Jacob. *The Idea of Purity in Ancient Judaism.* The Haskell Lectures, 1972–1973. Studies in Judaism in Late Antiquity from the First to the Seventh Century 1. Edited by Jacob Neusner. Leiden: E. J. Brill, 1973.

Newlin, Dika. "The Later Works of Ernest Bloch." *Musical Quarterly* 23, no. 4 (October 1947): 443–59.

———. "Self-revelation and the Law: Arnold Schoenberg in His Religious Works." *Yuval* 1 (1968): 204–20.

Newman, Ernest. "Bloch's Sacred Service." *Sunday Times* (London), 3 April 1938. Reprinted in *Ernest Bloch Society Bulletin* 4 (1972).

Newton, Michael. *The Concept of Purity at Quamram and in the Letters of Paul.* Cambridge: Cambridge University Press, 1985.

Niewyk, Donald L., ed. *Fresh Wounds: Early Narratives of Holocaust Survival.* Chapel Hill: University of North Carolina Press, 1998.

Oja, Carol J. *Making Music Modern: New York in the 1920s.* Oxford: Oxford University Press, 2000.

Olkhovsky, Yuri. *Vladimir Stasov and Russian National Culture.* Russian Music Studies 6. Edited by Malcolm Hamrick Brown. Ann Arbor, MI: UMI Research Press, 1983.

Ortega y Gasset, José. *The Dehumanization of Art and Other Essays in Art, Culture, and Literature.* Translated by Helene Weyl. Princeton: Princeton University Press, 1948.

Paoli, Domenico de, et al. *Lazare Saminsky: Composer and Civic Worker.* Eminent Composers of Hebrew Music. New York: Bloch, 1930.

Papp, Márta, and János Bojti, eds. and trans. *Modeszt Muszorgszkij: Levelek, dokumentumok, emlékezések* (Modest Musorgsky: letters, documents, reminiscences). Budapest: Kávé Kiadó, 1997.

Paz, Octavio. *Marcel Duchamp: Appearance Stripped Bare.* Translated by Rachel Phillips and Donald Gardner. New York: Viking, 1978.

Phleps, Thomas. "Zwölftöniges Theater—'Wiener Schüler' und Anverwandte in NS-Deutschland." (Twelve-tone theater—"Viennese students" and related figures in National Socialist Germany). In *"Entartete Musik" 1938—Weimar und die Ambivalenz: Ein Projekt der Hochschule für Musik Franz Liszt Weimar zum Kulturstadtjahr 1999.* Edited by Hanns-Werner Heister, 179–215. Saarbrücken: Pfau-Verlag, 2001.

Plotinus. *Enneads.* Translated by Stephen Mackenna. London: Faber and Faber, 1956.

Poorthuis, M. J. H. M., and Joshua Schwartz, eds. *Purity and Holiness: The Heritage of Leviticus.* Leiden: Brill, 2000.

Powell, Jonathan Anthony. "After Scriabin: Six Composers and the Development of Russian Music." Ph.D. dissertation. King's College, Cambridge, 1999.

Rabinovitch, Israel. *Of Jewish Music, Ancient and Modern.* Translated by A. M. Klein. Montreal: Book Center, 1952.

Rafael, Ruth. "Ernest Bloch at the San Francisco Conservatory of Music." *Western States Jewish Historical Quarterly* 9, no. 3 (April 1977): 195–215.

Rajner, Mirjam. "The Awakening of Jewish National Art in Russia." *Jewish Art* 16–17, no. 1 (1990): 98–121.

Ricoeur, Paul. *The Symbolism of Evil.* Translated by Emerson Buchanan. Boston: Beacon Press, 1967.

Rinder, Rosa Perlmutter. *Music, Prayer, and Religious Leadership, Temple Emanu-El, 1913–1969.* Oral history transcript, tape-recorded interview conducted by Malca Chall in 1968–69. Berkeley, CA: University of California, Bancroft Library, Regional Oral History Office, 1971.

Ringer, Alexander. *Arnold Schoenberg: The Composer as Jew.* Oxford: Clarendon Press, 1990.

Roberts, Deane Peter. *Modernism in Russian Piano Music: Scriabin, Prokofiev, and Their Russian Contemporaries.* 2 vols. Russian Music Studies. Edited by Malcolm Hamrich Brown. Bloomington: Indiana University Press, 1993.

Robertson Smith, William. *The Prophets of Israel and Their Place in History to the Close of the Eighth Century B.C.* New York: D. Appleton, 1897.

Rolland, Romain. *Jean-Christophe.* 2 vols. New York: Carroll & Graf, 1996.

Rosenfeld, Paul. "The Bloch Sacred Service." *New Republic* 78 (25 April 1934): 310.

———. *Discoveries of a Music Critic.* New York: Harcourt, Brace, 1936.

———. *Musical Portraits: Interpretations of Twenty Modern Composers.* New York: Harcourt, Brace, and Howe, 1920.

———. "The Music of Ernest Bloch." *Seven Arts* 1, no. 4 (February 1917): 413–18.

Rothstein, Edward, Herbert Muschamp, and Martin E. Marty, eds. *Visions of Utopia.* Oxford: Oxford University Press, 2003.

Rubsamen, Walter. "Schoenberg in America." *Musical Quarterly* 37, no. 4 (October 1951): 469–89.

Sabaneev, Leonid. "The Jewish National School in Music." *Musical Quarterly* 15, no. 3 (July 1929): 448–68.

————. *Modern Russian Composers.* Translated by Judah A. Joffe. New York: International Publishers, 1927.

Said, Edward W. *Orientalism.* New York: Vintage Books, 1978.

Saleski, Gdal. *Famous Musicians of Jewish Origin.* New York: Bloch, 1949.

Saminsky, Lazar. "Hebrew Song Lives in Modern Music." *Musical America* 41, no. 4 (15 November 1924): 4.

————. *Music of Our Day: Essentials and Prophesies.* New York: Thomas Y. Crowell, 1932.

————. *The Music of the Ghetto and the Bible.* New York: Bloch, 1934.

Schaer, Roland, Gregory Claeys, and Lyman Tower Sargent, eds. *Utopia: The Search for the Ideal Society in the Western World.* New York: New York Public Library/Oxford University Press, 2000.

Schiller, David M. *Bloch, Schoenberg, Bernstein: Assimilating Jewish Music.* Oxford: Oxford University Press, 2003.

Schoenberg, Arnold. *The Biblical Way. Journal of the Arnold Schoenberg Institute* 17 (1994): 162–329.

————. *Coherence, Counterpoint, Instrumentation, Instruction in Form.* Edited by Severine Neff and Charlotte Cross. Lincoln: University of Nebraska Press, 1994.

————. "Is It Fair?" In *Music and Dance in California and the West.* Edited by Richard Drake Saunders, 11. Hollywood: Bureau of Musical Research, 1948.

————. *Moderne Psalmen.* Edited by Rudolf Kolish. Mainz: Schott, 1956.

————. *Stil und Gedanke: Aufsätze zur Musik.* Arnold Schönberg Gesammelte Schriften 1. Edited by Ivan Vojtěch. Frankfurt am Main: Fischer, 1976.

————. *Style and Idea: Selected Writings of Arnold Schoenberg.* Edited by Leonard Stein. Translated by Leo Black. Berkeley: University of California Press, 1975.

————. *Theory of Harmony.* Translated by Roy E. Carter. Berkeley: University of California Press, 1978.

Schoenberg, E. Randol. "Arnold Schoenberg and Albert Einstein: Their Relationship and Views on Zionism." *Journal of the Arnold Schoenberg Institute* 10, no. 2 (November 1987): 134–87.

Schoenberg, Nuria, ed. *Arnold Schoenberg (1874–1951): Lebensgeschichte in Begegnungen.* Klagenfurt: Ritter Klagenfurt, 1992.

————, ed. *Arnold Schoenberg Self-portrait: A Collection of Articles, Program Notes and Letters by the Composer about His Own Works.* Pacific Palisades, CA: Belmont Music Publishers, 1988.

Scholem, Gershom. "Jews and Germans." *Commentary* 42 (November 1966): 32–38.

Schorske, Carl. *Fin-de-siècle Vienna: Politics and Culture.* New York: Vintage Books, 1981.

Schultz, Alfred. *Race or Mongrel.* Boston, L. C. Page, 1908.

Schwarz, Boris. "Musorgsky's Interest in Judaica." In *Musorgsky: In Memoriam 1881–1981.* Edited by Malcolm Hamrick Brown. Ann Arbor, MI: UMI Research Press, 1982.

Seiden, Rudolf, ed. *Pro Zion! Vornehmlich nichtjüdische Stimmen über die jüdische Renaissancebewegung.* Vienna: Samuel Insel, 1924.

Shiloah, Amnon. *Jewish Musical Traditions.* Jewish Folklore and Anthropology Series. Edited by Rachael Patai. Detroit: Wayne State University Press, 1992.

Shipman, Pat. *The Evolution of Racism: Human Differences and the Use and Abuse of Science.* New York: Simon & Schuster, 1994.

Sholochova, Lydmila. "The Phonoarchive of Jewish Folklore at the Vernadsky National Library of Ukraine." Translated by Illia Labunka. Kiev: Vernadsky National Library of Ukraine, 2001. www.archives.gov.ua/Eng/NB/Phonoarchive.php. Accessed October 2003.

———. *Stanovleniye i razvitiye yevreyskoy muzïkal'noy folkloristiki v rossiyskoy imperii v nachale XX st.* (Formation and development of the study of Jewish musical folklore in the Russian empire at the beginning of the twentieth century). Kiev: Natsional'naya Muzïkal'naya Akademiya Ukraini im. P. I. Chaikovskovo, 2000.

Sills, David L. "Bloch Manuscripts at the University of California." *MLA Notes* 42, no. 1 (September 1985): 7–21.

———. "Bloch's Manuscripts at the Library of Congress." *MLA Notes* 42, no. 4 ( June 1986): 726–353.

———. "Ruminations on *Macbeth.*" In *Ernest Bloch Society Bulletin* 18–19 (1986–87): 11–15.

Sitsky, Larry. *Music of the Repressed Russian Avant-Garde, 1900–1929.* Contributions to the Study of Music and Dance. Number 31. Wesport, CT: Greenwood Press, 1994.

Slobin, Mark. *Old Jewish Folk Music: The Collections and Writings of Moshe Beregovski.* Philadelphia: University of Pennsylvania Press, 1982.

Slonimsky, Nicolas. *Lexicon of Musical Invective: Critical Assaults on Composers since Beethoven's Time.* New York: Coleman-Ross, 1953.

———. *Music since 1900.* New York: Charles Scribner's Sons, 1971.

Solie, Ruth. "The Living Work: Organicism and Musical Analysis." *Nineteenth-Century Music* 4, no. 2 (fall 1980): 147–56.

Soltes, Avraham. "The Hebrew Folk Song Society of Petersburg: The Historical Development." In *The Historic Contribution of Russian Jewry to Jewish Music.* Edited by Irene Heskes and Arthur Wolfson, 13–42. New York: National Jewish Music Council, 1967.

Soussloff, Catherine M., ed. *Jewish Identity in Modern Art History.* Berkeley: University of California Press, 1999.

Spaeth, Siegmund. "Jews Interpreters More than Composers. Ernest Bloch Says It Is because in Music, as in Everything, They Assimilate and Imitate—More Sincere Jewish Art to Come." *Evening Mail,* 26 April 1917.

Stein, Erwin ed, *Arnold Schoenberg: Letters.* Translated by Eithne Wilkins and Ernst Kaiser. Berkeley: University of California Press, 1987.

Steiner, Ena. "Mödling Revisited," *Journal of the Arnold Schoenberg Institute* 1, no. 2 (February 1977): 75–86.

Strasser, Michael. "'A Survivor from Warsaw' as Personal Parable." *Music and Letters* 76, no. 1 (February 1995): 52–63.

Stuckenschmidt, H. H. *Schoenberg: His Life, World and Work.* Translated by Humphrey Searle. London: John Calder, 1977.

Symonette, Lys, and Kim H. Kowalke, eds. *Speak Low ( When You Speak Love): The Letters of Kurt Weill and Lotte Lenya.* Berkeley: University of California Press, 1996.

Taine, Hippolyte. *Histoire de la littérature anglais.* Paris: Librairie Hachette, 1864.

Tappy, José-Flore, ed. *Ernest Bloch, Romain Rolland, Lettres (1911–1933).* Collection "Les Musiciens." Lausanne: Editions Payot Lausanne, 1984.

Taruskin, Richard. *Defining Russia Musically: Historical and Hermeneutical Essays.* Princeton: Princeton University Press, 1997.

———. *Musorgsky: Eight Essays and an Epilogue.* Princeton: Princeton University Press, 1993.

———. *Opera and Drama in Russia as Preached and Practiced in the 1860s.* Rochester, NY: University of Rochester Press, 1981.

———. *Stravinsky and the Russian Traditions: A Biography of the Works through* Mavra, 2 vols. Berkeley: University of California Press, 1996.

———. "A Sturdy Musical Bridge to the 21st Century." *New York Times,* 24 August 1997.

Tasker, John Howard. *Our American Music: Three Hundred Years of It.* New York: Thomas Y. Crowell, 1946.

Taylor, William M. *Elijah the Prophet.* New York: Harper & Brothers, 1875.

Tchamkerten, Jacques. *Ernest Bloch ou Un prophète en son temps.* mélophiles. Edited by Jean Gallois. Geneva: Editions Papillon, 2001.

Tibaldi Chiesa, Mary. "Ernest Bloch." *La revue musicale* 15, no. 143 (February 1934): 123–34.

Tibaldi Chiesa, Mary, et al. "Il 'Servizio Sacro' di Ernest Bloch eseguito a Torino e trasmesso per radio." *Israel* 19, no. 17 (25 January 1934): 3–6.

Toch, Lilly. *The Orchestration of a Composer's Life.* Oral history transcript. Interviewed by Bernard Galm, 1971 and 1972. Oral History Program, University of California, Los Angeles. The Regents of the University of California, 1978.

Torberg, Friedrich. *Mein ist die Rache.* Los Angeles: Privatdruck der Pazifischen Press, 1943.

Trowbridge, W. R. H. *Jézabel: drame en un acte, en prose.* Paris: Edition de la Plume, 1903.

Vainshtein M. I. "Obshchestvo Yevreyskoy narodnoy muzïki kak faktor kul'turnoy zhizni Peterburga nachala XX v" (The Society for Jewish Folk Music as a factor in the cultural life of St. Petersburg in the early twentieth century). In *Etnografiya Peterburga-Leningrada: materialï yezhegodnïkh nauchnïkh chteniy* (Ethnography of St. Petersburg-Leningrad: Materials of the yearly scientific reading). Edited by N. V. Yukhnyova, 29–38. Leningrad: Nauka, 1988.

Vinaver, Chemjo, ed. *Anthology of Jewish Music: Sacred Chant and Religious Folk Song of the Eastern European Jews.* New York: Edward B. Marks, 1953.

Vorspan, Max, and Lloyd P. Gartner. *History of the Jews of Los Angeles.* Regional History Series of the American Jewish History Center of the Jewish Theological Seminary of America. San Marino, CA: Huntington Library 1970.

Wagner, Richard. "A Communication to My Friends." In *Richard Wagner's Prose Works.* Vol. 1, *The Art-Work of the Future.* Translated by William Ashton Ellis. New York: Broude Brothers, 1966.

———. *Judaism in Music.* In *Richard Wagner's Prose Works.* Vol. 3. Translated by William Ashton Ellis. New York: Broude Brothers, 1894.

Waite, Geoffrey C. W. "Worringer's *Abstraction and Empathy:* Remarks on Its Reception and on the Rhetoric of Criticism." In *The Turn of the Century: German Literature and Art, 1890–1915.* Edited by Gerald Chapple and Hans H. Schulte. Modern German Studies 5. Edited by Peter Heller, 197–223. Bonn: Bonvier Verlag, Herbert Grundmann, 1981.

Webern, Anton. *The Path to the New Music.* Edited by Willi Reich. Translated by Leo Black. Bryn Mawr, PA: Theodore Presser, 1963.

Weininger, Otto. *Sex and Character.* London: William Heinemann, 1906.

Weisser, Albert. "Lazare Saminsky's Early Years in New York City (1920–1928): Excerpts from an Unpublished Autobiography." *Musica Judaica* 7, no. 1 (1983–84): 1–37.

———. "Lazare Saminsky's Year in Russia and Palestine: Excerpts from an Unpublished Autobiography." *Musica Judaica* 2, no. 2 (1977–78): 1–20.

———. *The Modern Renaissance of Jewish Music. Events and Figures: Eastern Europe and America.* New York: Bloch, 1954.

———. "The Music Division of the Jewish Ethnographic Expedition in the Name of Baron Horace Guinsbourg (1911–1914)." *Musica Judaica* 6, no. 1 (1981–82): 1–7.

White, Pamela C. *Schoenberg and the God-Idea: The Opera* Moses and Aron. Studies in Musicology, No. 83. Edited by George Buelow. Ann Arbor, MI: UMI Research Press, 1983.

Worringer, Wilhelm. *Abstraction and Empathy: A Contribution to the Psychology of Style.* Translated by Michael Bullock. London: Routledge and Kegan Paul, 1953.

*Yevreyskaya entsiklopediya (Svod znanii o yevreystve i yego kulture v proshlom i nastoyashchem)* (Jewish encyclopedia [collection of knowledge concerning Jewry, its culture in the past and in the present]). Edited by Simon Dubnov. St. Petersburg: Izdaniye Obshchestva dlya nauchnïkh yevreyskikh izdaniy i Izdatel'stva Brokhaus-Efron, 1906–13.

Zemtsovsky, Izaly. "Jewish Music: Values from Within Versus Evaluation from Without." In *Representations of Jews Through the Ages.* Studies in Jewish Civilization 8. Edited by Leonard Jay Greenspoon and Bryan F. Le Beau, 131–52. Omaha: Creighton University Press, 1996.

Zuckerman, Marvin, and Marion Herbst, *The Three Great Classic Writers of Modern Yiddish Literature.* Vol. 3, *Selected Works of I. L. Peretz.* Malibu, CA: Joseph Simon Pangloss Press, 1996.

# INDEX

and on the new island of utopia] (More),
201

Dessau, Paul, 248, 251, 312

*Deutschjudentum*, 205–8

Diaspora, 4, 6; intellectual pursuits and,
228; Jewish nationalist debate over,
17–18, 54; Orientalism identified with,
91, 151; pilgrim festivals in tradition of,
128; Yiddish as linguistic marker of, 68

difference: celebration of, 151; denial of,
175; elimination of sexual difference,
231–32

Disraeli, Benjamin, 97–99, 115

dodecaphony. *See* twelve-tone system
(dodecaphony)

*Don Quixote* (Strauss), 138, 144

Dorian mode, 71, 72, 74, 78, 178

Douglas, Mary, 340

Downes, Olin, 105, 106, 150–51, 164,
371n32; on *America*, 166; Bloch's ideas
on race and, 158, 195, 197; on Bloch's
Orientalism, 160; on *Sacred Service*, 172;
on *Survivor from Warsaw*, 292, 293, 296–
97, 393–94n59

Drachevski, 20, 21

"Dream and Reality" (Krämer), 215

*Dreimal tausend Jahre* (Schoenberg), 304,
*305–6, 307–8*, 308–9, 316; *Prisma*
magazine and, 306, 395n18; State of
Israel and, 306, 321; utopian political
ideals and, 301

Dreyfus affair, 96

"Du, finstere nechtele" [You, dark little
night] (Rubinstejn), 25

Dubnov, Simon, 17, 18, 19, 54, 56

Duchamp, Marcel, 337, 338, 347

Dumas père, Alexandre, 153

"Du meydele, du sheyns" [You pretty girl]
(Zhitomirsky), 29

*Dybuk* (An-sky), 62

Echod hu Elohenu (in *Sacred Service*), 171,
177, 186

*Écoute Israel* (Fleg), 111

Efros, Abram Markovich, 55, 56, 83, 89

Eichmann, Adolf, 294

Einstein, Albert, 209, 217, 225, 321,
380n6

"Einsteins falsche Politik" [Einstein's
mistaken policy] (Schoenberg), 217

"Der Ejberster is der mchuten" [God is the

father-in-law] (in *Zamelbukh*), 24. *See also*
"Der eybershter iz der mekhutn"

"Ejlijohu hanowi" [Elijah the prophet] (in
*Zamelbukh*), 24

"Ejlijohu hanowi, Ejlijohu hatischbi" [Elijah
the prophet, Elijah the Tishibite] (in
*Zamelbukh*), 24

"Eli, Eli" [My God, my God] (Shalit), 29

*Eli Tsion* (Tseitlin), 31, 78, *80*, 81, *81–82*, 82

"Eli Tsion ve'areha" [Wail, Oh Zion and thy
cities] (dirge), 78, *80*

"Eli Zijojn w'oreho" [God of Zion and its
cities] (in *Zamelbukh*), 24

Ellis, Havelock, 343, 349

"El yivne hagalil" [God will rebuild Galil]
(Saminsky), 31

empathy, art and, 277

*Encyclopedia Judaica*, 208, 345

Engel, Yoel (Yuliy), 20, 21, 23, 38, 71, 88;
debate with Saminsky, 65–69; on Milner,
46; as Stasov's convert, 62–65; *Yidishe
folkslieder*, 45; Zionism and, 69, 363n36

English language, 296

Enlightenment, 212, 344

Ephros, Gershon, 218

*Erwartung* (Schoenberg), 256, *261*, 262;
*Begleitsmusik* compared with, 278, 280,
282, 285; comparison with Strauss's
*Salome*, 263, 265–66, *267–68*, 269;
musical signs of fear in, 262–63, *264–
69*, 265–66, 269–70, *271*, 272; "Premonitions" compared with, 272, 274–
75; *Survivor from Warsaw* compared with,
285, 295–96

"Es falt a thoj" [Dew is falling] (Mendelsohn
in *Zamelbukh*), 25

*Essai sur l'inégalité des races humaines*
(Gobineau), 108

essences: Jewish, 7, 97, 98, 152, 158, 209,
338; in modern art and architecture,
203, 348; national or ethnic, 1, 4, 10, 18;
Platonic, 340, 348; racial, 117, 154, 156

essentialism, 7, 299; national characteristics
and, 99; in philosophy, 346–47; Schoenberg's interest in Judaism and, 322;
Wagner and, 5

*Esther* (Engel), 62

"ethnic," as term, 3

ethnic cleansing, 115, 339

Etz Chayim (in *Sacred Service*), 171, 177, 182,
183, 184

German language, 45, 68

German music, 99, 102

Germany, Nazi: Bloch and, 113, 173–74; race as "man's most dangerous myth" and, 95; Schoenberg and, 204, 205, 207, 214, 216, 335

Germany and Germans, 2, 5, 98, 100, 157, 285; Jewish assimilation in, 103; Reform Judaism in, 242; in World War I, 205–6

Gerstl, Richard, 30, 257, 259, 394n2

"Das gesegenen sich fun a jeger" [The goodbye of a hunter] (Mendelsohn in *Zamelbukh*), 25

"Di gilderne pave" [The golden peacock] (Shklyar in *Zamelbukh*), 24, 29

Gilman, L., 173

Gintsburg, Asher, 16

Gintsburg, Baron David, 63

Gintsburg, Ilya, 63

Gintzburg, Vladimir, 19

Ginzburg, Saul, 19, 62

Glinka, Mikhail, 14, 20, 51; Jewish melodies used by, 21; *Prince Kholmsky*, 56; *Ruslan and Ludmila*, 15, 56; search for "Jewish Glinka," 14, 15, 51, 52, 90; "Yevreyskaya pesnya" (Hebrew song), 23, 56–57, *58*, 74

"A gnejwe" [A theft] (in *Zamelbukh*), 24

Gnesin, Mikhail, 21, 31, 52, 53, 90

Gobineau, Count Arthur de, 108

God, representation of, 236, 320; *Adonay* in liturgical music, 318, *319*, 320; prohibition on, 329–30

Godet, Robert, 97, 99, 116, 150, 181, 365n16; anti-Semitism of, 105–7, 152; Bloch's liberal views against, 196–97; Chamberlain's *Foundations of the Nineteenth Century* and, 97, 108–9, 110, 379n117; essentialized self-image of Bloch and, 151; falling-out with Bloch, 110–13; *Sacred Service* and, 195; Wagnerian vision of, 113–15

Goebbels, Joseph, 207, 377n81

Goethe, Johann Wolfgang, 109

"golden cockerel style," 55

Goldfaden, Abraham, 3, 34

Goldmark, Karl, 156

*Götterdämmerung* (Wagner), 251

"Gottes Wiederkehr" (Runes), 303, 304

grace notes, 56, 57, *126*

Gradenwitz, Peter, 8–9, 206, 232, 238

Graetz, Heinrich, 110, 367–68n59

*Les grandes légendes de France* (Schuré), 118

Great Depression, 202

Greenberg, Clement, 278, 346

Gregorian melodies, 64, 170, 178, *179*, 377n91

"A Gruss" [The greeting] (Mendelsohn in *Zamelbukh*), 25

Guilbert, Yvette, 164

*Gulliver's Travels* (Swift), 341

Gurovitch, S., 30

*Gurrelieder* (Schoenberg), 289, 313

"A gute Woch" [A good week] (in *Zamelbukh*), 25

"G'wald te Brider" [Oy, brothers] (in *Zamelbukh*), 24

Halpern, Benjamin, 312

"Hamawdil bein kojdesch l'chojl" [He who distinguished between the sacred and the weekday] (in *Zamelbukh*), 24

harmonic progression, 38, 250, 251

*Harmonielehre* [Theory of harmony] (Schoenberg), 203, 232, 348

harmony, 5, 72, 85, 194, 306, 391n18

Harrison, Thomas, 259

Hasidic music, 52, 65, 66, 70, 358n40

Hasidism, 19, 162–63, 168

*haskalah* (Jewish enlightenment), 15, 62

"Hatikvah" [The hope] (Imber), 29

Haudebert, Lucien, 153

*hazzanim*, Eastern, 181

Hebraism, musical, 82, 88

Hebrew language, 18, 140; Bloch and, 156, 163, 171, 372n7; as element of Yiddish, 68; Engel and, 62; poetry, 83; "racial purity" debate and, 68–69; in Schoenberg's works, 311, 313; in *Survivor from Warsaw*, 296

"Hebrew Melodies" (Byron), 43

Hebrews, ancient, 8, 56, 70, 150

"Hebreyish melodye" [Hebrew melody] (Achron), 31

"Hebreyish tants" [Hebrew dance] (Achron), 31

"Hebreyish viglid" [Hebrew lullaby] (Achron), 31

"Der hejliger Schabbes" [The sacred Shabbat] (Rubinstein in *Zamelbukh*), 26

"Helf uns Gottenju" [Help us, our God] (in *Zamelbukh*), 24

"Un reb Elyezer hot gezogt" ("Omar fun Elosor") [And Eliezar told us] (Saminsky), 33
"Unsane Toykef" (Milner), 32, 313
"Unser Rebeniu" [Our rabbi] (in *Zamelbukh*), 25
"Unter di grininke beymelack" [Under the green trees] (Milner), 32
"Unter soreles vigele" ['Neath little Sarah's cradle] (Saminsky), 29, 31, 72, *73*
utopianism, 2, 203–5; in Bloch's music, 144, *149*, 150, 169; elimination of sexual difference, 231–32; essential binarisms and, 335; history of idea of, 201–3; space of, 222, 231; twelve-tone system and, 278. *See also* purity, utopian vision of

Vaanachnu (in *Sacred Service*), 177
Variations sur le thème Hébraïque "Eil ivne hagalil" (Achron), 33
Varshavsky, Mark, 34, 66
Veohavto (in *Sacred Service*), 177
"A viglid" [A lullaby] (Rosovsky), 31
"Viglied fun dem Apten Row" (Saminsky), 34
Vinaver, Chemjo, 312–13, 318, 320, 396n40
Vinaver, Maksim, 19
Violin Concerto (Bloch), 168
Violin Concerto, op. 36 (Schoenberg), 252
Volhynia district (Ukraine), 19
"Volokhl" (Lvov), 30
*Voskhhod* [Sunrise] (periodical), 17, 19, 66, 355n9
"Vos vet zayn mikoyekh burikes" [What will be about the beets] (Lvov), 30, 38, *43*
"Vos vet zyn mit reb Yisroel dem frumen" [What will become of pious reb Israel] (Kopït), 32, 38, *41*

Wagner, Cosima, 108
Wagner, Richard, 9, 97, 152, 165; Bloch and, 99, 100, 102, 154; Chamberlain and, 108; on creative impotence of Jewish composers, 156, 157; *deutsche Kunst* concept, 100; Disraeli compared with, 97–98; *Götterdämmerung*, 251; influence of, 4–5; on Jewish assimilation, 102–3; *Judaism in Music*, 4, 6, 96, 98, 207; *Kol nidre* (Schoenberg) and, 250–51, 252; leitmotifs in music of, 123; on myth and human condition, 114; *Parsifal*,

178, *179*, 262, *262;* Schoenberg on spirit of, 207–8; *Tristan und Isolde*, 270
"Der Wald" [The forest] (Mendelsohn in *Zamelbukh*), 25
Warburg, Felix, 164, 171
Warburg, Gerald, 171, 176
Warsaw Ghetto uprising, 288, 292, 295
Webern, Anton, 208, 257, 274, 396n55
Weill, Kurt, 238, 386n22, 388n65
Weinberg, Jacob, 21, 54
Weinberger, Jaromir, 289
Weisser, Albert, 15, 53
"Welcher jojm-tojw is der bester?" [Which holiday is the best?] (in *Zamelbukh*), 25
Wellington, Duke of, 302
Werfel, Franz, 228
Whitman, Walt, 350
Whittall, Arnold, 256
Wilde, Oscar, 118–19, 202, 369n9
Willette, Adolphe, 300
"A Winterlied" [A winter song] (Mendelsohn in *Zamelbukh*), 25
Wise, Rabbi Stephen, 169, 210, 217, 218, 290
Wolitz, Seth, 89, 90
women, misogynist representations of, 118
World Jewish Congress, 217
World War I, 154, 205–6, 224–25, 382n37; expressionist malaise and, 259; racialist expression in art and, 155; utopian politics and, 202
World War II, 3, 97, 205, 294, 295; genocidal purification during, 339; horror of, 299; racist politics of, 335; Schoenberg's rejection of politics and, 301
Worringer, Wilhelm, 256, 276–77, 278, 346
"Wos wet sajn, as Moschiach wet kumen" [The Messiah will come] (in *Zamelbukh*), 25
*Wozzeck* (Berg), 257, 260, *261*, 262, 270, 282

"Yaaleh" [May it rise] (Yom Kippur hymn), 242
Yair, Pinhas B., 342
Yasser, Joseph, 3, 4, 54, 359n59
"Yerusholayim, Yerusholayim" [Jerusalem, Jerusalem] (Shklyar), 29, 38, *42*
*yevrei*, music of, 69–72
*yevrei* and *zhidï*, distinction between, 78
*Yevreyskaya Entsiklopediya* (Jewish Encyclopedia), 63

Text:   10/12 Baskerville
Display:   Baskerville
Compositor:   Integrated Composition Systems
Music Engraver:   Don Giller
Indexer:   Alexander Trotter
Printer/Binder:   Thomson-Shore, Inc.